GERMAN CITY,
JEWISH MEMORY

THE TAUBER INSTITUTE SERIES FOR
THE STUDY OF EUROPEAN JEWRY

Jehuda Reinharz, *General Editor*
Sylvia Fuks Fried, *Associate Editor*

The Tauber Institute Series is dedicated to publishing compelling and innovative approaches to the study of modern European Jewish history, thought, culture, and society. The series features scholarly works related to the Enlightenment, modern Judaism and the struggle for emancipation, the rise of nationalism and the spread of antisemitism, the Holocaust and its aftermath, as well as the contemporary Jewish experience. The series is published under the auspices of the Tauber Institute for the Study of European Jewry—established by a gift to Brandeis University from Dr. Laszlo N. Tauber—and is supported, in part, by the Tauber Foundation and the Valya and Robert Shapiro Endowment.

For the complete list of books that are available in this series, please see www.upne.com

NILS ROEMER

GERMAN CITY, JEWISH MEMORY

THE STORY OF WORMS

BRANDEIS UNIVERSITY PRESS
Waltham, Massachusetts
Published by
University Press of New England
Hanover and London

BRANDEIS UNIVERSITY PRESS
Published by University Press of New England
www.upne.com
© 2010 Brandeis University
All rights reserved
Manufactured in the United States of America
Designed by Eric M. Brooks
Typeset in Plantin and Typeface Six and Seven
by Passumpsic Publishing

*This project was published with the generous support
of the Lucius N. Littauer Foundation.*

University Press of New England is a member of the
Green Press Initiative. The paper used in this book meets
their minimum requirement for recycled paper.

Library of Congress Cataloging-in-Publication Data
Roemer, Nils H.
German city, Jewish memory: the story of Worms/
Nils Roemer.—1st ed.
    p. cm.—(The Tauber institute for the study of
European Jewry series)
Includes bibliographical references and index.
ISBN 978-1-58465-921-1 (cloth: alk. paper)—
ISBN 978-1-58465-922-8 (pbk.: alk. paper)
    1. Jews—Germany—Worms—History.
    2. Worms (Germany)—Ethnic relations. I. Title.
DS134.36.W67R64   2010
943'.4352004924—dc22   2010026560

5 4 3 2 1

CONTENTS

ILLUSTRATIONS

ACKNOWLEDGMENTS

The coexistence of archival collections in Jerusalem, Worms, and New York about Worms underscores the central contentions of this book concerning the dislocated shape of local memory. In addition to the existing archives in the narrow sense, text and images can be found in the library of early modern Jewry, in the reports of travelers, and in Jewish historical texts, travel accounts, city histories, tour guides, and various German, German Jewish, and foreign newspapers and archives.

Following the trail of these scattered documents led me to work and research in various libraries and archives. I want to thank Gerald Bönnen of the Stadtarchiv Worms for his help and support in bringing various collections to my attention. I am also grateful to the staff of the library of the Leo Baeck Institute in New York, where I intensively studied over the past years. I consulted the rich holdings of the British Library; the Library of Congress in Washington, D.C.; the New York Public Library; the archive and library of the Jewish Theological Seminary in New York for some of the printed material; the Stanford University Archives; the Wiener Library in London; the Hartley Library at the University of Southampton; and the McDermott Library at the University of Texas at Dallas. I also want to express my gratitude to my research assistants — Janet Brohier, Frank Garrett, James King, and Blake Remington — for helping to prepare the manuscript, and to the University of Texas at Dallas for affording them to me. Dennis Kratz, Hobson Wildenthal, Debbie Pfister, and Zsuzsanna Ozsvath are also on my list of gratitude for their ongoing support. Last but not least, I want to acknowledge Michele C. DeNicolo, who with her good spirit encouraged me to bring this book to completion and assisted in many other ways.

During the later stage of my project, I was fortunate enough to make contact with several former members of the Worms community, who generously answered my questions about their ongoing relationship with the city. These oral and written testimonies provided me with powerful evidence and allowed me to delineate more clearly the varied forms of remembrance during the postwar period. Annelore Schlösser, who, jointly with her husband, chronicled the fate of the persecuted and expelled members of the community, introduced me to many of them. Her work illustrates the enduring, if painful, ties that exist between members of the congregation and the city. I want to thank in particular Mrs. Schlösser, Gerhard Spies, Miriam Gerber, Frank Gusdorf, Paul Gusdorf, Izhak Kraemer, and Liselotte Wahrburg.

This work emerged out of an initial encounter with the history of Jewish martyrdom and memory during graduate seminars with Professor Yosef H. Yerushalmi at Columbia University. Worms initially provided me with important examples to illustrate a larger point about the impact of historical writings upon the German Jewish culture in my subsequent book on German Jewish historical writings in nineteenth-century Germany. During 1999–2000, I participated in the fellowship program on Christian Hebraists at the Center for Advanced Judaic Studies at the University of Pennsylvania and was struck by the extent to which seventeenth-century scholars debated the authenticity of the historical traditions of Worms. Slowly the idea for this book took shape. Once I had decided to work on this topic, I began to come across Worms everywhere, which quickly reshaped the chronological scope of this study.

I was fortunate enough to be able to present parts of this book at conferences at Princeton University, the German Historical Institute in Washington, D.C., and Stanford University, as well as various lecture seminars in the United Kingdom and Germany. I am particularly thankful for the many helpful comments and suggestions made by participants at the conferences. The research for this book would not have been possible without a research grant from the University of Southampton and the matching research leave awarded to me by the Arts and Humanities Research Board (AHRB).

GERMAN CITY,
JEWISH MEMORY

INTRODUCTION

In 1987, Chaim Herzog became the first Israeli president to tour the Federal Republic; he spent five days there in return for Richard von Weizsäcker's visit to Israel in 1985. Herzog commenced his tour at the Bergen-Belsen concentration camp before arriving in Worms in the company of the West German president. Once there, Herzog prayed in the city's synagogue, stood in front of the graves of Meir of Rothenburg and Alexander von Wimpfen, and recalled Rashi's lasting legacy. For him, the city of Worms, situated along the river Rhine in the Rhineland-Palatinate and otherwise known for the *Nibelungen,* German emperors, and Martin Luther, appeared as "a symbol of the great and tragic drama of European Jewish fate as it is symbolic of the remarkable interweaving—for better or worse—of German and Jewish life for a thousand years."[1]

The inclusion of Bergen-Belsen and Worms on Herzog's itinerary paid tribute to the remembrance of destruction, the German Jewish legacy, and Germany's strides toward the mastering of an unmasterable past. The synagogue in which Herzog prayed had been reconstructed and rededicated only in 1961; the nine-hundred-year-old house of worship had been set ablaze on November 9, 1938, and was razed in the years following. At the same time, Herzog's visit retraced the path of generations of pilgrims, rabbis, scholars, poets, and tourists. Throughout the community's history, this assortment of visitors prayed and inspected the graves of rabbinical luminaries and martyrs and visited Worms's famous synagogue and Rashi Chapel.

This book traces the recollection and invention of local Jewish historical traditions in religious commemorations, historical writings, the preservation of historical monuments, museums, and tourism's transformation of "sites" into "sights." My analysis of a multiplicity of participants in the process of remembrance aims to blur the lines between high and low culture and to view the production of culture and identity as the outcome of numerous practices. Instead of privileging, for example, the circle of learned rabbis and scholars over local archivists, novelists, pilgrims, and tourists, I seek to capture the often varied and conflicted but also overlapping voices in which Worms was not only remembered but also experienced. These many custodians of Jewish sites

FIGURE 1. *Map of Germany.*

and artifacts constitute changing communities of memory over the course of a millennium.

Organized in a roughly chronological fashion, this work highlights the trajectory from medieval and early modern rituals of remembrance and inventions of local traditions to modern reconfigurations of the local as sites of memory and its fundamental transformation into destination cultures of remembrance after the Holocaust. Chronicles, inscriptions, histories, liturgies, literatures, anthologies, travel guides, and archives have created a past that has been in turn reinforced by rituals, historical pres- ervation, traveling, and public celebrations.

My focus on a single community allows me to map out the changing sources of memory and practice over a long period of time in a city that became in fact increasingly peripheral to both German and Jewish history. Even during the Middle Ages, the Jewish communities of Speyer and Mainz overshadowed the Jewish community of Worms. Despite this marginality, however, Worms and its heritage remained vital to constructions of Jewish identities. The city and its Jewish population exemplify the importance of smaller regional communities for the larger history of German Jewry, however exceptional Worms's particular history may be.

Despite the radical changes brought about by recurrent expulsion and devastation, Jews' social advancement, the cultural and religious renewal of the modern age, and the community's destruction during the Holocaust, Worms's sites always displayed a remarkable degree of continuity. This significantly contributed to the construction of its distinct urban Jewish cultures, memories, and identities. During the Middle Ages, Worms was considered one of the foremost Jewish communities in Ashkenazic Europe, and it prided itself on its rabbinic leaders and martyrs. The advent of the First Crusade massacres illustrated the precarious status of the Jews and the extent of anti-Jewish hostility and violence. Yet the fate of the community paradoxically bound the surviving members even more to their location as they commemorated their martyrs there.

In the early modern period the third largest Jewish congregation in the Holy Roman Empire resided in Worms (after Prague and Frankfurt). Preservation, restoration, and innovation intermingled in the creation of a distinct local heritage that centered on rabbinical luminaries, religious martyrs, narratives about the community's mythical origin, and alliances to emperors, dukes, and local dignitaries. As the Jews of Worms delineated local Jewish customs and anthologized accounts about their past, they transferred oral traditions, rituals, and practices into books. Placed into circulation, these local traditions were able to cross denominational boundaries and attract pious and curious travelers as well as Christian scholars, historians of the city, and authors of travelogues. With the printing revolution, textual remembrance started to weaken the close relation between religious customs, memory, and place as the production of the local past increasingly occurred both inside and outside the city.

In the nineteenth century, Worms's physical remains, together with its textual traditions, were mobilized to bolster and shape Jewish local cultures. The rediscovery of medieval narratives about persecution and martyrdom, the unearthing of fantastic legends about some of the community's sages, and the preservation of the historical sites provided Worms's Jewish citizens with a powerful means of navigating their way between change and continuity. The local heritage production at the same time fashioned Worms's iconographic status and turned the city into a destination for tourists. By preserving their historical traditions and artifacts, the Jewish community of Worms both asserted and forged a particular local identity and contributed to the authentication of a far more complex construction of German Jewish culture during the late nineteenth and early twentieth centuries.

Despite the erasure of its community and synagogue, the legacy of Worms's Jews was reactivated in the postwar period as local memory politics commingled and collided with the interests of Jewish survivors, displaced persons, and Jewish members of the U.S. Army, who visited the city to view its remains. With the synagogue destroyed and the survivors scattered around the globe, the restoration of the house of worship in a city without a Jewish community fundamentally reconfigured the marker of destruction and violence under the banner of restoration that initially silenced the memory of the Holocaust. Today, despite the absence of a Jewish community, the recreated past to which Herzog's visit paid homage has influenced Worms's local culture as the city continues to reinvent itself as a popular destination for Jewish and non-Jewish tourists alike.

This evolving local heritage infused and sustained the sense of a Jewish community beyond its shared religious norms, practices, and ordinances, while memory also in turn reconfigured new communities of remembrance, with both Jews and non-Jews inside and outside the city participating in the acts of preservation and recollection. Embedded in these changing communities, remembrance became a dynamic and fragile endeavor that not only preserved historical reality but also shaped and created it, as historical remnants became invested with new meanings. Some aspects of the community's past fell into oblivion, only to be retrieved at a later stage, while other important artifacts were preserved due to serendipitous findings. What remained from the past was, therefore, neither neutral nor natural. The recording of some events coincided with the silencing of others. Even a building like the synagogue had to be created and preserved and thus became a conspicuous artifact embodying the ambiguities of remembrance.

Historical preservation and remembrance has attracted considerable scholarly attention, but the existing collaborative and multivolume works on German and French realms of memory operate within the arena of territorial-national or national-cultural concepts. The ambiguity of the central categories of French and German memory spaces is hardly explored, but a national perspective is constantly assumed, which in turn relegates Jewish sites to a few fleeting references. Moreover, in conceiving homogenous national frameworks, these otherwise pathbreaking works fail to consider the local modalities of the production of national heritages.[2]

Instead of conceiving memory as the result of a culturally cohesive local or national community of remembrance, this book places the investigation of local memory into networks of contacts and exchanges. As Doreen Massey has emphasized, places are not only constructed out of articulations of local social relations; their local distinctiveness is "always already a product of wider contacts; the local is always already a product in part of 'global' forces."[3] Situated on the Rhine River, Worms has always inhabited a space that, as the French historian Lucien Febvre argued during the 1920s, brought different cultures into contact and proximity.[4] To limit remembrance therefore solely to the boundaries of the city, its rabbis, historians, and archivists would have to subscribe to the view that men and women are the makers of their surrounding culture, as Clifford Geertz has argued.[5] Against the underlying perception of located, coherent cultures, a view that occludes the importance of relations, James Clifford points out that "the old localizing strategies" may obscure as much as they reveal.[6]

Following up on this insight, here I attribute a central role to the encounter and cooperation of locals and visitors in the formation and remembrance of the local Jewish heritage. Whereas on the surface, the Jewish burial ground and the Rashi Chapel in Worms appear to be mere constructions of stone, they derived their particular meaning from textual traditions and public actions in which both locals and visitors participated. Locally produced texts and actions, literary and historical narrations, archives, and a museum, as well as pilgrimage and tourism, all played central roles in forging a local heritage in Worms. Remembrance emerged also as a space of negotiation when Worms rebuilt its destroyed synagogue in the face of, at times, vocal opposition from several former members of the community who favored maintaining the rubble of the building as a site of memory for the segregation, expulsion, and

6 | annihilation of the community. Despite the presence of these competing voices, resistance to traveling to Germany waned and greater numbers of Jewish tourists began to readopt the reconstructed synagogue. It must be noted, however, that these Jewish travelers, as agents of their own agendas, invested the sites with different meanings. Although the rebuilt synagogue and the accompanying exhibition showcase seventeenth-century German Jewish life and culture, for many Jewish visitors, the absence of any current community presents an uncanny reminder of the city's involvement in Nazi atrocities and breaks through the surface in their personal travel accounts. At the same time, the close contacts between former members of the community and city representatives, and those members' donation of treasured artifacts to the archives and the museum, formed a reciprocal relationship. These newly established ties signify more than simple generosity; they are gifts that place an obligation upon the city to preserve them.

The notion of realms of memory as contact zones between otherwise geographically separated people who together invest in and negotiate the evolving meaning of monuments underscores the contested, conflicted, and conflicting nature of these local memory landscapes.[7] Yet studying the invention of local heritage within a wider context does not diminish the importance of place. The presence of physical markers gives legitimacy and force to local tradition, as Maurice Halbwachs observed in his classical study on collective memory.[8] The physical perseverance of the synagogue, the burial ground, religious artifacts, and historical documents anchored remembrance and bestowed continuity.

To medieval and early modern Jews, the presence of Jewish martyrs and learned rabbis made the cemetery a holy ground where God would more willingly receive prayers. During the modern period, the historical sites became locations in which observance of religious traditions ceased to exist or at least became radically altered. Yet the preservation and promotion of the city's local heritage constructed and defended Jews' local identity, legitimized change, and asserted their loyalties to their ancestors. In the postwar period, Worms functions as an *Erinnerungsort* (place of memory) for families with a long-standing attachment to a city, its holy sites, and its places of remembrance as well as for other Jews and Christians.[9]

In his groundbreaking work, Pierre Nora sees this transformation as a shift from "environments of memory" (*milieu de memoire*) to "sites of memory" (*lieu de memoire*).[10] A place of remembrance is hence the place of what has remained of an otherwise absent past. Nora contextualizes the shifting meaning of memory spaces within the paradigm of modernity and thereby overstates the homogeneous and stable nature of premodern remembrances, however, as well as the discontinuity and rupture that are implicit in the transition to modernity. In Worms, the traditions that had been associated with the synagogue and the cemetery evolved especially during the early modern period and became profoundly transformed in the course of religious reform during the nineteenth century.

Moreover, local remembrance and the importance of Worms as a destination for Jewish travelers exemplified the extent to which Jewish Diasporas comprised historical sites that conjured images of origin and belonging. As Yosef Yerushalmi has suggested, Jewish life in the Diaspora vacillated between concepts of exile and domicile—that is, an awareness of an unfulfilled state in dispersion and a profound sense of attachment to particular places.[11] During the Middle Ages, members of the community and pilgrims regularly visited the Worms graveyard, which had already acquired its religious significance. German Jewish travelers, as well as the famous Polish Jewish author Sholem Asch, sought in Worms lost traditions and the beginnings of Ashkenazic history. During the Weimar Republic, when urbanization had peaked and larger cities like Berlin became associated with rapid change and historical amnesia, small-town communities that prided themselves on their remnants of the past represented themselves as the last vestiges of a vanished world. During these years, Worms's Jewish past offered reassurance to German Jews, who were becoming infatuated with rural communities and their traditional piety. What had served the community in the formulation of its distinct local heritage now provided Jews in Germany with a long-standing and ennobling ancestry.[12]

The importance of domicile, which had led Jews to invest their surroundings with tropes and metaphors from their religious traditions, contradicts a tendency in recent theoretical writing to celebrate the dislocated and disenfranchised members of a diasporic community. To these critics, Jewish history seems to oscillate between land and book.[13] The German Jewish writer Heinrich Heine's often-cited proverb about the Bible as "a portable homeland" helped these thinkers to untangle Jewish history from the Zionists' territorialization of Jewish life.[14] For the literary scholar Sidra DeKoven Ezrahi, its authors' distance from the sacred

:nter of Jerusalem irrevocably marks Jewish literature in the Diaspora. ιilding on George Steiner, who deems texts to be Jews' only "natural" _meland, Ezrahi views homecoming as an illusionary, stifling alternative to the more vibrant and culturally productive life of the Diaspora, in which home becomes an exclusively literary engagement.[15]

At issue here is neither the binary view of Jewish history as center and periphery marked by expulsion and homecoming, nor an enchantment with the Diaspora that in effect mimics the Christians' interpretation of Jews' eternal damnation.[16] More central to my argument is that in order to sustain this view of homeless Jews, the crucial role that place played in the formation of Jewish cultures and identities is minimized, or even reduced, to a fleeting illusion.

This view renders remembrance as a disembodied act of recollection. To be sure, in the Jerusalem Talmud, R. Simeon b. Gamliel commented that a memorial should not be erected for righteous persons, as "their words are their memorial."[17] In line with this perspective, nineteenth-century German Jewish historians portrayed written and oral Jewish tradition as territory that Jewish communities inhabited in the Diaspora. Drawing upon the talmudic dictum "fence around the law" (Pirke Avot 1.1), the nineteenth-century Jewish historian Heinrich Graetz saw the Talmud itself as transforming every observant Jewish household into an extension of the Holy Land.[18] This claim seems to substantiate a delocalized reading of Jewish remembrance. For this reason, at the beginning of the twentieth century, the Jewish journalist and novelist from Galicia, Karl Emil Franzos, searched almost in vain for monuments to famous German Jews.[19] Their scarcity throughout Germany reflected the traditional Jewish opposition to making images of people, which prompted rabbis still during the nineteenth century to oppose plans to honor famous Jews with a monument.[20]

However, this opposition did not translate into a disregard for physical structures and religious artifacts. Already during the Middle Ages the cemetery had acquired an important role for the local community and visitors in the commemoration of Jewish martyrs. Pious travelers chiseled their names on the backs of tombstones and the Rashi chair. During the nineteenth century, Jews from various communities donated money for the restoration of gravestones and historical sites, while travelers purchased postcards of those sites. With the experience of the Holocaust and the ensuing scarcity of tangible relics of the Jewish past, the evocative appeal of the sites in Worms as places of remembrance only intensified.

I

FROM MEDIEVAL ORIGINS TO THE ENLIGHTENMENT

OBSERVING THE PAST

SACRED REALMS

Within the medieval world, Ashkenazic communities embodied authority and legislative competence and exhibited a degree of autonomy derived from imperial, ecclesial, regional, and local powers. Despite networks of contacts, webs of exchanges, and temporary supra-communal rabbinical councils, these medieval Jewish communities displayed a high degree of independence from neighboring congregations. While the communities shared sacred Jewish traditions, their religious customs nevertheless exhibited significant local variations. To the communities, the customs of their ancestors were no less sacred than and even could take precedence over Jewish law, provided that they did not contradict the laws of the Torah or Talmud. These local variations, often reverberating within the communal recollection of historical experiences, contributed to the creation of distinct local cultures and memories that sometimes contradict historical fact.

Today, for example, scholars have dismissed the contention that Jewish communities were present in the Rhineland continuously from the Roman period onward.[1] Jewish life and culture in Ashkenaz instead likely commenced in the mid- to late tenth century when Jews, as international merchants, moved along the trade routes across the Alps and from the Mediterranean coast of southern France into the Rhineland, where they adopted various medieval German dialects (from which Yiddish originated). This adaptation of local vernaculars probably functioned early on as the primary vehicle for cultural contact and exchange. To be sure, these emerging communities, led by an elite of wealth and learning, became tightly knit, but they would never become wholly segregated from the surrounding culture and its people.

In Worms, historical evidence points to the Jews' settlement in the city at the end of the tenth century. While these settlers were not restricted to the emerging "Jewish lane" until at least the fourteenth century, a cluster of buildings quickly arose that places Jews firmly within the walled space of the city at the southeast corner. By 1034, a synagogue, built by Christian masons, was inaugurated through the "munificence of the childless couple." Mindful of the importance of this act, synagogue authorities extolled the donation in an inscription and recounted it in a special prayer on the Sabbath well into the modern era.[2] With the building of the synagogue, the community acquired both a central place for worship and a space that could preserve events in their history, in addition to a burial ground, which they attained a few decades later.

Building activity during the eleventh century reflects the growth of the community that included probably a few hundred individuals, with families averaging two or three children each, like their Christian counterparts. Among these early residents were famous rabbinic authorities such as Jacob b. Yakar and Isaac ben Eliezer, Rashi's teachers, who resided in both Worms and Mainz and had studied with Gershom Me'or ha-Golah. Born in Troyes in 1040, Rashi was possibly attracted by the reputation of these sainted scholars and apparently spent some time with them before returning again to France.

When Henry IV rewarded the Jews and the city for allowing him to take refuge there during the Investiture Conflict in 1073, the Jews' presence became even more established. In recognition of their help and economic relevance, the emperor granted the "Jews and other burghers of the city" tax freedom in 1074.[3] The prominent naming of the Jews in this document underscores their important role as merchants and traders. In 1090, Henry IV further extended the privileges of the Jews in ways that illuminate their economic functions and life in the city. They were permitted to own houses, gardens, and above all vineyards, to employ Christians in their homes and at work, and to trade in wine, dye, and medicine. The granting of these rights established a lasting alliance between the Jews and the emperor that became a salient feature of local memory in Worms. Like other medieval emperors, Henry IV saw himself as an anointed ruler, and he based this last charter on those that Louis the Pious had already granted the Jews. Henry IV, however, went beyond these traditions and gave the Jews not only comprehensive protection but also jurisdiction over internal disputes.[4]

Despite these extensive rights, crusaders and burghers attacked the Jews during the 1096 campaign and devastated the community. Eco-

nomic competition between Jews and other city dwellers, the still ongoing Investiture Conflict between the popes and the German emperors,
and, above all, religious zeal contributed to this outburst of hostility. The
chroniclers explained that this violent episode in Worms was instigated
by a rumor that the Jews had boiled and then buried a Christian corpse.
Worms's Christian citizens accused Jews of pouring the resulting con-
coction into the city's water supply to poison the population. This charge
functioned as the local pretext for the first attack on the Jewish community, and many Jews committed acts of martyrdom on May 18, 1096 (the
23rd of Iyyar in the Hebrew calendar), when burghers and crusading vag-
abonds, led by Count Emicho, assaulted Worms's Jews.[5] The Jews initially
sought refuge in the bishop's palace, which led to a siege by the coalition
of crusaders, burghers, and villagers from the surrounding area. Most of
the city's Jews perished seven days later, on the new moon, the first of
Sivan, save those few who were forcibly baptized.[6] According to the Hebrew chronicle, approximately eight hundred Jews died in Worms, while
the *memorbuch* (book of memory) lists around four hundred who were
killed between the two attacks, with many having sanctified God's name.[7]

The crusade massacres illustrated the precarious status of the Jews
and the extent of potential anti-Jewish hostility and violence, but at the
same time the fate of this community paradoxically bound its surviving
members even more to their location, insofar as they commemorated
their martyrs. As Jeremy Cohen has observed, hostility and alienation did
not obviate the Jews' involvement in Christian culture.[8] In the holy campaign's aftermath, Henry IV allowed those Jews who had been forcibly
baptized to return to Judaism, and the community reestablished itself in
the city of Worms. In 1112, Henry V renewed his father's tax-exempt status for the Jews. Nevertheless, Jews' legal position remained uncertain in
the following decades, as the struggle between the emperor and the pope
regarding authority over earthly and religious matters intensified. This
conflict was somehow resolved by the Worms concordat of 1122, which
brought an end to the investiture struggle, if not to the rivalry between
pope and emperor. The agreement established an even closer alliance
between the emperor and the Jews, who, with the confirmation of the
Charter to the Jews of Worms in 1157, became "serfs of the chamber,"
a formulation that had already been used in an eleventh-century charter
to the Jews of Worms.[9]

To the survivors and returnees, the presence of hundreds of corpses,
buried only in mass graves, must have intensified the horror of the events.

The Hebrew chronicler from the twelfth century, who vividly recalls the destruction of the community, describes how several Jews decided during the attack to succumb to the approaching enemies when they saw members of the community lying naked: "Let us do their will for the time being, and then go and bury our brethren."[10] While these converts fulfilled their obligation to bury the dead, it is uncertain as to exactly where they did so. Today, with the exception of two graves dating from 1100, no other visible remains subsist on the burial ground.[11] Even if we were to accept the possibility that other graves had existed, most of the Jews who died during the First Crusade could not have had a proper burial.

In the minds of medieval Ashkenaz, martyrs who had not received a decent burial at times seem to have haunted the community of survivors. The medieval compilation *Sefer Hasidim* (Book of the pious) records the Jewish martyrs whom temporary converts had laid to rest. The converts purified themselves in water and brought the corpses of the martyrs to the cemetery before placing them in a large pit. On the way to the cemetery, the body of a woman fell off the body cart and was left behind. It is alleged that she later angrily reappeared in one of the survivor's dreams until her lost body was located and put to rest.[12]

The perceived distress of the deceased martyrs and the absence of places of memory in Worms might explain later attempts to locate the resting place of twelve community leaders that came to be associated with the martyrdom of the community.[13] According to a narrative strand in one early modern text, the leaders were among those who had remained in the bishop's house and fallen during the second attack. When a priest employed a mystical goose to illuminate their place of hiding, they ran along the city wall until they jumped from the tower to the cemetery, where the earth miraculously swallowed them.[14] The miracle here, then, serves to explain the absence of a grave,[15] but later generations appear to have felt more compelled to associate the memory of the martyrs with a distinct location. Thus in his description of customs, the same seventeenth-century author believed that the resting place of the community leaders was clearly identified. Whereas on other days throughout the year, the community encircled the cemetery's circumference, on the first of Sivan they "did not encircle it but visit[ed] the graves of the twelve *parnasim* and pray[ed] at their graves," he explains.[16] Yet no real grave seems to have existed, and the associated uncertainty prompted another seventeenth-century compiler of local customs to validate this claim by referring to an inscription on the cemetery wall.[17] During the nineteenth century, excavators unearthed an older plaque stating "Twelve parna-sim—1096." This inscription had existed adjacent to an alternative marker of the past: "Twelve parnasim."[18]

These traditions identifying a resting place in the vicinity of the plaque are, however, of later origin and probably, if anything, reflect the uncertainty surrounding the legend and burial place. It might have been the absence of graves in the immediate wake of the atrocities that motivated the liturgical innovations and creation of rituals that would function as conduits of memory. As Ivan Marcus has argued, from the commemoration of these martyrs "a nearly universal cult in memory of the dead" developed in Ashkenaz.[19] Roughly between the end of the First Crusade and the 1140s, the Hebrew chroniclers created an "epic of defeat," as Robert Chazan has noted, that depicted the fate of a small and hopelessly outnumbered group, representative of a higher form of civilization, whose ultimate victory would transcend their immediate trials.[20] Reflecting the hostile crusading ideology of the twelfth century, the chronicles are permeated with the language and symbols of their Christian surroundings, thereby demonstrating that the piety of the martyrs was unsurpassed by Christian sacrifices.[21]

Couched in allusions to biblical and talmudic models, the narratives and liturgical laments about the destruction of the Rhineland communities gave rise to a distinct culture of remembrance in Worms that recalled Jewish unity in the face of danger and the unwavering piety of the community. And just as the chronicles and laments clarified the perspective of those who survived, they also sharply demarcated differences between Jews and Christians to counter the increasing doubts among Ashkenazic Jews regarding the boundaries between themselves and Christian society. The pressure to choose between death as a martyr and baptism had fostered a degree of indecisiveness that loomed large in the minds of twelfth-century Ashkenazic Jewry.[22] Valorizing the heroic deeds of men and women like Isaac ben Daniel and Minna of Worms, and calling upon God to avenge the Jews' fate, reasserted Jews' differences vis-à-vis their Christian environment.[23]

Moreover, the chroniclers depicted a community that readily opted for martyrdom instead of conversion. Insofar as the survivors comprehended and enshrined the memory of the destruction, they had to contend with the community's unprecedented acts of martyrdom, which were in apparent violation of rabbinic law against suicide and homicide. To be sure, the Talmud advocates sanctifying God's name in martyrdom as a form of submission to avoid transgression, but it does not command the inflicting of death upon oneself and others.[24] The chroniclers' effort to comprehend and explain therefore did not refer to the halakhic discussion but slotted the events into existing narratives of destruction, persecution, and sacrifice as they apostrophized and memorialized the Jewish martyrs. Central to the chroniclers' narrative was the notion of Yitzhak's sacrifice.[25]

Whereas destructions of communities had traditionally been interpreted as divine punishments, the idiom of sacrifice created a new framework for comprehending the devastation. As Alan Mintz has observed, the self-perception of the Jews of Mainz, Speyer, and Worms did not permit a correlation between destruction and transgression.[26] In response to the enormity of the devastation, a new paradigm emerged that viewed the persecution as a divine test.[27] Replete with literary references, the so-called *Mainz Anonymous* alludes to Genesis 22 and the story of the sacrifice of Isaac when retelling the way Meshullam ben Isaac of Worms sacrificed his son before the approaching enemy killed him and his wife.[28] The description relies on the biblical idea of a sacrifice but replaces Abraham with Meshullam ben Isaac.[29] Using Yitzhak's sacrifice, the chronicler conveyed the belief that the Rhineland Jews had shown their unswerving dedication to God and thereby asserts that the Jews surrendered to their approaching enemies only after assuming that God had decreed their destruction. Instead of falling victim to persecutors, the Jews "placed their trust in their Creator, and offered true sacrifices, taking their children and wholeheartedly slaughtering them in witness to the Oneness of the Venerated and Awesome Name."[30]

Insofar as the Hebrew chronicles narrated the crusade's destruction according to its geographic unfolding, they focused on the fate of those communities for which the narratives fulfilled an important role in the commemoration of actual events. Gerson Cohen has conjectured that the chronicles were to be read in the synagogue as "hagiographic commentaries" to underscore their relationship to the martyrs' memorializing within individual communities.[31] Indeed, all of the chronicles, to varying degrees, interlace their narratives with poetic dirges. The longest chronicle, by R. Solomon b. Samson, quotes from Isaiah 64:11 and cries out, "Wilt thou restrain thyself at these things, O Lord?" His account not only bemoans the devastation but also prays for the rewarding of the martyrs, and for God's revenge.[32] In Rabbi Eliezer bar Nathan's narrative, the martyrs are bound up in the bond of eternal life and "garbed in the eight vestments of clouds of glory, each crowned with two diadems, one of precious stones and pearls and one of fine gold; and each bearing eight myrtles in his hand."[33]

The chronicles' celebration of the Jews' courage and willingness to die as martyrs and to sacrifice their community became intimately connected with a theology of vengeance through which the laments aimed to arouse God. God is challenged to "avenge the spilt blood of Your servants."[34] Thus the narratives established a reciprocal relationship between the martyrs, the community of mourners, and God. Matching these calls for vengeance, the chroniclers likewise voiced the survivors' anger toward Christianity. Written only for an internal audience, the accounts are sated with anti-Christian invectives. The crusaders are described as those "who wander in error," and baptism is seen as "sullying." This language denigrated Christianity and reaffirmed the boundaries that even forced conversion threatened to blur.[35]

The number of surviving manuscripts in Hebrew, Yiddish, and German that were copied between the fourteenth and the eighteenth centuries underscores this chronicle's lasting impact on Ashkenazic culture.[36] In addition, well over twenty laments were composed in the immediate wake of the destruction during the early twelfth century. Unlike the chronicles, the laments focus less on the fate of individuals than on the memory of all of the martyrs, while remaining largely silent about cases of conversion.[37] In his dirge that entered the Worms liturgy, Eliezer ben Nathan, the author of one of the chronicles, describes not only the readiness with which the Rhineland community sacrificed themselves but also the destruction of Torah scrolls, a crime he too calls upon God to avenge.[38] Kalonymous ben Judah names Speyer, Worms, and Mainz in his lament, mourning those sanctified in God's name in Worms and portraying them as adorned with crowns.[39] The significant inclusion of this prayer in the Ashkenazic liturgy for Tisha be-Av placed the memory of 1096 alongside that of the destruction of the two temples and other subsequent calamities.[40]

Best known is the prayer *Av ha-rahamim* (Merciful Father), which in Germanic lands originally was said only twice a year on the Sabbath before Shavuot and Tisha be-Av. The prayer, by an unknown author, eulogizes the martyrs and calls upon God to avenge their death. In a striking analogy to the legendary origins of another famous prayer from this period, *u-netaneh tokef* (Let us declare the mighty holiness), attributed to Rabbi Amnon of Mainz, a seventeenth-century source stipulates that

Av ha-rahamim was in fact found on the reader's table in the synagogue after the Crusade massacres.[41] Reflecting on the miraculous appearance

of this prayer, the *Minhag* book (Book of custom) of the Jewish community of Worms reports that the patriarch Abraham, whose name is contained in an anagram in the opening words, composed the lament.[42] This fictionalized authorship legitimizes this form of commemoration.

The inclusion of these dirges in the liturgy for Tisha be-Av reflects the impact of the Crusade-related destruction but also indicates a general reluctance to institute new days of mourning within Judaism. As the traditional day of mourning, Tisha be-Av served to commemorate not only the destruction of the ancient temple but all atrocities that had befallen Jewish communities. The traditional opposition to new fast days even found expression in one of the compositions about the Rhineland martyrdom by Kalonymous ben Judah: "However, we cannot add a day of mourning over ruin and conflagration . . . Instead today, I will arouse my sorrow wailing, and I will eulogize and wail and weep with a bitter soul."[43]

The traditional resistance toward new fast days and, more importantly, the fact that individual communities suffered on different dates explain the absence of a universal observance of the Crusade atrocities. In Worms, however, the memory of the Crusade was preserved with the inauguration of a specific local day of fasting on the 23rd of Iyyar with a prohibition to perform marriages, haircuts, or the trimming of beards. R. Eleazar b. Judah, who was born in 1160 in Mainz and died in Worms in 1238, recorded the tradition of a daylong fast and described the differences in observance between Worms's memorial fast and those of other communities.[44] On that day the community fasted, recited prayers and dirges, and visited the graves of the martyrs. References in the following centuries point to the continued observance of this day until the nineteenth century.[45]

Aside from the chronicles, the laments, and the communal day of fasting, books of memory memorialized the calamitous destruction of the Crusade as well.[46] The extant *Memorbuch* of the community details the list that begins with the martyrs of 1096 on the separate days and stipulates that it is to be read on the Sabbath preceding the holiday of Shavuot.[47] According to rabbi and codifier of Ashkenazi customs Jacob b. Moses Levi of Mainz (Maharil), during the fifteenth century, outside the Rhineland, only the names of the communities that had been attacked during the First Crusade were recited. The full list of martyrs was only obligatory for the Rhineland communities themselves.[48]

The atrocities of the First Crusade thus created a culture of remembrance that became in turn part of the cherished local traditions during the period when Yehuda he-Hasid (1185–1217), the co-author and editor of the *Book of the Pious*, led the sectarian followers of what came to be known as Haside Ashkenaz until he was succeeded by Eleazar of Worms (1165–ca. 1230). Eleazar of Worms significantly strayed from Judah's more radical sectarian program for accommodating the devastated communities.[49] Despite the mixture of innovation and tradition in the *Sefer Hasidim*, those associated with this group sought always to faithfully preserve received traditions.[50]

This compilation reflects already a much larger change in northern Europe in the eleventh and early twelfth centuries that came to bestow more authority upon written documents. A significant rise in Hebrew texts occurred during the period, and the Talmud acquired a more prominent place in medieval Ashkenaz as well. Along these lines, R. Eliezer bar Nathan (1090–ca. 1170), the author of one of the chronicles, compiled responsa and halakhic rulings following the order of the Talmudic tractates, while traditions and narratives that circulated in the Rhineland about the sages of Ashkenaz would also be inserted into the thirteenth-century *Sefer Hasidim*. This later collection promotes a utopian sectarian lifestyle and instructs the reader in the theology, ethics, and, above all, discipline required to attain salvation. The extent to which this work represents a pious ideal that became a social reality of sectarian followers, however, remains unclear. In line with the twelfth-century glorification of Jewish martyrdom, this ethical anthology celebrates the ideal self-sacrifice as tantamount to that of the martyr while commending those who had converted in order to bury their fellow Jews.[51]

More pertinent yet, the succession from Yehuda he-Hasid to Eleazar involved a geographic transfer that situated Worms as a new center of learning that had once paled in comparison to Speyer and Mainz. Already during the twelfth century, according to a decision at the rabbinical synod in Troyes, the three Rhineland communities had acquired judicial power over their German congregations. At the first meeting in 1150, it was decided that the *Shum* (Speyer, Worms, and Mainz) communities should regulate internal disputes among the communities of the German lands. Despite confirmation of their role in subsequent synods in 1223 and 1250, their authority was never formally accepted but depended instead on the presence of charismatic leaders. Yet whereas during the early medieval period, leaders of the community had been scholars and rabbis

Sacred Realms

who functioned as intermediaries with the non-Jewish authorities, the Rhineland synod declared in 1250 that an excommunication could be decided only by *parnasim* and rabbis.[52]

These apparent changes in rabbinic power notwithstanding, the self-understanding of individual communities continued to rest on the presence of individual rabbinic teachers, who carefully safeguarded the transmission of their knowledge and the divine name in a ceremony of purification, the wearing of white cloth, and the utterances of specific blessings, as Gershom Scholem has explained.[53] Moreover, these leaders inscribed themselves into elaborate chains of transmission. Initially, narratives of the beginning of the rabbinical academies in the Rhineland portrayed Kalonymous the Older as having arrived in either Mainz or Worms to found an academy. These genealogies created a cultural self-image that asserted the Rhineland community's superiority over the newly emerging centers of the Tosafists in France and linked the beginning of Jewish life in the Rhineland to its royal alliance. As Ivan Marcus has observed, they "bragged that they and they alone were the First Families of Ashkenaz."[54] The fact that Mainz and Worms are named interchangeably with regard to Kalonymous might indicate more than simple uncertainty; the conflicting accounts might illustrate the competition between the two centers of rabbinic learning in Ashkenaz.[55]

Such a rivalry would not have been the only reason for the creation of these chains of learning. The devastation of the community and the deaths of his son and Yehuda he-Hasid must have compelled Eleazar to put the esoteric oral traditions in writing. His chain, which had been significantly disrupted by the First Crusade, retraced a geographic transfer from the Babylonian center to Italian Jewry, to Mainz and Speyer, and, finally, to Worms. In his detailed account, Eleazar defended his versions of prayers against changes that had been introduced by the rabbis in France. In his commentary to a prayer book, Eleazar therefore outlined the chain of transmission of inherited traditions not only back to Babylonia and the Kalonymide families that had been brought to Mainz by Charlemagne but also up to himself, who received the teachings from Yehuda he-Hasid. In this self-serving reconstruction of transmission history, Eleazar portrayed himself as the sole and legitimate successor to the esoteric learning that had made its way from Babylonia to the Rhineland.[56] Moreover, this very personalized chain emphasizes the importance of individual teachers. In recognition of Eleazar's own reputation, in turn, during the thirteenth century his name became associated with a study house in Worms that had been erected in 1175 that contributed to the lasting renown of the community.[57]

Eleazar also penned a very personal account of his wife, Dolce, and their two daughters following their murder in late 1196, in which he elaborately expressed his loss.[58] Based on Proverbs 31, he praised Dolce's economic, familial, religious, and educational qualities and recounted how she served not only the members of the large household but also the women of the community as a religious leader, probably as *sangerin*. Recounting the ambush, Rokeah relates that it was Dolce who escaped to seek help, only to be cut to pieces in the street outside the house.[59] Dolce was not the only woman commemorated in this fashion. Urania of Worms's tombstone similarly praises this "daughter of the chief of the synagogue singers" for her "sweet tunefulness" as a women's prayer leader during the thirteenth century.[60]

Despite the relative importance of these women for subsequent generations, it was a rabbinic leader who would become most intimately associated with the community of Worms. Rabbi Meir of Rothenburg, who consolidated rabbinical authority and aimed to establish unity among the disparate communities of the Rhineland, exemplified the new brand of charismatic leadership. Born in Worms, most likely around 1220–23, he studied Talmud with R. Isaac Or Zarua in Wurzburg in 1235 before stopping in Mainz en route to Paris to study with the great Tosafist of the period. During his sojourn on the Seine, Meir witnessed the burning of the Talmud in 1240 that had been instigated by the Jewish convert Nicholas Donin in the Paris disputation. In 1247, Meir settled in Regensburg until his father's death in 1276 or 1281, when he returned to Worms. While traveling to the Holy Land, he was captured in Lombardy with his daughters and son-in-law and died in prison there in 1293.

The unfortunate conclusion of Meir's journey mirrors Yehuda Halevi's failed pilgrimage to Jerusalem. What remains of Halevi's trip is his well-known poem *Zion ha-lo tishali* (Zion, will you not ask?), which expresses his undiminished devotion to and longing for Zion and the patriarchs' graves at Hevron.[61] Meir, witnessing the burning of the Talmud, expressed his bereavement in a poem that carefully echoes Halevi's, titled *Sha'ali serufah be-esh*.[62] Whereas Meir, like Halevi, empathized with suffering in exile, he longs for the Torah, not Zion. Nevertheless, in either case the object of the desire of their laments, which became part of standard Ashkenazic liturgy for Tisha be-Av, is elsewhere than their domicile in the Diaspora. Yet the body of the deceased Meir became an object of

Jewish communities' ambition following their failed efforts to secure his ransom. When Meir was finally laid to rest in the cemetery of Worms in 1307, his tombstone recalled him as "our teacher" and retold of his imprisonment, death, and eventual burial. His ultimate fate was probably responsible for an inscription expressing the hope that "he may rest among the souls of the righteous of the world in the garden of Eden."[63]

The concern that was extended to Meir of Rothenburg's body suggests that his remains had acquired a religious importance comparable to the Christian sacred relics that proliferated during this period in northern Europe.[64] To be sure, relic veneration is not easily reconcilable with the ritual status of graves in Judaism, but the tombstones of martyrs and rabbinic leaders nevertheless became the objects of reverence. A special request by Alexander Wimpfen in the thirteenth century (he had invested his fortunes to pay the ransom of Meir of Rothenburg's body) substantiates this reading. Before Wimpfen passed away in 1307, he asked that he be granted the "fortune" to be buried adjacent to the rabbinic scion, as his tombstone recalls.[65] Not just Meir of Rothenburg's grave but the resting places of other martyrs acquired a religious function from which Jews sought assistance. For an increasing number of Jews outside the community as well, the cemetery had come to matter as a place for rituals of remembrance and prayers. A religious obligation existed for the descendents of those buried to annually visit their graves, and other Jews followed the custom of journeying to the graves of venerated scholars as well.

All of this in fact follows a very well established practice that is, however, difficult to document.[66] To visit graves, to commemorate the deceased, and to ask them to intercede on behalf of the living all imply a reciprocal relationship between the living and the dead that would become fundamental to the culture of remembrance. Instead of representing two opposite poles, life and death were placed on a sliding scale. Death did not connote a fundamental break but instead a transformation (this was also the case for Christians).[67] Already the Talmud describes how Caleb traveled to Hebron "to prostrate himself" at the graves of his ancestors and ask God to guard him against spies.[68] Recording the contested nature of this practice, however, the Talmud in another place reports a difference of opinion between R. Levi b. Hama and R. Hanina. According to one view, Jews go to cemeteries to underscore that they are "as the dead before Thee," while others hope to petition the dead to intercede for mercy on their behalf.[69]

Medieval commentators took it upon themselves to explore and negotiate these different textual traditions, which had already become part of a dispute with the Karaites, where the issue of worshiping at graves featured also in intra-religious polemics.[70] In his code, the philosopher and halakhist Moses Maimonides interpreted the talmudic references from *Ta'anit* 16a as directed only to visits to the cemetery to pray for rain (*Ta'anit* 4:17). He contended that visiting graves, however, made clear that humans are "as the dead before Thee." In contrast, the thirteenth-century *Zohar* took the same textual tradition as the basis for a discussion of prayers to the departed to intercede on behalf of the living.[71] Within the Ashkenazi orbit, Rashi noted the practice of students who gathered at the grave of their teacher to study on the occasion of the *yahrzeit*.[72] Individuals recalled the deaths of their parents in the time of the *yahrzeit* and expanded the liturgical remembrance of departed relatives in addition to the Day of Atonement, Sukkot, Passover, and Shavuot as opportunities to read the memorial prayers.[73] Other texts were mindful to emphasize the differences between Jewish and Christian practices. While Jews might have prayed at the graves of rabbinic sages, they did not share the Christians' enchantment with relics, at least according to a polemical fourteenth-century treatise titled *Sefer Nizzahon Vetus* (The old book of polemic), in which the anonymous author describes as impure the Christian practice of taking the bones of the dead for holy relics.[74]

Despite these varying opinions, within Ashkenaz the legend about Caleb served to legitimize intercessory prayers.[75] *Sefer Hasidim* recalls a story about a community that was threatened with extinction if the members did not pay tribute to the dead.[76] The compilation even notes that the dead are pleased by visits to their graves and the recitation of prayers to them.[77] Reflecting the growing prevalence of these customs, Yehuda he-Hasid's grave in Regensburg became a popular stop on pilgrims' itineraries for centuries. Some visitors even chiseled their names into his tombstone.[78] Responding to the popularity of these practices, R. Haim Paltiel, a student of R. Meir of Rothenburg, claimed that this custom was not in accordance with Jewish law. He particularly spoke out against women and uneducated men visiting graves to pray to the deceased.[79] R. Jacob Moelin (Maharil), an important codifier of Ashkenazic customs and a prominent Jewish leader in nearby Mainz, voiced his tacit opposition to this practice as well when he discussed cases in which individuals had vowed to visit the graves of their ancestors, righteous ones, or saints. Maharil argued that they could easily be absolved from their vows because many authorities had condemned this practice as "inquiring from the dead." Clearly uneasy, Maharil suggested directing one's prayers to God instead of the dead person's body. Nevertheless, he acknowledged that due to the presence of righteous souls (*zaddikim*), a cemetery is a holy place in which to pray.[80] Reflecting more on existing practice than on its larger meaning, Maharil unequivocally stated that on the eve of Rosh ha-shana, everyone went to the cemetery to "prostrate themselves on the graves of the *zaddikim*."[81]

Thus the memory of 1096 had become joined together in texts and rituals both inside and outside of the community. These channels of remembrance promoted attachment to the place and expressed verbal hostility toward Christianity. Whether these invectives necessarily reflect an existing gulf between the two communities or represent an attempt to introduce some distance remains unclear. Regardless, however, the local memory culture enshrined new elements within it that underscored the Jews' royal alliance and historical roots in the Rhineland.

The alliance, however, came at a price. During a period of economic prosperity, when Worms was one of seven free imperial cities and belonged to the founders of the Rhineland city league of 1254, increasing financial demands were placed upon the Jewish community. Despite their substantial financial contributions during this period, Jews were perpetually in danger of being disenfranchised from the corporate structure of the medieval world.[82] Their precarious situation only intensified with the ritual murder accusation, and when urban internal uprisings spread throughout various cities in Germany. In response to these challenges, the Jewish community began to encourage the view that it had originated during the Second Temple period.[83] These foundation myths, which both reflected the community's vulnerability and elevated its self-understanding, became particularly popular during the period of the Black Death when Jews faced renewed religious hostility. The foundation myth that located Jews' origin in the Rhineland before Jesus's birth helped to refute the age-old accusations that the Jews had killed Jesus.[84]

Narratives like these reinforced traditions concerning the Jews' royal alliance when, over the course of the thirteenth century, the bishop acquired jurisdiction over the Jews in criminal lawsuits and litigations that involved Christians. Along with the emperor, the bishop collected taxes from the Jews, while the city and municipal council determined their civic status. In Worms, although the bishop maintained the title of *Statt-herr*, a community council emerged that liberated itself from the administrative yoke of ecclesiastical domination. Nevertheless, in 1313 the bishop confirmed and then restructured the self-government of the Jewish community by placing twelve community leaders at its head.[85]

The erosion of the traditional royal alliance during the fourteenth century reflected changing power relations between the emperor, the churches, and the city, and the shift in their rights threatened to unravel the legal protection of the Jews, particularly given the increasing anti-Jewish animosity of this period. After the Romanesque cathedral in Worms had been completed at the end of the twelfth century, several alterations were made to its southern part between 1310 and 1320, including a typological representation of the victorious Church and the defeated synagogue. Drawing on Lamentations 5:16–17 and Jeremiah 48:16, the figure embodying *Synagoga* is blindfolded and holding a broken scepter, which illustrates her loss of power. A ram's head under her right arm denotes the carnal lust of Israel. Above her left shoulder, the tablets with the Ten Commandments are falling down (fig. 2). *Ecclesia*, in contrast, carries a goblet in which she collects blood from her wound, wears a crown, and carries an intact staff, representing Christian power and rule. Furthermore, prophets are juxtaposed with evangelists from the New Testament, thereby establishing a connection of promise and fulfillment. Depicting the Jews with their medieval Jewish hats, the monument fuses biblical and contemporary times. Further down, the monument envelops *Synagoga*, who turns her head forward, forcing her crown to slide off. In this portrayal, *Synagoga* is placed in company with *Caritas*, *Infidelita*, and the women of the world, who represent arrogance, thereby underscoring even further the low position of Judaism.[86]

The monumental degradation of Judaism was representative of the renewed danger Jews faced at the turn of the thirteenth and fourteenth centuries, with the Rindfleish massacre in 1298, the Armleder riots in 1322, and the outbreak of the Black Death in 1348. The plague in particular marked a turning point in the history of Western European Jewish life, ushering in the Christians' expulsion of Jews from almost all urban centers. As in many other cities, the citizens of Worms accused Jews of promoting the disease by poisoning the water supplies. Emperor Charles IV set the stage for trouble as well, when in 1348 he temporarily waived all royal rights over the Jews in favor of the city, leaving them at the citizens' mercy.[87]

Anti-Jewish violence soon broke out in the city, forcing some Jews to flee to Sinsheim, Heidelberg, and elsewhere. According to an early

FIGURE 2.

Photo of Synagoga *at the entrance of the cathedral. Stadtarchiv Worms, Germany*

modern Jewish chronicler of Worms, some burghers apparently took pity upon the Jews and hid them in their houses. Others used a magic goose, he reported, to reveal the Jews' location. A learned Jew, who had befriended a local priest, disguised himself and delivered a sermon in which he encouraged compassion among the Christians. Asking whether they would rather ascribe to reason or to a magic goose, he pointed to the goose that alerted the congregation to the presence of a Jew in the church. Since the members of the church believed there were no Jews among them, the goose could hardly be deemed reliable. Impressed by this, the congregation stopped harassing the Jews; soon thereafter, the goose metamorphosed into an eagle that is still visible on the St. Martin's church.[88] The facts differed significantly from this account, unfortunately. In the face of this threat, many members of the Jewish community gathered together and then set themselves ablaze. No fewer than four hundred Jews died, and the fire destroyed parts of the women's synagogue; only the cemetery remained unharmed.[89] The *Memorbuch* lists the hundreds who perished during this time.[90]

The ravages of 1349 destroyed numerous communities; others, crushed by constant financial demands by the cities and the emperor, simply ceased to exist in the following century. After 1349, then, the Jewish presence in urban centers plummeted, and the Rhineland was no exception: Speyer's Jews left in 1435, Heilbronn's in 1437, and Mainz's in 1438.[91] Unlike these cities, Worms saw its Jews return relatively soon (the community of Mainz, for example, would only reconstitute itself in 1583). Following the attack, Charles IV noted in a privilege for the city that the destruction of Jews and their property had also damaged the city and its citizens.[92] Moreover, the city authorities quickly realized that the confiscated property of the Jews would not cover the claims of former creditors and decided to allow the Jews to return to the city in 1353.[93] Upon their return, however, the surviving members of the community were subjugated to the magistrate; the bishop maintained his authority over them; and the Palatine duke increasingly interfered in their internal matters as well.[94] In contrast to life prior to the violence and destruction, then, Jews now found themselves even more restricted to the *Judengasse*.

Within this period of intense uncertainty, the community commemorated the destruction in 1349 with a new perpetual day of fast on the 10th of Adar. On this day, the community prayed and recited *Av ha-rahamim* along with other prayers, read the names of the martyrs from the *Memorbuch*, circled the cemetery, and offered their supplications at the graves of the *kedoshim* (holy ones).[95] R. Meir's prayer for the 10th of Adar eloquently captures the despair of a community confronted by enemies approaching them from all sides: "Gebal, Ammon, Amalek, they all act treacherously and lay to waste." He couched his outcry in language that Jews of the community would have been familiar with from the liturgical stanzas for the martyrs of the First Crusade, with each stanza concluding with a line from Isaiah 64:11: "At such things will you restrain Yourself, O Lord?"[96]

Despite the absence of many individual headstones, the Worms cemetery features the aforementioned tombstone dedicated to the memory of
twelve *parnasim,* who also became associated with 1349. The legend was passed down that twelve community leaders had attacked the magistrate prior to the destruction of the congregation. When their intervention in the town hall was unsuccessful, it was said, they then assailed the city councilors. However, no historical evidence substantiates this account.[97] Still, the memory of the 1349 destruction remained vivid within the community when, roughly thirty years later, several Jews signed an official document as sons of those "who may rest in the Garden of Eden," of which "the memory of the righteous is for a blessing" and where "the Lord may avenge his blood."[98]

Despite the Jews' return to Worms, then, the situation was precarious and grew more so when, after 1406, burghers succeeded in abrogating certain rights over the Jews to the magistrate. Tension between the magistrate and the bishop, who succeeded in 1407 in freeing the local clergy from many city customs taxes, also acted to unsettle the city. Despite these intensifying struggles and the increasing influence of the Count Palatinate, though, Worms remained an imperial city. As the various powers competed for authority within it, new regulations made Jews legally more reliant on the city and bishop than on royal favor. Given this arrangement, then, the magistrate became more invested in their protection. In 1410, for example, Jews became the target of ritual murder accusation; however, the city—in exchange for a handsome sum—defended them against the local bishop and the Count Palatinate.[99]

Changes to the status of the Jews (and to their taxes) continued to unsettle the relations among the competing powers and social groups, until in 1431 the emperor validated the Jews' right to collect money from their debtors. Farmers besieged the city and demanded the surrender of the Jews, which the magistrate denied. In 1432, the conflict was finally resolved; the compromise stipulated the lowering of interest and the postponement of repayment.[100] Once again, the magistrate's protection had come at a financial cost.

All of this newly acquired protection proved less effective against other forces arrayed to the Jews' detriment, among them the Dominican preacher Petrus Nigri (1435–83), who had recently returned from Salamanca to become a professor of scholastic theology at the University of Ingolstadt. In the second half of the fifteenth century he delivered zealous conversionary sermons in the cathedral at Worms.[101] Nevertheless, the Jews of Worms persevered and their protection was somehow reasserted when the Palatine duke Philipp and his son Ludwig IV visited the synagogue in 1495 to hear them sing and instructed the local subordinates to deal kindly with them. A year later the German empress Bianca Maria Sforza, the second wife of Emperor Maximilian, also inspected the synagogue.[102]

The relief that the royal visit might have brought was short-lived, however; a fanatical apostate, Johannes Pfefferkorn from Moravia, who also attached himself to the Dominicans, soon thereafter published a number of anti-Jewish tractates. Pfefferkorn called for the expulsion of the Jews from the few cities that still had sizable Jewish communities, including Frankfurt, Worms, and Regensburg. With the help of the Dominicans, he gained access to Emperor Maximilian, who empowered him to confiscate "offensive" Jewish books. Pfefferkorn's call for the erasure of Jewish literature became part of an extended public debate that involved the German humanist and Hebrew scholar Johannes Reuchlin upon the invitation of Johann van Dalberg, the scholarly bishop of Worms. According to the emperor's letter from Padua, Worms became the target of Pfefferkorn's ambitions because it was assumed that the prestigious community possessed many books.[103] Upon the emperor's order, the magistrate ordered Pfefferkorn to confiscate books he deemed blasphemous in Worms on December 18, 1509. Aware of Pfefferkorn's actions in nearby Frankfurt, the Jews of Worms might have been able to safeguard some volumes before his arrival; the list of confiscated manuscripts and books that would be destroyed at least does not feature polemical anti-Christian texts like *Sefer Nizahon* (Book of polemics) or *Toldot Jeshu* (The generation of Jesus).[104]

Pfefferkorn was not content only with excising Hebrew books, however. He also celebrated the expulsion of the Jews from Regensburg in 1519 and gleefully counted the cities from which Jews had been barred at the time, including Cologne, Augsburg, Strasbourg, and Nuremberg. For Pfefferkorn, the presence of Jews in Worms, a community that boasted many talmudic students, remained a thorn in his side. To complete his onslaught, then, he urged the magistrate of Worms to do its share and expel the Jews from the city. The emperor supported Pfefferkorn's quest and likewise urged the expulsion of the Jews, along with the razing of their synagogue in favor of a church or monastery in the same spot. Yet Pfefferkorn's plea was to no avail, and Jews remained in Worms.[105]

With Jews' status in the city constantly endangered and the dispute over the Hebrew books in abatement, the Jewish cemetery in turn suffered great losses during the sixteenth century, when Worms citizens decided to build an underground pathway using its tombstones. In response to the Jewish community's intervention—they reminded the magistrate that the headstones were protected under Roman imperial law—these desecrations ceased.[106] It might have been the constant insecurity and the increasing fragility of their channels of remembrance that compelled the community to compile the liturgy and their religious customs during this period.[107] Preserving the markers of the past also motivated Elieser b. Samuel Braunschweig from Worms; his inclusion of the synagogue's interior and exterior inscriptions in a manuscript in 1559 suggests that he saw the synagogue as a crucial part of the community's heritage.[108] Braunschweig's inventory of the inscriptions provides a new form of historical connection informed by Renaissance sensibilities about the study of the past, which accorded historical artifacts an unprecedented importance. Indebted to these new historical sensibilities, Braunschweig also recalled the fate of Rabbi Amnon and transcribed the testament of Judah the Pious. His attempt to preserve even the fading or overgrown inscriptions was indicative of this period, in which the community became defined not only by its religious customs, legal autonomy, and particular organization but also by the historical heritage.

Over the preceding centuries, Jewish memories had become marked by the conflict with Christianity and the political tension within the city. Yet it was the experience of violence during the First Crusade and the Black Death that paradoxically bound the Jews to the vicinity of the city and their cemetery. Moreover, the violence against Jews, the destruction of torah scrolls and tombstones, and the monumental degradation of the culture were all echoed in the chronicles' verbal attacks upon Christianity and calls for vengeance as well as the liturgical dirges. Nevertheless, the way in which Jewish victims of the First Crusade and subsequent persecutions were depicted as religious sacrifices gave meaning to their deaths and underscored the extent to which Christian concepts functioned as interlocutors of Jewish memories. Notwithstanding the apparent opposition between Jews and Christians, the chroniclers and authors of liturgical laments expressed the ideal of martyrdom in the idiom of twelfth-century Christendom.[109] During the early modern period, the religious antagonism that had governed the construction of Jewish memory was sidelined by the invention of new historical traditions. To be sure, the accounts of seventeenth-century persecution and expulsion would continue to reverberate with the textual traditions of previous attacks. The motif of vengeance would recede, yet the emotional attachment to Worms would strengthen.

BETWEEN RITUALS AND TEXTS

During the early modern period, preservation, restoration, and innovation intermingled in the making of a local heritage in Worms centered on rabbinical luminaries, religious martyrs, narratives about the community's mythical origin, and alliances to emperors, dukes, and other local dignitaries. This process engendered both uniformity and difference in response not only to renewed challenges, expulsion, and destruction but also to modern printing presses. As Jewish culture evolved into one of the book, textual representations were placed alongside the medieval memory culture of rituals and customs. Against the standardization of Jewish law and practice in printed codes and the fixing of oral traditions in anthologies of Jewish legends, the Jews in Worms defended, redefined, and asserted their own religious and historical traditions. This affirmation, however, also involved the adaptation of traditions that hitherto had been associated with other communities. Nevertheless, remembrance continued to remain entrenched in traditional cultural practices and thus acted to cloak the significant innovations that would come to define the local past.

The political regionalism of the Holy Roman Empire made the creation of local and regional identities in an imperial city viable. At the beginning of the sixteenth century, Worms counted politically as one of the great cities of the Holy Roman Empire—it was where, during the Diet of Worms in 1521, Martin Luther appeared before Emperor Charles V. It was for this reason that the humanist and renowned sixteenth-century cartographer Sebastian Münster included Worms in the collection of important city prospects in his *Cosmographia*. Financed by the magistrate of the city, Münster portrayed Worms in a 1550 woodcut as a proud imperial city marked by towering churches (the significantly shorter

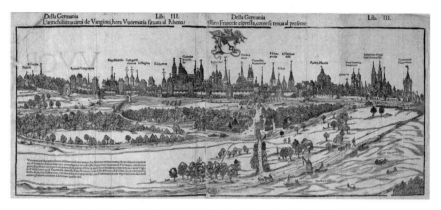

FIGURE 3. *Sebastian Münster,* Cosmographia *(1550). Stadtarchiv Worms, Germany*

synagogue remained invisible). The caption of the print elevated the importance of the city as home to Roman monarchs, Frankish kings, and German emperors (fig. 3).[1]

After the almost complete expulsion of Jews and destruction of urban Jewish life in the German lands at the end of the Middle Ages, only a handful of imperial cities continued to tolerate Jews. Worms's urban Jewish community was in fact the third largest in the Holy Roman Empire after Prague and Frankfurt during the sixteenth and seventeenth centuries. In recognition of this elevated status, the synod of Frankfurt in 1603 tried in vain to revive centralized rabbinical courts in cities like Worms in order to counter the increasing fragmentation of Jewish communities during this period within the Ashkenaz orbit.[2] Far from being relegated to an incidental space within the city proper, the Jews of Worms actually inhabited a central location in proximity to its marketplace. Notwithstanding their circumscribed living in the *Judengasse* and their religious differences, they shared many elements of a common culture with other inhabitants of the city. Not only Jewish men but also Jewish women actively engaged in the local economy, to the extent that a late-seventeenth-century rabbi in Worms conceded to economic reality in lifting the otherwise common prohibition against Jewish women being alone at any time with a Gentile male.[3]

In 1610, the *Judengasse* contained about 765 individual Jews, crammed into approximately one hundred houses in a city of no more than six thousand inhabitants in all. Emblems such as a star, moon, rose, green

tree, rod of oak, kettle, or goose adorned Jews' houses and served as a
marker of origin.[4] These emblems were also featured on torah binders

(*Wimpeln*). The German Jewish torah binders were, according to custom, made in honor of the birth of a baby boy, at times from the diaper
used at his circumcision. This practice bound the individual to his family, the house, and, above all, the community and its religious tradition.
The boy would bring the *Wimpel* with him to his bar mitzvah as well as
his wedding.[5] Location, religious custom, and identity all converged in
this particular ritual.

Jews' association with the city also influenced their visual representation during this period. In his encyclopedic survey of sixteenth-century
knowledge, the *Thesaurus picturarum*, Marcus zum Lamm (1544–1606)
portrayed city dwellers according to their social and political standing.
Traditionally, an insignia like a cross or crown held in the hand represented the power of those who were being depicted. On the other hand,
Lamm represented a Jewish man as dressed in a cloak and chaperon,
marked by the yellow badge and carrying garlic, while a Jewish woman
wore a cloak and veil and held a goose in her hand (fig. 4). The association of Jews with garlic features prominently in the arsenal of antisemitic
stereotypes. In this case, however, the garlic is less freighted, indicating
simply this Jew's prominent status and association with the communities
of Speyer, Worms, and Mainz, which were often abbreviated as *Shum*
(garlic). The goose invokes the name of a house in the *Judengasse* and
a legend about the magical goose. The woman holds in her left hand
a midwifery toad, which refers to childbirth and underscores women's
central role in Jewish genealogies.

Reflecting their elevated status as members of the *Shum* communities, Jews in Worms during the early modern period engaged their past
in various ways. The community had long been home to rabbinical luminaries. Many rabbis in communities in Austria, Germany, and Poland
originated from there. In the synagogue, the naming of seats after these
scions and their burial in the cemetery's "valley of the rabbis" helped to
preserve their memory.[6] The oldest extant tombstones (Jacob and Sa-
gira b. Samuel) are adjacent to the valley of the rabbis, while the graves
of R. Meir of Rothenburg and Alexander Wimpfen are close to the cemetery's entrance. The placement of rabbis' tombstones in a secluded location in the cemetery seems to have commenced already with R. Jacob
Moellin (Maharil) in 1427, followed by the cabbalist Elijah ben Moshe
Loanz (1564–1636).[7] Placing later rabbis next to the codifier of Ashke-

WORMS

J U D E N.

ZWEITE HÄLFTE DES 16. JAHRHUNDERTS.

FIGURE 4.

Marcus zum Lamm,
Thesaurus picturarum
(1577–1606).
Hessische Landes und
Hochschulbibliothek
Darmstadt, Germany

naz customs and the Baal Shem illustrates the lofty self-understanding of the following generation, which happily aligned itself with these exceptional rabbis. Within the empty pages of the thirteenth-century festival prayer book or *Mahzor*, a similar lineage was preserved when individual cantors and sextons inscribed their names from the sixteenth century onward out of gratitude for having been able to serve the Worms community.[8]

These different memorial practices both created and reflected the community's self-understanding in periods of transition, and these practices became ever more clearly defined through the observance and codification of local customs, the collection of legends, and the preservation of physical sites. With the onset of the printing press, which replaced the manuscript culture and shook the status of oral traditions, new conduits of communication emerged that refashioned local remembrance yet again. In Ashkenaz, the printing of large editions of halakhic, mystical, and philosophical treatises, which until this time had been in the possession of only a small elite, forged important new channels for the construction of memory. Bibles, prayer books, and moral primers appeared in greater numbers as Yiddish book production grew to meet the rising demand of men and women who lacked sufficient Hebrew.[9] Historical works like Solomon ibn Verga's *Shevet Yehuda* (Cracow 1591) and David Gans's *Zemach David* (Frankfurt 1698) were published in Yiddish, and compilations of legends that had only ever existed in the classical rabbinical writings and in oral traditions surfaced on the book market during the sixteenth century. This form of "mass" communication, however, soon acted to standardize practices and undermine local differences.[10] When the Sephardic codifier Joseph Caro in the Ottoman Empire compiled a comprehensive guide on Jewish law and customs, the Polish rabbi, Moses Isserles, added a commentary of his own to counter the power of the printed *Shulhan Arukh* and safeguard Ashkenazic traditions.[11] Apparently not entirely satisfied with these compilations, Jews in Worms worked to ensure also the preservation of their own distinct customs at this time.

Coincident with these broader changes in Ashkenazic culture, the community of Worms continued to face its own challenges during the early modern period, even though Carl V had renewed the community's privileges in 1551. Ongoing internal power struggles within the city continued to threaten the status of Jews. In 1524, the city of Worms gave its Jewish residents communal regulations (*Judenordnung*) for the first time. These decrees comprised twenty articles, which were confirmed with only minor changes in 1541. By 1584, even more comprehensive directives ordered Jews' lives in the city.[12]

Even given these extensive legislative measures, the status of the Jews remained precarious. In the sixteenth century, Jews again became the target of a ritual murder accusation that arose out of a conflict between the city and the bishop of Worms over the right to tax the Jews. Under the duress of these accusations, the city council obtained from Emperor Ferdinand I the right to force the Jews out, a move that was contested by Bishop Dietrich of Worms.[13] The dispute dragged on until 1570 and ultimately came to incorporate new ritual murder accusations that were made to the magistrate in 1563 and that eventually led to a protracted trial.[14]

The growing infringement on the emperor's prerogative during this period illustrates that Worms was technically not a *Reichsstadt* (imperial city) but a *Freie Stadt* (free city). Within its walls, a small, thirteen-person council governed the city and seventeen guilds chiefly represented the citizenry. The city indeed had acquired a high degree of autonomy and even liberated itself from its former dependency upon the bishop. However, the bishop still inhabited an autonomous realm within the city walls; it encapsulated the cathedral and his palace and catered to the Catholic minority. He also remained the *Stattherr*, investing the city's magistrate and maintaining the right to install Jewish elders. Over the years, some of the bishop's rights had been further delegated to his treasurer (*Kämmerer*), a member of the Dalberg family, who represented another powerful voice with a fiscal interest in the Jews. Lastly, the city remained technically subjugated to its protective lord, the Elector of the Palatinate, as well as to the laws and ordinances of the Holy Roman Empire.

In light of these complicated and overlapping power relations, conflicts concerning the Jews could be momentous, and not just for the community—any change in the regulation of the Jews endangered the established balance of powers that controlled and governed the city as a whole. Expelling the Jews, for example, would not only destroy one of the last remnants of urban Jewish settlement in the Germanic lands but also threaten to decrease the rights of their protector. Whereas throughout the Middle Ages, citizens of various cities, often with the tacit approval of the emperor, did expel the Jews from within their city walls, the authorities of the Holy Roman Empire during the seventeenth century typically opposed attempts to purge Jews due to their fiscal and political interests.[15]

When in 1613 the *Judenordnung* was up for renewal, the citizenry took the opportunity to protest against the presence of Jews and attempted to renegotiate the terms of their existence or even to expel them. The ensuing conflict revealed the tension between the magistrate and the guilds as much as that between Christians and Jews. The guilds accused the patrician council of unduly cooperating with the Jews and further complained about the interest that Jews leveled on loans. Economic competition mixed with social and religious hostility formed a particularly fraught backdrop for their petition, which the bishop and Dalberg quickly countered with their appeals to the imperial court. With the Jews petitioning the emperor and, at least initially, resisting attempts at intimidation, the emperor, as well as the Elector Frederick V of the Palatinate, intervened in the local conflict to assert their authority and relieve pressure on the Jews.[16]

The conflict, however, did not subside. In 1615, opponents of the magistrate published Jewish ordinances and a favorable report from the supreme court of the empire that supported the reduction of interest on loans. The subsequent arrest of one of these rebelling burghers by Frederick V escalated tensions further.[17] In the midst of these ongoing deliberations and negotiations, the Fettmilch uprising in nearby Frankfurt erupted out of similarly strained relations between the patricians and the guilds. Led by Vincenz Fettmilch, a grocer and pastry baker, the struggle brought about by the guilds included attacks on local Jews.[18]

Almost in tandem with the events in Frankfurt, a delegation of seventeen guildsmen in 1615 ordered the Jews to leave Worms, according to a German pamphlet of the time. A Jewish source even claims that up to six hundred city residents attacked the ghetto, and indeed, enraged burghers destroyed and desecrated the synagogue, the *bet midrash*, several hundred tombstones, and a building in the cemetery.[19] Given that the original economic motives for this conflict had by now faded, this struggle had come to represent a movement to purge the religious minority, remove its holy sites, and create a new citizenry. Rioters believed that their acts of destruction in turn validated their own faith, all of which almost resulted in the erection of a crucifix on the site of the destroyed Jewish cemetery. A city council member encouraged the destruction of the cemetery by noting publicly that the "people who lie here are not worthy of having such considerable and permanent memorials."[20]

Most of the Jews fled across the Rhine in the wake of the uprising against them and found shelter in Palatine villages, where, according to Christian sources, "they tore their clothing, strewed sand and ashes on their heads, fasted and prayed."[21] Juda Löw Kirchheim, a Jewish eyewitness to the expulsion of 1616, vividly captured the sense of loss when he wrote that in the midst of the persecution, several Jews had successfully fled the city and found themselves in "exile (*galut*) across the Rhine."[22] Far from losing themselves to despair, however, the Jews promptly appealed to the emperor, and four thousand Palatine soldiers eventually arrived in Worms, arrested several citizens, and forced all of the residents to renew their oath of loyalty to the council. A rare woodcut from a contemporaneous pamphlet depicts the deliberations within the city, the expulsion of the Jews, and the arrival of and work by the heavily armed soldiers of Frederick V's army (fig. 5).[23]

This turn of events gave momentum to the reinscription of the Jew's expulsion into traditional patterns of God's providence using historical songs, which represented a new genre in Jewish writings. Nahman ben Eliezer Puch of Prague composed a historical song shortly after the

FIGURE 5. *Woodcut from* Kurtzer unvergreifflicher Bericht *(1615).*
Stadtarchiv Worms, Germany

events in 1616 to convey "good news of deliverance and comfort." Such
songs, often intended to be sung to a well-known tune from the Jewish
liturgy or German popular music, acted like newspapers to inform and
educate the public about the destruction, migration, and return of the
Jews in Frankfurt and Worms. This long song praised God's providence
in past and present and recalled the revolt in Frankfurt and the execu-
tion of the rebels. It also described the events in Worms up until the Jews'
return. By attributing a miraculous quality to this return, Puch bestowed

a religious significance upon the events in relation to God's providence. In line with this religious interpretation of the events, Puch concluded his
song with moral instructions and a prayer for redemption.[24]

As these pamphlets placed the events into the cultural memory outside the city walls as well, the Jews returned to the city with the emperor's support in 1616. In addition to defending their economic interests, the emperor and the elector had turned against the uprising to affirm their own power vis-à-vis the city, its council, and its citizenry. Upon their return, the Jews noticed that one tombstone had partially survived among the many destroyed graves; it was believed to have been fifteen hundred years old, as a later note in Kirchheim's manuscript suggests. The writer, unconcerned by the question of historical veracity, then observes that remnants of the tombstone were sent "across the sea."[25] Kirchheim thereby underscores the apparent veneration for this tombstone, which held the promise of corroborating the community's claims about its origin during the Second Temple period.

Initially, the community struggled to observe the new fast day that was established in 1617 on Rosh Hodesh Shevat, the day of their return to Worms, during which they recited elegies and supplications.[26] Nevertheless, the community's self-imposed imperative regarding observance indicated a desire to preserve, and restore when necessary, its traditions and artifacts. Relying on older manuscripts (discovered in 1616 when the rubble from the destroyed synagogue had been removed) as well as on his own observations, Kirchheim recorded the existing communal customs in 1625.[27] Not unlike Juspa Hahn, who recorded the customs and laws of the community of Frankfurt, Kirchheim compiled a vast collection of local practices, inserting even records such as Eliezer b. Nathan's description of the Crusade and the Rokeah's account of the death of Dolce.[28] Conscious of the uniqueness of the community's customs, which differed from all "other places and countries," Kirchheim's compilation aspired to safeguard the congregation's memory and ensure its observance at a time when many Jews "grope[d] in the dark." Kirchheim believed that the Jews should not deviate from "the customs of our forefathers in our hands," since they are the law (Torah).[29]

Paralleling Kirchheim's efforts, the synagogue's restoration itself became an exercise in historical preservation and remembrance when David Joshua Oppenheim, the first *parnas*, contributed one hundred King's Taler to rebuilding the prayer platform (*bimah*) and other parts. While the *bet midrash* remained in its desolate state, Oppenheim restored the wall around the cemetery, erected a new building in the graveyard for the ritual cleansing of the dead, and constructed a small chapel adjacent to the synagogue in 1624.[30]

In line with Christian practices during this period, the architects of the rebuilt house of worship consciously aligned it with its pre-expulsion counterparts to reforge a link with that era.[31] Rendered in a contemporary baroque style, the synagogue nevertheless preserved many medieval elements from earlier columns and capitals. Likewise, the early baroque reading pulpit of 1620 either incorporated or replicated a late gothic precursor, while the circumcision chairs seemed to have been based on medieval models. Similarly, the chapel gestured to the past. Built in 1624, the chapel featured a Romanesque rectangular structure with equally sized apses into which a throne of stone with a half-rounded back-end had been placed. Following medieval models, a narrow stone bench encircled the chapel, and its entrance copied features of the synagogue's doorway.[32]

Despite the reestablishment of the community and the completion of the physical restoration, the congregation continued to face upheaval that further shaped its culture of memory. During the Thirty Years' War (1618–48), Worms's buildings suffered severe damage, and its population endured much hardship. With the Swedish invasion of the early 1630s, most Jews in Germany temporarily came under Swedish control and were heavily taxed. Despite these new financial demands, several Jews of Worms, among them members of the prominent Oppenheim family, managed to negotiate business transactions that extended to cities like Amsterdam, Prague, and Vienna. They loaned large sums of money, traded in wine and hides, sold jewelry and clothing, peddled wares to Jewish and Christian households, and involved themselves in agriculture. Women even took part in various commercial transactions and acted as both business partners and storekeepers. Nevertheless, its financial situation had become so strained by 1641 that the community was forced to tax married individuals in order to reclaim pawned synagogue ornaments.[33]

Reflecting the community's increasing economic reliance on particular individual members, the *Memorbuch* became a record of the munificence of the Oppenheim family and other generous donors. Building on medieval models, this prevalent resource in the Jewish communities of the Germanic lands functioned as a cherished conduit of local remembrance during the early modern period that in turn supported communal

identity.[34] Possibly reflecting the changing constituency of the community, this book further absorbed the historical memory of newly arrived

congregants; in 1655, for example, it listed the individuals who had perished in the Eastern European pogroms in 1648.[35] The *Memorbuch*,
which was read aloud preceding the holiday of Shavuot and Tisha be-
Av, also included occasionally elaborate hagiographic accounts of rabbis like Yair Bacharach and famous women like Eva Bacharach, who was
born in Prague around 1580 and died in Sofia in 1651 but lived for a
short while in Worms.[36]

The impact of the cycle of destruction, expulsion, and return might
have compelled Juspa Shammes, who was born in 1648, to follow in the
footsteps of Juda Kirchheim and extend his compilation of local rituals
and customs. Juspa, the sexton of the community and a native of Fulda,
eventually became by default the chronicler of the communities' traditions. He both justified and preserved current customs by tracing their
origin and affirming their continued observance, especially in those cases
that deviated from standard Jewish practice or law.[37] His interest in local
customs was probably also motivated by the upheavals of these decades,
which saw some community members leave the city while others arrived
there. These newcomers would have been required to observe the local
fast days, whatever their previous habits.[38]

The observance of the oldest customs was apparently in decline as
well, and probably for this reason, Juspa voiced his opposition to changes
and bemoaned any deviation that occurred within the community.[39] His
work also presumably filled both descriptive and prescriptive functions
as he detailed the various fast days that had been inaugurated to commemorate the fate of the community during the First Crusade, the Black
Death, and the expulsion at the beginning of the seventeenth century.
According to Juspa, for example, the community observed the fast day
of the 23rd of Iyyar to recall "the holy souls that were murdered here in
the holy community of Worms on the day of the persecution of 1096."
After the recitation of prayers, the congregation would proceed to the
cemetery and recite supplications at the graves of the holy ones.[40] For
Rosh Hodesh Adar, Juspa composed a special prayer for the members of
the Jewish burial society, who fasted on the preceding day and recited *selihot* in the synagogue. Wearing black coats, they pleaded for forgiveness
from the deceased and asked God to remember those women and men
who had died as martyrs in all persecutions.[41] The burial society subsequently adopted Juspa's prayer whenever they carried out a new burial

and encircled the cemetery. Like Kirchheim before him, Juspa reported that, between these fast days and Rosh Hodesh Sivan, luxurious activities like banquets and festivities were forbidden.[42]

Juspa sprinkled his depictions of local rites with references to historical events and legends associated with the Worms community. He also treated those things separately in his *Sefer Ma'ase Nissim*, where he recorded legends about the community's origin; moments of divine deliverance in the face of persecution; accounts of some of the community's renowned members; and other fantastic tales. Originally written in Hebrew, the work was translated by his son into Yiddish and published in 1696 in Amsterdam. It proved to be very popular, and nine more editions followed.[43] It is unclear exactly what role Juspa played in the published compilation. Existing tales suggest that he utilized both written and oral sources, and his son may have done more than simply translate the text. Juspa shared several of his stories with other compilers of this period as well and drew from accounts of persecutions that were familiar from other early modern Jewish historical texts.[44] By uniting these divergent oral and textual traditions, however, he created a distinctly local collection of narratives.

Yet while *Ma'ase Nissim* came to be seen as a celebration of local traditions, some of its stories in fact undermined the Worms community's self-elevation. At the outset, Juspa states that he received information about one narrative from his former teacher in Fulda, the current Worms rabbi Eliah Ba'al Shem, who himself knew the account through a commentary on the *Shulhan Arukh* by Joshua Falk, the sixteenth- and seventeenth-century head of a Polish yeshiva and renowned halakhist.[45] According to this controversial narrative, the Jews of Worms did not return from their exile in the Rhine valley to Jerusalem after the rebuilding of the Temple in the sixth century BCE. They replied to letters from Jerusalem that there was no need for them to go to Jerusalem for the festive pilgrimages because they lived in the "lesser Jerusalem." For their refusal to return, the community of Worms was punished.[46] This story transformed the foundation myth that otherwise existed in *Toldot Jeshu*, the medieval pseudo-history of the life of Jesus, creating from it a compelling cause for the community's later persecution.

Memory of their righteous ancestors serves to promote the ideal of faithfulness among the contemporary community. Juspa therefore coupled his descriptions of martyrdom with references to the community's remembrance of their deeds. He described one imminent threat of persecution, for example, that was deflected when two foreigners, whom Juspa speculated might have been angels sent by God, gave themselves up on behalf of the community. A prayer for the two strangers was recited ever afterward on the seventh day of Passover, and Juspa reminded his readers about the fast day for the martyrs of 1349 as well.[47]

From his biographies of some of the community's most venerated past rabbinical leaders, it is evident that Juspa did more than simply compile accounts; he drew upon, incorporated, and often revised some of the most popular hagiographical anthologies of the period, such as the *Maysebukh*. This compilation of over 250 tales represented one of the most comprehensive repositories of legends in circulation at the time. The oldest existing edition of 1602 conjoined talmudic and midrashic material that Jacob ibn Habib had already assembled in his *En Yacov* (Venice, 1566) with narratives lifted from Gedaliah ibn Yahia's *Shalshelet ha-kabbalah*, which encompassed yet other oral and textual traditions.[48] The immensely popular *Maysebukh* featured legends about biblical figures like Abraham, David, and Solomon but also included post-biblical rabbis, most notably Samuel he-Hasid from Speyer and his son Yehuda Hasid from Regensburg. Their inclusion reflected an increasing interest in Haside Askhenaz that also resulted in the publication of *Sefer Hasidim* in 1581 as part of the growing body of ethical literature of this period that was intended to strengthen religious values.

The inclusion of medieval sages and hagiographic narratives in compilations of local customs reflected a new genre within Jewish writing that became particularly popular and grew to incorporate accounts of the kabbalist Isaac Luria, the Ari, and the praises for the founder of Hasidism, Israel Baal Shem Tov. This hagiographic material both preserved and expanded historical memory.[49] Within this emerging literature, Worms initially lagged behind other Ashkenazic centers. Yet through this process of adopting existing narratives and applying them to Worms, locals invested their space with the presence of rabbinic scions and martyrs and thereby asserted and enriched their particular traditions as well.

An example of Juspa's Worms-friendly embellishment involved his description of the erudite Eleazar, who, endowed by magical powers, taught the medieval kabbalist, philosopher, and physician Moses bar Nahman (Nahmanides) in Spain. Whereas in the *Maysebukh*, Yehuda he-Hasid of Regensburg is at the center of this story, Juspa's *Ma'ase Nissim* bestows that role upon Eleazar and describes his flight on a cloud to Spain and his meeting with Nahmanides to highlight the importance of Worms. In

comparison to the glorified leaders of the past, Juspa deemed his generation to be undeserving of such miracles and asked God to consider them
worthy through the merit of their ancestors.[50]

Juspa also revised a story found in Gedaliah Ibn Yahia's *Shalshelet
ha-kabbalah* (1587) and in the Yiddish *Maysebukh* (1602) about an encounter between Rashi and the duke of Lower Lorraine, Godfrey of
Bouillon, that was meant to establish Rashi's superiority and the rule of
divine providence. The existing accounts described a meeting in which
Rashi predicts that Bouillon will conquer Jerusalem but remain in charge
for only three days, at which point the Muslims would regain possession
of the city and leave Bouillon with only three horses. Angered by this
prospect, Bouillon threatens to kill Rashi if he should return unharmed.
Bouillon does and seeks out Rashi but is discouraged from harming him
by a stone that falls from the top of the city gate and kills one of his remaining soldiers. While trying to make amends, he then learns that Rashi
has already passed away. Whereas *Shalshelet ha-kabbalah* and the *Maysebukh* describe Rashi as living in France at the time of the story, Juspa
assures his readers that the scholar instead resided and taught in a *bet
midrash* named after him in Worms.[51] Due to the success of Juspa's collection, later editions of the *Maysebukh* actually switched to Juspa's rendition of the story set in Worms.[52]

Juspa's *Ma'ase Nissim* likewise fundamentally altered the existing portrayal of Dolce; scholar Judith Baskin suggests that Juspa was motivated
to do so by new anxieties over appropriate male and female behaviors.
In his version, then, Dolce remains unnamed and is murdered at a time
when no men are present. Neither her important role in Eleazar's household nor the fact that she sought help are mentioned, whereas it becomes
Eleazar who is injured when he pursues the murderous gentile students.
Juspa appears to have deliberately transferred Dolce's early heroic acts to
the male figures of the story.[53] Yet it should be remembered that the historical evidence is in fact ambiguous, and local remembrance remained
at best multivalent and muddled at times the fate of other women with
the fate of Dolce herself.[54]

In line with an overall attempt to be more inclusive in his influential
act of remembrance, Juspa apostrophized both the male leaders of the
community and the women for their heroic response to the Black Death.
In his retelling, the story of the Jews' passivity and martyrdom comes
to demonstrate instead their bravery: the twelve community leaders kill
the members of the city council, while the rest of the community fights

the burghers in the streets. In this highly staged presentation of the Jews' readiness to defend themselves, women too appear as active martyrs, set-

ting fire to the four corners of the town. To be sure, this account most likely reflects how Jews of the early modern period wished to remember the past, rather than the historical reality.[55] The story of this armed resistance is certainly absent in Kirchheim's earlier rendition, and Juspa might very well have again conflated existing accounts about Worms with traditions about the Jews of his hometown of Fulda.[56]

The tranquility of this period in the aftermath of the Thirty Years' War proved to be short-lived.[57] While France established its dominance in the negotiations concerning the peace of the Pyrenees in 1659, Louis XIV continued to claim territories in the West. In the Regensburg Treaty of 1684, Germany and Spain conceded to France's recent gains. Nevertheless, in the ensuing Palatinate war of succession from 1688 to 1697, the Rhineland territories became part of the European conflicts between France and the Holy Roman Empire as well as the Spanish in Habsburg. A coalition of European forces confronted the French army, which quickly seized Heilbronn and Heidelberg. Speyer and Worms were not part of the Kurpfalz but were surrounded by it and therefore dragged into the conflict; in October 1688, Worms surrendered to the approaching French armies. In the midst of these events, the Jewish community petitioned for a letter of protection from the French marshal, who promised to guard it against possible attacks by the soldiers. The letter was hung outside the *Judengasse*, replacing the emperor's coat of arms with the French king's.[58]

The letter of protection, however, proved to be worthless when French troops ordered Jews and other city dwellers to destroy the towers and parts of the city wall, which put the *Judengasse* in great danger—many of its houses had been built directly into the wall itself. For a while all was well: "God protected us so that no harm befell a soul," as one Hebrew source recalled. French soldiers reassured the community at first that they would spare Worms, "for she is an ancient city." After a few months, however, French officials ordered all citizens to leave Worms, and the Jewish community had to temporarily transfer many of its religious ornaments to Metz.[59] Once the city was deserted, French troops set it ablaze in May 1689. In addition to the synagogue and the Rashi Chapel, the fires also destroyed the *Judengasse* itself.

In response to the enormity of the destruction, many narrative and pictorial descriptions of the devastated city began to appear. All of the citizens shared a sense of loss, displacement, and expulsion, and both Jews and Christians utilized a language of exile to express it. In 1691, when a minister conducted a service in the burned-out Magnus church, worshipers sang Psalm 137.[60] In a similar vein, a native of the city, Rabbi Yair Bacharach, who had fled with his wife to Metz, recorded these events with a sharp sense of dislocation. Bacharach describes how he has been forced into a state of "wandering" after the destruction (*hurban*) of "our congregation, the mother and city in Israel."[61] A native of Worms, the wealthy and learned rabbi David Oppenheim echoed this sense of loss of the "mother and city in Israel" and "the land of my birth and my father's house."[62]

Concurrently, Juspa's son Zekli composed an elegy for his father's *Ma'asse Nissim* that betrays a literary familiarity with the chronicles of the First Crusade. His Yiddish account describes the unfolding destruction, and every stanza closes with a quote from a biblical text, primarily Lamentations—the first ends with "and nobody helped her." Citing Lamentations 1:7 and 2:8, Zekli likens Worms's devastation to Jerusalem's. A few lines later, he compares the *hurban* of Jerusalem to the destruction of Worms, then adds the Hebrew quote from Jeremiah 9:17, "that our eyes may run down with tears, and our eyelids gush out with waters." How should we leave our holy community, the Yiddish text asks.[63]

Associating Worms with Jerusalem in this way reinforced the community's self-perception that it continued to exist, even in dispersion. In Metz, the Jews of Worms carefully recorded the income and expenses, changes of ownership, and names of the deceased, and they noted all of the synagogue's properties that had been brought to Metz for safekeeping.[64] In addition, Rabbi Bacharach stipulated that the Jews of Worms had to observe the community's fast days, even while they resided outside of the city's walls. For him, the community continued to exist and merely awaited its opportunity to return home. Its exile did not constitute its destruction (*hurban*) along the lines of a *gerush* or flight (*berikha*) of the old community, because "the holy torah scrolls, religious ornaments, and the community records" had been saved.[65] Bacharach's argument demonstrates the central role that religious artifacts and observance had acquired in ensuring the community's continuity even during the "exile of Worms" (*golah warmaiza*).[66] Despite the comforting presence of these traditional elements, however, the dispersion must have strained the bonds among the community's members, whose return to Worms was by no means a forgone conclusion.[67] Nevertheless, in anticipation of their return, the community of Worms sent out emissaries to other Jewish communities in midsummer 1698, asking for assistance in rebuilding the synagogue, the *bet midrash*, and the *Judengasse*.⁶⁸

In 1699, following the peace treaty of Rijswijk, negotiations between the city and the members of the community were completed, and the Jews finally returned to Worms with the religious objects they had been safekeeping in Metz.⁶⁹ With the help of donated money, they restored their synagogue, rebuilding it in much the same style, as is evident from the *Aron ha-kodesh* and the reader's pulpit. The Torah shrine, which had been partly damaged by French troops, was not replaced but rather built into a new shrine in 1704–5.⁷⁰ While reassembling their religious artifacts and restoring their buildings, the community also worked to incorporate the memory of those members who had perished while in dispersion. The *Memorbuch* therefore included several individuals, like Isaac Blin, the son of Elieser Sussmann, who died in 1695 and whose tombstone in Frankfurt names him as a refugee from Worms. The memorial book also lists Juspa Shammes's other son, Samuel, who died in 1699 in Frankfurt.⁷¹

In recognition of Rabbi Bacharach's effort to maintain the community during its temporary dispersion, the *Memorbuch* recounted his life upon his death in 1702, listing his publications, noting his wide-reaching erudition, and praising his fame. This hagiographic account also related that during the "difficult times" (*yamin noraim*)—most likely in reference to the destruction of the community in 1689—Bacharach had brought joy to God and the people of the community. He was buried next to his father, Rabbi Simon Bacharach, who had died in 1670. In recognition of his renown, and reflecting the apparently formidable role of women in the Worms community, Bacharach's wife, Sarlan, was laid to rest in the valley of the rabbis as well.⁷²

Although devastated by the experience of destruction and exile, the community continued to recover its lost treasures. In 1720, the *bet midrash*, which had been destroyed during the Fettmilch uprising in 1615, was rebuilt as a gathering place for scholars and students by Juda Loeb Sinzheim, the influential Jewish financier in Vienna and son-in-law of Samuel Oppenheim.⁷³ For this renewed construction, a separate *Memorbuch* was completed in 1730 that stated at the opening that it was copied from an existing book to be read out loud every Saturday in the *bet midrash*. Still, at this point the *Memorbuch* identified this building as the *bet ha-knesset* of Rashi, not the chapel.⁷⁴

The renovated synagogue and the rebuilt chapel indicate a desire to emphasize the community's continuity with its past at a time when religious rituals, compilations of communal customs, and the repertoire of Jewish legends all reflected both continuity and change. The notion of the Jews' exile from Worms and the community's continued viability in dispersion underscores the extent to which a local identity based on the community's past had been forged. As members continued to observe their fast days, their new liturgical laments, though akin to the Crusade poems, nevertheless represented a departure from previous forms of remembrance. Instead of calling for divine vengeance, these dirges call for divine protection for God's chosen people. Whereas the eleventh-century community saw their destruction as the supreme test and sacrifice, the seventeenth-century community saw theirs in the context of traditional Jewish responses as a divine punishment for their sins.[75]

During the early modern period, communal traditions that hitherto had existed only in oral forms were gathered and more formally attached to the Jews of Worms. These traditions celebrated devout and heroic ancestors and documented more completely than ever Jewish Worms's ancient origins, as well as its royal alliance—Jews continued to rely on the support and protection of the emperor and physically commemorated this with candelabras crowned with an eagle in the synagogue.[76] Emperor Charles IV confirmed in 1714 the privileges of the community and gave it the right to place the imperial coat of arms at the entrance to the *Judengasse* as a visible reminder that the Jews lived under his protection.[77] This legacy of emblematic patriotism for the Reich would resurface in nineteenth-century representations of the Jews in texts and images that sought to document their German nationalism.

CHRISTIAN INTERLOCUTORS AND JEWISH MEMORY

Historians of the early modern period have highlighted the extent to which printing presses, colonial expansion, and traveling, especially the educational Grand Tours of the continent, brought people and cultures into contact. In his classic study of the emergence of the Enlightenment, Paul Hazard traced the origins of this turning point in Western European intellectual history to the act of traveling.[1] Others have subsequently emphasized the importance of border crossings and the ways in which cultural encounters changed the interacting groups.[2] As the Jews of Worms solidified their local customs and practices and anthologized narratives about their past, they transferred oral traditions, rituals, and practice into books. Placed into circulation in this way, these local traditions crossed denominational boundaries both inside and outside the city. Instead of continuing to practice in isolation from each other, Jews and Christians in some ways began to reconfigure their respective cultures in response to this cross-community interaction.

This shift toward text-based forms of remembrance contributed to the proliferation of local traditions that in turn attracted pious and curious travelers as well as Christian scholars, historians of the city, and authors of travelogues. The lasting formulation of Worms's Jewish heritage during this transitional period occurred within (and sometimes despite) these overlapping fields of cultural production. Worms was not isolated, even though the city's relevance had waned ever since the magistrate and bishop in 1659 turned down Karl Ludwig of the Pfalz's offer to replace Heidelberg with Worms as the second residence and university city of the Palatinate. Mannheim accepted the offer, and Worms's political and economic influence began to decline. Similarly, the city's Jewish community, which was one of the few urban congregations to survive the sixteenth and seventeenth centuries, lost stature when, under absolutist rulers, Jews were once again encouraged to settle in German cities and towns.

As the Worms community weakened relative to their counterparts in the region, the city began to curtail the Jews' legal privileges even further. Despite the magistrate's successful appeal to the emperor and to the Imperial Diet against the reintroduction of Jews' payment of royal homage, the community continued to turn to their royal protector in cases of disagreement with the magistrate. With both sides asserting their fiscal interest in the Jews, hefty taxes soon followed.[3]

Increasingly impoverished and threatened by their ongoing battles with the magistrate, community members adopted a conservative mien as they tried to remain steadfast to their heritage.[4] More individuals took their house emblems for their family names, complying with the increasing external administrative pressure to fix those names.[5] The community repledged itself to its continuity through the remembrance of rabbinic leaders by adding Naphtali Hirsch Spitz (1712), Menachem Mendel Rothschild (1732), and Moses Brod (1732) to the famous valley of the rabbis in the Holy Sand cemetery.[6] Moreover, during religious services in the house of worship, the Worms *Mahzor* of 1272 remained in use until the nineteenth century, and various cantors and sextons continued to record their names in the book.[7] As mentioned previously, the retrospective style of the synagogue's interior likewise testified to an ongoing affection for the past. The wooden circumcision chairs that were donated in 1730/31 displayed a Romanesque style, and the torah ornaments (*rimonim*) continued to imitate medieval models even as other German Jewish communities were choosing tower shapes for theirs.[8]

Religious customs also held to Worms-specific precedent whenever possible. The community prayer books that were printed during the first half of the eighteenth century detailed the traditional customs and prescribed the continued observance of the local fast days. Similar to its seventeenth-century predecessors, the 1714 edition of the prayer book made clear that its contents were intended to counter both encroaching liturgical changes and diminishing knowledge of the community's own customs.[9] Those customs or stories that had been ambiguous became more clearly fixed. During the 1600s, for example, Juda Kirchheim failed to mention the tombstone of the twelve community leaders, while Juspa supplied a long narrative about their heroic deeds but associated their deaths with the destructions of both 1096 and 1349. In contrast, the eighteenth-century edition related that members of the community had always encircled the cemetery and visited the graves of the twelve community leaders on Rosh Hodesh Sivan, the day of remembrance for the martyrs of 1096, not 1349.[10]

Once again these gestures of preservation of the past seek to maintain continuity and forge cohesion in a period of social, political, and economic change. Increasing numbers of travelers likely encouraged retrenchment in a city that, due to its storied past, was featured on the itineraries of the early modern British Grand Tourists. Though on the whole less visited than cities in Italy and France, German cities nevertheless attracted their fair share of curious travelers, who then would appear to inspect the historical remnants of the Jewish community as well. Despite its allure, however, poor transportation, frequent customs barriers, and a placement away from main traffic arteries made Worms a demanding destination.[11] Travelers who took the more popular route from Frankfurt to Heidelberg skipped Worms only with some regret, since they all desired to see the city "where Luther made his first appearance before the Emperor."[12] Those (largely British) Christians who did visit Worms noted that the city "shewes great antiquity, and wantes not magnificence."[13] Worms's inclusion in one of the most widely read travelogues of this period no doubt raised such expectations, but the French travelbook author Maximilian Misson was surprised to observe that while he had expected the city to be as large as Frankfurt, he found that it was instead "poor, and ill peopled."[14] Interestingly, whereas early modern travelers frequently commented on the Jewish communities in Venice, Amsterdam, and London, Christian visitors to Worms were mostly interested in the city's churches and made little mention of the presence of a Jewish community there.[15]

Travel at this time, however, was not limited to Grand Tours, whatever their renown, and Jews too began to take more interest in visiting Jewish historical sites. To be sure, travelogues and travel writings are not much present in the corpus of Hebrew and Yiddish writings of this period. Yet the scope of this literature certainly expanded with the Yiddish translation of medieval travelogues as well as the publication of pilgrim's guides for the holy places in Palestine.[16]

Travel itself and travel writing became important channels through which the heritage of the local community was both consolidated and sent beyond the city walls. Travel reports of Worms reveal that by the eighteenth century at the latest, a fixed series of sites and narratives had emerged that every visitor to Worms would encounter. He would tour the cemetery, for example, inspect the synagogue, and learn about a torah scroll that the locals attributed to Meir of Rothenburg, contrary to the evidence provided only a few decades earlier in Juspa Shammes's book of customs.[17]

Abraham Levie traveled across Europe between 1719 and 1723 and wrote about it. Levie, whose family belonged to the prosperous circle of merchants and court Jews in Germany, first observed that Worms Jews were forced to wear a yellow cloth to distinguish themselves from non-Jews. He did not question the identification of the chapel with Rashi. Indeed, the chapel carried a particular significance for him; he was happy to be able to report "that I sat on Rashi's chair." Levie also was sure to spot the goose on St. Martin's church and paraphrased the legendary account of how the outside wall of the synagogue had opened to save a woman. Apparently unaware of the divergent textual tradition in this regard, however, Levie did not identify the woman as either Rashi's mother (based on R. Gedaliah ben Yosef ibn Yahia's *Shalshelet ha-kabbalah*) or the mother of Yehuda ha-Hasid (based on the account of Juspa).[18]

The emissary from Jerusalem in this period, Haim Yosef David Azulai, traveled widely in the second half of the eighteenth century to collect money on behalf of the Jewish communities in the Holy Land and arrived in Worms in 1753 via a once-weekly coach from Frankfurt. In his travel diary he describes how uncomfortable the trip was for the many cramped passengers in a vehicle otherwise loaded with merchandise and pulled by eight horses over the rocky terrain. In Worms, which Azulai deemed very ancient, based on Juspa Shammes's tales, he was shown the synagogue, the Rashi Chapel, and the cemetery with the tombstone of Rabbi Meir of Rothenburg. He also inspected the "miracle wall," which he was told had saved Rashi's mother and about which he had apparently read in R. Gedaliah ben Yosef ibn Yahia's *Shalshelet ha-kabbalah*.[19] Despite his apparent interest in the community, however, in his subsequent compendium on Jewish sages, *Shem ha-gedolim*, Azulai said that the Rashi Chapel had been closed when he visited Worms. In addition, he implied that the chapel's association with Rashi was less a historical fact than a traditional belief favored by the Jews of Worms.[20]

Unlike both Azulai and Levie, however, most Jewish travelers held to the model of traditional Jewish pilgrimages that continued to be more common at this time. Whereas medieval travelers like Petahiah of Regensburg had searched for holy shrines in Mesopotamia, their successors also visited the cemeteries of Ashkenaz.[21] Since the late Middle Ages, pious pilgrims had visited the graves of martyrs and rabbinic luminaries like Meir of Rothenburg, Alexander Wimpfen, Elijah Baal Shem, Juspa Shammes, and Bacharach. While initially rabbinical opinion regarding praying to the dead was, to say the least, divided, the opposition to it was weakened during the early modern period through the publication of books like *Ma'aneh lashon* (expression of the tongue), which appeared in Hebrew in 1615 and was promptly translated into Yiddish. These sorts of Yiddish books containing prayers to honor or petition the departed proved to be immensely popular.[22] Reflecting the growing acceptance of these practices, Joel Sirkes, an eminent Polish rabbi of the late fifteenth and early sixteenth centuries, rejected R. Haim Paltiael's opposition regarding cemetery prayers.[23]

Particularly on fast days, Jews from elsewhere as well as local community members would visit cemeteries. Those who paid tribute to the deceased hoped to derive protection through their visit and prayers and therefore recited supplications.[24] Before the High Holidays, Jews would likewise make a pilgrimage to certain revered individuals' graves, since many regarded the deceased as the most appropriate intermediaries before God. They directed their prayers to them as well, particularly in times of illness. Between Rosh Hashanah and Yom Kippur, women recited special prayers as they measured the individual graves as well as the circumference of the cemetery. Upon their return from the graveyard, they turned their measuring threads into candles. To this end, Simeon Frankfurt, for example, composed in his *Sefer ha-hayyim* (Book of Life) a special prayer based on material in *Sefer ma'aneh lashon*. It appears that the light of the candles facilitated the supplication and pleas for divine forgiveness.[25]

The textual tradition for this practice of pilgrimage to cemeteries was respectably long. The author of *Sefer leket yosher*, R. Joseph ben Moses, who lived during the fifteenth century, transmitted the case of a community leader from Augsburg who had vowed to visit all of the cemeteries of the famous Shum communities.[26] Rabbi Solomon ben Jechiel Luria (Maharshal), who was born about 1510 in Poznan, Poland, and died in 1574, recounts that his promise to pray at the grave of his mother in Worms brought him to that city.[27] During the seventeenth century, the popularity of the cemetery was evidenced by Juspa's observation that "many visitors travel to Worms to visit the graves of the Maharam and pious Alexander."[28] For the benefit of these visitors, Yair Bacharach entertained the notion of transcribing the inscriptions of several tombstones that were becoming increasingly difficult to decipher.[29] Several visitors even carved their names into the Rashi chair in the chapel or inscribed themselves, for example, onto the back of Jacob b. Moses ha-Levi's (Maharil) tombstone.[30]

The practice of leaving one's name implies that a visit forged an intimate relationship between the visitor and the religious artifact, in the same way that Protestant travelers broke off pieces of the bench where Luther had miraculously been saved from drinking a glass of poisonous wine.[31] Other Jewish visitors linked themselves to the Worms community by donating funds to refurbish the synagogue's interior. David Oppenheim's sister Frummet followed in his generous footsteps and provided the sanctuary with new circumcision chairs and a curtain.[32] The son of David Gans, Ischachar Moses, donated a Hanukkah candelabra to the community in 1656.[33] Bluemlein, the wife of Rabbi Koppel Levi, had been born in Worms (she later resided in Mannheim) and bequeathed a torah pointer to the synagogue; the sons of the court Jew Michael May gave the community a torah curtain in 1744 in memory of their grandmother, Rechele.[34]

Insofar as Jews and Christians traveled among each other during this period, narratives about the community's past crossed confessional boundaries. Personal contacts between Christian scholars and rabbis in Worms had existed already during the fifteenth century.[35] Yet during the early modern period the dissemination of local legends raised new questions about the community's past. Christian interpreters critically reviewed local traditions. Hebraists and historians of the city debated the veracity of some of these Jewish historical traditions. At the same time, the Hebraists' compendium of Jewish beliefs, customs, and lores served as the basis for the depiction of the Jews in Worms in some eighteenth-century travel guides. It should be noted, however, that while these Hebraists and guidebook authors disputed Jewish traditions at times, their publications still contributed to the dissemination of the local Jewish heritage of Worms.

In contrast to the often-contentious medieval exchanges between the faiths, the early modern Christian Hebraists, who engaged in lengthy refutations of Judaism, intertwined critical debates about Jewish theological concepts with detailed descriptions of their customs. The first stage in Christian-Jewish polemics, which extended from the beginning of Christianity until the twelfth century, had centered on the interpretation of the Holy Scriptures, while later conversations centered on the Talmud.

Christian Interlocutors and Jewish Memory ¦

Particularly during the twelfth and thirteenth centuries, the increasing Christian familiarity with Jewish texts gave credence to the Christian belief that Jews had significantly deviated from biblical precepts. During the early modern period, Christian scholars, often led by converts, sought to familiarize themselves with the entirety of the Jewish tradition, where the initial missionizing motif slowly waned. These studies displayed a new ethnographical curiosity in addition to a protracted polemical interest in what they perceived to be the anti-Christian elements of Judaism. At this stage in the Christian-Jewish disputations, the customs and practices of individual communities gained an unprecedented importance. Quarrelsome literature written by converts to Christianity, the translation of the *Maysebukh* in 1617 by the Giessen professor of Hebrew language Christoph Helwig, the publication of the controversial *Toldot Jeshu* in Latin, and a generally greater familiarity with Jewish historical texts starting in the sixteenth century among Christian scholars provided the emerging European republic of letters with easily accessible information about Jewish traditions and local communities.[36]

The Hebraists branded the community of Worms as steeped in superstitious beliefs and customs. They felt compelled to refute its legendary origin and alleged devoutness, and they were particularly suspicious of a legend that had been immortalized in one of the most radical anti-Christian Jewish tracts of the Middle Ages. *Toldot Jeshu*, a purported history of Jesus, relates that the Jews of Jerusalem sent letters to the various communities about Jesus, whereupon Worms's Jews replied that Jesus should be left alone and not condemned to death. Many manuscripts existed of this text, and it was also translated into Latin at the beginning of the eighteenth century. Taken at face value, of course, this account provided a powerful testimony to the antiquity of the community as well as a defense against the traditional Christian accusation of the Jews.[37] But it also attracted less welcome attention from those who sought to undermine the faith.

The Jews' reliance on these traditions and their acceptance by Christian authors grew more pronounced during the Renaissance, as whole cities, regions, and kingdoms sought (and, in a sense, competed for) their ancient origins.[38] Basing his work on similar accounts from the city of Trier, Jacob Twinger claimed in his influential chronicle of Strasbourg that during the fifteenth century BCE, Trebeta, the son of the Assyrian king Ninus, founded Strasbourg as a refuge. In a race for antiquity among the various cities, chroniclers in Zurich, Mainz, Cologne, and

Basel all adapted this textual tradition in order to assert that their city, too, predated Rome.[39]

In comparison to many other cities, then, Worms developed its distinct historical traditions quite late.[40] Drawing from the existing accounts of other German cities, Worms's first comprehensive chronicler, Johannes Heydeken, provided the city with its ancient tradition only at the beginning of the sixteenth century. He went one better, however, adding to the familiar tradition the claim that the Christian citizens of Worms had participated in the destruction of the temple in 70 CE. After the battle over Jerusalem, they brought Jewish female captives to Worms, which implied in turn that the city's Jews were the descendents of mixed marriages instead of a proud biblical lineage. The replacement of the Jewish version of their descent with a narrative of enslavement and mixed marriages enabled Heydeken to underscore their presently debased nature.[41] Despite his critical agenda, however, he nevertheless unintentionally substantiated the Jewish community's roots in antiquity, whatever story one was inclined to believe.

These various historical traditions justified the Jews' legal standing as much as they helped to consolidate their local identities. Juspa Shammes therefore sought to counter the Hebraists' negative portrayal of the community's origin by inserting a local bishop into the foundation myths, which underscores the increasing regionalism of Jewish culture at this time. Moreover, the prominence attributed to the Dalbergs in Juspa's account might also reflect his personal relationships, particularly with Johann von Dalberg (1445–1503), the bishop of Worms, who was known for his interest in Hebrew scholarship and his significant collection of Hebrew books.[42] In his book on Jewish customs, Juspa explained the absence of the prayer 'adon 'olam (Lord of the world) by pointing out that the Jews of Worms believed that since their congregation antedated the writing of this prayer, they need not recite it.[43] At the same time, he used his anthology of local legends to revise certain narrative elements from Heydeken's chronicle. In Juspa's version, Ashkenazic Jews saved a member of the Dalberg family in antiquity, for which the family handsomely rewarded them. Subsequently, other members of the Dalberg family were instructed to deal kindly with the Jews, and they paid the ransoms for Jews who were captured during a siege of Jerusalem and then brought to Worms. Juspa, who had heard about this legendary story, insisted that it was still recorded in the annals of the house of Dalberg. He believed that this tradition was the basis for the customs of Dalberg servants serving as pallbearers at every Jewish funeral and also accompanying couples to their wedding canopy, as were both still observed during Juspa's time.[44]

The partial endorsement of this foundation myth by some Christian authors was a pressing issue for those Hebraists and converts to Christianity who wanted to contest the local traditions. *Shalshelet ha-kabbalah*, for example, included several legends about the community and specifically related that God's name had been written on the ceiling of the synagogue but was covered by cobwebs.[45] Enraged by this report and its implication that Worms's synagogue was a temple comparable to that in Jerusalem, the convert Samuel Friedrich Brentz, in his *Juedische abstreifter Schlangen-Balg* (1614), reported on his personal inspection of the synagogue: "I have freely got on the way for a time / and went to Worms / since the Jews regard Worms as the small temple (*Bet mikdash*), that is / for the holy temple / and say: God resides here in a spider web / and their synagogue is filled with spider webs, which once someone wanted to remove / at which point the vault lowered itself toward that Jew / that he had to refrain from it / about which the Jews pretend / what their signs and miracles had occurred / about which a whole book could be written."[46] Salomon Zvi Aufhausen vigorously disputed Brentz's entire diatribe, pointing out in his Yiddish rejoinder that God does not dwell in spider webs.[47]

Brentz was not alone in his ridicule and criticism of the Jewish community in Worms. Unsettled by the proliferation of its mystical and holy traditions, the eminent Christian scholar Martin Diefenbach applied his critical sensibilities and Christian prejudices to the community's history at the end of the seventeenth century.[48] For Diefenbach, ultimately, the Worms Jews' resistance to conversion arose from their local tradition, which he regarded as a "fable."[49] To refute Jewish beliefs in general, Diefenbach chose to take issue with the particularities of Jewish customs in the town. Instead of devoutness there, the Hebraists found religious ostentatiousness. Diefenbach turned particularly to the Worms accounts of a messianic pretender who emerged in 1222 in Worms as a sign of their impiousness—this was a popular and fraught topic in Christian writings about Jews in the aftermath of the Jewish messianic movement led by Shabatai Zevi during the 1660s.[50]

Another story widely circulated since the Middle Ages, this one of seduction, featured prominently in Christian debates about Jewish messianism. In Caesarius of Heisterbach's thirteenth-century collection of moralistic tales, *Dialogus miraculorum* (Dialogue on miracles), he employed the cultural stereotype of the beautiful Jewess and her attractiveness to Christians.[51] Caesarius used the trope to combine debauchment and gullibility with violence: "In the city, I think, of Worms, there lives a Jew, who had a beautiful daughter." To cover up the unnamed woman's pregnancy, the cleric who had seduced her convinces her to tell her parents that she is a virgin who will give birth to the messiah. The parents accept this story and look forward to the birth, but when she then gives birth to a girl, one of the members of the community kills the newborn.[52]

When Jacob Eisenmenger, in his notorious anti-Jewish compilation, retold the story, it had acquired a more sinister tone. Rather then their gullibility, his story proclaimed the Jews' dangerous and vengeful character, as it is now the mother herself who smashes the baby against a wall, committing *Kindesmord*.[53] It may be that Eisenmenger's portrayal of a woman capable of killing her children is partly informed by First Crusade chroniclers' reports of the acts of martyrdom committed by women. While some medieval writers interpreted Jewish martyrdom as acts of heroic piety, others saw those acts, especially when committed by women, as evidence of an innate cruelty. The latter interpretation fueled Franciscan debates over forced child conversions in particular and buttressed antisemitic stereotypes of the late medieval period in general.[54] The later Hebraists, however, like Johann Jacob Schudt in his vast book on Jewish history and lore entitled *Jüdische Merkwürdigkeiten* (Jewish curiosities), at least occasionally reverted to Caesarius's more charitable rendering.[55]

These Christian critics in turn functioned as interlocutors of Jewish memory when Juspa revised their accounts in his own work. In his rendition of this story, a student employs a sorcerer to put the only daughter, who lived in the house named *Zu den Springbrunnen* in the *Judengasse*, under a spell to seduce her. When the girl realizes her impending danger, she informs her father, who invites ten rabbis to study in his house and form a circle around the girl to protect her. When midnight strikes, everyone except the girl has fallen asleep, and the student appears. She then declares, "I would rather die than sleep with you" and kills him with a knife. The Jews who respond to her cries are finally able to dispel the magic, and the story ends with her exoneration by her Christian neighbors as well as the local authorities. The moral is obvious: "Thus, dear people, you see that God regards the pious and faithful for everything."[56]

The various versions of this tale demonstrate the extent to which Jewish and Christian cultures intersected and engaged with each other, and the retelling of tales represented one way in which Jews and their traditions were represented and debated. Hebraists sought to ridicule Jewish character and religiosity, but they also questioned the origin of the community itself. Diefenbach was not alone in his annoyance about the foundation myth.[57] Johann Christoph Wagenseil took issue with it upon learning that the Jews of Worms had bolstered their arguments to the emperor by claiming that they were descendants of those who had settled in Germany before the birth of Jesus.[58] Their alleged origin then helped them to negotiate their privileges, to the Hebraists' dismay.[59] In the community's collections of privileges and ordinances was a copy of their regulations from 1570; it was claimed that the city had originally issued this document in 70 CE.[60] During the seventeenth century, even Christian community leaders repeatedly alluded to the Jews' ancient roots when they petitioned the emperor to help them.[61] In the conflicts at this time over the status of the Jews that led to their temporary expulsion, local pastor Stephan Grün, for example, upbraided Christian burghers for acts of violence against the Jews. Accepting the legendary dating of a tombstone as over 1,600 years old, he argued that the Jews of Worms shared no guilt in the death of Jesus because their community predated his existence.[62]

At issue here was not simply the question of Jewish versus Christian precedence but also the Jews' use of the origin myth to their advantage when they negotiated their legal status.[63] The Hebraists felt even more compelled to refute these claims given that some early modern German chroniclers, theologians, and philosophers had uncritically regurgitated them. Jacob Schudt counted even the Dutch Renaissance scholar Hugo Grotius among them.[64] In contrast to these Christian "believers," Schudt emphatically rejected the evidence provided by *Toldot Jeshu*, even speculating that the Jews of the community must have convinced the author to falsify his account.[65] Despite his conclusion, however, Schudt conceded that the community must have originated around the time of Jesus.[66] Not unlike Juspa Shammes, Schudt saw the Dalberg legend as evidence of longevity, given its continuing manifestation in the dues Jews paid for their weddings and burials.[67] Maximilian Misson, the author of a comprehensive travel guide to Europe, also perused the Latin translation of *Toldot Jeshu* during his sojourn in Worms and reported on the Dalberg legend.[68]

Similarly, the first comprehensive history of the Jews, by the French Huguenot Jacques Basnage, was entitled *Histoire du people Juif depuis*

60

Jésus Christ jusqu' à present, pour sevir de continuation à l'histoire de Jo-
seph (1706–11). It became a standard work during the eighteenth century and it, too, questioned the evidence. Basnage was suspicious from ┊ 61
the start: "But those [Jews] of Worms pretend to have given Proofs to
the Emperor, and the States of the Empire, that they had no hand in our
Saviour's Crucifixion, and that from time immemorial, they have been
settled in this City, which is the reason they have been granted Privileges,
which others are deprived of." Reviewing the claims based on Huldrich's
Latin translation of *Toldot Jeshu*, Basnage concluded by flatly denying
their reliability.[69]

Ludvig Holberg, the Danish author of another comprehensive history
of the Jewish people that appeared in a German translation in 1747, recounted the Dalberg legend based on Misson's early modern travelogue.
With Schudt and Basnage, Holberg also deemed the account in *Toldot
Jeshu* to be both wanting and doubtful. Nevertheless, Holberg concluded
that the Jews must have lived in Worms during the time of Jesus, though
he joined other Hebraists in questioning their legendary devoutness;
like Diefenbach, he even insinuated that the community was "low" and
"bad," and that their many persecutions proved that this was so. In particular, he charged the Jews with deceit for cooperating with the French
troops during the occupation of the city at the end of the seventeenth
century.[70]

Despite their ongoing critical reviews, ridicule, and dismissal, however, travelogues published through the mid-eighteenth century included
in their expanded discussions of Worms further details about the Jewish past. Whereas German travel writer Johann Hermann Dielhelm's first
guide neglected to describe Worms's major attractions, a later edition included a lengthy account. In it he associated Trebeta, the son of the Assyrian king Ninus, with the foundation of the city, thereby situating the
beginning of urban life in Worms in the time of Abraham. Dielhelm believed that the other available sources vindicated him—his comprehensive historical account of the Rhineland further reported that the local
synagogue prided itself on being the oldest in Germany, and that Rashi
had taught there. In the end, nonetheless, Dielhelm dismissed the Jews'
early settlement claim in Worms, but his language notably lacked the
harshness that characterized the Hebraist debates.[71]

In line with Dielhelm's more tempered approach, local Christian historians in Worms likewise affirmed the Jewish tradition, which enabled
them to place Worms's origins in the Roman period. This argument

became important in that it established a basis for reasserting the idea of Worms as an imperial city that was free from ecclesiastical influence. Despite the Christian Hebraists' dismissal of the relevant sources, these local historians carried out excavations in the Jewish cemetery, attempting to locate a Jewish tombstone from the Roman era—such a discovery would have proven that Worms predated Christianity and was exempt from Church rule. Johann Wendelin Jung, who had served as rector of the local gymnasium since 1720, searched the cemetery in the 1740s and determined that the community had been in existence since the sixth century BCE. Löw of Hanau supplied the relevant alleged text from the badly damaged tombstone in question.[72]

When two other local historians reviewed the city's history during the 1750s, an ongoing conflict between Worms's magistrate and the Church further occasioned a reassertion of the Jewish tradition of their pre-Christian origin. Johann Friedrich Moritz endorsed the magistrate's position against the diocese and responded to the Church and their spokesman, Johann Friedrich Schannat, who had been commissioned by Franz Georg von Schonborn, the Archbishop of Trier and Bishop of Worms. Finding the general historical evidence to be lacking, Moritz contended instead that Jung's discovery of the ancient tombstone, as well as the narratives in *Ma'ase nissim*, substantiated his claims.[73]

The insertion of the Jewish foundation myth into the chronicles of the city ensured its future relevance at the very time when the city's Jewish heritage was becoming better known beyond its walls. Newly published chronicles like Menahem Man Amelander's *Sefer she'erit yisra'el* (Book of the remnant of Israel) in 1743 valorized the heroism of Ashkenazic communities like Worms during the First Crusade and the Black Death. Amelander contended that chronicling persecution was a holy duty, but he failed to link the twelve community leaders with the events of 1096, which would have endorsed local remembrance in Worms.[74]

At this point, in fact, this particular identification still seems to have been limited to local forms of memory. A new version of *Ma'ase nissim* by Abraham Wallerstein in 1767 likewise continued to associate the fate of the community leaders with events in 1349. Capitalizing upon the community's renowned past, Wallerstein claimed that his book contained miracles and wonders about Rashi and other righteous Hasidim as well as accounts of various persecutions.[75] He also indicated that the latest persecutions threatened to obliterate the memory of earlier attacks on the community, which made it all the more important to publish his

work.[76] To emphasize the ongoing miraculous character of the community, Wallerstein even added to its traditional legends an excerpt from the
pinkas of the burial society.[77]

At the same time, Yehiel ben Solomon Heilperin's *Seder ha-dorot*
(Order of the generations) retold the story of the miracle wall but also
reiterated that the Jews of Worms had failed out of arrogance to return to
Jerusalem. More importantly, he significantly altered the medieval Spanish Jew David Kimchi's exegesis of Judges 20:15. Whereas Kimchi had
stipulated that the tribe of Benjamin ventured to Romania, Heilperin
claimed instead that they journeyed to Germany (and Worms). Heilperin's exegesis affirms the extent to which the Worms community was
seen to be the oldest German Jewish community by the end of the eighteenth century, surpassing its sister communities in the Rhineland.[78]

As these many and various traditions began to inform the reputation of
the community in Europe, the Jews of Worms became objects of mockery. A "Worms miracle" became synonymous with a claim so extraordi-
nary that it was likely to be untrue. The community's recurrent reference
to its antiquity became enshrined in a slightly deprecatory fashion. While
Worms Jews explained their origins in reference to their omission of the
'adon 'olam prayer, which postdated the community's founding, a common saying became, "The people of Worms can pride themselves on
having existed before God (*'adon 'olam*)."[79]

This mockery reflected the dramatic historical changes in Europe that
were transforming Jewish life. In the same year that the French Revolution proclaimed universal equality, Worms commemorated the destruction of the city one hundred years before. For some contemporaries,
including Professor Böhmer, who lectured on the historical event in the
local gymnasium, the destruction of Worms by French troops in fact anticipated the fate of Paris in 1789.[80] Echoing these sentiments, the Jews
reaffirmed their royal alliance during the course of the anniversary of the
destruction; they even threatened to fine community members who left
Worms on the day of celebration. After the community recited psalms,
members clothed in their Sabbath garments gathered in front of Rabbi
Samuel Wolf Levi's house and paraded in pairs through the city. They
carried a sign, adorned with the emperor's coat of arms, that read: "Here
lives his royal majesty and highness and all burghers and Jews!"[81]

When in October 1792 French troops captured the left side of the
Rhine and occupied the city, the French challenged Jews' traditional
alliances to the German emperor. The importance of those abiding

alliances, coupled with the memory of the last French occupation of the city, made it impossible for community members to view the arrival of 64 | the French troops as a good thing. Despite the initial antagonism, however, the community underwent rapid changes. Michael Gernsheim, the so-called bishop of the Jews, had died earlier the same year, and the position would only be refilled five years later. When Herz Abenheim was sworn in to the post, the community leaders insisted that his appointment followed their longstanding traditions. Yet the times had markedly changed, and the position would become largely obsolete under Napoleon's new regime.[82]

Prior to Abenheim's installment, the Jews were asked at the *Konventskommision* in March 1793 to renounce the privileges that had been extended to them by the emperor, the city, and the bishop of the city. If they failed to comply, the commission threatened to confiscate their fortunes and draft them. Even these threats did not compel their leaders to renounce their traditional loyalties, however, and soon they, along with other community members, were imprisoned and tortured. To escape the impending danger, Rabbi Samuel Levi fled the city. Upon his return, the mayor of the city and other city officials convened every evening in front of his house, where Levi paraphrased the content of French newspapers.[83]

The Jews' stubborn resistance to their French occupiers illustrates the extent to which the royal alliance (and its memory) had become an inseparable part of their culture. Yet outside of Worms, a new group of Jewish intellectuals had started to promote dramatic changes and challenge their traditional authorities. These Jewish enlighteners advertised themselves as leaders who would advance Jews' cultural, religious, social, and economic renewal more effectively than those presently in power. They sponsored a new educational program in response to the radically changing cultural and political landscape of these decades. Whereas in Worms the commemoration of the destruction of the city in 1689 led to a renewed commitment to the Jews' traditional alliances, these Jewish *maskilim* viewed the French Revolution instead as a promising sign that could quickly ameliorate the status of the Jews in the Germanic lands. Inspired by Europe's societal turbulence, the *maskilim* promoted a new liturgy that had been cleansed of its medieval references to persecution and destruction. Isaac Euchel, the Jewish enlightener from Königsberg, might have overstated the group's accomplishments when he noted that many communities had already excised prayers like *Av ha-rahamim* out of the liturgy, although this was certainly in line with the maskilic agenda.[84] Despite all such efforts, however, it appears that Worms's Jewish community remained relatively unbothered by the maskilic movement, which flour- ished mainly in the major urban centers of northern Germany, such as Berlin, Königsberg, and Breslau.[85]

The ongoing tumult in Paris did redirect those British travelers who had hitherto experienced the Rhine Valley, if at all, only on their return from France and Italy. By the end of the eighteenth century, the Rhine Valley was a well-established tourist destination in and of itself, especially for British travelers who had become infatuated with the valley's landscape under the banner of a new aesthetic that sought after the sublime in nature and admired the Rhine as a picturesque and awe-inspiring place. Alongside the river's new enchantment, and influenced by an ongoing revival of the gothic, a sentimental curiosity for the region's crumbling ruins emerged as well. Those British travelers who "delight[ed] in picturesque country" passed through Worms in transit and described its urban space as wretched and impoverished throughout.[86]

Still, the new aesthetic sensibilities of this period ensured the elevation of the Rhineland among poets, historians, artists, and travelers, and this eventually permitted Worms to regain its regional importance. The rediscovery of Shakespeare's writings during the *Sturm-und-Drang-Periode* injected the ideal of sublimity into German literary culture. This also prepared the ground for a Rhine-centered German romanticism, though it would focus mainly on the region between Bingen and Bonn. This area offered what was perceived to be a particularly dramatic natural landscape, interspersed with castles, churches, and ruins, and it drew thinkers like Johann Gottfried Herder and Johann Wolfgang Goethe as well as a bevy of natural scientists. Inspired by Goethe's description of the beauty of the Strasbourg cathedral, for example, sworn German Romantics like the poet and philosopher Friedrich Schlegel traveled along the Rhine as well.

These cultural developments laid the foundation for the unprecedented popularity of the Rhineland as a travel destination in the decades to follow. The new sensibility, and an uncomfortable awareness of discontinuity in German life that had been intensified by the experience of the French Revolution, turned the Rhineland's ruins into the romantic remains of a bygone age. The modern concepts of irreversible time, change, and progress turned the Rhineland into a landscape dotted with memorable vestiges of German culture. In response to the

Enlightenment's rationality and universalism, then, the later Romantics celebrated the historical particularism of this region, which contributed to its transformation into a poetic space that helped nineteenth- and twentieth-century German nationalists integrate it into their national perspective.

Yet while those German Romantics quickly became enthralled with German ballads, folklore, natural landmarks, and castles, they were much less taken with regard to Judaism. Worms and its Jewish community barely factored in Romantic travelers' celebration of the historic German landscape. Within the Rhine region, only the famous Frankfurt *Judengasse* attracted any attention, and it was not complimentary.[87] Eventually, however, Jewish traditions came to claim some recognition. On their tour of the Rhine in 1802, Clemens Brentano and Achim von Arnim collected songs and ballads, which they later published in their *Des Knaben Wunderhorn*. If their inclusion of the famous Passover song "Had gadya" signaled some curiosity about Jewish customs, though, their inclusion of a story about the Crucifixion and the Passau host desecration of 1477 exposed a counterbalancing antisemitism.

Alongside these iconic elements in the antisemitic arsenal, Arnim and Brentano also included the song "The Jewish Woman." It acquired a canonical status through this publication and became even better known through the setting of Johannes Brahms.[88] Mirroring the stories of seduction and conversion that had circulated since the Middle Ages, the song mourns the fate of a beautiful Jewess who, in this version, chooses suicide over conversion despite her attraction to a Christian scribe.[89] Thus, for Arnim and Brentano, the song emphasized the irreconcilable differences between Christians and the Jews; other ballads in the collection further denigrated Judaism as alien and dangerous. While the Romantics obviously could not open the revived cultural landscape of the Rhineland to all faiths, changes were slowly taking place. The portrayal of the Jewish women of Worms in literature, for example, which had been traditionally dominated by sorcery, violence, and murder, was being refashioned through stories of seduction, conversion, and self-assertion, thanks to song collections like Arnim and Brentano's.

Politically more benign, but equally unable to contend with cultural divergence, the enlightened societal sensibilities (and the French revolutionary armies) that brought civic equality to the Jews in many locations in Europe initially disregarded Worms's Jewish past. The city became part of France in 1797, and Samuel Wolf Levi became a member of the

French Sanhedrin in 1807, which assembled rabbis and other notables to answer questions concerning relationships between Jewish authorities and the French state, and Jews and other Frenchmen. In the course of these deliberations, the Jewish representatives declared their undivided loyalty to the French nation, and so emancipation proceeded in the conquered territories. New French legislation applied equally to Protestants, Catholics, and Jews, though there were a few exceptions. When in 1816 Worms once again came under the tutelage of the Grand Duchy of Hesse and by Rhine, a member state of the German Confederation, this status of equality was maintained. During the 1840s, the remaining restrictions were rescinded, such as the *Moralitaets-oder Handelspatent*, which had compelled Jews to acquire a certificate from the community vouching for their moral impeccability and to take a Jewish oath.[90]

Both the new politics of equality and the Enlightenment's general criticism of Jewish tradition threatened the memory of the community, which had always been enacted in religious rituals and recalled in textual traditions. Written in Hebrew and Yiddish and tied to religious observance, these fragments became weakened during the nineteenth century, when Jewish religious reformers excised medieval *piyyutim* from the liturgy and even canceled the observance of inherited fast days. Moreover, the Jews' longtime alliance to the city and the emperor became outdated in an age that promised to level differences and institute universal citizenship while promoting a new attachment to the emerging German nation.

Yet German nationalism did not override local patriotism; one's city and region continued to matter. Despite the radical changes that the Enlightenment and the French revolutionary wars had brought to the Rhineland, local traditions manifested a great deal of continuity. When local historians (Jews and non-Jews alike) embarked on the study of the community during the first half of the nineteenth century, they began with its diverse premodern textual traditions. These legacies were recognized as important elements in Worms's heritage and provided the Jews with a powerful means of negotiating their path between change and continuity. During the modern period, then, the premodern Jewish traditions and local and regional loyalties became part of a web of historical preservation, local patriotism, German nationalism, German Jewish cultures, and the production of tourist destinations.

II

MOVING LOCAL JEWISH HERITAGE INTO MODERNITY AND ITS DESTRUCTION

RESTORING THE LOST MEMORY

From the arrival of the Napoleonic armies to the foundation of the Second German Reich in 1871, Jews in Germany navigated their way into modernity on their own terms. They pursued cultural renewal and religious reform within the frameworks of the cities they inhabited, expressing their German nationalism, local patriotism, and sense of Jewishness. At the same time, dislocation and modernization created for them a culture of nostalgia. And as the Jews moved out of the *Judengassen* and away from small, rural regions, they recalled a past that was quickly vanishing.[1]

The famed German Jewish writer Rahel Varnhagen, who hosted a literary salon in Berlin in the early 1800s, worried about the radical disjuncture that threatened to unhinge all traditions: "How are old customs supposed to maintain themselves?" she asked in 1816.[2] In Worms, the community curtailed their traditional commemorative practices by excising medieval dirges from their liturgy and abolishing the observation of fast days devoted to medieval and early modern calamities. Yet as the community modernized, the members' rediscovery of those narratives and legends about sages and the preservation of historical sites provided them with a powerful means of negotiating their path between change and continuity. Far from representing a backlash against the forces of modernization, this rediscovery of diverse traditions helpfully evoked the security of their forbears even as the community radically departed from them in the process of constructing and legitimizing their local Jewish identity within the newly emerging citizenry of Worms. The nostalgic recovery of the past simultaneously asserted Jews' cultural and religious difference and promoted their integration into the city's larger heritage. Their faithfulness to their ancestors thus represented a reappropriation of the past at a time of considerable cultural and religious discontinuity for all.

Under French occupation, it must be recalled, Worms lost its status as a free imperial city, and the Jews gained their emancipation. Legal equality for the Jews was part of the larger transformation promoted by the French revolutionary army, whose leaders sought to reform the outdated economic structure and its guild system as well as to ameliorate the political tension among the various religious groups. Unlike in the other French-occupied German territories, the defeat of Napoleon did not end this period of civic improvement in Worms. At the Vienna Congress in 1815, the *Grossherzogtum Hessian* was reconfigured, and it ceded Westphalia to Prussia in exchange for several territories to the west of the Rhine, including Worms, which together came to be known as Rheinhessen. The sudden turn of fortunes notwithstanding, the regulations stipulated that in Rheinhessen, the Jews' emancipation would be upheld.

The city declined economically during the first half of the nineteenth century; though its population gradually increased from five thousand to ten thousand people between 1800 and 1860, Worms itself never expanded beyond the city wall.[3] Though international tourism to the Rhineland had increased to the point that the German writer Heinrich Laube claimed that French and British travelers took the Rhineland to be Germany itself, Worms remained unable to compete for attention with more famous destinations.[4] In his 1836 travel guide to the continent, John Murray presented a decaying city to his readers: "On entering within its gates, large enclosures, some waste, some turned into vineyards and gardens, are seen on either hand; these were once covered with populous streets and fine buildings. Grass now grows even in the existing streets, many houses are untenanted or falling to ruin, and the whole city has a decayed and inanimate aspect." The only commerce, Murray writes, "is in the corn, rape oil, and wines produced in its neighborhood." Nevertheless, he continues, it remained "the once important Imperial Free City of Worms; still venerable even in its decay from historical associations connected with it, such as few other cities in Europe can boast of."[5] The Romantic French author Victor Hugo echoed Murray's dour assessment when he visited the city in October 1838. Probably deluded by Muenster's majestic portrayal of the city, Hugo was dismayed to find it in such poor condition. Impressed only by its cathedral, Hugo dismissed its dilapidated, sleepy, and narrow streets: "A dying city!" he cried. Yet, like Murray, he too redeemed the crumbling town, fallen from its former glory alongside the Rhine, as a "beautiful, peculiar city worth seeing."[6]

For the small Jewish community, the introduction of civic equality in this peculiar and hardpressed town happened to coincide with rapid internal religious and cultural changes. Religious modernization received a strong backing in Worms. When in 1822 Rabbi Isaac Adler, who had served the community since 1810, was buried in the "Holy Sand" cemetery in Worms, his tombstone was placed in the valley of the rabbis alongside the famous medieval and early modern luminaries of the city. He would be the last man added to this lineage, which had for centuries conveyed a sense of continuity in the transition of leadership via the cemetery's many monuments.[7]

More immediately perceptible than this were the alterations that were made to the synagogue service at the end of the revolutionary epoch in 1815. Expectations and aspirations that were attributable to the emancipation era made the Jews in Worms abrogate around 1815 the fast day that memorialized the death of approximately eight hundred Jews on the 23rd of Iyyar 1096. Rabbi Koeppel of Worms approved the abrogation based upon a talmudic discussion that allowed the abolition of a previously accepted communal fast once the social and political conditions had changed.[8] Positing modernity as just such a break in continuity justified these changes as well as the reformers' overall position vis-à-vis the Jewish tradition. It might also have been responsible for the 1816 over-painting of an inscription on the synagogue wall from Kings I, 19:4: "For I am not better than my fathers."[9]

These early signs foreshadow the radical social and political transformation of Jewish life in Worms during the modern period. Unlike those many other German Jewish communities that lost their civic equality in the aftermath of the Vienna Congress, the Jews of Worms retained their full emancipation with only minor restrictions, such as the need for a certificate of good conduct that vouchsafed for the proper moral standards of Jewish businessmen or the taking of the oath *more judaico*, both of which remained in place until the 1840s. With the symbolic shattering of the *Judengasse*'s locks in 1801 by the city's mayor, Jews moved out into the city in great numbers and experienced upward social mobility — within two generations, the community had turned into a largely middle-class social group.[10] Philippine Landau, née Fulda, who was born in Worms in 1869, recounts in her memoirs that the *Judengasse* was quickly divested of its original character; only the poorest members of the community remained there, "intermingled with wretched, lowly workmen and poor people of other faiths." Wealthy members of the community had abandoned the *Judengasse* for good.[11] Accompanying this move out and up, Jews increasingly participated in local culture and politics. Abraham Adler worked as journalist for the *Wormser Zeitung*, in which he favored a radical democratic agenda, while Ferdinand Elberstadt became, for a short while, the mayor of the city in 1849.

With partial sponsorship of the local government under Elberstadt, Reform Judaism quickly took hold in Worms, despite often vehement Orthodox opposition.[12] During the 1840s, Orthodox rabbi Jacob Koppel Bamberger had to contend with competition from both preacher Samuel Adler (who, in 1857, became the rabbi of the influential Reform synagogue Temple Emanuel in New York) and, a little later, his brother Abraham Adler. The Adlers participated in all three Reform rabbinical conferences in the 1840s, which aspired to unify the most common Reform agendas.[13] In Worms, for example, Reform-oriented members of the community wanted to ensure a more orderly service, so they decided to substitute movable chairs with pews. They then explained that the age-old *almemor* would have to be replaced by a new pulpit at the front to give all congregants the same view. During the ensuing debate, community leaders requested statements from both Adler and Bamberger. While both acknowledged the need for rethinking the interior of the synagogue, Bamberger drew the line at the removal of the *almemor*. Community leaders then secured three additional rabbinical *responsa*, each of which approved of the entire plan. Only Bamberger continued to oppose the renovation, out of his "all too great reverence for the old stones," according to the final proposal to the city's magistrate.[14] Religious reform here overpowered historical reverence. Guided by the same spirit, the community also decided between 1841 and 1842 to remove the wall that traditionally had separated men and women in the synagogue, replacing it only with a small wooden barrier.[15]

This apparent disregard for historical preservation manifested itself further in changes to religious services. Echoing the 1845 Frankfurt rabbinical conference's calls to reduce the role of Hebrew in the liturgy, the community of Worms, on Passover in 1847, conducted a German-language service for the first time while removing the wooden fence that separated men and women once and for all, including both sexes in the historic occasion. The community further reprinted the prayers in the vernacular for the first day of Passover, and the publication attracted the attention of many other communities by proudly noting that Worms had managed to introduce these changes "without the tearing apart [of the community] that has occurred elsewhere in the course of the battles."[16] Despite the radical changes, then, the reformers in Worms, some of whom joined Samuel Adler in participating in the revolutionary movement of 1848, continued to profess a spirit of reconciliation. These reformers, who resembled the radical Frankfurt Reform groups of the 1840s, promoted in 1848 the abolition of "a mass of ordinances"; the introduction of German; and the erection of a new "Temple in which past and future are reconciled and from which once again a burgeoning fresh and free wind blows to animate our ambitious youth."[17]

These far-reaching reforms were at least partly legitimized and inspired by the radical Jewish scholarship of the 1820s that dismissed post-biblical history in favor of an aloof ideal of a pristine biblical Judaism. Jewish historians tried to distinguish the elements of "authentic" Judaism from its later accretions, and its early historians rejected the "degenerate" Ashkenazic past while enthusiastically appropriating the Sephardic tradition. Isaac Jost, the first Jewish author of a comprehensive Jewish history, composed his *Geschichte der Israeliten* (History of the Israelites, 1820–28) under the spell of the myth of Sephardic supremacy. He contrasted the meager culture of the Ashkenazic Jews of the Middle Ages, which he linked to their continuous persecution, with the prodigious achievements of their Sephardic counterparts.[18] In line with these critical sensibilities, the first German Jewish periodical *Sulamith* carried a lengthy article on the history of the Worms community in which it questioned their claim to have originated in antiquity.[19] In the 1820s, Leopold Zunz, the founding father of *Wissenschaft des Judentums* (Science of Judaism), denigrated the Ashkenazic hagiographic literature as the product of rogues and liars who were willing to cast Rashi as a miracle worker before Duke Godfrey and have him converse with Maimonides. Zunz ridiculed the local traditions of Worms and called the city's Jews *"Märchen Juden"* (fairytale Jews) for falsely claiming ownership of Rashi's chair.[20]

These scholarly investigations thus specifically targeted the historical traditions of the community, which still resonated strongly in Orthodox circles during this period. Two decades later, Rabbi Bamberger of Worms claimed to have deciphered a Worms tombstone that dated from the third century CE. German and German Jewish newspapers widely discussed the evidence but ultimately dismissed his claim.[21] Yet Bamberger was not alone in his belief. Joseph Schwarz, a native of Bavaria,

FIGURE 6.
*Abraham Neu's drawing of the
interior of the synagogue (1830).*
Stadtarchiv Worms, Germany

settled in Eretz Israel in 1829 and authored a geographical study of the
Holy Land in which he confidently recounted how a member of the Dalberg family had been saved by a Jew, thus placing the origin of the community in antiquity.[22]

Cognizant of the rapid changes, several artists hurried to depict the
still unaffected synagogue before it was too late. Abraham Neu donated
his lithograph of the synagogue, which was deliberately reminiscent of
early modern woodcuts, to the "Association for the Improvement of the
Status of the Israelites in Worms" (fig. 6).[23] Heinrich Hoffmann, erstwhile soldier and later a painter, was garrisoned in Worms and became
an autodidact who painted many of the city's Romanesque buildings,
including the synagogue. In 1854, interestingly, he was less concerned
with the synagogue's contemporary appearance than its unaltered interior (fig. 7).[24]

The preservation of the visual appearance of the synagogue hints at a
slowly emerging reverence for history that also manifested itself in modern Jewish historiography from the 1840s onward. Despite *Wissenschaft*'s
fundamentally critical stance, Zunz, Jost, and Heinrich Graetz still con-

FIGURE 7. *Heinrich Hoffmann's drawing of the interior of the synagogue (1854).* Stadtarchiv Worms, Germany

tributed to the recovery of local history in Worms. At this time the now classic formulation of the *Leidens- und Gelehrtengeschichte*, the history of suffering and learning, emerged. Leopold Zunz opened his book, *Die synagogale Poesie des Mittelalters* (The poetry of the synagogue during the Middle Ages, 1855), with an exhaustive introduction entitled "*Leiden*" (Suffering), which summarizes the experience of the Jews from the triumph of Christianity to the Reformation in the following manner: "If there is a ladder of suffering, then Israel has reached the top. If the span of pain and the patience with which it is borne ennoble [the sufferer], then Jews surely are a match for the nobility of any land."[25] Heinrich Graetz summed up Jewish history in a similar fashion in his introduction to the fourth volume of his *Geschichte der Juden* (History of the Jews): "To study and wander, to think and endure, to learn and suffer, these are the hallmarks for this long era."[26]

In tandem with this ongoing reorientation of German Jewish scholarship and in response to the community's religious polarization, spiritual leaders worked to recover elements of Worms's Jewish past despite the ongoing push for religious reform. Hoping to constructively link past and present, Moses Mannheimer published in 1842 a small history of the community itself, the first ever such work, in which he notes the contemporary status of its various historical sites. While suspicious of some of the evidence provided for the antiquity of the community, Mannheimer nevertheless at least engaged with the assumption.[27] His attitude toward the community's past demarcates distance, rupture, as well as an affinity that is established in the historical narration.

Mannheimer's study followed the path of Worms's historical sites, describing the synagogue and its religious customs and then the "Holy Sand" cemetery. This work more closely resembles an account in a travel guide than a comprehensive history of the community, an impression underscored by Mannheimer's use of a tour's narrative patterns, such as "before we enter the threshold of the holy temple."[28] Constructing the sites in his community as historical monuments for tourists created some ambivalence for Mannheimer; lacking a profound nostalgia for the community's past, he nevertheless empathized with Jewish victims of persecution. He queries the reliability of some of his sources but ends up retelling many place-related legends without any critical distance at all.[29] Mannheimer points out, for example, that the legend about the Worms synagogue's wall appeared in various writings, then observes that visitors had inscribed their name into the walls of the Rashi Chapel, calling this a "book of descent" (*Stammbuch*). He also retells the legend about the two foreigners and points out that the memory of the two anonymous saviors is still alive in the *maskir neshamot* on the seventh day of Passover, then he notes various ongoing structural changes to the synagogue. He also embellishes the legend about Meir of Rothenburg's torah scroll. Drawing upon apparently local traditions, Mannheimer believed that the torah scroll attributed to Meir of Rothenburg had miraculously made its way over the Rhine to Worms. Yet even Rabbi Bamberger doubted the veracity of this tradition, as one of the leading rabbis of neo-Orthodoxy, Benjamin Hirsch Auerbach, reported later.[30]

Mannheimer's narrative creates continuity beyond its obvious rupture between the present immediately before him and the recent and ancient pasts. Recollection and abandonment commingle here. On one hand, and contrary to other evidence from the same period, he relates that the community still observed the fast days.[31] On the other, he recounts radical changes in Worms with little dismay, observing, for example, that the old *almemor* would soon be replaced—"one has already started with the work."[32] He further informs his readers that Rashi's *bet midrash* still exists but attributes more importance to the chapel, where he believed Rashi taught.[33] Finally, the cemetery, with its rabbinic scions, martyrs, mothers, fathers, and children, appears to him marked by tears of melancholy (*Wehmut*) and pain, and he concludes his survey with a plea for tolerance in his own time, in which prejudices still had not fully subsided.[34]

Mannheimer's study reflected the interest that the major historians of *Wissenschaft des Judentums* were devoting to the history of Jewish martyrs in particular, which contributed to a lachrymose conception of Jewish history.[35] In his introduction to Mannheimer's work, Isaac Jost too describes Jewish history as an endless line of suffering and scenes of mourning, but he counters the grimness with his elevation of the courageous Jewish martyrs: "The Spirit never dies, even in the suffering of mankind it develops . . . And proves itself worthy of its moral endeavor, which cannot be ruled by any earthly power."[36]

Alongside these initial efforts to recover or at least recall the past, several of the medieval and early modern legends about the community became anthologized. Next to Prague's legendary heritage, which Wolf Pascheles had rediscovered and popularized in his *Sippurim* (1847–64), Worms represented the best storehouse for such foundational narratives. Both communities prided themselves on Rashi's alleged close association with their synagogues.[37] In particular, Abraham Moses Tendlau's popular anthology ensured a continuing familiarity with Worms's Jewish legends beyond the city.[38] The revitalization of these narratives in a modern anthology and their republication in periodicals in Germany and abroad (based largely on Juspa Shammes's early modern compilations of local legends and Gedaliah Ibn Yahia's *Shalshelet ha-kabbalah* [Chain of tradition]) repopularized the community's past among Jews who had already moved beyond the traditional observance of ritual and customs of remembrance.[39]

The curiosity, both Jewish and Christian, that persisted regarding Ashkenazic history demonstrates the importance of the Rhine to Jewish as well as German worldviews. So the German Jewish poet Heinrich Heine has the river comfort Sarah as she and Abraham escape a pogrom in a boat in his *Rabbi of Bacharach*: "For in truth old, kind-hearted Father Rhine cannot bear that his children shall weep, so calming their crying, he rocks them on his most golden treasures, perhaps even the ancient long-sunken *Nibelungen* hoard."[40] Alongside its Germanic pedigree, the river also "seemed to murmur the melodies of the Haggadah" to Sarah.[41] Moreover, when the pair finally reaches Frankfurt, Heine uses a cantor from Worms to represent the strength of the Ashkenazic tradition, the beauty of its "ancient, solemn melodies," and the purity of its religious devotion in the synagogue. Sarah's delight at the spectacle is promptly contrasted with the reaction of a member of the Frankfurt community, who exclaims that she heard far better singing in the Sephardic communities of Holland.[42] Heine's guarded admiration for Ashkenazic tradition stands in sharp relief to the otherwise common belief in Sephardic supremacy that, for example, informed Herman Reckendorf's 1856–57 work *Die Geheimnisse der Juden* (The secrets of the Jews). Reckendorf contrasts the Jewish martyrs of Worms with his Mesopotamian-Spanish protagonist in order to distance him from the world of Ashkenaz.[43]

Heine's poem, partly written during the 1820s, appeared at a time when he critically reviewed the German and French nationalist literary feud along the Rhine in the 1840s in his *Germany: A Winter's Tale* (1844). Though the jingoism even led August Heinrich Hoffmann von Fallersleben to compose his "Song of the Germans," which claimed the river as German, it soon subsided again.[44] Nor was Heine alone in viewing the Rhine as the location of German and Ashkenazic traditions and not simply as the cradle of German or French traditions. The archivist and popular German author Ludwig Bechstein intended his anthology of legends from the Rhine to sustain the German people's love for their *Heimat* and *Vaterland* through their folk traditions.[45] Here he once again recounted Worms's Jewish origins in antiquity as well as the well-known story about the community's response to their peers in Jerusalem regarding Jesus, based on *Toldot Jeshu* (The generation of Jesus).[46]

Tendlau's anthology in particular inspired various new poems that evoked a world that was still governed by God and that mourned the transition to modernity despite the premodern prevalence of anti-Jewish measures and violence. Common to these poems is an interest in persecutions and divine interventions; they depict an endemic suffering that could only be ameliorated by the community's faith and God's protection. Already with a certain nostalgia, the miraculous saving of Yehuda Hasid's mother was converted into a sign of God's providence in a poem whose "guide" contrasts the divine intervention of the past with the dolor of his own time, which, because it lacks in faith, does not experience miracles. Another poem celebrated the heroic deed of the two unknown saviors, assuring readers that the martyrs were still commemorated to the present day with two burning candles.[47]

This emerging enchantment with martyrs of the past was not limited to either German Jews or the German-language publications of the period. The local and national were not the only realms of cultural interaction and production; Jewish Diaspora communities were emerging to form affiliations that went beyond linguistic, cultural, or political boundaries. The publication of newspapers, historical novels, and scholarly literature in the nineteenth century contributed to a transnational Jewish realm of communication. From the beginning, the Jewish periodicals *Allgemeine Zeitung des Judenthums* (1837), *The Jewish Chronicle* (1841) and the French Jewish periodical *Les Archives Israelites* (1840) explored local as well as global aspects of Jewish life during this period for readers from many countries.

It should therefore come as no surprise that Worms's local heritage also attracted attention beyond the Germanic lands. The Anglo-Jewish writer Celia Moss (1819–1873) wrote about the two martyrs in a short piece in the American Jewish journal *Occident*, further informing her readers, "The Synagogue at Worms is one of the oldest in the world; it is supposed to have been built at the time when the second temple was erected."[48] The editor of the newspaper, however, observed in an accompanying piece that such assertions rested "rather more on legendary than any actual historical authority." Still, he continued, "[That] several of our places of worship in Germany are very old admits of no doubt; probably the Jews arrived in that country immediately after the destruction of the second temple," adding that he would certainly accept such claims if they were furnished with proper evidence.[49]

Notwithstanding this slightly patronizing editorial alongside her article, however, Moss was a rare female voice in the otherwise male-dominated realm of Jewish heritage production during the nineteenth century. In 1843, she and her sister Marion (1821–1907) published a three-volume work entitled *The Romance of Jewish History* that collected tales of the

Jewish past from Jonathan's martyrdom and the Maccabees to the martyrs of Worms. Inspired by the historical novels of Sir Walter Scott and compilations like Henry Neele's *The Romance of English History* (1827) and Leitch Ritchie's *The Romance of History, France* (1831), the two sisters adapted the genre to their largely female audience. Responding to English conversionist literature that denounced Jewish women as prone to surrendering their faith, the Moss sisters invented new historical models to redeem them.[50] Writing for both Christian and Jewish audiences, they drew upon historical research to buttress their claims about, among other things, the martyrs of Worms. *Occident* would later republish this particular story, reminding its readers at the conclusion that "our fair correspondent has woven a pretty wreath of fancied incidents to fill up, though somewhat varied, the meager outlines of the Two Martyrs."[51]

The Moss sisters had indeed reworked the original sources to center the story on the faithful Jewess Esther, who attracts the greedy Count Elric. When Elric sees her face, he is instantaneously drawn to her, asking himself, "How tame did the fair skin, blue eyes, and flaxen hair of [my] Adelaide appear when compared with the rich olive tint, the speaking eyes, the jetty hair and dimpled cheek of the bright daughter of the East." Elric attempts to kiss one of "Judah's stately maidens," whereupon her brother hits him. When in response to this challenge, Elric attempts to take Esther, her sister, and their brother, Zillah, to ransom them against their wealthy father, Judah Hallevy, two mysterious foreigners appear to save the daughters; Elric imprisons the son.[52] Just as Shylock in *The Merchant of Venice* and Isaac in *Ivanhoe* both forsake their wealth for their daughters, Hallevy surrenders his riches in exchange for his son. The Moss sisters then relate the traditional plot element in which the two foreigners trample a Holy Communion wafer in the marketplace, then make their escape. In the ensuing confusion, the entire Jewish community finds itself accused and held hostage until the two interlopers are delivered to the local mayor. At the deadline, the men, who have taken refuge with Hallevy, step forward and sacrifice themselves to save the community.

Situated in Worms, the story echoes other writings by Anglo-Jewish writers of the period in countering the stereotype of the suffering Jewess who becomes the target of Christian desire (popularized by Scott's successful *Ivanhoe* [1819], among other stories).[53] Certainly the role of women in the Moss sisters' rendition extends far beyond the original narrative, inspiring the editor of *Occident* at the time, Isaac Leeser, to note admiringly that although "the story of Miss Moss is fiction, still it is a faithful sketch of what *we* suffered." The priority here was not historical authenticity but rather a religious and moral education. Leeser, a native of Westphalia who had migrated to America, took the opportunity here to place the obligation to remember squarely on his readers: "And shall all the blood that has been shed, have flowed in vain? Will Israel, now in prosperity, forget the truth which they preserved when fear was their only companion, and rapine and murder the lot of many?"[54]

The remembrance of Jewish martyrs was not limited to the realm of literature but also informed the preservation of Jewish cemeteries as historical sites, as did the lachrymose conception of Jewish history. The cemetery was not just a place where historical acts could be unearthed but also a place where they should be remembered. To counter the reformers' historical amnesia, German Jewish historians joined the poets and novelists in promoting the notion of the community's devout and steadfast Jewish ancestors, who willingly died for their faith. Along with Speyer and Mainz, Worms had always prided itself on the memory of the martyrs of 1096. It was now time to reassert this fact.

Religious piety and the modern historical sensibility came together in a profound way when, in 1845, Leopold Zunz, who had also visited Worms to decipher tombstone inscriptions, published his *Zur Geschichte und Literatur* (On history and literature). He dedicated approximately 150 pages to a historical analysis of the ways in which the Jews commemorated their righteous dead. He particularly stressed the historical value of tombstones and epitaphs, calling upon his contemporaries to preserve the memory of their Jewish heroes before the ravages of time or persecution destroyed their monuments.[55]

Whereas Zunz perhaps sought generational reconciliation through his history of ritualized remembrance, the Worms community as a whole would benefit from this work as well. The reorientation of German Jewish historiography coincided there with a lessening of the radical polarization of religious platforms during the tenure of Rabbi Ludwig Lewysohn in the 1850s. Following the failure of the revolution of 1848/49 in particular, the religious feuding lost some of its political relevance, and historical preservation in turn became a new focal point for the community. Specifically in response to Zunz's call, community leaders launched an initiative that brought together Jews of different religious backgrounds. The "Committee for the Renovation of the Jewish Monuments in Worms" comprised Orthodox representatives like Rabbi Bamberger as well as followers of the Reform movement like Lewysohn and

Moses Mannheimer. In July 1853, they published a call to donate money toward the restoration of the Rashi chair and chapel as well as several

tombstones in the cemetery. The declaration, which appeared in German Jewish, French Jewish, and Anglo-Jewish periodicals, reaffirmed that Worms still had a chapel that dated back to Rashi, a tombstone of martyrs from the First Crusade, and the graves of several famous rabbis.[56] The circular promised that the names of generous donors would be inscribed into a special memory book and honored in a yearly service in the synagogue. While the latter event never materialized, the authors thought a promise like this would curry much-needed financial support: "May belief and confidence grow stronger from the immortal memory of these great men, and may that promise become reality: Those who practice charity and always strive toward love, will find happiness and honor in life."[57] Despite the traditional religious rhetoric, the circular, which equated historical preservation with the age-old custom of honoring the deceased, carried out an important elision from religious observance to cultural commemoration when it stressed that these landmarks would vanish if they were not renovated.

This local event quickly gained in stature throughout the European Jewish communities, given that the writers of the circular had already obligated all Jews to contribute in light of the stream of visitors from different religious backgrounds that encountered these sites.[58] The major German Jewish periodical, the *Allgemeine Zeitung des Judentums*, tracked the donations for the restoration from various German Jewish communities as well as Bordeaux, Alsace, Vienna, Rotterdam, London, Lemberg, and Tarnowitz.[59] Lewysohn then kept the readers of the *Allgemeine* informed about his research and the ongoing renovations to the synagogue.[60] With the donated money, he raised many sunken tombstones, renovated the synagogue, and apparently rebuilt Rashi's chapel. During this work he also rediscovered the tombstone of the twelve community leaders, which had, over the years, faded in the blackened southern wall that surrounded the cemetery. It was hidden behind a juniper bush, while another one adjacent to it read *12 parnasim tatnu* (fig. 8). In order to better link the twelve community leaders with the Jewish martyrs of the crusade, Lewysohn proposed that the initial stone had been covered up out of fear of vandalism to something so obviously important.[61]

These efforts led also to the publication of Lewysohn's *Nefashot zaddikim* (Souls of the righteous), which contained sixty inscriptions from tombstones in the cemetery and tried thereby to establish Rashi's pres-

ence in Worms. Playing on the already established valence of some of the tombstones, Lewysohn relates, for example, that Juspa's grave had always attracted many visitors.[62] In Lewysohn's eyes, keeping alive the memory of those who sanctified God's name was imperative for his contemporaries: "This painful and extensive, anguished and glorious past may teach Israel the task for the present and its obligation for the future: to live and to die for God, the only one, and to remain dignified for the ancestors, to whom we thankfully say: Your memory will be preserved forever!"[63] The Rashi chapel underwent renovation in 1854–55, while Rashi's *bet midrash* was renovated and turned into a house for the elderly, thereby fulfilling its charitable purpose. A special inscription was placed on the southern wall of the chapel to remind visitors that the generosity of supporters from "near and far" had enabled its restoration from "ruins."[64]

In the following decades, elements of the community's past continued to gain relevance in various ways. Tendlau's anthology reappeared

during the 1870s, following his new collection of Jewish proverbs in
1860 that described the Jews of Worms as faithful but also slightly gull-
86 | ible.[65] Whereas publication of these sorts of legends during the 1840s
had largely occurred in Reform-oriented publications, their proliferation
in the 1860s indicates a cross-denominational expansion of their readership. Tendlau also published some of the legends in *Der Israelit*, founded
in 1860 by Marcus Lehmann, which provided its readers with "small,
appealing stories and descriptions about the Jewish past and present."[66]
Der Israelit regarded Jewish history as a realm in which God's providence manifested itself; along those lines, neo-Orthodox scholars had
long complained about the absence of a properly written history of the
Jews in the spirit of their tradition.[67] Republished legends from the Middle Ages filled this gap with, for example, Tendlau's poetic rendition of
the life of Meir of Rothenburg. The fact that *Der Israelit* was able to draw
upon anthologies of German legends for these narratives indicates how
widespread this material was by this time.[68]

Beyond the proliferation of the legends, followers of *Wissenschaft des
Judentums* eventually took an interest in the community's past as well.[69]
Beginning in the 1850s, they transferred the traditional *Luah* (calendar)
into yearbooks that not only included information regarding the holidays but also articles devoted to Jewish history. These yearbooks were
regarded as the "channels through which *Bildung* and knowledge is directed unto the lowest classes of the people."[70] Zunz used the Gregorian
calendar as an instrument for the creation of a Jewish collective memory
by summarizing two millennia in his *Die Monatstage des Kalenderjahres*
(The days of the month of the calendar year). Beginning with the month
of January, the *Monatstage* contained the *yahrzeit* of some eight hundred
Jews, including various events associated with Worms as well as the death
of Dolce and her children.[71] The inclusion of a relatively small number
of women was telling with regard to this scholarship, which continued to
portray the history of learning and suffering predominantly with regard
to Jewish men. Thus also Heinrich Graetz, the author of *The History of
the Jews*, counted Worms among the oldest German communities, but
in his detailed description of the Jews' suffering during the first crusade
and the Black Death, he noted only in passing that "women killed their
tender babies."[72]

Despite this slow but powerful transformation of the *Wissenschaft*
from a scholarly discipline to an agent of public education, marked differences persisted between the followers of modern Jewish historiogra-

phy and local Jewish historians. In contrast to the luminaries of German Jewish scholarship, the local historians inhabited a space at the intersection of historical research, preservation, and the burgeoning field of tourism. Their publications appeared most often in German Jewish newspapers rather than in scholarly periodicals and thereby also contributed a great deal to the increasing popularity of the Rhineland as a travel destination.[73]

As mentioned previously, the Rhineland had already featured prominently in the itineraries of the Grand Tour since the eighteenth century. In the midst of the Napoleonic Wars, German Romantics discovered the Rhineland as well—the ruins offered an image of endurance as well as a place from which a German historical tradition could be shaped in opposition to the ideals of the French Revolution. In particular, the campaign to complete the cathedral of Cologne underscored a new sensibility concerning historical ruins, as well as a national agenda.[74] Yet German tourism emerged only slowly as a new cultural practice during this period, whatever the Romantics' fetishization of the Rhine. With the establishment of a regular steamship service on the river in 1827, English tourists increasingly ventured across the channel to see the area's natural beauty and castle ruins—up to half a million passengers by the 1830s. Recognizing the comparatively backward status of internal German tourism and its slow expansion during these decades, the famous Baedeker travelogues addressed themselves to the international market and not to German travelers.[75]

While more research must be done on this important question, it is clear that from the 1850s onward, travel to Jewish sites of interest was an important leisure activity for modern Jews in Germany, especially as rail networks and the German tourism industry continued to expand. As those Jews began increasingly to identify with the virtues of the German middle class, they came to regard travel (particularly in the form of a *Bildungsreise*) as an important element in the education of the individual. The prestigious scholarly periodical *Monatschrift für die Wissenschaft des Judentums* celebrated the railroad for its ability to transport all sorts of passengers and thereby level social differences.[76] Travel descriptions of German Jewish historical sites became more frequent during the 1850s and included the history of individual communities, their social-political status, and their religious institutions and practices.[77] These "travels through the German countries," as one Jewish traveler dubbed them, combined a historical review with a contemporary travel report.[78]

Alongside the satisfaction of a nostalgic desire, German Jewish travel at this time also expressed a certain hope for the blessings of modernity and especially its promise of civil equality. Like Isaac Jost's surveys of emancipation in his comprehensive Jewish history, these travel descriptions comprised a form of inventory taking. One traveler, for example, drew attention to the radical changes that had occurred in Worms. Whereas medieval chamber serfdom and the ghetto had marked the city's past, citizens had now changed to such an extent that they had recently voted Ferdinand Elberstadt into the office of mayor.[79]

Concurrent with this celebratory observation, the citizenry found itself part of Germany's ever-expanding rail network upon the dedication of its train station in August 1853 along the Mainz-Worms Hessian Ludwig line. In 1855, the first bridge across the Rhine was completed; it would receive its own train station by 1867.[80] As travel became a new form of leisure activity, reports about the Jewish sites appeared in one of the first guides to the attractions along the Ludwig train line.[81] Following the successful historical preservation of Jewish sites in Worms, they began to receive more attention in English, German, and Jewish travelers' handbooks to the continent. Indeed, the portrayal of these Jewish landmarks is all the more remarkable given that these new types of guidebook concerned themselves not with what *could* be seen but what *ought* to be seen.[82] At the same time, the Leipzig *Illustriete* and the American *Jewish Messenger* provided short historical surveys of Worms's Jewish sites.[83]

In line with this new respect for and recognition of Worms's synagogue, a proposal to alter the building's interior met with severe opposition at the beginning of the 1860s.[84] Preserving the precise historical layout of the building had become very important to the members of the community. Mirroring the increased care that was devoted to Worms's Jewish heritage in the 1850s, city authorities likewise established a society for the renovation of the cathedral in 1856.[85] A few years later, the *Rheinisch Herold* promoted the idea of a general historical association and museum in Worms; they further argued for the economic development of the town in light of its role as a spiritual center. Just as the newspaper had previously argued for the establishment of the railroad, it now promoted recognition of the historical legacy of the city. While many cities had historical associations, Worms lacked one: "In order to maintain our sense of belonging to this city and our pride, we have to preserve our heritage." For the *Herold*, this heritage encompassed the Jewish past; the

FIGURE 9. *Postcard of the Luther Monument (ca. 1900). Private collection, Nils Roemer*

editors observed that the city "as well as the Jewish community are supposed to have a great number of historical documents."[86]

Following up on this initial appeal to recall its own history, the city commemorated the father of the Reformation with the unveiling of the Luther monument in 1868 (fig. 9). Subscriptions, mainly from German Protestants, allowed for the sculpture, which featured Luther towering in the center of a group that includes Petrus Waldus, Wickliffe, Huss, and Savanarola. Presented by a cross-denominational Christian citizenry, the formal dedication of the monument brought together the kings of Prussia and Wurttemberg, several German Protestant princes, two thousand clergymen from Germany and abroad, and some ninety thousand visitors to the city. In addition to numerous international speakers, the Catholic mayor and a representative of the local Protestant church gave speeches as well. The mayor announced that Luther's famous declaration—"I have not been convinced, I cannot retract, here I am, I cannot change, may God assist me"—had altered European history by asking everyone to bring common sense to bear on their religious traditions, whatever they might be. No Jews fulfilled any official functions at the ceremonies, and they may in fact have been absent at the monument's unveiling. Yet the general emphasis of the festivities on Luther's role as a promoter of the German language, rather than as a Christian reformer, would certainly have allowed for the Jews' attendance. Moreover, the historically rather unexpected insertion of Reuchlin, who had defended the

Jews of Worms against Pfefferkorn's demands, among Luther's supporters in the monument would even have invited a limited Jewish identification with it.[87]

The unveiling of the Luther monument in Worms raised the city's profile among Christians in Germany and abroad. Yet Jewish heritage was also becoming part of the general local lore; Friedrich Fuchs, for example, published a history of the city in the same year that was not only printed by a Jewish book dealer but also included detailed descriptions of the Jewish sites.[88] Fuchs's recognition of Jewish history foreshadowed the impending convergence of local heritages in the formation of the city's past. At the same time, the placement of the Luther monument just outside of the city's walls signaled an intention to expand Worms that in fact came to fruition during the *Kaiserreich*, when the population would reach thirty-five thousand people by 1900.[89] Promoted by all of the members of the community and facilitated by the increasing cooperation between Jews and non-Jews, this cultivation of Worms's past resulted in a local realm of memory that would prove to be important for modern Jewish cultures beyond the city's boundaries as well.

5

JEWISH TRAVELING CULTURES OF REMEMBRANCE

The unification of Germany in 1871 finally universalized Jewish emancipation and promised the possibility of unity without homogeny as it brought diverse regional and religious cultures together into one nation. The nation-state that Bismarck created was little more than a federation of largely sovereign individual states, however; even under Wilhelm II, Prussia's political dominance in Germany did not significantly weaken the country's regional cultures and identities.[1] This diversity provided ample justification for the Jews' self-assertion as a distinct ethnic group and renewed their attempts to overcome internal disunity. The foundation of the second *Reich* spurred the creation of Jewish national organizations and the drive to create a distinct German Jewish culture that involved both the imagining of a community across all time and space *and* the reinvention or renewal of local historical traditions.

The creation of an encompassing German Jewish identity arrived relatively late and never fully unseated the local. Elements of this hybrid identity emerged from the battles over emancipation and religious reform, but overall its boundaries remained in flux.[2] When Germany was finally united in 1871, the Jewish communities had to replace their existing political alliances to localities with a new loyalty to the *Kaiserreich*. In response to this expectation, several of the southern Jewish communities expressed anxiety as early as 1871 over the potential for domination by Prussia and its Jewish communities.[3] Many of the smaller communities, as well as some of the larger ones, initially opposed any attempts to centralize German Jewry. While German Jews at times envied associations like the *Alliance Israélite Universelle*, the Board of Deputies of British Jewry, and the Board of Delegates of American Israelites for their ability to powerfully represent Jewish interests, the support for the *Deutsch-*

Israelitische Gemeindebund (German Israelite community organization), formed in 1869, was slow to come about as communities fought to uphold their age-old autonomy. It was only during the 1880s and 1890s that the *Gemeindebund* finally succeeded in enlisting the support of the majority of German Jewry. Reflecting the rapid growth of the Jewish population in Berlin from 1870 onward, in fact, the *Gemeindebund* moved from Leipzig to Berlin in 1882.[4]

The emergence of local Jewish historical societies beginning in the 1880s ultimately resulted in the need for an umbrella organization with headquarters in Berlin. While the center in Berlin, called the Association for Jewish History and Literature, sought to place the larger Jewish past at the center of a reshaped German Jewish subculture, the local branches emphasized their own heritages as well. In Worms, a local branch of the association existed between 1897 and 1900 with a significant following of thirty active and sixty passive members. By 1900, however, the association seems to have folded.[5] It would appear that by this time the group's efforts might have been seen as "mainstream" enough to obviate the need for a distinctly Jewish organization.

Through the later 1800s, however, local Jewish communities continued to assert their right to represent their own history. Thus, a plethora of local community studies, including new works on Worms, began to appear from the 1860s onward in order to document the integration of Jews in Germany. In fact, Jewish communities competed to demonstrate most forcefully that their roots reached back to antiquity or at least to the celebrated Middle Ages, when modern Germany was though to have emerged.[6] While Jews' persistent recourse to antiquity and the medieval world asserted their place within the German society, the celebration of antiquity and the medieval age goaded some Germans during the *Kaiserreich* to formulate an anti-modern agenda that often intersected with antisemitism. Their claims concerning the origin of the German nation, most often located in Arminius's battle in the Teutoburg Forest against the Romans, were often exclusively jingoistic. Even Gustav Freytag, the liberal-minded popular author and supporter of a constitutional state, offered in his *Die Ahnen* (The ancestors) in 1872 a history ranging from the fourth century to the revolution of 1848 that did not consider Jews to be equal members of the German nation.[7]

Despite the confluence of nostalgia and reactionary political rhetoric in Wilhelminian Germany, Jews continued to inscribe their past into regional heritages. By preserving their historical traditions and artifacts, as they had in the decades preceding the unification, the Jewish community of Worms both forged a local identity and authenticated the far more complex construction of German Jewry. Moreover, this recovery of historical monuments helped to improve the city as a tourist destination, which in turn contributed to its notion of its Jewish heritage. In Worms, both local and national German and Jewish identities coexisted in an ongoing process of negotiation.[8]

Various groups evoked the community's past to bolster their program of cultural and religious renewal. Some scholars seized on the historical commemoration of the community in particular and republished parts of the *Memorbuch*.[9] Their work reflects the increasing importance of both the idea of commemoration in Jewish public discourses and of the cemeteries for the narration of local histories.[10] Some historians became very invested in the notion of the devout community, recommending its heroic steadfastness to contemporary Jews as they faced renewed challenges from the antisemitic revival and the ongoing cultural integration of the *Kaiserreich*. Along similar lines, Moritz Kayserling included Dolce in his gallery of Jewish heroines and villains of the past as a moral and educational precursor to contemporary attempts to include women in the emerging German Jewish culture.[11]

Kayserling's pantheon insisted that the veneration of Jewish heroines was compatible with Jews' integration into German society. His admiration for Dolce countered the representation of the Worms Jewess as simply prey to a Christian seduction. At a time when authors like Franz Grillparzer, in his *The Jewess of Toledo* (1855), projected Christian resentment at the Spanish king's seduction by a beautiful Jewess, Wilhelm Brandes, the long-time director of the Wolfenbüttel high school, composer of numerous ballads, and friend and editor of the German author Wilhelm Raabe, published the short play *The Jewess of Worms*.[12] His beautiful Jewess falls in love with Emperor Henry. Her father, the rabbi of the community and a devout follower of his faith, is blinded to the emerging danger by his love for his daughter. Significantly, it is her mother who ultimately questions the girl's idle talk about her devotion to the emperor.[13] The story, which was even set to music just before the outbreak of World War I, depicts the processes of integration and conversion as both liberation from and a betrayal of the Jewish tradition. The preservation of a sense of Jewish particularity and integration into German society thus seemed irreconcilable.

Theodor Gassmann too combined seduction and persecution in his historical drama *The Jews of Worms*, which used the persecution of the Jews during the Black Death as a foil for the promotion of religious tolerance.[14] In this book, the driving force behind the persecution is the beautiful Marie, who is promised to the Christian Detlev but realizes and embraces her Jewish origin when the burghers threaten the Jewish community. In contrast to the dramatic situation in Brandes's play, Gassmann indicates that Detlev's unremitting desire not only motivates Marie's return to Judaism but also is ultimately responsible for the destruction of the community, including the deaths of Marie and her mother, Rebecca. Jewish self-assertion comes here at the price of a community's destruction, as its rabbi leads its members to martyrdom.

These two historical literary works present Jewish life as marked by danger and headed for destruction, and they are not particularly encouraging about the present either. At the same time, they do reflect the growing integration of local Jewish history into various modes of historical writing. Gassmann carefully weaves several of the legendary accounts about the Black Death and the community's past into his historical drama, which he most likely encountered in the regional compilation of Rheinland legends titled the *Rheinlands Wunderhorn*. The book's illustrations, by Richard Püttner (1842–1913), feature a cemetery with its oversized tombstones, suggesting a dramatic, mythical and awe-inspiring past of the community (fig. 10).[15]

Whereas some literary portrayals of the Jewish past centered on a threatened but homogeneous and united community, the contemporary population remained divided along religious lines. Confirmation ceremonies of boys and girls became the norm and, in 1868, an harmonium was placed in the medieval synagogue, further intensifying the religious friction within the community (the harmonium was replaced in 1877 by an organ). Toward the end of the 1860s, Leopold Levy, a wealthy fruit merchant, transformed his warehouse in the *Judengasse* into a new synagogue for what had become the Orthodox minority. The exterior was completed in a Romanesque style at the beginning of the 1870s, while work continued on the inside of the building until 1877.[16] The construction of a separate Orthodox synagogue encapsulated the religious polarization of German Jewry during this period. Cognizant of the potential danger of a neo-Orthodox separatist community, Levy stipulated that the new synagogue would always belong to the community associated with the old synagogue and expressed his hope that the new synagogue would renew rather than damage community unity.[17]

FIGURE 10. *Richard Püttner, "Der Judenfriedhof in Worms," Carl Trog, Rheinlands Wunderhorn (1882–84). Stadtarchiv Worms, Germany*

Also in the name of reconciliation, Alexander Stein, a graduate of the Breslau Jewish Theological Seminary, became in 1867 the first religious leader of the community who combined the roles of rabbi and preacher, thus bridging a gap in the community that had existed since the 1840s. Stein's son Nathan recalled in his autobiography that his father's tenure was fraught with bitter feuds within the community, where there had developed next to a "justified pride of the historical tradition a petty conceitedness in customs and traditions."[18] Still, while Frankfurt's neo-Orthodox Jews, under the leadership of Samson Raphael Hirsch, left the main community to found a separatist congregation, these religious differences were mitigated in Worms by the community's pronounced reverence for its past. The old synagogue was still considered the main synagogue, and the community conducted separate services in the two synagogues only on high holidays.[19] Even less observant families continued to partake in the synagogue's services out of respect for the old traditions as well as peer pressure within the close community. Recalling her time as a child, Philippine Landau of Worms noted that while her parents were not actually religious Jews, they still observed, for example, the High Holidays, "not so much from an inner need, but rather . . . from custom and habit, and, also, under the influence of the eyes of the small Jewish community, which would have regarded an abandonment of the show of external solidarity with Judaism by the descendents of such pious forbearers . . . [as] a sacrilege."[20]

Coincident with the building of the new synagogue, members of the community stumbled across archival records and other artifacts when a two-story house adjacent to the old synagogue was razed between 1876 and 1878. This serendipitous discovery contributed to the foundation of an Antiquity Society in 1879 and a Worms city museum in 1881. Several Jews of Worms were founding members of the society, and it was within the framework of this association that local Jewish historians carried out their work.[21] Thus the Jewish legacy became an integral element of the city's past at a time when Worms was also advancing itself as the city of the *Nibelungen*.[22]

The cooperation between Jews and other Germans on the historical preservation of Worms indicates rather more benign relations than did the heated debates and hostility on the national level. Certainly German nationalism developed in multiple ways. As the nationalists asserted an ideology of belonging by establishing boundaries among groups, they repeatedly encountered multiple regional, religious, and ethnic minorities that begged the question of who would be called "German." At the university in Berlin, Heinrich von Treitschke had since the 1870s celebrated Germany's unification as the natural culmination of a centuries-long struggle. Combined with his indictment of German Jewry, Treitschke's theories inspired the protracted scholarly debates that came to be known as the *Berliner Antisemitismustreit*. After all, German nationalism was not a homogeneous movement, and while the nationalists' descriptions of Germany reflected their ambitious goals, others were more cognizant of the reality. For Theodor Mommsen, who responded to Treitschke, the German nation was "based . . . on the cohesion and the blending of different German *Stämme*," of which Jews were part, "no less than the Saxons, Swabians, or Pomeranians."[23]

For both Treitschke and Mommsen, then, nations had to be *made*, however one chose to recognize (or deny) their population's diversity. Local historians, on the other hand, reveled in that diversity. In Worms, for example, the city archivist, August Weckerling, lamented at the 1883 conference of the Union of the German Historical and Antiquarian Societies the devastated status of Worms's famous *mikvah* (ritual bath), which had been used as a cesspool throughout the nineteenth century. Together with the local teacher, Samson Rothschild, Weckerling would arrange for the renovation of the *mikvah* twelve years later.[24] Along simi-

FIGURE 11. *Photo of the interior of the conference room with painting by Hermann Prell. Stadtarchiv Worms, Germany*

lar lines, when the regional German monument preservation association created its comprehensive inventory, it favored mainly churches, castles, and town halls, but—in a nod to Worms's infatuation with the Middle Ages—it also listed Worms's synagogue.[25]

The apparent interest among local historians and archivists extended to the renovation and extension of the city hall during the 1880s in light of Worms's aspirations and historical traditions. Like similar structures in many other cities in Wilhelmine Germany, the design in Worms consciously evoked the Roman Empire's federal structures.[26] By depicting German emperors, a painting in the town hall's conference room fused nationalism and particularism. Another piece of art in the conference room featured the eleventh-century bishop Burkard beneath two cherubs, carrying the coat of arms of the German *Kaiserreich* with its one-headed eagle and holding a model of the cathedral and the coat of arms of the city. This carefully staged emblematic display attempted to unite the city's complex history, incorporating the legacy of Catholicism and German emperors into local heritage. Moreover, Nikolaus Reinhart, the

FIGURE 12. *Photo of the interior of the archive. Nils Roemer*

owner of a leather factory, donated a painting for the conference room by the historian and artist Hermann Prell (1854–1922) that depicted Henry IV's granting of the privilege of 1074 to the city. Evoking the foundational document of imperial Worms, which named Jews as members of the city even before other citizens, the painting captured the significance of the historic moment.

Local, regional, national, and imperial historical traditions also commingled in the interior decoration of the newly established Worms city archive, which was located in a building attached to the town hall. The painted vault displayed the German eagle as well as heraldic images of Worms's imperial, Catholic, and Protestant histories, and it alluded to Pirke Avot 4:17 through images of the crowns of the king, the priesthood, and the Torah (fig. 12).[27]

Probably inspired by these advancements in historical recollection of Jewish heritage, Samson Rothschild, who was hired in 1874 as the first Jewish teacher at the coed city school, took over the newly created community archive.[28] Moreover, the synagogue inscription dating from 1212/1213 was renewed and placed in its western portal. At the begin-

Raschitor am Martinsplatz   Hofphotograph Herbst, Worms

FIGURE 13. *Postcard of the Rashi Gate by Christian Herbst (ca. 1900).*
Private collection, Nils Roemer

ning of the twentieth century, Julius Goldschmidt and Rothschild unearthed in the attic of the synagogue other remnants of the community's
archive, including hundreds of bindings, called *Wimpel*, that dated from
1570 to 1914. In addition, in conjunction with the Jewish historian David
Kaufmann, Rothschild and the cantor, Julius Rosenthal, transcribed inscriptions and preserved tombstones in the old cemetery around the turn
of the century.[29]

In 1907, a newly erected gate adjacent to the *Judengasse* was named
Raschi-Tor, because the alteration had obliterated Rashi Street, which
had existed since the late 1880s (fig. 13).[30] With the naming of the new
gate, Worms's collective rediscovery of its Jewish past became much more
publicly visible, and a Jewish museum soon followed that also housed the
local archives within the Rashi Chapel (fig. 14). Several historical objects
were already on display in 1895 in the chapel, including the Rashi chair,
commentaries, and several *mahzorim* (Jewish prayer books) with illustrations. To improve this collection even more, community leaders pledged
special funds in 1912 for the creation of a new museum. The outbreak of
World War I, however, halted these plans.[31]

To varying degrees, Jewish history surfaced as well when, in 1889, the

FIGURE 14. *Postcard of the Rashi Chapel by Christian Herbst (1905). Private collection, Nils Roemer*

city commemorated the two hundredth anniversary of the 1689 destruction and made Otto von Bismarck an honorary citizen. Friedrich Soldan, whom the city commissioned to write a history of those calamitous events, treated the Jews sympathetically in his account.[32] Similarly, Oscar Canstatt, writing for the *Wormser Zeitung*, used a Jewish source in his description of the event. Dedicating his work to Chancellor Bismarck to honor him for establishing the German Reich, Canstatt sought to inspire affection for the *Heimat* (home, but also birthplace and place of belonging) and expressed the hope that the new Germany would never again be as powerless as it was in 1689. Yet despite his enchantment with German nationalism overall, he nevertheless defended the Jews against the charge of disloyalty in their welcome of the French troops at that time. He thought that this simply reflected their overall treatment during the seventeenth century.[33]

Historical remembrance and preservation not only bolstered local pride but also served to promote the city as a tourist destination at the turn of the new century as more diverse guides to the city and the region appeared. Local and regional suppliers challenged the dominance of Karl Baedeker's guides, which had long attended to various Jewish historical sites.[34] Yet in addition to a narrative, the Baedeker guides also featured a map of the city that visually represented the various Jewish

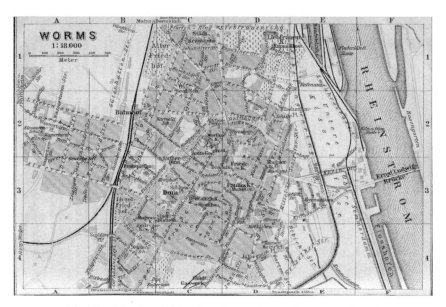

FIGURE 15. *Karl Baedeker,* The Rhine from Rotterdam to Constance *(1896).*
Private collection, Nils Roemer

landmarks alongside the rest (fig. 15). Competing with Baedeker, Leo
Woerl's popular *Reisehandbücher* series offered books on the larger population centers as well as a wide selection of travel brochures that featured
mid-sized German towns. The affordable, pocket-sized books addressed
a slightly less affluent market segment. The Woerl guide to Worms described all of the Jewish sites and had six editions published within fifteen
years. August Weckerling's *Beckmann-Führer*, which appeared in 1902
and was rapidly reprinted in a French translation as well, also featured
Worms and its Jewish sites.[35] Other guides to the city also reported extensively on the Jewish sites and integrated them into their recommended
tours.[36] Ludwig Heilmann, a local schoolteacher, presented visitors with
a survey of the city and locals with a "complete picture of the historical
significance of their ancient city and placed the still preserved monuments in front of their eyes." As a local author, Heilmann was more sym-
pathetic to the Jewish foundation myths as well.[37]

The inclusion of the Jewish past in the city's heritage mirrored Jews'
overall social integration and acceptance—in small towns, at least, the
Jews formed a fairly well-integrated element of the local population, according to their memoirs. Philippine Landau, for example, writes that

the Jews dressed festively for religious holidays and walked undisturbed through the streets of Worms.[38] Yet these memoirs, written after the Ho-

locaust, might well present sanitized versions of their authors' childhood years in Worms in order to draw a sharper contrast with the virulent antisemitism of the twentieth century.[39] Antisemitism was never entirely absent in the city; there was, for example, vandalism in the cemetery in 1885, and the Jews of Worms would form a local branch of the *Verein zur Abwehr des Antisemitismus* (Association for combating antisemitism) following its national foundation in 1891. The membership of this association comprised mainly educated and wealthy members of the Jewish middle class but also a significant number of Christians. In Worms, the association succeeded in eliciting the support of the lord-mayor; among its most active members nationally was Charles L. Hallgarten, the Frankfurt banker and philanthropist who was born in Worms.[40] Yet, on balance, there is little evidence to counter the positive portrayal of Jewish life during the *Kaiserreich* in Worms, a time otherwise often associated with the rise of German antisemitism.

From this level of relative cultural ease arose a business in Jewish memorabilia as well. The photographer Christian Herbst created a variety of "Greetings from" illustrated postcards that featured Jewish (and other) landmarks, which he sold in the tourist office opposite the Luther monument. Such postcards dated back to the 1860s, and Germans became their leading producers and consumers; by the end of the century, depictions of topographical views and landmarks featured prominently on them (fig. 16). These postcards were not only used for writing but also became sought-after collectors' items.[41] During the 1890s, Herbst captured a whole series of images of the synagogue, the mikvah, the cemetery, and individual tombstones (figs. 18, 19, and 20). These images acted to canonize particular views of sites through their subsequent reappearance in various tour guides, newspaper articles, and history books. Several other local companies offered similar postcards.[42] Along with the expected postcard themes of the synagogue and cemetery, the well-known indentation in the synagogue's outside wall was portrayed as well.

Herbst also published tour guides that listed Jewish sites among the city's attractions. He was a seasoned promoter. No other city "from the Maas to the Memel" could compete with Worms's historical riches, he exclaimed. It is through Worms that we might best encounter the heroic period of German history, most notably the *Nibelungen* legends.[43] Herbst's enthusiasm, in the style of August Heinrich Hoffmann von Fall-

Die jüdische Gemeinde wünscht hebräisch ein gutes Neues Jahr; rechts im Kreis die Synagoge des

FIGURE 16. *New Years greeting card from Worms (ca. 1900).*
Stadtarchiv Worms, Germany

FIGURE 17. *Postcard of the synagogue by Christian Herbst.*
Private collection, Nils Roemer

FIGURE 18.
*Postcard of the
mikvah by Christian
Herbst (1905).
Private collection,
Nils Roemer*

FIGURE 19. *Postcard of the cemetery by Christian Herbst (1906).
Private collection, Nils Roemer*

Die Rajdji-Kapelle mit Rajdji-Stuhl.
Verlag und Photographie von Karl Herbst Wwe.
(Jede Nachbildung verboten)

ersleben's "Song of the Germans," extended to the Jews, whose old land-marks gave additional weight to the historical importance of the city. In addition to the *Nibelungen* and Luther, Herbst's guide also describes the cemetery, synagogue, and Rashi chair.[44] Far from pursuing solely antiquarian interests, local Jewish historians appear to have provided the burgeoning tourism trade with information that they could immediately repurpose. Instead of linear narratives of the city's history, and in contrast to the modern Jewish historiography, which critically dissected the historical material, these local historians preferred to paraphrase and gloss medieval and early modern legends and descriptions of Worm's various sites.

Responding to the interest in the community's history that was inspired by the tour guides, the local teacher and community archivist Samson Rothschild composed a small pamphlet that soon found interest outside of Worms. Whereas it first appeared in nearby Mainz, the major Jewish publisher of this period, Kauffmann in Frankfurt, then published all of the subsequent editions.[45] Herbst's photographs of the cemetery for the pamphlet, interestingly, remove its subjects from the flow of history and thereby bestow upon the simple stones an aura of authenticity. Another photograph depicts the Rashi chapel as a study room, with volumes open on a table and two chairs (fig. 20). In addition to this staged presentation of the chapel, the guide pictured the Jewish cemetery with a view toward the city's cathedral, thereby linking the two sites.

Jewish Traveling Cultures of Remembrance ¦

This association visually represented Jewish-Christian coexistence; more importantly, it established the Jewish burial ground as a historical site of equal importance to the cathedral.

The guide also provided photographs of the exterior and interior of the synagogue and recounted many of the more common legends, referred to Meir of Rothenburg's torah scroll, and described the synagogue's inscriptions.[46] Subsequent editions incorporated better photographs and significantly longer texts, as well as a short historical survey, augmented to contain all of the legends from *Ma'ase nissim*; descriptions of the newly created archive and the *Wimpeln* collection; and a photo and portrayal of the restored ritual bath. In addition to these updated texts, newer images staged the Jewish memory landscape more clearly. A new photograph of the cemetery focuses on the tombstones in the foreground and relegates the cathedral to a barely distinguishable silhouette in the distance. The tombstones, along a curved path, are now pictured surrounded by trees. The synagogue is captured in a slightly more off-center frontal view, which brings the left indented wall that allegedly saved the mother of Yehuda he-Hasid into view.[47] The text and especially the images highlight several of the candelabra with the imperial eagle that were placed in the synagogue. This was in line with other guides to the city, which presented to visitors the eighteenth-century candelabra as a symbol of Jews' German patriotism (fig. 21).[48]

Despite its inclusion in these travel books, Worms had stiff competition from the urban centers of German national heritage, especially those situated along larger railroad lines like nearby Frankfurt. For tourists, time was always of the essence as well. In the age of the steam engine, some travelers would race from Frankfurt to Mainz "without paying a visit to the city of Worms," as one newspaper noted. Nevertheless, by the turn of the century those newspapers were consistently promoting it as the site of important events in German history and including Jewish landmarks alongside Christian ones. The purported antiquity of the community likewise elevated Worms's historical interest. Newspaper articles, as well as several tour guides, recounted how the Jewish community had tried to intervene on behalf of Jesus, introducing the Jews of Worms as loyal German citizens who did not harbor any anti-Christian sentiments.[49]

For Jews, a trip to Worms took on a unique significance as the city worked to validate the German Jewish self-understanding of an integrated but distinct minority. Such visits had also become common during the second half of the nineteenth century, as many Jews migrated

FIGURE 21. *Photo of the women's synagogue and the eagle candelabra by Christian Herbst (1914). Private collection, Nils Roemer*

from rural areas and small towns to larger cities to advance themselves socially. In 1871, about 30 percent of Jews lived in big cities; this figure increased to 70 percent by 1910. Memories, as well as extended family networks, however, continued to connect these urban Jews to their former hometowns.[50] Leo Schönmann, who was born in Worms in 1886 but moved to Darmstadt with his family, repeatedly returned to his former hometown to visit his family's house in the *Judengasse* and the cemetery. Reflecting on this changing network of relations and memories later in his life, Schönmann recalled the many times that he had arrived in or passed by Worms and the way his mother always pointed out the cathedral that dominated the city's silhouette.[51]

Indeed, for all Jews, not just those who had been born in Worms, the physical presence of such timeworn artifacts provided a means of negotiating the tension between tradition and modernity. Revisiting Worms provided continuity in an age of rapid change. In his account of what he deemed the "old European Jewries," David Philippson came from America to inspect various Jewish locations, including Worms, just before the turn of the century, "for memories linger about these spots which bring their history vividly to mind."[52] These memories, however, could be contentious, as when, for example, Abraham Epstein's 1896 research trip challenged local Worms historians regarding the idea that the Rashi chapel had anything at all to do with Rashi.[53] Epstein had found a tender spot; the association of the chapel with Rashi had become central to local heritage production, and the now elderly Ludwig Lewysohn forcefully rejected Epstein's claims.[54] Rashi's historical relations with Worms remained important when, in 1905, the Jewish world commemorated the eight-hundredth anniversary of Rashi's death, and Worms received particular attention.[55] Community leader Max Levy suggested honoring this occasion with an essay competition on the questions "What did Rashi mean for his time, what was his subsequent importance, and what importance do his writings have for the present?" Jewish banker Salomon Loeb from New York financed the competition in commemoration of his parents, who were from Worms.[56]

Nostalgia notwithstanding, however, divergent views of the historical sites surfaced in travelogues, and the traveler's encounter with the German Jewish past in Worms remained ambivalent. Jews' engagement with the past often remained attached to their trust in progress, not to nostalgia's subversive aspect as an expression of dissatisfaction; therefore, they tended to seek comfort and encouragement from the local sites, with varying degrees of success. To some Worms tourists, the cemetery landscape in particular offered the solace of the permanence of the past, a place where the cathedral "greet[ed] his contemporary, the old Jewish cemetery." The view of tombstones ravaged by the medieval crusades did not overwhelm this experience of reassurance but instead functioned as a "reminder whereto religious and racial hatred lead."[57] For the French Jewish author Bernard Lazare, in fact, the burial ground represented an affirmation of life and perseverance: "The stones stand up in a great open meadow; with their feet in the thick grass, they stand up."[58]

For others, the past functioned as a reminder of a distant ideal, and its discrepancy with the present was nowhere more obvious than in the presence of the synagogue's organ or the absence of dividers between the men's and women's sections.[59] To some neo-Orthodox visitors, the encounter with Worms's historical sites at least initially exacerbated a sense of loss. In a relatively long article in 1885, an anonymous writer at the neo-Orthodox periodical *Der Israelit* used two images of the synagogue to comment upon Rashi's mother's miraculous escape. Alongside the above indiscretions, the writer expressed his shock at another recent change: "In the presence of the monument of the great and holy men and women there is a tombstone, which was placed for a young woman, who died about two years ago. This tombstone carries the marble bust of the deceased! We do not believe that something like this can be found anywhere else in the world."[60] Despite this overtly critical stance, the same newspaper would later print Rothschild's lengthy and more generous account of the same synagogue.[61]

Among those who visited Worms early in the new century was the Polish Jewish Yiddish author Sholem Asch, who settled for a while in Cologne and traveled throughout Europe and Palestine in 1908. Echoing Heine, Asch observed that the Rhine is the place not only of German legends but also of traditions associated with the martyrdom of the Jews during the First Crusade and with Meir Rothenburg's torah scroll that floated from Bacharach to Worms. For Asch, the Rhine was "holy" and culturally more important to Jews than the Jordan in Palestine, because Ashkenazic Jewry originated there.[62] Asch's elevation of the river Rhine over the Jordan helped him to critically engage the Zionist infatuation with their old-new Heimat. The comparison between the two rivers was not coincidental. Thus, the *Ha-tikva* with which the fifth Zionist congress in 1901 closed was not only inspired by the song "Wacht am Rhein" but was also translated into English by Israel Zangwill as the "Hebrew Wacht am Rhein."[63]

In his trip along the Rhine, Asch mourned the absence of historical monuments in Mainz while discovering tombstones there that had, centuries before, been removed from the cemetery and used in the construction of houses.[64] In his description of Worms, titled "The oldest Shul in the world," he encountered instead the very old *Judengasse* and synagogue, inspected the famous indentation in the wall, and paid his tribute to the cemetery, including the graves of Rabbi Meir of Rothenburg and the twelve *parnasim*.[65] Indeed, he found that for any Jew, religious or not, a visit to Worms produced a strange sensation: a "holy shiver goes through your body" upon viewing the synagogue.[66] To him, the Worms sites were markers of Jewish defiance and perseverance. Impressed by the extant synagogue, he nevertheless joined much more conservative Jews in lamenting the presence of the organ.[67]

These travelers' reports indicate that part of what made tourism popular was its educational value. The young Gershom Scholem made this link in 1914, when he wrote in his diary: "Culture, that is a book with red binding" (referring to the signature Baedeker cover).[68] So, for both enlightenment and inspiration, many secular and religious dignitaries visited the Jewish historical sites of Worms as well.[69] Protestant clergymen wrote in the synagogue's guest book that Jews and Christians share a belief in one God. Anglo-Jewish translator of Hebrew poems Nina Davis toured the sites with Rothschild, while the Lubavitcher Shalom Dov Ber Schneersohn inspected Rothenburg's scroll.[70] Another very notable visit took place just prior to the outbreak of World War I, when delegates at the annual meeting of the Society for the Promotion of the Science of Judaism, which took place in nearby Frankfurt, made an excursion to Worms. The mayor as well as the local community welcomed the national and international visitors. A group of approximately one hundred people toured the synagogue, the Rashi chapel, and the *mikvah* and viewed a collection of artifacts on display for this occasion in the community house. At the end of the tour, Worms's mayor invited the visitors to the city hall, where Rabbi Nobel from Frankfurt emphasized that the historical sites of Worms represented fertile soil for the great ideas of Jewish history.[71] For these visitors, Rothschild also compiled a collection of Herbst's photographs of the synagogue for purchase that featured not only the well-known sites but a few of the items on display in the Rashi chapel, such as Emperor Carl V's privilege granted to the community, a circumcision chair, the goblet of the burial society from 1609, bindings, facsimiles of the thirteenth-century *Mahzor*, and a Juspa Shammes book on Jewish customs.[72]

The small community, which numbered 363 members in 1911, had thus made significant strides in the promotion of their city as an important site of Jewish memory and the quintessential signifier of Jews' overall belonging in Germany.[73] The recovery of historical monuments and encouragement of historical remembrance continued apace in the city, partly on the basis of this interest. The opening of a new Jewish cemetery in 1911 provided the opportunity for a lengthy review of the community's past, particularly in light of some renovation work that was carried out on the old cemetery.[74] In midst of the construction, tombstones from the underground path that had been built during the early modern period resurfaced.

The process of recovery had also become by now a *public* event, one deserving of being recorded and photographed. In one image by Christian Herbst, Samson Rothschild stands in front of piles of rubble and several broken tombstones on the ground. He directly confronts the camera, slightly ill at ease, in the act of taking notes on artifacts he has presum-

FIGURE 22. *Photo of Samson Rothschild by Christian Herbst (1911–12).*
Stadtarchiv Worms, Germany

ably taken from the rubble.[75] The image attributes great significance to
the act of excavation. In keeping with this reverence, the rediscovered
tombstones were placed into the inner side of the wall surrounding the
cemetery, and Rothschild was careful to include the inscriptions of these
stones in his list of epitaphs (figs. 23 and 24).[76]

Despite the evident and growing importance of local and regional histories in the *Kaiserreich*, the preservationist efforts carried out in Worms
were quite exceptional when compared to the famous Frankfurt *Judengasse* nearby. When in 1869 several older Frankfurt houses fell into ruin,
the local press and larger German Jewish newspapers carried relatively
long articles on the history of the *Judengasse*. When the *Judengasse* vanished due to the city's urban expansion, only the Rothschild house was
restored, following large-scale city alterations, "with piety according to
the old one."[77] The German Jewish press welcomed the *Judengasse*'s dissolution, with the *Allgemeine Zeitung des Judentums* applauding the disin-
tegration of this "monument of disgrace."[78]

Yet despite the discrepancy between the two cities, it must be remembered that as much as Worms worked to preserve its Jewish historical
landmarks during this period, city officials never showed any interest in
its former *Judengasse* per se. The underlying perception of the medieval

FIGURE 23. *Photo of the discovered tombstones by Christian Herbst (1911–12).*
Stadtarchiv Worms, Germany

remnants of the ghettos in Frankfurt and Worms underscores the critical
distance that German Jews had placed between themselves and certain
aspects of their past. But German Jewish history in general, particularly
in Berlin, would be vital to facing renewed cultural challenges in the late
1870s and early 1880s. Responding to the antisemitism movement, the
Berliner Antisemitismusstreit, and the revival of ritual murder accusations,
the *Gemeindebund* launched an initiative in 1885 to alter the public's perception of Judaism. Under its auspices, the *Historische Commission* was
established and enlisted three Jewish and three Christian medievalists.
Referring in particular to the famous *Monumenta Germaniae Historica,*
which had since 1819 published important sources in the name of both
scholarship and German nationalism, Harry Breslau used the commission's announcement to claim that previous historians had failed to make
any real progress. Relevant sources had not been utilized, claimed Breslau, because most historians lacked the ability to understand German
Jewish history as an integral part of German history.[79]

Yet the commission struggled to secure sufficient support, and among
the many Jewish communities that refused to help out was Worms.[80] It
managed to publish several valuable sources during its few years of exis-

tence, including a *Memorbuch* and the medieval chronicles from the First Crusade.[81] The collection and publication of Hebrew sources in particular made this history accessible to the non-specialist while demonstrat-
ing the rootedness of German Jewry in the Germanic lands. At the end of 1892, though, Breslau announced that the commission would disband because of declining financial support from the Jewish communities.[82] It was the first comprehensive attempt to forge a German Jewish historical tradition, and the bibliography in its short-lived periodical on studies of individual communities reflected the attention that their histories had received, beginning with Moses Mannheimer's study of Worms. Various Jewish and non-Jewish periodicals had published up until the 1880s over one thousand articles on these topics.[83]

The commission's interest in converting local and regional traditions into a German Jewish heritage presaged a greater movement after Germany's unification and the growth of the Berlin Jewish community. Along with the central role Berlin played as the new capital of the country, the city also became a focal point for the commemoration of the German past. Chancellor Bismarck promoted German nationalism through the mediation of local and regional loyalties and traditions, and this led to the even more unified and nationalist agenda under Wilhelm II, who supervised the *Siegesallee* in Berlin, dedicated in 1901, as well as the Reichstag and several museums.[84]

Mirroring the aspiration to display Germany's past in Berlin, new Jewish associations and institutions emerged there to promote a German Jewish identity based on new historical research. Collecting and preserving documents became a quasi-sacred duty at this time. With the expulsion of Jews from most of the urban centers by the end of the Middle Ages, many physical remnants of Ashkenazic history had been destroyed. Moreover, when the German states mandated that German become the official language of legal documents from the late eighteenth century onward, those that were still written in Yiddish or Hebrew promptly lost their value and were abandoned. Finally, negligence of and contempt for documents that reminded Jews of their dark past caused even more destruction.[85] At least this was Ezechiel Zivier's assessment as he traveled through southern Germany in 1904 to survey the situation following his 1903 proposal for a central archive to members of the B'nai B'rith Lessing lodge in Breslau. According to his report, relatively few community archives existed in Worms, Darmstadt, or Frankfurt, and Zivier insisted that it was a "holy duty" to preserve whatever remained.[86] Along

similar lines, the editor of the *Allgemeine Zeitung des Judentums*, Gustav Karpeles, asserted the pressing need to gather and thereby preserve
the slowly disappearing traces of German Jewish history. Karpeles noted
that his generation had "the obligation . . . to rescue what can be saved
before it is too late."[87] Subsequently, Eugen Täubler founded the *Gesamtarchiv der deutschen Juden* (Central Archive of the German Jews) in
October 1905 with the support of the *Deutsch-Israelitische Gemeindebund*,
the B'nai B'rith, and the financial assistance of several larger Jewish communities like Berlin, Frankfurt, Breslau, and Hamburg.[88]

Nevertheless, the actual work of moving archival collections from individual communities to the central archive proved difficult. By this time,
various German Jewish communities had already carried out, within the
framework of local German historical associations, the first studies of
Jewish communities that inscribed the Jewish past into the annals of
urban centers. In light of this, as the Jewish historian Martin Philippson
noted at the time, several communities refused to hand over their archives, out of what he saw as an "unjustified particularism and local self-
consciousness." Täubler branded the opposition to the *Gesamtarchiv* as
motivated by a "poorly thought out local patriotism." Yet he admitted
that the thought of uniting all Jewish archives would worry not only local
patriots but also professional archivists, since "documents are part of
the foundation upon which they grew." Removing documents from their
original sites appeared counterintuitive from both scholarly and cultural
points of view, in that the most obvious connection between the past and
the present in individual communities would be broken. To counter opposition by Täubler and others, the *Gesamtarchiv* eventually stipulated
that the individual communities would remain the legal owners of their
materials.[89]

The tension between the reassertion of localism and the impetus for
centralization indicates that the work of the *Gesamtarchiv* involved more
than the simple collection of otherwise neglected material. It wanted to
illustrate the close historical ties between the Jews and the Germans, as
Philippson explained.[90] By dismissing the local patriotism of individual
Jewish communities and suggesting their lack of sufficient expertise, the
administrators of the *Gesamtarchiv* asserted their own particular vision
of German Jewish history, one that involved Berlin's physical claim upon
the remnants of the German Jews' communal past. They also declined
the Frankfurt Jewish community's offer to house the archive; Philippson
pointed out that the central Jewish archive had to be located in the Ger-

man capital, within the Berlin Jewish community.[91] Worms is not specifically mentioned in these debates, but we did note previously that the community there did not hand over its archive. Instead, it created its own archive and forged its own forms of commemoration, often in conjunction with the city.[92]

The new center of research that took shape in Berlin came into conflict with local forms of historical research, which were at times already fully developed. Those historians who contributed to the new cluster of research on a German Jewish history played freely with local research in their comprehensive accounts. In his richly illustrated and beautifully decorated coffee-table book, Adolf Kohut presented German Jewish history as a bricolage of these individual places and cultures, linking past and present using photographs of various historical sites, including Worms. These images, above and beyond the historical sites they captured, aimed to recover the past.[93] Within the subsuming context of an overarching history of German Jewry, historians like Kohut viewed Worms through the lens of its medieval and early modern history of both learning and suffering. *Wissenschaft* historians, then, elevated chiefly those elements of the local community that they deemed to be typical of German Jewish history at large.

These historians likewise emphasized the antiquity of the entire German community, and Worms in particular seemed to reinforce the Jews' claim of belonging in Germany even when most of them had moved to the big urban centers. Worms's antiquity ornamented the notion that German Jews were one of the many German tribes (*Stamm*).[94] In line with Gabriel Riesser, the nineteenth-century advocate for Jews' emancipation, these historians emphatically rejected the portrayal of German Jews as homeless cosmopolitans, and Worms was proof of their claim.

Yet the idea of Worms also served the critics of modernity and even German Jewish integration. Reflecting on the long history of Jews in the Rhineland, Fabius Schach, in the Zionist newspaper *Die Welt*, contended that Rhineland culture had totally merged with its Jewish elements, and Jews felt right at home there: "The sentiment has become that of the Rhineland yet the spirit remain[s] Jewish."[95] Schach's view resonated with Zionist critics of modernity like Arthur Ruppin and Felix Theilhaber, who at the beginning of the twentieth century associated urban centers with decay, fragmentation, rampant assimilation, and intermarriage. For the Berlin dermatologist Theilhaber in particular, rural Jewry, in contrast, "represented an indestructible capital of biological health and fertility" and was representative of a "deeply rooted Jewishness."[96] Whether as a symbol of longevity or purity, then, communities with heritages like Worms's represented the last vestiges of a world that had vanished.

The widely celebrated identification of the Rhine with the quintessential German landscape made the inscription of this realm with emblems of the Jewish tradition all the more meaningful to contemporaries. In his autobiography, Gershom Scholem recalls the literary penchant of his mother, who composed for her son his school essay on the Rhine as a witness to German culture. The young Scholem happily accepted her help as long as she also described the fate of the Rhineland communities during the First Crusade.[97]

In addition, when the president of the *Centralverein deutscher Staatsbürger jüdischen Glaubens* (Central Association of German Citizens of Jewish Faith) republished Riesser's works, he filed this fighter for emancipation under the slogan "Glaube und Heimat" (Faith and homeland).[98] The chairman of the C.V., Eugen Fuchs, also pointed to this slogan to emphasize his critical distance from the radicalized German Zionist who favored emigration above all else.[99] In a lengthy article Fuchs evoked various definitions of nation in order to describe himself in the following manner: "I am a German national, [and] Jew from religion and tribe," adding that his own identity had been shaped by his Prussian and Silesian upbringing. His identity thus fused cultural, religious, national, and regional elements.[100]

Although Worms was increasingly seen as the German Jewish *Heimat* —a view that emphasized the compatibility of *Deutschtum* and *Judentum*—it also maintained an association with the martyrdom of the Jews during the Middle Ages. Gustav Karpeles charged that Jews in Germany had for too long neglected their history in the hope of a better future; Worms's Jewish history of martyrdom and faithfulness represented defiance and steadfastness.[101] Familiarity with the continuous mission of the Jewish people and their glorious history was imperative to making a "certain modern martyrdom plausible."[102] Moreover, Jewish history both informed one's comprehension of the present and provided solace, courage, and pride, as one observer noted: "The sufferings of the past have to console for the manifold pains and tribulations of the present."[103]

The martyrdom of the Rhineland Jews formed one of the central literary models of the Eastern European poets as well as they tried to come to terms with the impact of the pogroms of the 1880s and the Kishinev violence in Czarist Russia. Whether they celebrated those Jews for their willingness to sanctify God's name or, like Saul Tchernichovsky and Hayim Bialik, aimed to critically subvert the idea of *Kiddish ha-Shem*, the textual traditions of the crusade chronicles and the narratives of the Rhineland Jews became the touchstones of their quest for reorientation. Whereas in his poem "Baruch of Mainz" Tchernichovsky compares the religious piety of Isaac to the guilt of those who sacrificed their children and converted, Bialik even more boldly renounces the ideal of martyrdom in his poetry about the Kishinev pogrom. Others, however, continued to recall the sainted martyrs of the First Crusade during this period. Abraham Shalom Friedberg significantly enlarged and revised Herman Reckendorf's 1856–57 *Die Geheimnisse der Juden* (The secrets of the Jews) in the last decade of the nineteenth century. In Friedberg's Hebrew version, the section titled "The Slaughterknife" celebrates the medieval martyrs as members of a cohesive and faithful community against the Sephardic Jewry.[104]

Taken together, the Hebrew, Yiddish, and German versions of the history of the Rhineland and Worms's Jewish community underscored the city's popularity and the multivalence of its historical heritage. Whereas during the first two-thirds of the nineteenth century the rediscovery of Worms's Jewish traditions helped the community balance continuity with change, the popularity of those sites aided Jews' efforts during the *Kaiserreich* to legitimize themselves within the new citizenry. In the Weimar Republic, dynamic reciprocities would emerge even more fully between local and regional belonging and the heritage of German Jewry.

WORMS | A JEWISH *HEIMAT* ON BORROWED TIME

The Weimar Republic is rightly associated with the prestigious accomplishments of German Jews in the arts and sciences at a time when the size of the Berlin community dwarfed all other German Jewish congregations. Yet the fast-paced life of the metropolis, associated with rapid change and historical amnesia, also gave a new importance to the small-town communities that prided themselves on being the last vestiges of a world that had otherwise vanished.[1] The prolific novelist Georg Hermann's article "Großstadt oder Kleinstadt" prompted a flood of responses concerning the differences between Berlin's Jews and those in the rural villages and small towns.[2] Jews of the larger urban centers appeared to be stuck in self-imposed isolation, in contrast to Jews of the small-town communities, who were represented as thoroughly enmeshed in the local and regional lives of Germans. Those metropolitan Jews, therefore, lived vicariously through the memories of the older rural communities.[3] Partly marred by antisemitic stereotypes, the debates nevertheless reflected the accelerated urbanization and centralization of an increasing number of Jews in Berlin, a trend that had separated many of them from their older communities and heritages.

The dichotomy between rural, small-town communities and those in larger urban centers also turned on the question of Jewish identity. During the Weimar Republic, when the process of urbanization had peaked, Leo Baeck considered it to be responsible for the shift from what he called *Milieufrömmigkeit* (piety of the milieu) to *Individualfrömmigheit* (piety of the individual). Within this binary opposition, Baeck viewed urbanization as a rite of passage from a location in which Judaism had governed every aspect of life to a location dominated by non-Jewish customs.[4]

Urban German Jews became infatuated with rural communities at the same time as Jews in Germany were increasingly being viewed as foreign elements among the German people, so the commitment to one's local *Heimat* signified ownership and belonging. *Heimat* allowed German Jews to mediate among different Jewish identities and conceptualize the interactions between Jews and other Germans. Indeed, in the context of the Weimar Republic—and even after the erosion of democratic structures with the establishment of the Nazi state—Jews negotiated and debated their affiliation and cultural heritages within overlapping German, Jewish, local, urban, and metropolitan communities by seizing the language of local *Heimaten*. Precisely because these concepts were subject to interpretation and contestation, Jews promoted their local heritages to define their place in the national community of the Weimar Republic. For many Worms Jews, pride in the community's past and a profound German nationalism went hand in hand. Their "resistant nostalgia," to use Svetlana Boym's formulation, coincided with the community's efforts to honor its fallen soldiers of the First World War with monuments and memorials, which Weimar-era tourist guides described.[5]

The complexities of German Jewish identity formation as they were repeatedly invoked in contemporary scholarly discussion remained unstable, contingent, and culturally constructed. Again during the Weimar Republic, the harnessing of a larger German Jewish tradition remained significantly tied to the history of individual communities. Reviewing the current scholarship in 1929, the German Jewish historian Adolf Kober observed that no history of German Jewry in fact existed, though the history of individual communities had been "enthusiastically looked after."[6] This provincialized grounding of Jewish traditions made concepts of a German Jewish identity more tangible and local histories more relevant. It was only with the Nazis' rise to power and the first anti-Jewish measures that comprehensive histories of German Jewry began to appear—a time, of course, when many Jews reassessed the German Jewish past and its prestigious pantheon of heroes.[7]

Within the framework of a German Jewish renaissance of sorts in the Weimar Republic, the Jewish legendary accounts of Worms received renewed attention as part of the recovery of the folklore of the Jewish past. Bertha Pappenheim, the social activist and women's advocate, republished the *Maysebukh*, and Sholem Asch's writings about Meir of Rothenburg and Juspa Shammes appeared in German translations.[8] Legends from the East and West merged in the works of Eastern European scholars as well. Micha Josef Berdyczewski, who was born in the Ukraine but lived in Germany from 1890 until his death in 1921, published the first volume of his *Legends of the Jews* in 1913.[9] Such compilations made premodern Jewish myths and legends again available to the German Jewish reading public.[10] Despite Berdyczewski's call for a Nietzschean trans-evaluation of Judaism that might again base the faith on traditions that had been suppressed within rabbinical Judaism, its German Jewish readers like Arnold Zweig viewed the twelve-volume work simply as a re-opening of the "paradise of our youth."[11] Similar to the way that the Grimm brothers' compilations of German legends fostered German nationalism, Berdyczewski's tales nourished a new concept of a German Jewish past, and even included a few legends from Worms.[12] In 1924, the Hebrew poet Saul Tchernichovsky, who resided in Germany during the 1920s, composed one of his best-known poems about the divine rescue of Yehuda he-Hasid's mother. To Tchernichovsky, the synagogue's wall represented a world that was still governed by faith and divine intervention at a time when the Jews of Eastern Europe had experienced large-scale persecutions in the aftermath of World War I.[13]

These Eastern European Jews were, however, not the only ones to seize upon Worms to reinvigorate their Jewish culture. The locals continued to plumb its depths as well. During the Weimar Republic era, Worms's plans to open a Jewish museum finally came to fruition under the guidance of Isidor Kiefer, a tin manufacturer and chairman of the Jewish community of Worms who had been born there in 1871. The museum was officially opened on the synagogue's three hundredth anniversary in November 1924, to link it with another famous restoration project: the rebuilding of the synagogue. The museum, which was promptly featured on illustrated postcards, displayed medieval privileges, bindings, prayer books, a *Memorbuch*, Juspa Shammes's collection of legends, circumcision chairs, and torah ornaments.[14] Photographs of the interior of the museum indicate that religious objects and historical documents were placed alongside each other to demonstrate their integration in the community's past. Kiefer attached explanatory plates to some of the items and guided tourists through the museum (fig. 24).[15]

The display of Jewish artifacts in Worms had an impact well beyond the perimeters of the city. Worms became one of the formidable icons by which the German Jewish past—and culture—came to be represented in the Weimar Republic. The Jews of Worms and the Rhineland also had a significant part in the 1925 Cologne installation entitled *Thousand-*

FIGURE 24. *Postcard of the Jewish Museum (1925). Private collection, Nils Roemer*

Year Exhibition of the Rhineland, part of a year of wide-ranging festivities to celebrate the region's German cultural heritage.[16] Introduced by Cologne's mayor, Konrad Adenauer, this public display of age-old German history fulfilled obvious political ends at a time when France still occupied parts of the Rhineland. The exhibition's section on the Jews presented their traditions as the foundation of contemporary German Jewish culture. The display of Constantine's privilege from 321 CE functioned as a "discrete propaganda tool," as the co-curator of the Jewish section, Elisabeth Moses, described it, because it situated Jews in the Rhineland already in late antiquity.[17] Moreover, the presentation showcased documents, models of Jewish baths, images of synagogues, a map with Jewish settlements in the region prior to 1349, *Memorbücher,* letters of protection, medieval *mahzorim,* bibles and *mohel* books, replica tombstones, and a seder room.[18] It also exhibited copies of important documents from Worms, Herbst's photographs of the synagogue, and a model of Worms's *mikvah.*[19]

The major periodicals of this period, such as the *C.V.-Zeitung* and *Israelitische Familienblatt,* extensively reviewed the exhibition's section about the Jews' rich history in the Rhineland. For the C.V., the exhibition succeeded in its mission by demonstrating that the "synthesis of *Deutschtum* and *Judentum"* was more than the mere construction of great and intemperate Jewish German scholars. The Rhineland, the papers opined, was the first place where Jews had settled on German soil and, therefore, its culture remained as evidence of the German Jews' longstanding attachment to Germany.[20]

Traveling to Cologne to visit the exhibition was one way Germans could express their solidarity with the occupied areas, and their trips helped to prop up the local economy as well. To this end, in the summer of 1925, German newspapers outside the Rhineland urged their readers to travel to Cologne. Likewise, *Die jüdische Frau* wrote, "German women, Jewish mothers and men, come to us to the Rhine."[21] Along with German Jewish associations of rabbis, cantors, and teachers, the West German branches of the Central Union of the German Citizens of the Jewish Faith responded to the exhibition by moving one of their meetings to Cologne.[22] "Who wants to miss this celebration?" the C.V. newspaper asked its readers.[23] The meeting commenced with a special concert in the Cologne opera house performed by the city orchestra and also included a talk from Kober, who, with the assistance of Elisabeth Moses, had created the exhibition. Ludwig Holländer, chairman of the C.V., greeted the 250 delegates with his hope that the convention in Cologne would express "the intimate attachment of German Jews with the German *Heimat*."[24] Under the title "The German Jew on Rhineland Soil," his newspaper emphasized that Jews in the Rhineland had contributed to the creation of its particular regional culture and had, therefore, acquired a right "to this soil and to this people."[25] Similarly, the *Reichsbund jüdischer Frontsoldaten* (Reich Federation of Jewish Front Soldiers) held its general assembly in the Rhineland to underscore German Jewry's age-old association with that region. For Leo Löwenstein, the founder of the *Reichsbund* and a retired captain in 1919, the Rhineland was "the cradle of German Jewry."[26]

Worms certainly seized the opportunity offered by the Cologne exhibition. Its newspaper celebrated the recognition of the city's past, including that of the Jewish community.[27] Within weeks of the special meetings of the C.V. and the *Reichsbund* in Cologne, Rothschild contributed to the series "Aus jüdischen Gassen" by writing about the Jewish sites of Worms.[28] Rothschild presented Worms as a popular destination for Jewish travelers, observing that the city had many more historical documents, artifacts, and monuments on view than nearby Speyer.[29]

Heeding the calls to travel that deemed it a national duty, the *Reichsbund jüdischer Frontsoldaten* brought hundreds of delegates to Worms. To

FIGURE 25.
Postcard of the interior of the synagogue (1923). Private collection, Nils Roemer

the members of the *Reichsbund*, after all, the synagogue there represented a memorial to the "right of the Jewish community to celebrate with the German people the thousand-year anniversary of the German Rhineland" (fig. 25).[30] With Isidor Kiefer, Friedrich Illert, the director of the city library, and Erich Grill, the director of the city collection, the delegates toured Jewish attractions in Worms as well as the special exhibition in Cologne. In addition to the delegates, many individual visitors came to Worms, and within a few weeks, one thousand people had seen the special exhibition, as Rothschild proudly noted. In comparison, a local exhibition by Worms's Protestant community attracted only five hundred visitors over the span of a few months (fig. 26).[31]

The close affinity between German and Jewish historical traditions that

FIGURE 26.
Photo of the Reichsbund
jüdischer Frontsoldaten
in Worms (1925).
Stadtarchiv Worms,
Germany

was evident from the Cologne exhibition influenced other Weimar-era
artistic refutations of the Zionist interpretation of the Diaspora. One
prominent example was the *Haggadah*, published in 1927, of Siegfried
Guggenheim, a lawyer living in Offenbach on the Rhine. According to
Guggenheim, the traditional conclusion of the *Haggadah* prayer, *le-shanah
ha-ba'ah bi-yerushalayim* (Next year in Jerusalem), referred to Jews' hope
for a time when all men walk in the light of God, and when the *Wahn* (in-
sanity) is ended and all weapons are destroyed. He noted, however, that
a Moravian author of one fifteenth-century *Haggadah* with which he was
familiar had added the words "or in Brünn" to the conclusion. He then
added that his own family in Worms replaced the conclusion altogether
with the sentence, "Next year in Worms-on-the-Rhine, our *Heimat*."[32]

Guggenheim's carefully crafted *Haggadah*, of which only three hundred were printed on handmade paper in a Bible-esque Gothic type,
recorded his family's tradition of observance in order to authenticate
his version: "The Seders, which I had experienced in my father's house
under the eyes of my grandparents and parents, led me to hold on in
my own family to the custom of the private (*häuslichen*) Seder celebrations."[33] The title page underscored the family's association with the city
by featuring the Guggenheim coat of arms (*Hauswappen*). The Worms
newspapers viewed Guggenheim's at once personal and political *Haggadah* as having "come forth" from the soil of Worms, announcing that
it "breathe[d] the spirit of the Rhineland's depth of feeling and cheer."[34]
The journal of the *B'nai B'rith* agreed that the work's characteristic
cheerfulness constituted part of its particular religious virtue.[35] Its pronounced regional flair inspired the celebrated writer Stefan Zweig to

conclude that this *Haggadah* merited a place "at any German exhibition on the art of the book"; Guggenheim had artfully implanted "Jewish tradition into German soil," he tellingly exclaimed.[36] For the *C.V.-Zeitung*, the *Haggadah* was further evidence of the proximity between German Jewish and German cultures. Herman Meyer, secretary of the Soncino Society for the Friends of the Jewish Book, heralded it in his review as "the dawn of the revival of Jewish religiosity, which draws the elements of its piety—as does your book—from Jewish heritage and the reality of life in Germany."[37] Like no other *Haggadah*, the book brought out the close relation between German Jews and German culture, noted the periodical.[38]

Guggenheim's *Haggadah*, like the Cologne exhibition, illustrates the complex interaction between German nationalism and various forms of Jewish self-understanding. The exhibition had a particularly lasting impact. For Adolf Kober, it helped further the study of Jewish local history in general and even spurred the creation of several local Jewish museums in later years.[39] Various communities in addition to Worms, including nearby Mainz, either created small exhibits of Jewish artifacts or displayed their collections within local German museums, localizing their Jewish institutions of remembrance.[40] But the question persisted: a central Jewish museum, local Jewish museums, or dedicated sections in existing regional and national museums? Erich Toeplitz, the director of the Jewish museum in Frankfurt, proposed the creation of a new Jewish museum in the mid-1920s inspired by Eugen Täubler's central archives. He was, however, keenly aware that Jewish communities would be reluctant to part with their treasured items. To counter this opposition, he picked up where Täubler had left off, arguing that limited resources, lack of knowledge, and vandalism in the local communities would endanger their historical treasures, which would be safer somewhere else.[41]

In the ensuing debate, Jakob Seifensieder, a teacher from Nuremberg, famously furthered the notion of German Jews' obligation to contribute to the Jewish collection in the national museum in Nuremberg. His article was immediately countered by voices from Breslau, Berlin, and Mainz, who favored a more broadly conceived Jewish museum that might encompass Jewish artifacts in their original locations.[42] Using the longstanding Jewish traditions of Frankfurt and Mainz as examples, these opponents argued that such a museum could only be created in these cities.[43] In his rejoinder, Seifensieder clarified his position and argued that the inclusion of a Jewish exhibition in the Nuremberg national museum need not be at the expense of other local museums. While he did oppose the creation of museums in small cities, he conceded that a central museum could be constructed in Berlin, Frankfurt, Mainz, or even Worms. That Seifensieder included Worms on this list reflects the high visibility of the community's past, a credit to its effort to preserve and display its heritage.[44]

The tension between the ideas of a centralized museum and local museums eventually also raised the question of original artifacts versus replicas, as new capabilities in mass distribution led to the commodification of images, for one, that then circulated via newspapers, travel guides, and illustrated postcards. In an important essay, the German Jewish philosopher Walter Benjamin highlighted the extent to which the mechanical reproduction of artifacts threatened to unravel the notion of authenticity altogether.[45] Original artifacts carried with them the guarantee of authenticity, in which the visitor could partake. For Erich Toeplitz too, reproduced historical artifacts did not provide the viewer with the same experience as the originals.[46]

Worms, of course, rated very well in this new hierarchy of authenticity. The city center had not been radically altered, so Worms appeared to travelers as still free of the forces of modernity; its longtime economic disadvantage now became a major asset, as its more modest modernization enabled visitors to "recapture the permanent spirit of the Rhineland."[47] Once again, the organ in the synagogue received the wrong kind of attention.[48] This lingering criticism notwithstanding, however, the Jews of Worms publicized their historical sites as places that offered visitors a "shuddering and deep reverence as with the bliss of mental uplifting," as Isaak Holzer, the rabbi of the community, put it. This authentic cognitive and spiritual experience was facilitated by the presence of the physical remnants of the past where, he contended, the "stones talk."[49]

The veneration for historical patina contributed greatly to Worms's popularity as tourism continued to grow. In the aftermath of World War I, the upper class gave up their extended visits to spa towns and joined the middle class on more limited ventures with overnight stays in economical accommodations, such as youth hostels. Package holidays were popular during this period and were even a common feature of newly negotiated worker contracts. Reflecting the diversification of the travel industry, the traditional dominance of the Baedeker guides gave way to a plethora of new tour books targeted at specific audiences.[50] Alerted to the rich legacies of the various German cities, serialized articles in the *Israelitische*

Familienblatt also invited Jews to places like Worms.[51] New brochures about Worms featured even more detailed descriptions of its Jewish sites, including new images of the *Judengasse*, the synagogue, and the cemetery, with its tombstones covered in supplications (figs. 28 and 29).[52]

Along with its allure for individual travelers, the city also attracted organized Jewish tours. The synagogue's guest book of this period reveals that journalists, politicians, rabbis, scholars like David Sasson and his family from Calcutta and London, the banker Otto Schiff and his brother Arthur, Jewish artists from the university in Moscow, and the scholar and Sephardic rabbi Moses Gastner all found their way to the synagogue. The precursor to Franz Rosenzweig's famous *Lehrhaus*, the Frankfurt *Gesellschaft für jüdische Volksbildung*, founded in 1919 by the liberal rabbi Georg Salzberger, enhanced its program of adult education with excursions to historical sites like Worms in 1922.[53]

A Jewish Heimat *on Borrowed Time* |

Der älteste israelitische Friedhof Deutschlands.   Grab des Rabbi Meir (1295) und Alexander b. Salomon (1308).

FIGURE 28. *Postcard of the tombstones of Meir of Rothenburg and Alexander von Wimpfen (1924). Private collection, Nils Roemer*

As the city increasingly engrossed Jewish visitors from afar, Roths-child, Kiefer, and the community's rabbi, Isaac Holzer, tirelessly pro-moted Worms in the German Jewish periodicals. Their close cooperation with Illert suggests that city officials endorsed their work. Rising anti-semitism, however, was already beginning to complicate things. In their propaganda, right-wing parties targeted and exploited the presence of Eastern European Jews in Worms, eventually compelling Karl Guggen-heim, the chairman of the local branch of the C.V., to attack antisemitism in his confessional speech in Worms on the fusion of Germanness and Jewishness.[54] When Holzer gave a dedicatory speech in 1932 at the mon-ument to the city's fallen soldiers of World War I, he expressed the hope that the commemoration would enhance the spirit of solidarity and unity for the benefit of their *Heimat* and for the blessing of the fatherland and the German people. For Holzer, the monument was to be a testament to Germany's transcendence of its social and religious divisions.[55]

And certainly all was not yet lost. Confidence and dedication moti-vated Kiefer in 1932 to reorganize the museum's holdings in a year when he also enlarged the collection through the acquisition of a painting of the interior of the synagogue. The revamped museum's entrance hall showcased tombstones that had, over the centuries, been stolen from the cemetery and used for buildings around the city. Upon the museum's reopening, Worms's mayor joined the director of the museum and the city archivist to pay tribute there; the local newspaper likewise noted that the Jewish museum had contributed greatly to Worms's international reputation.[56]

Ironically, the intensification of antisemitism in German spa towns during the early 1930s probably further contributed to the popularity of small towns like Worms on the vacation itineraries of German Jews. During these years, the C.V. kept these travelers informed through an increasingly elaborate system of information gathering and classification regarding specifically antisemitic spas and hotels. At the same time, German Jewish periodicals promoted German Jewish travel destinations, and from 1930 onward, the *Israelitische Familienblatt* published serialized articles on Jewish travel in Germany as well.[57]

Manfred Lehmann, who became a scholar on Worms's Jewish history after World War II, recalled that in 1931, his parents took him to the city, likely in response to such advertising. He wrote that his "late father wisely realized that such a visit would make a lasting impression on us." From the cemetery, the family went to the Rashi chapel, and Lehmann remembered "clearly the awe we felt when we visited the ancient synagogue of Worms, with 'Rashi's chair' where, according to tradition, Rashi had sat while he wrote his monumental commentaries on the Tanach and Talmud" (fig. 29). Next to the synagogue the Lehmanns "saw with our own eyes the vestige of a miracle that took place there," referring to the wall's indentation. Contrary to the caption on the illustrated postcards for sale at the site, but in line with many other visitors and commentators, Lehmann believed that it was Rashi's mother who had been miraculously saved there, not the mother of Yehuda he-Hasid.[58]

One of the most famous and frequent visitors to Worms during this period was Martin Buber. As he engaged in his musings on Christianity and Judaism in 1933, he related at the Stuttgart *Jüdisches Lehrhaus* that he occasionally visited Worms, whose old Jewish cemetery provided him with a telling perspective on the cathedral as well. For Buber, the cathedral consisted of individual elements crafted into a harmonious whole, while the Jewish cemetery contained only formless and directionless stones.[59] Buber contrasted the aesthetically appealing order and grandeur of the church with the remnants of the Jewish past: "One only has the stones and the ashes beneath the stones. One has the ashes no matter how much they have disappeared . . . I have them as a physical presence of my

FIGURE 29.

Postcard of the cemetery and the tombstone of Maharil (1924). Private collection, Nils Roemer

memory reaching far back in history, back to Sinai." The historical site thus functions for Buber as a pathway to the entirety of Jewish history. The cathedral does not. Seen from a distance, the silhouette of the cathedral converts historical differences into what Buber ultimately finds is a misleading sense of harmony, from his position in the cemetery: "I have stood there, connected with the ashes and, through them, the ancestors (*Urväter*). This is the memory of God's acts that is given to all Jews."[60] Whatever the splendor of the cathedral, it is the concreteness of the cemetery that is reassuring. Buber illustrated the point in his published dialogue with an often-reproduced view of the cathedral that could be found in tour guides and on illustrated postcards.[61]

The raging political clashes and increased anti-Jewish hostility in Germany did little to discourage American Jews from visiting the country at a time when Jewish tourism was emerging as a new field of leisure activity there. Less shaped by the political exigencies of the Weimar Republic, American Jews encountered the old Jewish memory landscape—and Worms in particular—from a more open, secular perspective as a cultural practice of remembrance. While scholars have noted that American travel agencies then targeted in particular Eastern European Jews, American Jewish tourism was not limited to this constituency.[62] It was for a far wider Jewish English-speaking audience that the *Menorah Journal* in America reported on various Jewish travel destinations and Marvin Lowenthal wrote his *A World Passed By* (1933), which was heralded as the first comprehensive Jewish travel guide. Lowenthal invited readers to "come with me to the forgotten sites of Jewish culture, art, history in Europe and North Africa."[63] Lowenthal brought his own prestige to the topic as a Harvard graduate, former editor of the *Menorah Journal*, representative of the Jewish minority interest at the League of Nations, and independent scholar in his own right. The guide, designed for travelers' "pleasure and use," organized its destinations conveniently along railways routes: "I have tried to keep an eye on Baedeker as well as on the Jews," he commented wryly, as he sought to bring to light some of the "old and often little-known seats of Jewish civilization."[64]

Lowenthal treated Worms extensively in a chapter entitled "A Thousand Years Along the Rhine." Like other visitors before him, Lowenthal found conflicting accounts of its legends, including the story about the miraculous rescue of a woman, whom he was told was the mother of Judah the Pious: " 'Not so,' said my friend, 'I too was in Worms, and the woman, I might tell you, was the mother of Rashi.'" Regardless of the local color, Lowenthal contended that, other than Prague, Worms was the only other place where "we come as close to touching the hem of the medieval German Jew," and he encouraged visitors to place a pebble on the tomb of Juspa Shammes, that "retailer of miracles and legends."[65] Unfortunately, traveling to Germany was fast becoming difficult for Jews, despite the flourishing of international tourism there in the 1930s. American travel guides began to caution prospective tourists about the Nazi seizure of power and its ramifications for the German Jewish community. While regional tourist offices kept advertising the Rhineland in the London *Times*, American travel guides warned Jewish tourists about visiting Germany.[66]

The intensifying harassment of German Jews by the Nazis and their accomplices affected local communities as well. Jews who might hitherto have had very little contact with the congregation now became forcibly part of it. The promulgation of the "Law Against Overcrowding in German Schools and Universities," passed on April 25, 1933, forced the children of the Russian-born Jew Illi Kagan, for example, to attend lessons at the school in a community building adjacent to the synagogue. For one of them, the young Vladimir, this coercion entailed an even bigger change, as he "until then had spent more time in Worms's famous cathedral than in the synagogue, and had never even attended synagogue services," he later recalled.[67]

In response to these changes, the Jewish community soon developed an autonomous and diversified cultural life beyond the previously dominant religious sphere. Educational activities, lecture series sponsored by the Zionist association, local sporting events organized by the Jewish War Veterans, and chess clubs all emerged. Members of the Worms community in 1935 conducted a memorial service for Theodor Herzl; they commemorated those who died during World War I; later, they celebrated the memory of Hindenburg in August 1938.[68] It was within this emerging, segregated Jewish landscape of local associations that the Jews in Worms memorialized the nine-hundredth anniversary of their synagogue on June 3, 1934. Commemorating the German Jewish past was not limited to Worms but indicative of the C.V.'s attempts to utilize history to assert German Jewish identity.[69] In Worms, the event's press release noted that it was hardly a time to celebrate, but that the anniversary could not be passed over. Nevertheless, designated ushers, wearing white buttonhole rosettes, welcomed guests at the train station on the day of the event and led them to the decorated synagogue, which was filled with members of the community dressed in festive attire. Long before the ceremony began, guests had filled the old synagogue, so organizers broadcast the service simultaneously over loudspeakers in the adjacent Levy synagogue. Among the guests were numerous community representatives from around the country as well as Leo Baeck, the chair of the *Reichsvertretung der deutschen Juden* (National representation of German Jews).[70]

The celebration did more than summarize the synagogue's by now well-established historical traditions; it also brought together various strands of earlier constructions of the local heritage, now linking it to the merits of the ancestors. Isaak Holzer, the rabbi of the community, equated the synagogue with the burning bush in his opening speech. Citing "Put off thy shoes, for the place is holy ground" (Ex. 3:5), he presented the building as a sacred site that illuminated the path for other communities. In his review of Worms's Jewish past, Holzer portrayed a devout Jewish community from which God's teaching emanated; it had long served as a model and leader for others. He became almost defiant as he elaborated upon the religious devotion that had enabled the Jews of Worms to endure many challenges and even die as martyrs when necessary.[71]

It was left to Leo Baeck to transform this local anniversary into a commemoration of German Jewish history. German Jews had the desire to "commemorate in a worthy manner the past generation by looking back reverently at the century-long Jewish history in Germany," he announced. Like Holzer, Baeck wanted to draw lessons from the community's past, because certainly the site that had existed for nine hundred years "speaks about our German Jewish nobility." German Jewry now had to "remain noble" and overcome their disunity, which contradicted "the old spirit of Worms." Baeck then concluded that nine hundred years signified *Heimat* in Worms's convergence of Jewish spirit and German soil.[72]

Central to the celebration of the synagogue was the idea that the Jewish past had again taken hold among the Jews of Germany in light of the Nazis rise to power: "We take hold of our past from a [perspective] of familiarity, which is not lectured, not deduced, but immediately verified by our experience," wrote one newspaper.[73] Along these lines, Max Grünewald of Mannheim explained in a special table talk that nothing obstructs historical memory more than history itself. As time passed and the Jews invested their hopes in a better future, the past became increasingly distant. But faith in progress and advancement, however admirable, had rendered historical documents, stones, and artifacts more and more impenetrable. The German Jews' radically altered situation in 1930s Germany, however, suggested new pathways to the understanding of the past and encouraged Jews to redeem their heritage. The contemporary experience of harassment and persecution made the examples of the Worms community's martyrdom much more immediate and profound, for example, stirring faith in the Jews' ability to endure: "That which we experience, they too experienced." Whereas the legends of the *Nibelungen* perhaps evoked death and downfall, Jewish legends demonstrated above all that the Jewish soul was ultimately "invulnerable and unassailable."[74]

All of the major German Jewish periodicals carried extensive articles. Through a tightly organized management of the press, Karl Guggen-
heim, the president of the Jewish veterans' association in Worms, who acted as the press liaison, provided news agencies and periodicals with news releases that formed the basis of their articles.[75] Therefore, the depiction of the celebration in newspapers was fairly uniform, even when the papers had special correspondents of their own in Worms. Most of them cited Leo Baeck's speech extensively, along with his notions of *Heimat* and German Jewish nobility.[76] Many newspapers also used the occasion as an opportunity to commission separate articles about the history of Worms's Jewish community. The C.V. published a special issue adorned with newly made sketches of the synagogue and the cemetery, accompanying them with a retelling of the legend of Rothenburg's torah scroll by Henriette Mannheimer.[77] The *Zeitschrift für die Geschichte der Juden in Deutschland* published a special commemorative volume. Its authors praised the community as a "mother in Israel" from the perspective of its significance to Jews in general and German Jewry in particular. The synagogue symbolized German Jews' constant presence in Germany as well as their devotion to their religion and culture, and this "great past" placed an obligation upon present-day Jews for the future.[78]

Despite the general unanimity, of course, slight differences in tone emerged in the Zionist press. The *Jüdische Rundschau* reminded its readers that the history of the Jews in Worms was full of both suffering and learning and even hinted that the community had silenced those accusers who believed that the Jews had always remained homeless. The paper then went on to stress, however, that current events were forcing German Jews to distance themselves from German society, whatever their history in that country, pointing out that the Jews of Worms would likely have disappeared if they had not remained so devoted to Judaism and its culture.[79] The neo-Orthodox press ridiculed the presence of an organ and choir in the synagogue but was impressed with Leo Baeck's speech.[80]

Beyond the extensive newspaper coverage, the celebrations garnered telegrams and other greetings from Germany and around the world. Many German Jewish communities noted that all of German Jewry shared in this celebration and took solace and pride in Worms's legacy.[81] In its congratulatory letter, the *Reichsvertretung der deutschen Juden* also emphasized that Worms's legacy implied an obligation for the future: "This celebration tells of a historical place and a historical task . . . that leads from an important past through the present to the future."[82] The

134

MOVING LOCAL JEWISH HERITAGE INTO MODERNITY

letter also echoed the by now familiar observation that the history of the Jews in Worms proved how deeply rooted Jews were in the German lands and culture: "This building testifies to the history of Jews in Germany more than scrolls and books. The attachment of German Jewry to the German *Heimat* finds a symbolic expression [here]."[83]

Similar notes arrived from abroad. The Board of Elders of the Congregation of Sephardic Synagogue Bevis Marks in London noted the history of Worms's learning and suffering and expressed the hope that "God may vouchsafe enlargement, deliverance and peace to the Jewish community of Worms and to all Israel."[84] The Jews of Worms also received a letter from the influential Congregation She'arith Israel in New York City, reminding them that the American congregation was likewise the oldest community in North America with a not inconsiderable history of 280 years: "In all the vicissitudes of its venerable history, from the martyrdom in the first Crusade to the sorrows of the present day, your community has withstood suffering with an unshaken faith and an unbroken courage that have been an inspiration to Jewish communities everywhere."[85]

The celebrations had been undeniably affected by the Nazis seizure of power and policy of intimidation and harassment, social isolation, and economic exploitation of German Jews, including the Worms community, which numbered around one thousand members in 1933. Already in 1922, a Worms branch of the National Socialist German Workers Party (NSDAP) had begun to act on behalf of the small but rapidly growing number of National Socialist supporters in the city. In January 1933, the city held a ceremony to make Hindenburg and Hitler honorary citizens, followed by a large torchlight procession on January 30 by the NSDAP through the city and the opening of Osthofen, the first concentration camp, not far from Worms.[86] In the run-up to their synagogue anniversary festivities, members of the Worms community had consulted with the C.V. and other associations about how to proceed. In their correspondence with Leo Baeck, community members feared that the celebration would bring numerous international guests to the city and thus too much attention to the community. In light of these concerns, it was decided to celebrate the occasion locally and only with guests from Germany proper.[87]

Though Jewish heritage had played a central role in both the city's local and destination culture, only one non-Jewish local journalist, Adolf Tschirner—as well as the chairs of the antiquity society, Cornelius and

Ludwig von Heyl—responded to the invitation; the rest of the local press remained silent.[88] With only one exception, German newspapers left the celebration unmentioned, and the situation continued to deteriorate. In December 1933, local members of the National Socialist party began to call for the renaming of the Rashi gate.[89] Already in March 1933, Isidor Kiefer had terminated his membership in the antiquity society, as had other Jewish members such as Leopold Nickelsburg, Siegfried Guggenheim, and Max Levy. One year later, Kiefer informed the Jewish community from Brussels that he had decided not to return from a trip abroad.[90]

Kiefer was not alone; in 1933, over 160 Jews left Worms, which was the highest number to depart in a single year. This figure was roughly halved in 1934 and declined to as low as thirty-two in 1935.[91] Isaac Holzer left that year, eventually arriving in the United States. Heinrich Rudolf Hüttenbach, who had been born in Worms in 1930, moved to Mannheim with his parents in 1935 before immigrating to Milan in 1936 and London in 1939. Cognizant of the slowly diminishing community, Herta Mansbacher, who had been a teacher in the city in the early 1900s, began to record the names and dates of those who migrated abroad between 1933 and 1941. Quoting Heinrich Heine's famous lines, penned in Paris about his German fatherland, Mansbacher wrote in the introduction to her "emigration book" that she expected these Jews to experience a nostalgic yearning for their former *Heimat*. Hopefully an awareness of their origins would help them to adjust in their new homelands.[92]

Just as Worms's Jews began to leave, the city also began to rewrite its historical heritage. Friedrich M. Illert, the local archivist and author of tour guides, who had a few years earlier promoted Worms's rich Jewish legacy, described the city instead as the birthplace of *German* legends in the 1935 official Worms tour guide. (Interestingly, the slightly abridged version still listed the Jewish sites as major attractions.)[93] Illert in particular sold the city as the source of the *Nibelungen* and even submitted a proposal to Joseph Goebbels in 1936 for a national celebration of the Reich in Worms. When its staging of Friedrich Hebbel's *Nibelungen* in 1937 was attended by Hitler's chief propagandist, it became very apparent that the city had made considerable progress in refashioning its historical heritage.[94]

The political shift to the right in Germany thus presumably brought many more anxious admirers of German emperors, the *Nibelungen*, and Luther to the city. But for Jews in Germany, however, traveling after 1933 became almost impossible, even to formerly popular Jewish travel

136 |

resorts like Norderney. The C.V.'s distinction between welcoming and antisemitic hotels and resorts had become meaningless at a time when hatred of Jews had become state ideology. Even in larger cities like Hamburg, hotels refused outright to accept Jewish guests, or took them only with discriminatory measures. Legislation followed here an already well-established pattern of exclusion. In 1937, the *Reichsstatthalter* in Hessen implemented a new regulation by the Reich and Prussian Ministry of the Interior that severely limited Jews' ability to visit German spas.[95] Of course, one response to such efforts to isolate Jews was to promote instead their only available tourism option, visiting Jewish historical sites. Yet organized group visits became dangerous and too difficult during this period as well, so that the community, for example, had to advise the Frankfurt *Jüdischen Lehrhaus* against a day excursion with about fifty people.[96]

Reflecting the radically changed circumstances of Jewish life, the commemorative celebration by the local branch of the patriotic Jewish war veterans' organization in Worms, the *Reichsbund jüdischer Frontsoldaten*, took on a defensive and somber mood.[97] Despite the challenges, the *Reichsbund* traveled in 1936 with some thirty guests from Frankfurt to Worms, a city that allowed them "to recall the past to gain strength from it for the present and future."[98] It was perhaps for a similar reason that Saul Lilienthal republished his *Jüdische Wanderungen* (Jewish walking tours), a collection based on articles that he had published from 1930 onward in the *Israelitische Familienblatt*. This description of various Jewish travel destinations took on the quality of a *Memorbuch* when Lilienthal noted that it was no longer able to fulfill its original intention: "Because, day by day, the existence of the Jews in Germany becomes more history, that is, something of the past." Therefore Lilienthal hoped only that his guide would act as more of an inventory of the sites while they were still there, travelers or no.[99]

One year later, during *Kristallnacht* in November 1938, the old synagogue was set ablaze in two consecutive attacks. At the same time, many shops owned by Jews were being demolished as well (fig. 30) as part of a new urban plan that was claimed to be more in keeping with the German *Volk*. Only the cemetery was left unharmed, possibly because the local archivist Illert, who would have a central role in the postwar rebuilding of the synagogue, perpetuated the legend that Heinrich Himmler had expressed a great interest in the cemetery during a visit in the early 1930s.[100]

A Jewish Heimat *on Borrowed Time* |

FIGURE 30. *Photo of the synagogue during* Kristallnacht *(1938).*
Stadtarchiv Worms, Germany

Despite mounting difficulties in procuring the financial resources and entry documents to other countries, around 170 Worms Jews emigrated between 1938 and 1939 in response to anti-Jewish legislative measures and violence. The Kagan family, for example, fled the country when they were threatened with deportation to the Polish border in January 1938 because of their Russian passports.[101] Given the accelerating migration of Jews from Worms, "emigration book" keeper Herta Mannsbacher in 1937 radically changed her interpretation of the process, viewing these migrants not as leaving their homes but as searching for a new *Heimat*.[102] Some who had already left Worms returned once more, if only briefly, including Max Guggenheim, who recalled in exile his last visit to the razed synagogue in 1938. He said *Kaddish* for the last time, removed a few stones from the *Aron ha-kodesh*, and collected the key to the building. He then left the "holy place, the city, in which I had been born and which had been the place of residence for 400 years for my family."[103]

For those who remained in the city, the situation became even more unbearable. In November 1938, a *Reich* law required all Jews living in Aryan quarters to be evicted by April 30, 1939. Under these conditions, the last rabbi of the community, Helmut Frank, left for America in

1939.[104] Henceforth, Jews could only be tenants in Jewish-owned or designated housing, an order that corralled them all into the Jewish Quarter, where the community still owned several larger buildings.[105] As the number of Jews living in Germany rapidly declined, communities struggled to find safe locations for their cherished documents and artifacts. Who could heed the C.V. newspaper's calls to communities to guard their historical collections?[106] From New York, Isidor Kiefer tried in vain to transfer the museum's collection to America, but he was resisted by the community members still in Worms, who were unwilling to part with it.[107] A few years later in February 1939, when Worms's historian Samson Rothschild left the city at the age of ninety-two to live with his daughter in London, such options no longer existed. Rothschild died that same year and an obituary noted the passing of the "Historian of the Jews of Worms," who had, on his ninetieth birthday, received over one thousand letters and telegrams from Jews and non-Jews alike. The family plot in the new Worms cemetery between his wife and sister would remain empty, as he was buried in East Ham Jewish Cemetery in London.[108]

Already in exile and living in a hotel on the Upper West Side in New York, Kiefer recreated the Jewish museum with the available photos in an album. He poured himself into this task of assembling a virtual museum because his "devoted love for the venerable Jewish community had experienced no change and suffered no loss." Dedicating this work to the memory of his parents and his *Heimat* community of Worms, Kiefer claimed that historical destiny had put him in the position of preserving its local heritage. Out of gratefulness for this opportunity, he wrote alongside the photos everything he knew about the items for future generations, in case the museum should be destroyed.[109]

Kiefer hoped that his annotations and photos might aid in the future reconstruction of the museum, but only a few more Worms Jews managed to escape Germany in 1940 and 1941, and the prospects grew dim. In October 1940, those who remained, together with Jews from Baden, Pfalz, and Saarland, were deported to Gurs in the south of France.[110] Some managed to migrate or simply escape from the camp, while many others were ultimately deported to the death camps in Poland. Herta Mansbacher had the opportunity to emigrate to Egypt but decided to stay in Worms until the last of her pupils was safely abroad. While still in Worms, she continued to record the emigration of the Jewish community, and, in March 1942, she was deported to Piaski, near Lublin, together with eight of the remaining children. She then perished in the same year in one of the nearby death camps.[111] At the same time, with few exceptions, most of the artifacts that had been on display in the museum were destroyed—unfortunately, Worms Jews had taken only a few items with them into exile.[112] Two silver cups and a goblet belonging to the Worms burial society were saved when, in 1942, the chair of the Jewish community in Worms requested help from Michael Oppenheim in Mainz to hide them. Oppenheim managed to safeguard them in Mainz's antiquity museum.[113]

In the course of a little more than twenty years, then, the Jewish community's remembrance of Worms had undergone a fundamental transformation. Already its nine-hundred-year celebration had balanced an emphasis on *Heimat* with an appreciation of the heroic martyrdom of the medieval community. During World War II, people continued to try and comprehend the unfolding horror and destruction that had befallen European Jewry through the lens of the community's medieval past; in Chile, for example, a Jewish newspaper even reprinted a poem about medieval persecution in Worms during the 1940s.[114] These Chilean emigrants were not alone in using medieval textual traditions to experience the gravity of the horror. In his "Ballads of Worms" (1942), the Hebrew poet Saul Tchernichovsky evokes the arrival of the Black Death in the *Judengasse*: "He's come! He's come! He's here!" In its medieval context, members of the burial society would be calling upon the citizens to witness the first victims of the plague, who are Jews, therefore proving the community's innocence against allegations of well poisoning. In the poem, the first victim alerts the reader to the annihilation of European Jewry and highlights Jews' powerlessness. The cyclical nature of the persecution also informs Tchernichovsky's poetic rendition of the story about the two foreigners who gave themselves up to save the community.[115]

Dislocation and remembrance featured also in the Hebrew poet Agnon's fable *Ba-derekh* (On the road), where a lonely protagonist hides in a cleft of rock, like Moses when God revealed himself to him. In the protagonist's revelation, he sees two men and two women on their way to the synagogue. Although he thought Jews no longer lived in that town, he comes to realize that despite their persecution, some remain and continue to meet on Rosh Hashanah, Yom Kippur, and the first of Sivan, the day of the First Crusade destruction of the Jewish community of Worms. Encapsulated in these days is the remembrance of persecution. The narrator, who moves from the twelfth to the fifteenth century, learns the customs and rituals of the Ashkenazic community. The devout society, however, is steeped in blood. The narrator eventually leaves and embarks on a train to Eretz Israel. It seems that he can only proceed with his trip once he embraces his Ashkenazic heritage.[116]

Agnon's fable depicts a last embrace of the Ashkenazic past before it is left behind, and it relies upon a certain continuity of historical remembrance, despite the obvious geographic break between the Diaspora communities and the emerging *Yishuv* in Palestine. Indeed, for the members of the Jerusalem school, the medieval past remained an important lever into their terrible present. When, in 1945, Abraham Haberman published the Hebrew chronicles and medieval liturgical dirges, he hoped that through these texts, the Jews' mourning for the Holocaust could find its first expression until other forms of remembrance could be found. Quoting from the Babylonian Talmud (Shabbat 13a), he expressed his inability to comprehend, let alone find words for, the erasure of European Jewry. In the meantime, Haberman hoped that these medieval sources, which vividly depicted the martyrdom of the Rhineland communities, would in turn hint at the horror of the death camps.[117]

In the midst of the ongoing dislocation and destruction, Mannsbacher's chronicle and Kiefer's account of the Jewish museum anticipated new means of remembrance that would surface after the Holocaust. These recollections ensured that despite the erasure of the community and the synagogue, the history of Worms's Jews was remembered in the postwar period, when local memory politics commingled and collided with the interests of Jewish survivors, displaced persons, and Jewish members of the American army who visited the city to view its remains.

AFTER THE HOLOCAUST

DISTURBING REMAINS

PLACE AND DISPLACEMENT OF MEMORY

The immediate postwar history of occupied Germany has often been described as a "zero hour," marked as it was by a profound lack of memory and an inability to confront the Nazi crimes. Most Germans saw themselves as victims rather than victimizers, though this view has since been rightly challenged. Their remembrances did not form a coherent whole but instead displayed various inclinations within what Frank Stern has called the historic triangle of occupiers, Germans, and Jews.[1]

In the midst of the many destroyed political and physical landscapes, Jews, who had been in hiding, soon resurfaced in several German cities. Others returned; large numbers of Eastern European Jews, in particular, sought safety under the Allied occupation. Approximately 300,000 Jews temporarily resided in Germany before most of them emigrated to America and Israel. They comprised survivors of the Final Solution, a small remnant of German Jews, and over a quarter-million East European Jewish "displaced persons," or DPs. During the liminal postwar period up until the establishment of the two German states, Germans and Jews were placed "on exhibit" to journalists, delegates, and representatives. Questions about the renewal of Jewish life and the ownership of their former property became enveloped within local and regional German power structures, commanders of the Allied Forces, international Jewish organizations, and representatives of the nascent Jewish state.

In addition, returning to Germany remained anathema to many of those Jews who had managed to flee Nazi Germany. In July 1948, the World Jewish Congress declared at its first postwar assembly in Montreal, Canada, that Jews would never again set foot on the "blood-soaked German soil."[2] While a rabbinical ban against living in Germany was never issued, it was widely held that living in Germany was, at best, a tenuous affair. After a 1946 visit to the country, German Zionist Robert Weltsch observed, "We cannot assume that there are Jews who feel themselves drawn towards Germany . . . Germany is no place for Jews."[3] The first Israeli consul in Munich, Chaim Yahil, declared in the *American-Jewish Frontier* in 1951 that all Jews should in fact leave Germany. Even those who had reestablished Jewish communities felt they were merely part of a "liquidation-community" that lived in a "stopping-place between the camps and the grave," as Moritz Abusch, an early postwar leader of Jews in Germany, graphically described it.[4]

On the other hand, some Jews both inside and outside of Germany took a keen interest in its postwar status, the reconstitution of its Jewish communities, and the cultural legacy of German Jewry. They came as individuals to revisit their former hometowns; as officials to assess the situation in Germany; as political representatives of various international organizations and institutions; and as tourists. Soon enough, Worms and its renowned Jewish historical sites attracted an intense interest among former members of the community, Jewish chaplains and other Jewish members of the Armed Forces, and many DPs. Mediated through their reports and articles, the desolate state of the destroyed synagogue and the remains of the former archive and museum became known to the wider Jewish public. The presence of these early visitors and returnees began the acts of preservation and rehabilitation that would become instrumental in shaping the remembrance of the Jewish past during a period in which almost nothing was done to remember Nazism and its victims at the former concentration camps in Germany.

The Jewish community of Worms had been destroyed. Its survivors were scattered across several continents, and its synagogue, many of its historical documents, and its torah scrolls torched (fig. 31). Only the ritual bath, a few remnants of the museum collection, and the cemetery had made it through relatively unscathed. Despite the prompt reconstitution of Jewish communities in Berlin, Munich, and Cologne, no such congregation reorganized in Worms. Already having confronted the difficult task of coming to terms with their new lives in Israel, South America, the United States, and the United Kingdom, most of the more than five hundred surviving former Worms Jews never did resettle there.[5] Still, many contacted the city or even visited it at some point. Spurred on by family memories and recollections of the venerable community, these survivors all attempted in their own ways to reconnect with the city that had forcefully expelled them only a few years before. They corresponded among

FIGURE 31. *Photo of the destroyed synagogue (1945). Stadtarchiv Worms, Germany*

themselves as well, creating yet other Worms-centered networks of communication. These contacts built upon the "emergency committee" that had been established in the late 1930s in the United States by Rabbi Helmut Frank in Philadelphia and Elke Spies in New York to stay abreast of the situation of those who were still in Worms or had been transferred to the camps.[6]

As these former members exchanged information and mourned the destruction of their community, they seldom expressed an interest in returning there. While their *Heimat* appeared lost to them, its memory was not. In 1946, Hannah Arendt evoked this feeling in a poem in which she converted Rilke's famous lines, "Lucky he who has a home," into "Lucky is he who has no home; he sees it still in his dreams."[7] The often-disturbing memory of the former hometown emerged at the intersection of place and displacement, as Maurice Halbwachs observed in his studies of collective memory. Memories, he noted, "are attached to a place, coalesce, divide, become attached to one another, or scatter, as the case may be."[8] The breaking up of the various local and national communities of remembrance that had shaped the representation of Worms throughout the ages refashioned its sites of interest and import in various ways.

Rather than simply representing the past by acting as depositories of historical memory, these sites became reinvested with multiple meanings in the postwar period. Memory now operated as a process of representing and integrating the past into different contexts.

As the past held sway over the German Jewish survivors, the act of remembering Worms was both haunting recollection and programmatic obligation. To Erich Guggenheim, for example, whose family had resided in Worms since 1550 but fled to Brazil in 1934, Worms never stopped appearing in his dreams as "what it cannot not be in reality: My home/land (*Heimat*)."[9] For Henry Huttenbach, writing many years later, the Jews of Worms had managed to maintain their sense of community. "Little Jerusalem dispersed," as he called the survivors, "had not lost [its] sense of a common heritage." Jewish Worms, while destroyed, "continues to enrich Jewish life through its dispersed exiles and their children."[10]

In March 1945, former Worms resident Max Guggenheim, Erich's uncle, who had arrived in Buenos Aires in 1939, published an article in a Jewish periodical in Chile informing his readers that the French army had reached Worms. During World War II, the Rhineland had been heavily bombed by the Allies, and Worms, like many other German cities, was left cratered and rutted. Without specific details about the destruction, Guggenheim was left to quote Jacob Rust's seventeenth-century poem about the devastation inflicted upon the city by French troops in 1689: "Courage is sinking indeed with sorrow, / Because Worms is done, the worthy city . . . What was standing for a thousand years, / Is destroyed in a day."[11]

Guggenheim's juxtaposition of the French impact upon Worms in the seventeenth century and the Allies' part in its havoc during World War II underscores the relevance of history to his ongoing experience of dislocation. His choice of comparison would have been very meaningful to those who were intimately familiar with Worms's history. Still, he preferred not to characterize the city solely as a victim of Allied air raids, whatever the larger tenor of the times, and recalled the destruction and dispersion of the Jewish community: "*Heimat* and existence have been taken from us—and alas how many had their lives taken."[12]

Guggenheim cited the same line in a short autobiographical account in which he described his last trip to the partially destroyed synagogue in 1938 before his emigration to Chile. Guggenheim had recovered the old metal key from the *Aron Kodesh* and bequeathed it to the Bezalel National Museum in Jerusalem after the war, with the provision that it would be returned to Worms once a Jewish community had reestablished itself there.[13] The defeat in the surrender of the key to Jerusalem is belied by the hope in the renewal of Jewish life in Worms. Concurrent with the key's transfer, Michael Oppenheim in 1945 discovered the goblets of Worms's burial society and arranged for their shipment to the Jewish Museum in New York. In a letter to Oppenheim, Stephen Kayser of the Jewish Museum welcomed the arrival of the goblets, which, he wrote, enriched the collection of mostly newer objects. Such additions were all the more important insofar as the museum had, in the course of the Holocaust, acquired a new meaning as a "monument for the remembrance of the Jews of Europe," Kayser explained.[14] The fate of the key and the goblets also indicates the ongoing scattering of Worms memorabilia around the globe in the immediate postwar years.

The foundation of German Jewish organizations around the world further cemented the dislocation of memory from the country itself. The Council of Jews from Germany, which had been set up toward the end of World War II by organizations of German Jews in Israel, England, and America, initially diverged with regard to its views on Germany. Hans Reichmann, representing the London Council of Jews from Germany, believed that the 1952 Luxemburg Reparation Treaty with the Federal Republic could allow Germany to become part of the council's cultural work. He proposed, among other things, the establishment of a Jewish museum in one of the old Jewish settlements like Mainz, Worms, Cologne, or Frankfurt. Reichmann, however, faced formidable opposition in the person of Siegfried Moses of the *Irgun Olei Merkas Europa* in Israel, who called on Jews to suspend all work in Germany and ridiculed Reichmann's proposal as a perpetuation of fantasies about a German Jewish symbiosis. By the end of 1955, the council had established the Leo Baeck Institute and its branches in Jerusalem, London, and New York as an institution outside of Germany that would be devoted to the task of keeping the memory of the German Jewish past alive.[15]

Despite the fundamental geographic shift of the centers of German Jewish life, Worms attracted the attention of many Jews in the immediate postwar period. In her programmatic 1955 survey of German Jewish and American Jewish history, the German Jewish historian Selma Stern, then residing in Cincinnati, testified to the importance of Worms. Comparing the historical consciousness of German and American Jews during the modern era, she reminded her English readers, "There was no chapel here where Rashi had taught, no memory book that told of sufferings and persecution." For her, German Jews' "sharing in a common past in common traditions in turn produced a strong historical consciousness."[16]

Historical memory also resurfaced soon after the war, as the Jews of Worms provided information to various organizations surveying the fate of heirless Jewish property. The debates about this recovered cultural property provided a "touching footnote to the passing of the scepter of Jewish life," in the words of Robert Liberles.[17] During the war Jewish organizations had considered the future of things like community archives and Judaica collections. Whereas these recovery efforts initially aimed to rebuild Jewish life, they became transformed by both the destruction wrought by the Holocaust and the larger plans for the reconstruction of Jewish cultural strength, especially in America and Israel. In Germany, the debate centered on legal representation for Jewish interests regarding looted property. During a conference held in London in April 1943 under the auspices of the Jewish Historical Society of England, the eminent Anglo-Jewish historian Cecil Roth argued that all heirless cultural property should be placed in the custody of the Hebrew University in Jerusalem.[18] In 1944, the Board of Deputies for British Jews instead called for the establishment of a Jewish trusteeship for each country liberated from Nazi or Axis control. This trusteeship was to represent the restitution or compensation interests of Jews in cases where property owners or heirs could not be located, or a Jewish community could not be restored.[19] Preparing the groundwork for any future claims regarding Worms, the Jewish chaplains who had been in the city in 1945 supplied Roth with a short survey of its existing cultural remnants.[20]

Similar efforts were put into motion in America already in 1941, when the American Federation of Jews from Central Europe was founded in New York City as the central representative agency of over thirty national and local organizations for victims of National Socialism from that region. The federation drafted lists of Jewish property and requested information, for example, from the former director of the Jewish museum, Isidor Kiefer, about the treasures of the Worms community.[21] Dovetailing these initiatives, the Conference on Jewish Social Studies in America established the Commission on European Jewish Cultural Reconstruction in the summer of 1944 under the leadership of Jewish historian Salo Baron from Columbia University. Hannah Arendt, the German Jewish philosopher cum historian, led the research performed by this commission in 1944. In conjunction with the first director of the commission, Joshua Starr, she prepared the publication of comprehensive lists of Jewish cultural property. Baron also turned to Isidor Kiefer for information about the belongings of the community.[22] The publication of the commission's "Tentative List of Jewish Cultural Treasures in Axis-Occupied Countries" in 1944 duly included Worms's Jewish properties.[23]

In 1947, the Jewish Restitution Commission (JRC) was recognized as an umbrella organization for various Jewish groups devoted to the task of restitution. The JRC collected information on Jewish artifacts and books from their office in Wiesbaden, from which the publicist Ernst G. Loewenthal, who had been active on behalf of the C.V. and the *Reichsvertretung* during the 1930s, corresponded with the city's archivist, Friedrich Illert, between 1949 and 1951.[24] To assess the situation on the ground, Professor Arendt, a refugee from Nazi Germany and now a visitor from the United States, traveled in Europe for six months between 1949 and 1950 and directed the operation that recovered about one and a half million volumes of Judaica and pieces of ceremonial art. In the course of her investigations, she went to Worms, where she detailed Illert's ongoing efforts to collect the community's historical documents, and his plans to rebuild the synagogue.[25]

The JRC's work met with substantial opposition in Germany, where the newly established government either opposed the recovery of former Jewish belongings or had already begun to hand over Jewish property to recently restored Jewish communities. The JRC, as Hannah Arendt observed, had to proceed with negotiations on a community-by-community basis.[26] In addition to Bavaria, Worms, at the time still occupied by French forces, was also unwilling to hand over its Jewish archives. Confronted with Illert's resistance to parting with the collection, Arendt asked the archivist instead to microfilm substantial parts of it; she also requested copies of the Worms *Mahzor* upon her return to New York.[27]

Despite Illert's former interest in the idea of casting the city of the *Nibelungen* as the birthplace of Nazism during the 1930s, he reinvented himself in the postwar years as the cemetery's rescuer who had safeguarded the remains of the synagogue and the archives. Within a carefully cultivated network of city representatives and former Jewish citizens, Illert became the postwar trustee of Jewish interests. He promoted himself (and Worms) through a combination of fact and fiction, making the truth difficult to pinpoint. According to a popular apocryphal account, the *Reichsführer-SS* and chief of the German police, Heinrich Himmler, had inspected the Jewish cemetery during the 1930s. Illert claimed that Himmler had placed the cemetery under his direct protection at that time, should it ever be endangered.[28] Whatever the truth of it, the account quickly spread unquestioned, not least because Illert's role seemed to validate Jewish faith in the miraculous survival of important remnants of their past. Thus a 1956 article in *Newsweek* about the possible reconstruction of the synagogue spurred the German Jewish newspaper in New York, *Aufbau*, to announce that it was only thanks to Illert that several remnants still existed at all.[29]

The city's renewal of interest in its Jewish treasures did not go unnoticed. The *Poale Zion* newspaper in Germany, which favored the transfer of Jewish artifacts to a central archive in Jerusalem, saw a financial interest in Worms's withholding of them.[30] Undaunted, Illert continued to defend the Judaica collection when a former Jewish citizen of Worms, Julius Schack, was authorized by the Hessian interior ministry in May 1948 to transport Jewish documents and a torah scroll from Worms to Israel. Illert successfully discouraged Schack's attempts, both at the time and later on, to have the Judaica moved to Israel.[31] Likewise, Illert frustrated Franz Landsberger, a professor at the Hebrew Union College in Cincinnati and former director of the Jewish museum of Berlin, when, in February 1950, he attempted to acquire parts of Worms's archival collections. When Landsberger requested the loan of Worms's famous *Mahzor*, Illert turned him down, pointing out that the JRC had a copy of the *Mahzor* he could borrow instead. Landsberger reiterated his interest and even offered to purchase certain items from him, but Illert could not be persuaded.[32]

By the late 1940s, after having fended off the initial attempts to relocate the archival collection and its cherished manuscripts, Illert began to preserve or collect Worms's extant physical sites, ritual objects, and archives. Motivated primarily by the desire to eradicate evidence of the Nazis' destruction, his efforts likewise buttressed his claim that the markers of Worms's Jewish past, whatever their nature, should remain in Worms. Illert also pointed to the temporary presence of former Jewish citizens, regional and national politicians, Jewish members of the armed forces, and Jewish displaced persons in Worms as his potential audience. Their ongoing visits to the city proved the reverence in which the local sites were held around the world. While these guests at times sought the transfer of some of the community's belongings as well, Illert viewed this as proof instead of their relevance for Worms.

Illert also began to hope that a future reestablishment of a Jewish community would be possible in Worms, despite the reality of the situation, and that his work might contribute to it.[33] Certainly there was interest. Looking back at his father's restoration of the synagogue in 1961, Georg Illert, who succeeded Friedrich as the director of the cultural institute of the city of Worms, related that immediately after the American troops' arrival in March 1945, the first Jews came to inquire about the historical monuments. These guests, including former members of the Jewish community, came and went, however, because Worms was no longer the place of living Jews, as one Jewish newspaper contended. Former Jewish burghers of the city wrote Friedrich Illert to inquire about the status of their family tombstones as well.[34] Karl Darmstaedter, who was familiar with Worms from a trip during the Weimar Republic era, was keen to find out whether Rothenburg's torah scroll still existed.[35]

The local newspaper reported on former community members' stopovers in Worms, cultivating a sense of connectedness between the city and its former Jewish citizens. In the early 1950s, Kiefer told those Worms Jews who had fled to Chile about his recent trip to the city, where he met Illert and toured the cemetery and the destroyed synagogue. According to the headline in the local press, Kiefer had remained faithful to his hometown and not severed his ties to the city.[36] Further reinforcing the notion of a citizenry beyond the boundaries of the city itself, the *Wormser Zeitung* also was careful to note the eightieth birthday of Alfred Langenbach, then living in London. Langenbach's "move" (*Übersiedlung*) had not severed his ties to his hometown, where he frequently vacationed to meet up with "wartime comrades." This reference was more than misleading; it promoted the essential message that Langenbach, a refugee from Nazi Germany, was a "good friend of his *Heimat* in Worms."[37] Features on Jewish Worms that appeared in the journal of Worms's high school and in the local historical association's periodical fulfilled a similar function.[38]

Among Worms's postwar Jewish visitors, as mentioned previously, were a considerable number of DPs from nearby camps in Bensheim, Lampertheim, and elsewhere. Inspired by the Partisan song written after the Warsaw ghetto uprising in 1943, the *she'erit ha-pletah* (surviving remnant) announced these people's survival to themselves and to the world: "We are here," it stated simply.[39] This conflicted combination of triumph and emotional and spiritual despair contributed to the DPs' heightened mobility overall, as Koppel Pinson observed in 1947.[40] The survivors set up a "Central Historical Committee," created by the Central Committee of Liberated Jews in the United States Zone of Occupation in Germany in December 1945, to coordinate local efforts to document Jewish life under the Nazis. At the same time, members of the camps chronicled the destruction of German Jewry in their newspapers.[41] Toward this end, inspecting sites of destruction in places like Worms provided the Jewish DPs with firsthand experience of this recent history while making their survival more immediately visible to the German population.

Among those who came to Worms were Orthodox Jews, who most likely traveled from DP camps such as Föhrenwald, Lampertheim, and Bensheim.[42] These Hasidim made up a small part of the Jewish survivors with temporary homes in the British and, especially, U.S. zones. They were part of a transitory and highly mobile society that nevertheless left its mark upon Germany, and particularly upon Worms.[43] Among the Hasidic Worms returnees were students of Rabbi Benzion Halberstadt, who had been killed by the Nazis in 1941.[44] For example, Lampertheim, situated between Mannheim and Darmstadt, housed over 1,200 DPs at its peak and boasted a significant library, an elementary school, a religious school, and its own newspaper, *Frayhayt*. Its Orthodox DPs were known to cross the Rhine regularly and go to Worms's Jewish lane, where they came upon the Rashi gate, the Levy synagogue, the ritual bath, and "a pile of stones and soil" that represented the destroyed old synagogue but evoked these visitors' memories of a ruined Warsaw. Together, the destruction of the two communities represented the "*hurban* [destruction] of the entire European Jewry."[45] Having arrived without a camera, the group made contact with a German photographer, who posed them in front of the damaged but still erect Levy synagogue (fig. 32). Led by a representative of the UNRRA (United Nations Relief and Rehabilitation Administration), the group viewed the city museum, where they inspected remnants of the destroyed synagogue and the archive. With the help of members of the Israel Agency and a rabbi, the group deciphered some of the Hebrew inscriptions before they progressed to the cemetery, where they assembled for another photo at the entrance (fig. 33). News about the Jewish guests traveled fast, and Illert caught up to them at the cemetery as well, equipped with the still existing *Mahzorim*, and told them about how he had saved some materials from destruction.[46]

Other frequent Jewish visitors to Worms included students from the Frankfurt Talmud Torah School, who annually mourned the ruins of the synagogue, and students from the Heidenheim DP camp's Klausenburger Hasidim yeshiva. For these visitors, Worms, with its Jewish cemetery, came to represent the "wailing wall of the twentieth century," one

FIGURE 32.
*Jewish displaced persons
outside of Levy synagogue
(1946). Stadtarchiv
Worms, Germany*

FIGURE 33.
*Jewish displaced persons
outside the cemetery
(1946). Stadtarchiv
Worms, Germany*

German Jewish newspaper noted.[47] As these Jews wrote about their tours of the city, they helped to familiarize the larger Jewish public with its once famous sites and inscribed the desolation into a narrative of destruction. They also provided Illert, as mentioned above, with more ammunition in his battle over the question of ownership of the Jewish community's belongings. To that end, Illert always tried to make contact with Jewish guests, exchange addresses, and even join in their photographs.[48]

Other Jewish visitors included a Leo Baeck student named Steven Schwarzschild, who went to Berlin in 1948 to temporarily take over the role of community rabbi. For him the experience of Worms was ambivalent at best. Taken around by a city guide, Schwarzschild was offended by the offer of photographs of the destroyed synagogue. He found to his dismay that the museum of Worms had become a "German museum," in which he had to pay admission to acquire a picture of a synagogue that "Germans" had destroyed. By contrast, the cemetery seemed less "tainted"—numerous stones and candles that had been placed on tombstones were comforting signs that other Jews had been there too. He joined many other visitors in celebrating the almost timeless appearance of the cemetery, which seemed to capture the memory of a thousand years as "a beautiful, and, at the same time, defiant picture."[49]

American soldiers also comprised a significant part of these early tourists. When in 1945 Major Max A. Braude, an Orthodox chaplain from Chicago who was stationed at the Seventh American Army Headquarters in Heidelberg, came to Worms, he inquired about the fate of the Jewish archives and was apparently taken to the remains by Illert. The *Aufbau* article that describes his visit also notes that many more of the cherished artifacts had survived than had originally been assumed.[50] Some of the American Jewish soldiers who came to Worms also conducted religious services in which they used some of the extant religious objects of the former Jewish community. As Illert reported, other visitors soon followed upon the "stream of rabbi tours":[51] they inspected the *Mahzor*, the torched torah scrolls and *Wimpeln*, the privileges from emperors, and the silver ritual objects. They looked at the Rashi chair and asked if they could take a little bit of the stone with them. In the cemetery, they sought out the tombstones of the sainted rabbinical figures Maharam and Maharil. Some of them lit candles and placed written supplications upon the graves. At times, they sang psalms and other parts of the liturgy, both in the cemetery and at the site of the destroyed synagogue.[52]

Among those American soldiers was the former executive secretary of the Centralverein, Bruno Weil, who had emigrated to America in 1935. In 1948, Weil wrote about his inspection of the old Worms cathedral, from which the swastikas had been chiseled off, though remnants of the Hitler eagle were still visible. Attracting considerable attention from the locals, he then made his way to the former synagogue in an American military vehicle. Known to Jews around the world "as a particularly holy place," the site, Weil believed, could serve as a reminder of Nazi atrocities. Before he departed, Weil took two pieces of the rubble and left wondering whether the synagogue might be rebuilt, either at its original location or in America, where many German Jews had found a new home.[53]

Jewish members of the American armed forces did not coincidentally stumble over Worms; many came with a sense of purpose, as well as with the newly released version of Marvin Lowenthal's pre-war Jewish travel guide *A World Passed By*. The National Jewish Welfare Board in the United States, which was also responsible for the recruitment of Jewish chaplains under the leadership of Rabbi Philipp S. Bernstein, had republished it in 1945.[54] The booklet supplemented the common armed forces resource *A Pocket Guide to Germany* as part of the National Jewish Welfare Board's program of religious, cultural, and educational services for Jewish servicemen.[55] Frank Weil, the president of the board, wrote that *A World Passed By* was to be offered to Jewish soldiers "at the cessation of the hostilities on the European front," and he recommended visiting "some of the places so charmingly described by Marvin Lowenthal." These places would give readers "much enrichment and enjoyment," but Weil noted that the traveler "may not be able to see all the places . . . [because] some of them may have been destroyed."[56]

In his own foreword to the new edition, Marvin Lowenthal announced that the book was essentially unaltered and that the descriptions reflected the status of Jewish historical sites before the war. He did rewrite some sections, however, and left out Spain, Czechoslovakia, and Poland, since members of the American armed forces would not be traveling there. He reminded his readers that every historical relic they would encounter represented a "token of one of the greatest and lengthiest struggles for liberty in the annals of mankind." This view of historical remnants as reminders of the struggle for liberty established the rationale for the Americans' interest and protection. Lowenthal made the connection even clearer when he declared that American forces were carrying on this fight for liberty, which would eventually usher in a new period of

freedom for the Jews, Europe, and all of humanity.[57] In his treatment of
Germany, Lowenthal observed that it was "difficult to know if any relics
of the sixteenth century of Jewish life in Germany survived; and mention is made of only the outstanding monuments—standing, that is, before Hitler seized power." The section on Worms remained unchanged.[58]

Responding to the interest in the city's history, Illert sought to ac-
commodate visitors by publishing a short booklet on Worms and its historical sites in English as early as 1945. In it he reported briefly on the
Judengasse in the northeastern section of the old town center, mentioned
the cemetery in passing, and observed that the synagogue had been destroyed a few years earlier without giving any more information. He was
also quick to point out that the Rashi chair, manuscripts, torah scrolls,
and communal archive had survived, and that the ritual bath buried
under the rubble of the destroyed synagogue would soon be unearthed
again as well.[59] Guidebooks like Illert's introduced travelers and locals
alike to a city that no longer existed, linking the devastated landscape to
a past that had vanished. A similar portrayal of Worms came out in 1949
from Andre Soutou, a French author probably stationed in Germany. In
this tour guide, rebuilding the city is captured as a process that "heals
Worms little by little from its inflicted wounds."[60] The guide reprints
photos of destroyed buildings and monuments in the context of ongoing
rebuilding work, and unlike Illert's guidebook, Soutou's travel guide included a picture of the rubble of the razed synagogue. While guides like
this charted the destroyed landscape, the visual representation of the demolished synagogue was rather exceptional as it served as a reminder of
the destruction of the Jewish community; all of the other guides to the
city filled this space instead with photos of the Rashi gate.[61]

These tour guides anticipated growing numbers of tourists from the
United States in general as the result of the opening of the German
Tourist Information Office in 1950 in New York and, soon thereafter,
branches in San Francisco, Chicago, and other North American cities as
well. The increase in American tourism propelled a similar surge in Jewish traveling overall. This was evident with the publication, beginning in
1954, of an annual Jewish travel guide (in this case by the Anglo-Jewish
newspaper *Jewish Chronicle*).[62] Similarly, a rather exceptional and short-
lived German guide appeared that included excerpts of speeches against
antisemitism by West German President Theodor Heuss, articles about
Jewish institutions and communities, and advertisements from various
German companies like Mannesmann and Mercedes.[63] Moreover, Ger-

man tourist activities were also being promoted again. Already by 1947, several German tourist offices had opened in occupation zones in Würtemberg, the Rhineland, Westphalia, Bavaria, and other regions.[64]

This confluence of official tourism, political observers, and Jewish pilgrims led Arendt to write in 1950 that Worms had become "a shrine of Jewish pilgrimage," as several German Jewish and DP newspapers likewise publicized the Jewish sites.[65] In *La Vie Juif*, the Hungarian banker and Jewish art historian Ernest Namenyi, who had migrated to Paris in 1949, wrote about his trip to the city of Rashi in the Rhineland. Given the absence of Jews in the city, Namenyi observed pilgrims who collected stones in Worms.[66] In 1953, the American German Jewish *Aufbau* reported that every year, Jews from all over the world went to Worms to commemorate its cultural importance over a span of nine hundred years. Moreover, the newspaper related that in light of the great interest in the city's Jewish landmarks, a plan to rebuild the destroyed synagogue was slowly starting to take shape. A few years later, the *Herald Tribune* and the *Frankfurter Allgemeine Zeitung* also framed Worms's Jewish sites as tourist destinations.[67]

The occurrence of antisemitic cemetery vandalism in Worms therefore now threatened the refashioning of the city as vital to Jewish memory, the ongoing work of reestablishing contact with its former Jewish citizens, and the rebuilding of the city's historical sites. Speaking at the 1949 Heidelberg conference, convened to review the situation of Jews in Germany, the U.S. High Commissioner for Germany, John McCloy, characterized Germans' attitude toward antisemitism as the "touchstone and test of Germany's progress."[68] Reports by the German Jewish historians Eva Reichmann, who resided now in England, and Hannah Arendt despaired of Germany's high level of anti-Jewish sentiment.[69] Antisemitism in the form of cemetery vandalism became prevalent enough during the late 1940s to compel the Wiener Library in London to monitor it.[70] At one point, the *Jewish Chronicle* featured a front-page story about the recent defacement of the graves in the Jewish cemetery in Worms. Confronted with national and international inquiries about the extent of the destruction, Illert nevertheless insisted that the newspaper reports had been exaggerated.[71]

The news nevertheless represented more than an embarrassment and threatened to potentially unravel Illert's ambitions at a time when the city was working hard to restore its former physical appearance after Allied air raids had reduced Worms's central marketplace to rubble and destroyed most of its factories. Like many other German cities, Worms sought to recreate historical continuity by restoring its historic buildings and celebrating its past. In 1948, Cologne celebrated the seven hundredth anniversary of the laying of the foundation stone of its cathedral, and in Frankfurt the Paulskirche was reconstructed to commemorate the centennial of the Frankfurt national assembly.[72] In Worms, to gain the support of the citizenry, the local government exhibited plans for the reconstruction to take place between 1945 and 1949, whereby a consensus emerged to retain the old urban pattern of the city. During the 1950s, the sense of a recovered city began to take hold.[73] As the reconstruction got underway, the churches took priority, as they represented the more striking and visible markers in the city's silhouette. Later editions of Illert's guide, while still noting the destruction, no longer featured pictures of ruins.[74] Of course, the restoration of these religious sites buttressed the city's symbolic association with a Christian European tradition, for the most part, and city planner Walter Koehler, who had been a member of the NSDAP since 1933, assembled plans that did not include the synagogue.[75]

It was thus left to the archivist Friedrich Illert to collect, preserve, and even restore Jewish historical landmarks. Aided in the coming decades by newly elected Social Democratic mayor Heinrich Völker, who assumed his post in 1948, the rebuilding of the synagogue eventually took place. Under Völker's tenure, the city erected a monument to the victims of fascism, though it displayed the all-too-common problem of neglecting to specifically refer to the mass murder of European Jewry.[76] Even before Völker, however Illert had the tacit support of the city's officials, and from the beginning, he showed a preference for the preservation of the medieval and early modern heritages. He was not too concerned about the nineteenth-century Levy synagogue, then, which was bulldozed in 1947.[77]

As Illert began his monumental task, several Jewish tourists also expressed their shock about the damage caused by the air raids and wondered about the possibility of restoration.[78] In response to these inquiries, Illert asked the mayor's office in June 1945 to reinstate the old cemetery attendant and began lobbying already the next year for the reconstruction of the cemetery.[79] The finance ministry of the city endorsed Illert's requests in 1946 but was forced to conclude that there was simply no money available.[80] Soon afterward, during a public meeting of the city magistrate in December, a member of the conservative Christian Demo-

FIGURE 34. *Photo of the erected portal (1949). Stadtarchiv Worms, Germany*

cratic party stated that Nazis had demolished several tombstones in the Jewish cemetery, which needed repairing in order to "eradicate a Nazi mark of shame."[81] The following year, Illert reported to Isidor Kiefer that the restoration of the cemetery had begun; the work would continue into the late 1950s.[82]

These earlier efforts at restoring the cemetery were pure works of preservation as well as means of restoring access to a vital component of Worms's tourist market. Thus, an article in the journal of the local historical society joined the travel guides in publicizing the existing cemetery as a tourist site. In addition, Otto Böcher, a student of theology, embarked on his research into the community, its synagogue, and the cemetery in 1955. In 1958, he produced the first guide devoted to all aspects of the old Jewish graveyard; it would be republished in many later editions.[83]

At the same time, Illert carried on a frequent correspondence with Kiefer, who supported the rebuilding of the synagogue.[84] In February 1946, Illert reported that he had secured all of the important remnants of the synagogue's architecture and inscriptions and deposited them in the museum for the future reconstruction of the building.[85] By the end of

1947, Illert believed that the reasons for the restoration of the synagogue were self-evident, as an act of both reconciliation with Jews and preserva-

tion of a historic monument.[86] Nevertheless, following the opening of the *mikvah* in 1947 and the erection of the northern portal of the synagogue in 1949 (fig. 34), work ceased until 1956, when funds finally became available. At that point, city tour books were taking it upon themselves to inform readers that the re-erected synagogue's portal had given the damaged building a slightly new appearance, which they hoped would usher in the complete rebuilding of the synagogue.[87]

The increasing sense of local expectation regarding the rebuilding of the synagogue resonated with a German political culture that displayed an avowed philosemitism. When the historian Eleonore Sterling, an erstwhile student of Frankfurt school philosopher Max Horkheimer, was asked to write entries on Jews and Judaism for the venerable German encyclopedia *Der Brockhaus*, she was told by the editors to place an image of the Worms and Saarbrücken synagogues alongside her text. She refused, arguing that these illustrations would be tantamount to falsely presenting Germany as again "covered with beautiful new synagogues—as if nothing had happened." If the *Brockhaus* wanted to showcase Worms's synagogue, then they ought to mention in a caption that the synagogue had been destroyed, Sterling contended in a letter to the German Jewish medievalist Guido Kisch.[88]

This tense exchange over the editorial policies of an institution of German middle-class education highlights the intermingling of the Jews' veneration for the Worms synagogue with an ambivalent German politics of memory. Germans' attempt to master their past, however, would become even more conflicted in the following years, as the city indeed pursued the rebuilding of the synagogue to forge continuity and recreate a sense of normality for itself. Local and national German initiatives collided with the interests of the Jewish survivors, who vigorously debated the plans for the synagogue among themselves and with city authorities. Moreover, the survivors continued to invoke a past that was partly veiled in the official process of rebuilding. Remembrance therefore became a space of fraught negotiations.

WORMS OUT OF THE ASHES

With the foundation of the Federal Republic, German society began the transition from the legacy of the National Socialist dictatorship to a stable democratic society. Konrad Adenauer led the nascent democracy until 1963, when Ludwig Erhard, the father of the West German economic miracle, took over. The next four years of unbroken Christian Democratic leadership brought with it political stability and economic security as the avowedly democratic society amnestied and integrated former supporters of the Third Reich and completed its separation from Nazism. The legislative, judicial, and executive activity of the Federal Republic also partially reversed the de-Nazification process initiated by the Allied powers in 1945.[1]

As the enablers of the German Nazi state appeared to be permitted to skirt issues of culpability and responsibility, the Germans' ruined *Heimat* was "pulled out of the rubble of the Nazi Reich as a victim, not a perpetrator," writes historian Celia Applegate.[2] Central to the new narratives of German suffering was, therefore, the plight of German refugees, expellees, and POWs, as well as the havoc that Allied air raids had wreaked upon German cities.[3] Indeed, while Germans were able to elaborate upon a past that was centered on their own suffering, many historians have noted their refusal to confront their moral responsibility for the Nazi atrocities, a situation that would not change until the student revolts and the screening of the television program *Holocaust* in 1979.

But this portrayal of postwar Germany has recently been challenged as historians have explored the many ways in which the reworking of German memory included debates about restitution and the establishment of diplomatic relations with Israel.[4] Moreover, Germans consistently encountered poignant reminders of the Nazi past on their own doorsteps, where they faced the ongoing plights of German Jews and forced laborers as well as the legacy of the death camps.[5] Still, at the time, Hannah Arendt, in her 1950 report on postwar Germany, was startled by the Germans' unwillingness to confront the "nightmare of destruction and horror." In the midst of the ruined cities, she explained, "Germans mail each other picture postcards still showing the cathedrals and market places, the public buildings and bridges that no longer exist."[6]

Mirroring the sentiment of these popular picture postcards, urban renewal efforts sought to restore the historical landscape of many German cities, masking political discontinuity by emphasizing cultural continuity. In their very influential study of the unimaginative and restorative urban renewal of the boom years, German psychologists Margarete and Alexander Mitscherlich saw an expression of the Germans' inability to mourn.[7] The reconstruction or preservation of prewar buildings thus served as a vehicle for the creation of a new normality by silencing the memory of Nazi destruction. Indeed, as German cities restored their historical buildings, some towns razed or rededicated synagogues for other purposes to eradicate the memory of the once vibrant German Jewish prewar history and the Holocaust.[8] Urban reconstruction during the postwar period represents an expression of Germans' complicated attempt to master their recent past, as Gavriel Rosenfeld argues in his study on Munich.[9] Yet whereas Rosenfeld contends that the urban landscape physically represents memory, remembrance in Worms instead took shape primarily through the interaction between locals and visitors.[10] Monuments, as James Young argues, can exhibit an interactive, dialogical quality.[11] But in the effort to rebuild the destroyed synagogue in Worms, local memory politics came into conflict with the interests of Jewish survivors. Remembrance emerged, therefore, more as a space of negotiations that also invoked the question of ownership of heirless Jewish property.

Despite the presence of these competing interests, the restoration of the synagogue—in a city without a Jewish community—fundamentally reconfigured this marker of destruction and violence under the cheerful banner of restoration, without, however, erasing the synagogue's other meanings. Memory and silence overlapped as it was rebuilt according to its early modern appearance, partly to disassociate the house of worship from the history of its destruction. Moreover, by turning the synagogue into the focal point of Worms's remembrance, attention in the city could be focused, at least initially, on 1938 and the *Kristallnacht* rather than on the Holocaust. This would change, however, when survivors began to insert their past into the local memory culture.

Initially, however, with the reestablishment of a Jewish community in nearby Mainz in 1948, Worms came under increasing pressure to transfer its extant archives, manuscripts, and ritual objects. As the only Jewish community in Rhineland-Palatinate, the Mainz congregation viewed itself as the legal successor to Worms's community. Thus, in 1948, Mainz demanded Worms's collection and petitioned the French military government toward this end.[12] In his own letter to the French military government, Friedrich Illert countered by stating that the archives should remain in the custody of the city until a Jewish community could be reestablished there.[13] At the same time, Kiefer, who otherwise endorsed Illert's plans to preserve the Jewish artifacts in Worms, suggested in 1949 that if the Judaica collection had to be removed, it should be transferred to the Jewish Museum in New York or the Jewish Museum of Hebrew Union College instead. Kiefer was particularly interested in the *Mahzor* and *Kaiserbrief*, among other things.[14]

When in 1952 the Branche Française de la Jewish Trust Co-operation for Germany was established, the question of Jewish property fell under its purview. After negotiating an initial agreement about the archive with the Branche Française, Illert then had to move against the group when it decided that the historical collections and artifacts would be housed in Israel.[15] The legal debates over this issue continued until 1954, when a compromise was reached that stipulated that the Branche Française indeed held the legal rights over the Jewish property.[16] Yet Illert again refused to submit, and the city repeatedly appealed the subsequent court's decision, while Kiefer also crafted a forceful statement in 1956 in favor of Worms as the location for all of its historical remains. Given its history of a thousand years or more, the temporary absence of a community in Worms did not perturb him, as he believed that a community undoubtedly would reconstitute itself there within two or three generations. It was for those future members that Kiefer wanted the artifacts to be kept in a fiduciary manner and preserved by the city. Claiming to speak on behalf of some forty to fifty former Jews of Worms, Kiefer objected to Israel's wish to have Worms's privileges by the emperor and prayer books transferred. Neither Israel nor the community of Mainz was prepared to maintain the cemetery. Kiefer argued that without such a comprehensive sense of obligation, their demands appeared to him to be "cherry picking." Kiefer asserted that if such plans were to proceed, the surviving members of the community would demand financial retribution.[17]

To strengthen Worms's case, Illert curried support, with the help of Kiefer, from former Jews of Worms. He sought approval for his own plans for restoration there and asked them to sign documents that stipulated their continuing association with the Jewish community of Worms. The prepared statement emphasized that "the forced emigration has not changed our belonging to the Jewish community of Worms . . . We wish that the rescued Judaica should remain entrusted to the city of Worms until the reestablished community provides the city with the opportunity to return these valuables."[18] Not all of the former members of the congregation unanimously endorsed this declaration, and several in fact crossed out the lines stating that they still regarded themselves as members. Nevertheless, with eighteen signatures on the declaration, Illert then asked the returnee Erwin Mayer to appear in court to plead Worms's case.[19]

During this protracted legal battle, Illert was also asking the German ministry for education and religion to consider the Jewish collection to be part of the larger German cultural collection and therefore prohibited from being transported abroad.[20] But the issue of ownership had already become entangled in international politics when the Israel Mission in Munich entered the dispute. The State of Israel, which rejected the view put forward by the mayor of Worms, engaged some of the basic premises then informing local efforts to confront the Nazi past. The conciliatory Israeli memorandum, crafted by the deputy director of the Israel Mission in Cologne, Chaim Yahil, first suggested the possibility of acknowledging Friedrich Illert's efforts on behalf of Worms with a place for him among the righteous people at Yad Vashem. Yahil went on, however, to reject the oft-invoked analogy between Worms's medieval persecution and the annihilation of European Jewry under the Nazis. The memorandum conceded that while the archive in Worms would continue to underscore the role Jews had played in "host societies," Israel had to forge a "Jewish historical consciousness" that spoke to all periods of Jewish history. Yahil hoped that Worms would accept its proper, if vaunted, place in the "view of history of the new generation in Israel." He then stated bluntly that the Nazi era had disqualified Germany as a "trustee of Jewish antiquities."[21] At issue here was not only the question of ownership or the relative value of the objects but, more importantly, the entanglement of Worms's artifacts in these conflicting projects of historical remembrance.

The differences in interpretation threatened to unsettle the rapprochement between Germany and Israel in the aftermath of the Luxembourg reparation agreement in 1952.[22] While the stakes had now been raised, the minister-president of the Rhineland Palatinate, Peter Altmeier, appealed to the German chancellor Konrad Adenauer to broker a compromise between Worms and Israel. In the meantime, the Branche Française had its claim regarding the Worms objects affirmed in another court's decision, which the city of Worms further appealed in 1956. To avoid a diplomatic confrontation with Israel at this point, Adenauer intervened in the dispute. In August 1956, Illert informed Kiefer that an agreement had been reached, stipulating that the Central Archives in Jerusalem would function as a custodian of the objects until a Jewish community could be reconstituted in Worms. Clearly exasperated by this news, Kiefer, in a last-minute proposal, suggested bringing the archive to the Jewish Museum of New York instead.[23] Yet this apparently did not prove to be a viable option, and finally, in light of the highly politicized nature of the deliberations, the local city council of Worms unanimously accepted the agreement with Israel.[24] As the English Zionist, lawyer, and scholar Norman Bentwich observed in 1958, "The sentiment for gathering the whole corpus of German Jewish original documents in Israel was too strong" to allow the Worms archive to remain in that city.[25]

German newspapers viewed the transfer of the archives alternatively as a painful blow and as an important contribution toward a German Jewish reconciliation, made possible by Konrad Adenauer's ultimate intervention.[26] The German Jewish newspaper *Allgemeine* asserted that the move had been carried out against the will of the former Jews of Worms, but beyond this it refrained from making its own view public.[27] In Israel, the arrival of the archives was greeted with satisfaction. For the Central Archives in Jerusalem, the collection of historical documents from Worms (and Germany) contributed significantly to a larger project to collect all dispersed Jewish records and artifacts. The Prime Minister's office emphasized that the arrival of these documents constituted an important phase in the "ingathering of scattered records of the nation."[28] In a formal celebration, the former chairman of the Jewish community of Worms delivered a conciliatory lecture in which he thanked Illert for having worked so diligently to preserve these archives.[29]

Despite this conclusion to the long deliberations about the archive, Illert found consolation in the fact that the objects' potential reparation appeared to guarantee the future of the stationary vestiges of Jewish culture in Worms.[30] To rally support behind his plans to rebuild the synagogue, then, Illert promptly publicized the community's history in American newspapers, never neglecting to mention his role in saving some of the remnants.[31] He insisted that his plan had the approval of "the dispersed Jews of Worms," as he called them, for whom the rebuilding of the synagogue offered consolation "from the distant past into the future."[32] Illert was again aided in this new effort by Kiefer, who also published widely on the community and its history in newspapers in the United States. Speaking on behalf of the Jews of Worms as well, Kiefer viewed the plans to rebuild the synagogue as a gesture of reconciliation with Germany that would serve a future Jewish community there.[33]

Despite all of Illert and Kiefer's work, however, conflicting visions about the synagogue's ultimate function eventually emerged.[34] Their vision of the reconstitution of an existing community, enabled by their preservationist work, proved to be rather more conflicted than the legal pleas and public campaigns would suggest. Working in Israel, Eugen Mayer, the grandson of Moses Mannheimer (the first historian of Worms's Jewish community), welcomed the notion of the rehabilitated synagogue with its symbolic reconciliatory meaning. Unlike Illert and Kiefer, however, he placed little faith in the possibility that Worms would eventually regain a Jewish community. The synagogue, he contended, would therefore serve only to remind people of the age-old relation of Jews to the city.[35] The former rabbi of Worms, Isaac Holzer, who migrated to the United States in 1935, questioned the rebuilding of the synagogue altogether, given the financial picture at the time. Holzer, who likely consulted with Salo Baron from Columbia University about this question in 1947, contended that it was unlikely that American Jews and Christians could provide the necessary funding in light of the tremendous help they had already afforded to survivors of the Holocaust. Even the Jews from Worms were asking Holzer whether everything possible for the survivors had already been done. In light of this, Holzer believed that the city of Worms itself, or descendants of Nazi activists, rather than the Americans should fund whatever restoration ultimately took place.[36] Similarly, the architectural historian Richard Krautheimer wondered whether the former Jews of Worms would be capable of supporting the project. He also doubted that there would be enough original material to rebuild the synagogue.[37]

Even more poignantly, after the *Aufbau* briefly reported on the potential plans, Elke Spies, a former member of the community who migrated to America in 1938, wrote that almost all of the earlier members of the community had unanimously rejected the idea. For whom should this rebuilding be done, she asked: "Should these unscrupulous destroyers of ┆ 169 Worms receive an object to view from which they can obtain income?"[38] Echoing Spies's concern, the former Jewish resident Carola Kaufmann-Levy contended that rebuilding a synagogue without a community would reduce the building to simply a historical landmark.[39] She also took issue with the restoration of the synagogue of the seventeenth century, given all of the Reform-oriented alterations that had been introduced to it in the nineteenth century: "It is as if one removes from a Catholic Church all the images and figures or conversely as if one decorates a Protestant church richly with saints."[40] Other emigrés, like Ferdinand Kaufmann, who resided in New Jersey, wondered whether some of the historical artifacts could in fact be transferred to Jerusalem. While he approved of the ongoing conservation work on the cemetery, he also regarded it as the responsibility of those who had made Jewish life in Worms impossible. But he rejected the idea of rebuilding the synagogue: "It is not needed as a house of worship. As an attraction for foreigners, I deem it unnecessary. As an exhibit (*Demonstrationsobjekt*) for Germans?"[41]

Confronted by this powerful opposition, Illert turned to new allies for his plans: the representatives of the city, regional, and state governments, for whom initiatives of reconciliation loomed large on the political agenda, alongside their attempts to eradicate antisemitism. In 1949, Karl Heyl, the Social Democrat director of the cultural office of Worms, appealed to the German president, Theodor Heuss, to support the rebuilding of the synagogue as an act of reconciliation by the new German Federal Republic and the German people. In January 1952, Heuss consulted with Chancellor Adenauer, who endorsed the plan; Kiefer then continued to appeal to Adenauer for help, asking him to accelerate the process.[42] Three years later, despite lingering doubts among and outright opposition from former Jewish citizens of Worms, the city, regional, and state governments pledged their financial support for the removal of the rubble from the synagogue space, in preparation for its eventual rebuilding.[43] With the backing of various political representatives, the reconstruction eventually broke ground in 1957. Illert, as well as the mayor of the city, Heinrich Völker, hoped that the rebuilding of the synagogue would be interpreted by all as a sign of reconciliation. With this in mind, Völker invited former Jewish citizens to the public celebration on September 9, 1959, as well.[44]

It would be a fraught occasion nevertheless. Despite wide-ranging German support for the restoration of the synagogue, there was some

confusion around coincident events of remembrance and reconciliation, not all of which were well articulated, as well as the ongoing revival of antisemitism. When the laying of the synagogue's foundation stone took place in September 1959, it overlapped with the highly politicized opening of a Jewish community center in the formerly destroyed synagogue on *Fasanenstrasse* in Berlin. At the same time, the first major exhibition on Jewish history in the postwar era opened in Recklinghausen. The German president Heinrich Lübke heralded the exhibition of Jewish ritual objects and works of art, a collaboration between Israeli and West German scholars, as a "sign of beginning recollection."[45] In September 1959, Adenauer also partook in the formal consecration of the synagogue in Cologne. These multiple symbolic gestures, coupled with the multiplying of antisemitic incidents beginning in 1958, brought members of the Adenauer government under intense international scrutiny regarding their Nazi pasts. This led to the dismissal of the minister of all-German affairs, Theodor Oberländer, in 1960. To counter the Federal Republic's increasingly tainted image, then, Adenauer jointly visited Bergen-Belsen with the president of the World Jewish Congress, Nahum Goldmann. He also had a widely publicized meeting with Ben Gurion in New York.[46]

The continuing professional advances of former supporters of the NSDAP in the political, judicial, and economic arenas, and the rising number of antisemitic acts of vandalism, confronted the German public with the legacy of Nazism. To counter the ongoing debates, the mastering of Nazism and the Holocaust became a project of political education. To this end, the Association for German Jewish Cooperation organized a conference in 1959; the Frankfurt school philosopher Theodor Adorno was the keynote speaker. For Adorno, *Aufarbeitung der Vergangenheit* (working through the past) was already a highly suspect concept, and he was quick to distinguish between Germany's coping with its Nazi past directly and its overcoming of that past by simply distorting or repressing it. To him, coming to terms with what had happened implied a "serious working through of the past, the breaking of its spell through an act of clear consciousness."[47] With these lines Adorno effectively squashed any anticipation for ready-made methods for coming to terms with the past.

Unfazed by Adorno's interjection into the memory discourse, the ceremonial laying of the foundation stone offered an opportune moment to advertise a new Germany to the numerous representatives of Jewish-Christian associations who were participating in the event.[48] Given the political stakes of Germany's international reputation and interest in mastering its past, the public celebration in Worms obviously attracted a great deal of national and international attention. Some of the Jewish participation remained rather restrained. At the cemetery, the Chief Rabbi of the State of Hessen, Ernst Roth, suggested following an old Jewish custom that directs the faithful to visit the graves of the parents during a wedding of orphans. He therefore opened the celebrations by asking those Jews who were buried in the venerated cemetery to participate.[49]

Mayor Völker followed this somber opening with a message that tried to smooth existing tensions and differences. Concerning the cemetery, he declared with "deep distress and shame" that "we have to think of that night on November 9, 1938."[50] He professed his hope that the renewed cooperation between the city, the Jewish community of Mainz, and the former Jewish citizens of Worms had made it possible to regard the rebuilding of the synagogue as a token of reconciliation. To support this view, Völker cited a letter by Karl Guggenheim from Santiago, Chile, applauding the reconstruction and wishing the city well with the traditional saying *Digna bona laude semper Wormatia gaude* (Worms worthy of high value, may happiness always be yours) that Emperor Barbarossa had chiseled into the cathedral's portal.[51] Following Völker, German minister for economic affairs and vice president Ludwig Erhard denounced antisemitism as blasphemous and reiterated the message of reconciliation and a new beginning for German Jewish relations (fig. 35).[52]

Illert, who had been instrumental in making this event happen, had apparently been forced into retirement over a dispute with the city government and did not go to the ceremony, but an elderly Kiefer came to participate.[53] Kiefer thanked Illert for his contribution. Attempting to dispel the lingering criticism about a synagogue in a city without a community, he emphasized that Jews could nevertheless be proud of it, evoking the familiar observation by Gabriel Riesser that the synagogue represented the fact that Jews had not migrated to Germany but had been born there. Kiefer's short and emotional talk expressed his joy at the rebuilding and his expectation that in the future this synagogue might serve a Jewish community.[54]

Rabbi Roth's speech registered the significance of the events in a different way. He drew attention to the loss and destruction of Jewish life in Worms, quoting from the Babylonian Talmud, "Give me the persons, and

FIGURE 35. *Laying of the foundation stone (1959). Stadtarchiv Worms, Germany*

take the goods to thyself" (*Nedarim* 32a) and then responding to himself, "but where are the people, who had once belonged to this synagogue?" (fig. 36).[55] He then read a special dedication that began with the traditional "Let them make me a sanctuary, that I may dwell among them" (2 Moses 25:8) and recounted the synagogue's history. The concluding lines placed the Worms event in a global context by declaring the date of this occasion, September 27, 1959, to be "in the 12th year of the existence of the State of Israel."[56] Subsequently, Roth, along with the chairman of the Jewish community of Mainz, Isidor Wenger, and Mayor Völker signed the dedication, and it was placed within the foundation stone. The ceremony ended with a rendition of *Kol Nidre* by composer Max Bruch (1838–1920) and an Adagio by Worms native Fritz Gernsheim.[57]

In the concluding reception in the town hall, the Minister of the Interior, Gerhard Schröder, conveyed to guests that he too regarded the soon-to-be-restored synagogue as a place of commemoration for victims of persecution and a visible sign of reconciliation. He called the destruction of the old synagogue a blatant example of the barbarian politics of the National Socialist regime, and he expressed his wish that Worms not only get its monument back but also become once again a destination for devout Jewish pilgrims.[58]

FIGURE 36. *Laying of the foundation stone (1959). Stadtarchiv Worms, Germany*

Schröder's evocative faith in a new beginning contrasts with the sentiments of Rabbi Roth, indicating that beneath the surface, perhaps, differences still had not subsided. For Hendrik van Dam, the general secretary of the Central Council of the Jews in Germany, for example, the synagogue represented less a gesture of reconciliation than a testament to the indestructible spirit of the holy writings. Second-guessing his fellow speakers, Dam declared that in light of the absence of an actual Jewish community, the synagogue would have primarily a cultural and historical value.[59] The Israeli ambassador further impressed upon the audience that the synagogue was now a "reminder" (*Mahnmal*) of the Nazi crimes.[60] On the other hand, Richard Lewisohn, from the Dresden Jewish community, thought that the steps taken in Worms indeed illustrated "good reconciliation and tolerance," while congratulatory telegrams arrived from other Jewish communities in Germany as well.[61]

Overall, the celebration comprised largely dissonant voices and conceptions, whatever the public face of it. Some had taken offense that Schröder, who repeatedly appeared on the list of German politicians with a Nazi party past, had even been invited to the event. Völker could only respond that Schröder had come at Adenauer's suggestion and that

Worms Out of the Ashes

it was not for him to question this decision.[62] Moreover, despite the emphasis that had been placed on the close relations between the city and
its former Jewish burghers, very few of those individuals who had survived participated in the dedication ceremony.[63] The fact that the mayor received numerous letters that declined the invitation, however courteously, suggests that among those former members, the opposition to the synagogue's reconstruction remained powerful.[64] Similarly, the *Allgemeine Wochenzeitung des Judentums* steered clear of the rhetoric around a "new beginning" when it noted the absence of a Jewish community in Worms and stated instead that the rebuilt synagogue would represent first and foremost a memorial to destroyed communities.[65] In the *Jewish Chronicle*, Norman Bentwich recognized Illert's aspirations, but his article's title, "Jewish Relics at Worms," made it clear to the reader that he saw it all as an act of historical preservation and not the beginning of a new Jewish community.[66]

The rebuilding of the synagogue entailed significant alterations in accord with a new historical perspective. The underlying historical preservationist agenda stipulated continuity despite the fissure between past and future. The preservationists argued that the building should be restored for its historical value rather than as a reminder of its recent history. Already the disregard for the still-intact Levy synagogue, which had been damaged only in 1947, indicated the disinterest in the more recent history of the Jews in Worms. When it came to planning the restoration of the synagogue, Kiefer therefore favored the rebuilding of the sanctuary as it was in 1620 and left aside the building's nineteenth-century alterations, including the balcony and the organ.[67] Silencing the issue of its destruction altogether, the association *Deutsche Kunst und Denkmalpflege* (German Preservation of Art and Monuments) at its meeting in 1963 welcomed the reconstruction solely on the basis of the synagogue's historical value.[68]

The packaging of the project as an act of historical preservation highlights the tensions that the public dedication artfully veiled. Yet Böcher promptly noted, for example, that the aging Illert was barely mentioned during the course of the ceremony, save by Kiefer. Böcher, who still expressed his anger quite openly in an article as recently as 2000, further implied that Rabbi Roth oversold his own particular perspective to the other participants. According to Böcher, Roth had also apparently prohibited the use of vertical windowpanes in the synagogue in order to prevent the appearance of cross-like figures there. Likewise, Roth forced the replacement of the eagle candelabrum with a simpler model.[69] Another contested aspect of the reconstruction involved Isidor Kiefer's offer of a *mezuzah* to be placed outside the synagogue. *Mezuzot* are commonly only placed outside private homes, but their use outside a synagogue reflected a particular custom of the Worms community, as Kiefer explained in a letter to Böcher.[70] When Böcher related these squabbles to the public in the local newspaper, Isidor Wenger attacked Böcher, a non-Jew, for unduly engaging in an internal Jewish matter that was of no concern to him.[71]

The reconstruction's orientation toward the Middle Ages and early modern period continued to stand in sharp contrast to the memories of the Worms survivors. Karl Guggenheim, in his recollection for a German Jewish newspaper, for example, cited not only Leo Baeck's speech on the occasion of the nine hundredth anniversary of the synagogue but also his own talk during the course of the celebration of a local branch of the *Reichsbund jüdischer Frontsoldaten* in 1937.[72] In accordance with the new post-Holocaust sensibilities, however, Guggenheim's memory was sacrificed in favor of the image of a distant, frozen history during the public reconsecration of the synagogue. When Kiefer composed an account of his youth for the local historical journal, he wrote about the buildings and streets of Worms and underscored the close relations that existed among the city's citizens. A small caption emphasized Kiefer's continued appreciation for the city. But the text is silent on his Jewish background, the community, and his experience of exile.[73] At best, then, Kiefer's recollection remained fragmentary.

Still, the work on the synagogue progressed, part of the still ongoing historical restoration of many German cities. In nearby Speyer, the restoration of the "German Kaiserdom" in September 1961 presented an opportunity to associate the German nation with the tradition of Christianity and the Western world.[74] At the time, the televised Eichmann trial in Jerusalem was focusing the public's attention on the specific fate of the Jews in the death camps, forcing people to contend with vivid images of the mass destruction of European Jewry.[75] Compared to the church restoration in Speyer and the deliberations in Jerusalem, the Worms dedication was to mark a very different Germany, according to its hosts. During the ceremony, which took place on the first day of Chanukah, the mayor of the city handed Isidor Wenger the key, then gave Chanukah presents to Jewish children.[76] In the course of the religious service, a light was lit for the memory of the two martyrs from the Middle Ages, according

FIGURE 37. *Reconsecration of the synagogue (1961). Stadtarchiv Worms, Germany*

to local tradition, and "the victims of persecution between 1933–1945" (fig. 37).[77]

About forty former Jewish citizens of Worms came from America, Israel, England, France, Sweden, Switzerland, and Italy to the public reconsecration of the synagogue in 1961, although none of them gave speeches. City and state representatives took charge of the ceremony. In the course of the solemnities, Mayor Völker again commended the synagogue as a symbol of a new beginning of Jewish life and German Jewish reconciliation.[78] Local branches of associations for Jewish Christian cooperation sent representatives and saw in the newly erected synagogue the beginning of a better future.[79] The local press shared this interpretation, labeling the synagogue a "symbol of love and understanding."[80] German television and radio stations transmitted the event, while both Jewish and non-Jewish German and foreign newspapers reported on it.[81] The German press unanimously remarked upon this symbol of a new beginning of Jewish life and reconciliation and congratulated the city for its efforts.[82] Otto Böcher echoed this view when he reiterated his hope that the "rebuilt synagogue will in the future inhabit again a Jewish community that peacefully live and pray to the God, who is both a God of the Jews and the Christians."[83]

In contrast to these announcements, however, the Jewish program participants offered an entirely different perception of the events. Whereas Leo Baeck in 1934 had emphasized the German Jews' "nobility" in their adherence to their long history in Germany, Ernst Roth interpreted Baeck's notion solely in relation to their religious tradition. For Roth, the example of Worms demonstrated the need to remain loyal to Judaism alone, since assimilation had provided no protection from Nazi persecution.[84] While the German speakers at the opening celebration glossed over the lack of a Worms Jewish community, the fact that this synagogue existed in a city without Jews featured much more prominently in Jewish publications.[85] The Jewish press, both in Germany and abroad, reported on the events, viewing the synagogue as a new building instead of a restored historical structure.[86] As opposed to a new beginning, the *Jewish Chronicle* instead titled an article "Europe's Oldest Synagogue Is Reconsecrated: Reminder of Nazi Crimes."[87] Likewise, Ernst Gottfried Lowenthal, in the German Jewish periodical *Aufbau*, reminded his readers that the synagogue could have been left in its destroyed state as an even more effective reminder of Nazi atrocities.[88] More subtly, Lowenthal elsewhere subverted the rhetoric of the "day of brotherhood" into a "day of conviction—a day of contemplation."[89] Different perspectives continued to appear over the years when the synagogue was featured in tour guides; Illert's newly released guide to the city reinserted images of the rebuilt synagogue as well.[90]

In the following decades, the city devoted additional resources to the renovation of the *Judengasse*, which follows the slightly curved perimeter of the medieval city wall. The planning occurred during a period of economic recession in the 1970s amid a growing dissatisfaction with the modernist rebuilding of German cities in the previous decades. While the German student revolt of the late 1960s had challenged the Adenauer administration about its inclusion of former National Socialists, the silence on the Holocaust held, by and large. Any local rehabilitation of the Jewish past therefore tended to focus on the fate of German Jews up until their deportations, and commemorated *Kristallnacht* instead of the death camps.[91]

Along those lines, then, the renovation of the *Judengasse* commenced during the 1970s with the approval of the citizens of the city.[92] The planners aimed to recreate the *Judengasse* as an important part of the old city ring, which linked many other historical landmarks as well. To maintain a sense of unity among the individual buildings, a limited but

FIGURE 38. *Photo of the* Judengasse. *Nils Roemer*

harmonious color scheme was employed. Badly damaged during the war, the nineteenth- and twentieth-century Jewish home for the aged had to be demolished in 1971, with the exception of the fourteenth-century cellar and a few wall fragments (fig. 38). When it was rebuilt in 1982, the building came to be known as the Rashi house and served as the location of the general city archive as well as the Jewish museum. The association of the museum with the archive underscores the central place of Jewish history in the city.[93] Similarly, Fritz Reuter has been Worms's archivist since 1964, and, like Illert before him, the city and Jewish community's 179 historian and producer of tour guides.[94]

From the beginning, Reuter envisioned the new museum as a place of learning. With this in mind, the permanent installation houses a few rare items but mainly focuses on introducing visitors to Judaism through the eyes of Worms Jews.[95] There are facsimiles, copies, and models that have some connection with Worms and displays of various historical documents that illustrate the history of Jews in the city, commencing with the facsimile of the privilege by Henry IV that extended tax freedom to them. To further the education agenda, exhibition designer Hans W. Herbert created in 1985–86 models of religious festivities to familiarize visitors with some religious festivals and the Jewish lifecycle. Together with Reuter, Herbert also created a model of the synagogue, as it was around 1620. Based on Moritz Oppenheim's nineteenth-century paintings, the miniature display effectively visualized Jewish customs in a highly sentimentalized fashion that silenced the potential association of Jewish life with its destruction.[96]

More than simply an attempt to master the past, the rededicated synagogue, the archive, and the museum also eventually revitalized the bonds among former members of the community, who were spread over several continents. During the late 1970s, they formed a committee that forged new networks of communications and channels of remembrance when Miriam Gerber, working at the Leo Baeck Institute in New York, became aware of Herta Mannsbacher's record of the exiled community. Gerber, née Sondheimer, had successfully made her way to the Dominican Republic after *Kristallnacht*, while many of her relatives perished in the Baden-Pfalz deportation. In Gerber's view, Mannsbacher kept notes on the disintegrating and dispersing community in order that they might one day reconnect: "She did this with the idea of 'roots' in mind, so that future generations would be able to trace their family history."

Born in Darmstadt in 1885, Mannsbacher was a teacher in Worms from 1906 until the end of the 1930s; she was deported to Poland in 1942. Her manuscript survived in Germany and found its way to Yad Vashem in 1957. The book enumerates 618 names with the usual data in each case, adding the country of destination and, in many instances, useful information on family connections. Henry Huttenbach, the director of the Russian and East European Studies Program at the City College of New York, published a detailed study of the record of emigration that Mannsbacher kept from 1931 to 1941. In line with the pre-war elevation of Worms as a symbol of German Jewry, Huttenbach believed that this emigration book would fill the void also for those communities that did not have one. At the same time, despite the trauma involved in sifting through familiar names, he worked to honor those who had died as well as to establish the historical truth.[97]

Mannsbacher, who alluded in her record to the importance of descent as an element in identity formation, would have welcomed the role of her work in the reestablishment of relations among the survivors of the community. Gerber and Huttenbach reached out to other former members of the community via a note in the newspaper *Aufbau*.[98] Through these efforts, a remnant of the former community constituted itself, despite the reluctance of several members, who wanted a complete break with the past. They preferred to simply assist those members who had survived and objected to the idea of making contact with Germany. Nevertheless, twenty people met in September 1979 and formed the Memorial Committee for Jewish Victims of Nazism from Worms. Another note in the *Aufbau* resulted in a mailing list of approximately 250 people with whom the committee began to correspond.

In the meantime, Huttenbach completed the manuscript for a Worms memorial book on behalf of the committee. His book meshed historical reconstruction with elements of *yizkor* books and included a list of 456 Jews, with biographical information, who perished in the Holocaust. For about a third of the featured individuals, the book reproduced the passport photos already marked with a "J" for Jew, as well as the obligatory Sarah and Israel.[99] Huttenbach said he wrote for those "prone to forget and for those haunted by memories."[100] Despite the fact that the book chronicles destruction and dissolution, it looks both forward and backward. It is dedicated to the last two Jewish children who were born in Worms—Hillel Weiss, born in 1939, who perished in Belzec in 1942, and Bela Mann, born in 1940, who survived. The accompanying poem, "Elegy for the Victims of the Holocaust from Worms," by Anne Marx, née Anneliese Löwenstein, exclaims, "We are the remnants, unraveled and torn / from fabric once sturdy, a proud congregation."[101]

About forty former Worms Jews, including spouses, traveled to the city in 1980, where the mayor invited them all to the town hall.[102] For Miriam Gerber the synagogue had not lost its appeal; she relates that "standing in it with a view to the 1,000-year-old cathedral . . . you get the feeling of our ancient history, continuity, suffering and even triumph. It is a feeling that comes close to being at the Western Wall in Jerusalem."[103] For the unveiling of a plaque in the synagogue, the 1980 group approached an American Jewish chaplain, William Greenbaum, from the American base in Heidelberg to conduct the service. The plaque, placed on the building's eastern wall, lists the names of the Jews from Worms and surrounding area who were murdered between 1933 and 1945. Gerber vividly recalled the group's sense of accomplishment: "It is impossible to describe the mood in the Synagogue where for the first time in 42 years there were enough Jews from Worms to make a Minyan." During the dedication, Huttenbach spoke of the miracle of the existing small community. Later in the service, eighteen members of the community read out the names on the plaque.[104]

The unveiling of the plaque served as a rallying point for the dispersed survivors, but not all of the German participants in the ceremony seemed entirely happy about it. Fritz Reuter's response to Otto Böcher that he too had to buckle under to the "American invasion" (*amerikanischer Zugriff*) suggests that tensions remained. Reuter and Böcher had favored a less prominent placement of the plaque outside of the synagogue, but to no avail.[105] This dissonance in the correspondence notwithstanding, the committee honored Reuter in the course of the ceremony as well.

While marked by both divergence and opposition, or even silence, the rebuilding of the synagogue, in conjunction with the historical preservation of the *Judengasse*, the opening of a museum, and the relocation of the archive, created a new structure for local remembrance that in turn drove other local initiatives. The later transfer of the archives and other precious items did nothing to diminish this interest. The local adult education school launched a lecture series on aspects of Jewish history in an effort to enhance the educational impact of the rebuilding of the synagogue.[106] At the same time, Worms's members of the Social Democratic party toured Israel and met with several former Jewish citizens of Worms.[107]

Aside from representing a formidable part of the local and national culture of remembrance, the work of historical preservation refashioned Worms as a place for inhabitants and travelers to be able to invest their surroundings with a variety of meanings. While initially the local and national historians and politicians set the agenda for the rebuilding, it would prove to be the focal point around which surviving members of the former community could connect. Notwithstanding the domestication of the process, former members of the community inscribed their own remembrance into the newly erected synagogue and the local culture of Worms. Though the synagogue's early modern appearance seems to disregard the modern destruction of the community, a perpetual flame crafted by the goldsmith Stefan Uri for the synagogue fittingly commemorates the Holocaust.

THE PRESENCE OF ABSENCE

The rise in tourism during the postwar period has been associated solely with the commercialized world of consumer culture. While visits to Worms apply here to an extent, viewing this particular traveling culture of remembrance only from the perspective of consumer culture fails to acknowledge its hybrid character or the contested nature of the tourist attraction. Travel guides informed tourists' encounters with Worms, but the tourists constructed the city's past and its meaning for their own ends. They experienced sites in turn as markers of remembrance, forgetting, reconciliation, and a palpably haunted destruction.

For many visitors, profound visual and textual representations of the past also shaped their encounters with Worms. Their perception of the city was often already shaped by postmemory that was distinguished by generational distance and lack of personal connection. This, however, did not sanitize the experience or render it devoid of perplexing ambiguities. Klaus F. Schmidt and Günther Sydow's collaborative work *Steinzeichen* (Stone signs) brings together poetic and photographic explorations of the Worms cemetery's landscape that are full of images of loss, destruction, mourning, and endurance. A poem, titled "memento," recalls those members of the community who, with their "contorted limbs, without kaddish, without songs of death, without names, without stones," perished in the death camps, while indicting their non-Jewish contemporaries, most of whom "kept silent in cozy houses."[1] While the next poem, "stones of souls" (*seelensteine*), cannot find words for the camps that are named, the photo alongside the text superimposes train tracks onto the cemetery, thereby establishing a visual link between the graves and the deportation.[2] Within the landscape of loss, the tombstones ("bending by time and crooked, / giving signs") (*zeitgebeugt und schief / geben zeichen*) appear as repositories of divine inscription.[3] In one of the photomontages, images of a busy street, construction work, and train tracks create a composite picture that is juxtaposed with the cemetery and the tombstones "that do not move."[4] The book is partly inspired by the way Martin Buber's interpretation of the cemetery came to be understood in the postwar period, whereby a photo of the cathedral is superimposed onto the landscape of the cemetery, a unity that is underscored by the poem placed alongside the collage.[5] The artistic visualization and narrative description mournfully captures this lost common ground in another poem entitled "feud between brothers" (*bruderzwist*).[6]

The individual and group memories of Jewish visitors to Worms underwent contradictory changes with the passage of time. Conducting a religious service in Worms or simply visiting the city played a decisive part in people's attempts to confront the Holocaust and reinsert the history of German Jewry into their culture. Rather than representing a passive nostalgic desire, organized Jewish tours sought to actively recover realms of Jewish memory. In addition, a biographical attachment to Worms drew former members of the Jewish community to the city. Inspecting the once familiar streets became for many of them an act of mourning. For many Germans, on the other hand, visiting Worms metamorphosed into a learning experience about Jews and their culture, a process of reconciliation that seemed to be vindicated by the sites themselves.

The persistent globalization of Holocaust remembrance in Europe, Israel, and America was accelerated and energized by the network television series "Holocaust" in 1979, the observance of consecutive anniversaries of the Nazi reign and its defeat during the 1980s and 1990s, and the opening of the Holocaust Memorial Museum in Washington, D.C. Together, these events turned the Holocaust into an all-pervasive cipher for the twentieth century. The multiplication of Holocaust sites around the world, however, gave new credence to local historical sites, while the commercialization of historical memory, as part of a developing leisure culture, increased the appeal of the "authentic" historical experience.

The rebuilt synagogue generated a disquieted and reluctant return of Jews, without, however, restricting remembrance to the local space. Instead, its iconographic status was renewed. In the year of the public dedication of the synagogue, the *New York Times* featured it in a list of the nine most famous Jewish houses of worship in the world.[7] When it opened in 1978, the Diaspora Museum, located on the Tel Aviv University campus, displayed not artifacts but scaled models, sculptured figures, and reconstructions to recreate the past of the Jewish Diaspora, including Alex Kaufman's scaled model of Worms's synagogue.[8] The Jewish Museum in Berlin—with its now renowned architectural voids, jagged windows, and Holocaust Tower—also commemorates the history of the Worms community. An elaborate virtual reconstruction of its top-ographical sites, with a rotating synagogue and ritual bath, introduces visitors to the community's past. Centered on the visual representation of the buildings as markers of Jewish life and culture, the presentation is accompanied by text and music, and visitors are able to watch medi-eval Worms taking shape. A transparent synagogue hovers in the virtual space that exposes the building's interior. The roof of the ritual bath is lifted to unveil the structure. A tour of the cemetery includes the story of the fate of Meir of Rothenburg in the context of the intensified antisemi-tism of the fourteenth century, which led to the expulsion of many Jew-ish communities. Outside of the video representation, photos of Worms's *Judengasse* are placed alongside one photo capturing the burning syna-gogue during *Kristallnacht*. Opposite these visual reminders, a gigantic bulb of garlic represents the interlinked communities of Speyer, Worms, and Mainz.[9]

The sites remained important in Worms itself as well. Following the synagogue's completion in the late 1950s, travel descriptions of Worms multiplied, and Böcher composed a popular guide to the synagogue.[10] For many Christians, the sites provided a resource toward a "Jewish ex-perience" that offered solace and religious introspection. The Protestant minister and poet Albrecht Goes toured the city and Jewish cemetery at this time and was inspired to envision the mossy tombstones in silent conversation with their visitors, petitioning God to "Hear us, O shepherd of Israel, who leadest Joseph like a flock of sheep. Show thyself, thou that art throned on the cherubim" (Psalm 80:1).[11]

Mass-market tourism to Jewish sites came to represent a much sought after "learning experience" during the postwar period. Alongside other media of memory, these trips offered encounters with original histori-cal places. As tourism reached new heights in West Germany during the 1970s, the travelers included significant numbers of international tour-ists as well, and many of them went to Worms.[12] To cater to them, the museum and archive released in 2003 a CD-ROM containing the names of exiled and annihilated former Jewish community members in order to facilitate genealogical research. Moreover, a DVD produced by the ar-chive offers nostalgic original film footage from the 1920s of the Jewish

FIGURE 39.

*Bar mitzvah celebration
(1992). Stadtarchiv
Worms, Germany*

sites, while also introducing viewers to the basic tenets of Judaism with
the help of the Jewish community of Mainz. A rather peculiar mixture of
Giora Feidman's interpretation of Klezmer music and the Zionist classic "Jerusalem of Gold," better known to a wider audience from the film
Schindler's List, accompanies the DVD.[13] Recent city walking tours include "A Walk Through Two Millennia," featuring the cathedral and the
Jewish cemetery, and a specially guided tour of Jewish Worms that focuses solely on the synagogue, the cemetery, and the museum.[14]

Over the last twenty years, an average of thirty-two thousand locals
and foreigners have inspected the synagogue annually, while the cemetery attracts about fifty thousand visitors, and the Jewish museum, about
twelve thousand. The discrepancies are attributable to the heterogeneity
of the visitors. Orthodox Jews, particularly from the centers of European
Orthodoxy like Antwerp, Basel, Zurich, and Paris, go mainly to see the
synagogue, the *mikvah*, and the cemetery rather than the museum. They
frequently conduct small prayer services in the synagogue and use the
functional *mikvah* before they go to the graves of rabbinic luminaries in
the cemetery.[15] Representing a different constituency, Jewish members of
the American armed forces from nearby bases are attracted by the ancient
synagogue's reputation and have marked Bar Mitzvah celebrations and
other religious festivals in the sanctuary, while the community of Mainz
regularly conducts religious services in the synagogue. These services,
while led by visitors, are part of the local culture in that they are often
noted in Worms's press and aid in the momentary transformation of a
historical monument into a working house of religious worship (fig. 39).[16]

In all, Worms has become a formidable German national site. Its proximity to the West German capital of Bonn lent great political significance to its monuments as well, and official guests of the German Federal Re- public have routinely toured the city. In addition to official guests like Heinz Galinski (chairman of the Central Council of Jews), Chaim Herzog (sixth president of Israel), Richard von Weiszäcker (German president), Teddy Kolleck (former mayor of Jerusalem), and Bill Clinton (former U.S. president), notable visitors and everyday tourists pour into Worms from around the world.[17] Chaim Herzog came to Germany in 1986 during an extensively covered five-day tour. Within his packed program, Herzog dedicated one day to the history of German Jewry and went to Worms. Together with German President Vogel, he stood in front of the graves of Meir of Rothenburg and Alexander von Wimpfen. He signed his name into the golden book of the city and was welcomed by the mayor, who called Worms the mirror image of German history—a place where Jews had repeatedly been victimized, from the First Crusade to Hitler's dictatorship. Herzog in turn bemoaned the absence of a Jewish community in Worms. Echoing the growing German fascination with Jewish tradition, Vogel underscored that "our culture" is not only Christian but also Jewish. In his answer, Herzog recalled Illert's efforts and Rashi's importance and highlighted the significance of the newly forged partnership between Worms and Tiberias.[18]

The prominence of these visitors should not detract, however, from the myriad other individuals who have journeyed to Worms. What is often missing in debates about Germans' confrontation with the Nazi past and their growing enchantment with Jewish culture is a discussion of the varied Jewish voices that inform that culture. Among Worms's former Jews, for example, the reopened synagogue failed to usher in a trend to return to the city, even though initial opposition to its rebuilding eventually waned.[19] When Siegfried Guggenheim, then residing in America, republished his *Haggadah*, it entailed new illustrations alongside some subtle changes. Whereas the first edition had underlined the intimate attachment of Jews to the city, the revised version expressed best wishes to the State of Israel. Guggenheim also excised the reference to his family's tradition of replacing "Next year in Jerusalem" with "Next year in Worms-on-the-Rhine, our *Heimat*."[20] Once dispersed, then, the Jews of Worms did not feel compelled to return, whatever the new fame of their birthplace.

Yet the city remained relevant to them as their place of origin. Spurred by the increasing popularity of Jewish genealogical studies, promoted by, for example, the Leo Baeck Institute in New York, former members of the Worms community have begun to compile their genealogical information. In Paul Gusdorf's case, his list today comprises some four thousand names.[21] Moreover, the rededication of the synagogue and the opening of the Jewish museum afforded those surviving community members a new means of coming to terms with the city. To honor the memory of Kiefer, for example, one of his grandchildren donated a silver ritual object to the synagogue in the summer of 1961. A small oil lamp in the Rashi chapel, bequeathed by Samson Rothschild's granddaughter (then living in London), brought the memory of her grandfather into the present with the inscription, "In memory of the teacher, Mr. Samson Rothschild, honorary archivist of the Jewish community in Worms from 1872–1927."[22] In 1984, Erich Guggenheim and his wife entrusted to the museum a silver goblet that had belonged to his mother.[23] Generous acts like these established a bond between members of the destroyed community and the city while prominently activating a form of family remembrance. They reinserted into the culture of Worms a Jewish presence that had been eradicated while placing upon the receiver an obligation to honor the gift, in turn signifying a new recognition of and respect for Jews and Judaism within the city.

Many former Jewish citizens remained reluctant to return. Liselotte Wahrburg decided to explore Worms after she heard from another former Wormser, then residing in Israel, about her visit. Wahrburg, who fled Germany in 1937 for Denmark and then lived in Sweden, welcomed the rebuilding of the synagogue. But when she was finally escorted into the synagogue by her German guide, she recalled, "It felt for me as if I was walking on the dead bodies of all my friends who ended [up] in Auschwitz and other camps, including my family." Nevertheless, out of this initially painful encounter, she went on to forge new friendships with former school friends, as well as the Schlösser family.[24] Paul Gusdorf traveled to Worms in 1976 after receiving an invitation from the city for former Jewish citizens. He, like Wahrburg, felt uneasy, "looking over my shoulder all the time."[25] Nevertheless, he went back again with several other former members of the community, including Wahrburg, in 1988 to mark the fiftieth anniversary of *Kristallnacht*.[26] Whereas the commemoration of *Kristallnacht* in Germany tended to silence the memory of the death camps for most Germans, in the minds of German Jews, the pogroms of 1938 were poignant harbingers of the Holocaust.[27]

Even individuals like Frank Gusdorf, Paul Gusdorf's cousin, who re-

mained consistently critical of the work of the Memorial Committee, returned in the end. He had previously seen the city as an American Jewish
soldier in the 1940s and early 1950s, then stayed there again briefly in
the 1980s. Gusdorf, who now resides in California, always intended to
sever his ties to his former hometown. For him, the history of the community was over, and with it, the five-hundred-year history of his family
in Worms as well. For that reason, he saw no purpose in the rebuilding
of the synagogue. "I honor history," he explained, and therefore saw the
synagogue work "as an insult," an act of forgetting instead of a remembrance of the atrocities. All of the historical restoration and educational
programs carried out there (often in conjunction with former members
of the community) were to him fruitless attempts to undo the past. After
a painful experience in Worms in 1986, during which he overheard a
tour guide make disparaging remarks about Jews, Frank Gusdorf vowed
never to return to Worms. Yet the loss of his wife compelled him to em-
bark on a "sentimental odyssey," which eventually brought him back in
2002. Like many others, he wrote in his diary about the buildings, shops,
and individuals that related to his family, a sentimental narration that is
quickly subverted by the story's end in harassment and deportation. Before Gusdorf even reached the *Judengasse* in his tour (and in his narrative), he was reminded of *Kristallnacht* and Herta Mannsbacher, who
sent him home to check on his father, who had just been arrested by the
Gestapo and was never to return from Buchenwald. Overwhelmed by
these recollections, Gusdorf writes, he sat in the synagogue on "one of
the rows of benches where I remember being seated next to my father
and family." Upon exiting the building, he recommenced his tour of the
city and came across the building in which he took shelter before he im-
migrated to England with the *Kindertransport*. After Gusdorf's short stay
in Worms, he left emotionally drained and eager to return to the United
States.[28]

Stories like these remind us of the multivalence of the sites and the
memories they engender, and of the way Germany's attempt to recreate cultural continuity beyond the abyss overlaps and interacts with Jewish remembrance. In 1989, surviving members of the Worms children's
choir met at the Hebrew Tabernacle in New York and sang portions of
the Friday evening service, as they had done fifty years earlier. During
the service, the former children of the community, including Henry Huttenbach, introduced themselves and stated their names and relation to
Worms, and many even provided their former Worms address, including

the house number.[29] To this day, Gerhard Spies annually informs an extensive mailing list of former Worms Jews about the latest city news, gathered from one of his recent trips, as well as information about members of the Memorial Committee and their families. Spies's newsletter chronicles the life events of the surviving community, including Bar Mitzvah celebrations, weddings, graduations, and deaths.

Worms's reputation entices individual German tourists and Jewish-Christian associations to travel there as well.[30] These particular visitors are symptomatic of a larger, more pervasive German curiosity for things Jewish. Over the years, books on Jewish topics have proliferated in the Federal Republic, and the Jewish Museum in Berlin attracted 350,000 people even before the installation of its permanent exhibition was complete.[31] To its German visitors, Worms symbolizes an element of recovered German and Jewish history, or "a piece of a rescued forgottenness," as Thomas Klein wrote in the *Frankfurter Allgemeine*.[32] For one tourist, the sites offered a "necessary and exact memory."[33] Some people continue to seek interaction with Jews to help shape their encounter with Worms as a place of reconciliation that signifies a tradition of religious coexistence. Members of one Christian-Jewish society felt, therefore, that joint trips enhanced their travel experiences.[34]

In light of these tourists' expectations, the city also named a street after Martin Buber. The naming followed the rediscovered link between the city and the German Jewish theologian and philosopher during the course of a large exhibition in Worms on the occasion of Buber's one hundredth anniversary in 1978.[35] Moreover, in 1997, the city decided to reopen what had become known as the "Buber view" in the cemetery, looking toward the cathedral. To facilitate this perspective, some large, old maple trees had to be cut down; the local press heralded this unusual act of "restoration" beneath the title "The Buber View Opened Again" (fig. 40). Whereas for Buber, during the 1930s, this view had authenticated the historical place of Judaism, the newspaper saw it instead as a "symbol for the connection between Jewish places of worship and Christian houses of God."[36]

Despite the recurring motif of reconciliation, however, visiting Worms can create uncomfortable tensions within mixed travel groups. For example, differences surfaced when the historian Björn Krondorfer organized a tour with third-generation Jews and Germans during the late 1980s that took them to the Holocaust Memorial Museum in Washington, D.C., as well as to Worms. German participants were not sure how

FIGURE 40. *Photo of the "Buber view." Nils Roemer*

to react to the emotional turmoil among their Jewish co-travelers.[37] In ensuing group discussions, one of the American Jewish participants explained that he "felt like the last Jew in Germany" in the synagogue in Worms.[38] Similarly, in 1996, Christian participants wrote in the Rashi House guest book that they did not want to know what the Israeli pupils, who accompanied them with tears in their eyes, were feeling.[39]

Jewish tourists continue to come to Worms, and especially the cemetery, around the High Holidays and place pebbles on the tombstones in the valley of the rabbis. Rabbinic opinions continue to vary about the significance of praying at the graves of righteous Jews, yet the practice nevertheless seems to have proliferated, particularly among North African and Hasidic Jews. The days before Rosh Hodesh are popular, especially the eves of the months of Nisan and Elul. As Norman Bentwich related during the early 1960s, based on a conversation he had with a tour guide in Worms, North African Jews who served in the French army went to the cemetery with small offerings of stones, honey, and wine. Others apparently lit candles and placed specially written prayers upon the graves.[40] Beginning with the invitations extended to former Jewish residents, individual travelers now arrive in Germany from around the world.[41] Today, the city attracts members of various German Jewish communities, Hillel groups, and organized Jewish heritage tours who pay their respects to the historical sites as well as to the former members of the community.[42]

Nevertheless, Jewish travel to Germany remained a complex issue during the early 1960s. Cecil Roth, the eminent Anglo-Jewish historian at Oxford University, promoted European sites to American Jewish tourists, reminding them that Europe offered "many Jewish memorials."[43] As Roth described sites of interest on the continent, he acknowledged that, traditionally, tours for Jewish travelers ought to include Germany. Yet anything of Jewish interest had been destroyed, he contended. The rebuilding of the synagogue in Worms did not change his mind, because as long as "present memory endured, Germany can no more be a land of light-hearted Jewish travel for the sake of sightseeing and diversion."[44] American-Jewish chaplain Mark Elovitz noted during the 1960s, "The radiance that once belonged to the Jewish community of Worms . . . is now only a shadow haunting the empty pews of the synagogue, the Rashi Chapel and the Holy Sand Cemetery."[45] For Elovitz, the sites evoke the rich medieval Jewish history but also the destruction of Jewish life during the 1930s and 1940s. When reporting in the *Times* about a trip to Germany in 1977, Julie Neuberger, a rabbinical student at the Leo Baeck College in London, noted that many Jews felt that by sightseeing in Germany, "They are betraying those who died on German soil or by German hands, that they are being disloyal to their ancestors, and that they are forgetting the past and allowing the memory of those who were murdered to sink into oblivion."[46]

In the context of Jews' reluctance to visit Germany as tourists, Werner Cahnman, a professor of sociology at Rutgers University, reported on his extended stay in the country as a Fulbright fellow at the University of Munich between 1969 and 1970. Cahnman, born in Munich in 1902, had worked as the regional secretary in Bavaria for the National Association of German Jewry. He left Germany in 1939 and arrived in America in 1940. In 1978, he founded the Rashi Association for the Preservation of Jewish Cultural Monuments in Europe, which aimed in particular in Germany to save testimonies about the past for the future of Judaism, as well as for Germans.[47] In an article in 1970, Cahnman described the relative isolation of the Jewish communities in Germany and concluded that it was vital that Jews from abroad come to visit.[48] He also wrote that Worms's synagogue was one of "our most precious treasures." Yet for Cahnman, such sites had been almost forgotten among contemporary Jews, whom he charged with "suffering from an attrition of a sense of history." While Jews were fairly familiar with Biblical heritage and the Holocaust, they lacked an understanding of Jewish history throughout the ages. It is this situation that tourism in general, and a visit to Worms in particular, could remedy. In Worms, Jewish travelers would be able "to enter . . . the core of the Jewish existence," and Germans would be able to learn about Jewish history.[49] Concurrent with this assessment, articles appeared in the Jewish press that lauded the city for having made a sincere attempt to confront the past.[50]

Despite this new rationale for touring Germany in general and Worms in particular, Jewish travelers to Worms typically viewed the historical sites within the overarching interpretive frame of the Holocaust. The duality of important historical monuments and an absence of Jewish life in the city led them to experience Worms in a highly ambivalent manner. "Worms—Tourist trap or recognition of infamy—how is the Jewish traveler to judge the restoration of the thousand-year-old Jewish quarter in this quaint, medieval city?" asked a Jewish journalist during the early 1980s. "Does an empty synagogue—visited occasionally by Jewish soldiers stationed at a U.S. base nearby in Heidelberg or by Worms school-children—sufficiently recall a thousand-year-old community . . . and the townspeople who watched or took part in its destruction?"[51]

Examples abound of painful encounters with Worms. When Erica Stachelberg fearfully decided in 1982 to fly to Germany to "understand," her decision triggered also "a serious case of angst."[52] In an added note to her travel diary, she recalls her ambivalence about the German landscape, where the "castle ruins appeared beautiful" but everything else was destroyed. Her visit to Worms began with the cathedral and the

Luther monument and ended at the synagogue, where she finally "felt at home."[53] Other tourists "seemed less impressed by the smell of moisture emanating from the old stairs leading down to the ritual baths, the *mikvah*, than by the absence of Jews. They did not appreciate the medieval building but could only see an empty synagogue" during a visit in November 1988.[54]

By the beginning of the 1960s, Americans traveling to Europe comprised students, pilgrims, war veterans, and former refugees; American Jews were also making the trip by the tens of thousands.[55] Yet while individual tourists came early on to Germany, formal Jewish tourism generally confined itself to Eastern Europe; these trips in fact significantly increased during the 1990s.[56] Lufthansa Heritage Tours signaled a new beginning in this regard in the early 1970s, however. Promoted in the pages of the *Aufbau*, a two-week trip to Germany, Austria, and Czechoslovakia promised to be "a bridge to the remnants of a proud heritage and a once flourishing Jewish community life that was brutally destroyed by Nazi tyranny." Organized by Rabbi Robert Lehmann of the Hebrew Tabernacle Congregation in New York, the trip represented the "refusal of Jews to forget their past and reaffirm the faith of our forefathers." The heritage tour thus became a collective quest that aimed to revive the memory of central European Jewish life among contemporary Jews.[57] It also shows that organized Jewish tourism to Germany remained at that point largely limited to the generation of Jews who still had been born in Germany. Lehmann was born in Germany, and his congregation had become home to many German Jews who had fled the Nazis.

The increasing interest in Holocaust remembrance during the 1980s heightened the visibility of other Jewish historical sites.[58] Tourism to those places in turn generated a plethora of new tour guides and numerous Web sites in the ensuing three decades.[59] During the mid-1980s, Jewish theme travel even began to be covered by features in newspapers and magazines.[60] Within this burgeoning market, the fall of the Berlin wall and the end of the Cold War began to spur Jewish tourism to Germany in particular. Yet the change came slowly to the Jews, so that general tour guides like Ben Frank's *A Travel Guide to Jewish Europe* (1992) continued to voice profound reservations about sightseeing in the country even in the 1990s. While Frank's chapter on Germany is subtitled "Jews Do Live There," the opening pages warn readers that the memory of the Holocaust will haunt them on their visit.[61] In light of these reservations, several groups specializing in Jewish heritage tours in the United States neglected to include Germany on their itineraries as late as 1995.[62]

The beginning of the 1990s saw the production of several new guides to Germany that informed travelers about the Jewish sites in Frankfurt, Berlin, and Worms.[63] Already in 1990, shortly after the fall of the Berlin wall, the German National Tourist Office in New York published its first guide for Jewish travelers to Germany, the arrival of which was duly noted in the *Jerusalem Post* as well as in the American press.[64] *Germany for the Jewish Traveler* invoked the Holocaust at the outset but quickly added, "It is neither the beginning of Jewish history in Germany, nor the end." The introduction frames Germany's Jewish sites within a paradox: "Throughout Germany today the traveler can see not only poignant signs of the Jewish absence, but historic and modern signs of the Jewish presence."[65]

The promise of authenticity in the Jewish sites is vital to Germany's mastering of its past as well as to the commercial tourist market. Within this brochure, the history of Worms is treated jointly with those of Speyer and Mainz, the communities that comprised *Shum* during the Middle Ages. After a short survey, the guide presents Worms's *Judengasse* and asserts that it is configured "as it was during the Middle Ages." While there are no places associated with Rashi in his hometown of Troyes, "Rashi disciples who want to experience the same atmosphere the great Talmudist lived in come to Worms." The guide goes on to advertise the cemetery, with its famous "valley of the rabbis." Appealing to Jewish tourists, the guide presents the historical landmarks as signs of Jewish perseverance. For example, the guide informs its readers, whereas the statues adorning the Worms Cathedral were sculpted to signify *Ecclesia* ("triumphant") and *Synagoga* ("defeated"), time has reversed this fate: while the blindfolded *Synagoga* has survived the centuries intact, *Ecclesia*'s arms have been broken.[66]

Despite this message of Jewish endurance, the sites of Worms conjure different images. In 1990, when the German radio station S3 transmitted a special talk show from the Rashi chapel, Cilly Kugelmann, coeditor of *Babylon*, charged that a synagogue without a community was not a living synagogue. The archivists and historians of the city responded that the synagogue was indeed used for religious functions.[67] The Worms situation prompted another Jewish tourist from America to note in the Rashi House guest book that it was "painful to see how little is left of my people here."[68] One traveler from Israel expressed his unease more forcefully (the note is in Hebrew): "This place is a big lie . . . This is a shocking place that intends to assuage the consciousness and there is nothing here that is specific to the Jews. Everything looks and feels here like one big lie."[69] This comment is followed by a similar remark on the same day, also in Hebrew: "This place is like a museum and not like a Jewish place."[70] Another Israeli tourist was compelled to view Worms as a symbol of both destruction and fortitude, leading him to write the traditional saying, "May the name Israel be remembered for eternity."[71]

Notwithstanding this common response to German Jewish sites, some Jewish tourists from the United States are motivated by a different set of goals (as well as divergent notions about what they will find); even restored buildings are perceived by some as fragmented but profound ruins of a once vibrant Jewish culture. For these Jewish tourists, visiting Germany has become a modern *Mitzvah*, a quasi-religious obligation that transforms leisure activity into "a kind of pilgrimage," as the American Jewish sociologist Joseph Greenblum writes. For these travelers, bricks and mortar are "sacred sites that keep alive the remembrance of the Jewish past" and help them to "overcome the attempt to eradicate the Jew and to erase Jewish memory." The recognition of the existence of a new Germany, together with the remembrance of the German Jewish past, may "help many Jews confront and transcend their pain and rage." Trips to Germany would, therefore, afford "a restorative experience," as Greenblum notes.[72] Another Jewish visitor to Germany explained, "To assure a rich Jewish future in New York, it is essential to visit the places where Jewish life once prospered before they . . . became a vision of the past."[73]

In light of their particularities, these trips were often advertised in a special way. YIVO Institute for Jewish Research, for example, promoted its tour to Germany, the Czech Republic, and Lithuania under the heading "A Jewish Heritage Mission."[74] Organized Jewish tourism acquires its "redemptive" function for Greenblum to the extent that it attributes a "tragic significance" to all Jewish sites. All Jewish sites are therefore ultimately viewed as reminders of the Holocaust: "A Jewish pilgrimage to Germany, particularly in an organized Jewish heritage tour, would symbolize, perhaps even more markedly, the failure of the Nazis to erase Jewish memory, for it was the Jewish civilization of that nation that was first targeted for extinction."[75]

This powerful reevaluation of Jewish tourism quickly entered a new phase with the help of the German Tourist Office (GNTO) when, in 1995, on the anniversary of the end of World War II, Germany was left out of the Allied victory and liberation celebrations (and the related tourism opportunities). In addition to making its own special effort to thank GIs for their service in Germany, the GNTO wanted to persuade them to return as tourists, and so "Nostalgic Journeys" with Galaxy Tours was created. The GNTO also published in 1996 a related booklet entitled *Exploring Jewish Germany: A Reporter's Notebook* by the American Jewish author Ruth Rovner, who had already established herself as a prolific writer on Jewish tourist destinations. Not intended to be a complete guide to Jewish Germany, Rovner's work sticks to the better-known sites in Berlin, Dresden, Düsseldorf, Wiesbaden, Mainz, Munich, Frankfurt, and Worms. Though she was reluctant at first to travel to Germany, she writes, she felt comfortable there in the end. For her, the Jewish sites had a different resonance precisely because they were located in Germany. She gained a new respect for Jews living there and an awareness of being "open-minded about modern Germany, not only as a place where Jews have chosen to live, but as a meaningful destination for Jewish travelers."[76] Under the title "Tracing Jewish History in Worms," Rovner described her tour of that city, which was even noted in the local press.[77]

Even though the American press took notice of her publication, the GNTO quickly replaced it with Geoffrey Weill's *Germany for the Jewish Traveler*.[78] The publication of Weill's guide coincided with that of Harvard academic Daniel Goldhagen's *Hitler's Willing Executioners* (1996), which paradoxically aided Germany's attempt to present itself to the world in a new light. While Goldhagen indicted prewar German culture for being enmeshed in an endemic eliminationist version of antisemitism, he did note in the paperback edition of his book that many Germans are willing to confront this horrific past, an "indication of how radically transformed democratic Germany has become in the second half of the 20th century."[79] Severing the ties between past and present, Germany's tourist brochures echoed this assessment in emphasizing the radical departure from and discontinuity between the Federal Republic and the Third Reich.

Weill's guide encourages Jewish travelers to view Jewish historical landmarks as "sacred sites that keep alive the remembrance of the Jewish past." Citing Greenblum's article, the guide notes that Jewish tourism aims to overcome the erasure of Jews and Jewish memory in Germany.[80] With its introduction by the former President of the Central Council of Jews in Germany, Ignatz Bubis, the booklet presents a new, self-confident Germany as the center of a vibrant Jewish community. For that reason, the booklet strikes a very different chord from the rather chilling accounts of Germany in some of the older guidebooks. Its recurrent references to the increasing numbers of Jews living in Germany illustrate not only the beginning of a new Jewish life in the country but also the validity of Germany's transformation as well. Bubis welcomes potential visitors "from America and around the world" to Germany. He emphasizes that currently some seventy thousand Jews live in Germany, making it the fastest-growing (and third-largest) Jewish community in Europe. "Germany has learned from its history," he observes, and its people can take pride in its old and new synagogues, lively Jewish community centers, fascinating museums, and other "outstanding tourist attractions . . . where visitors pay homage to the memory of those who perished at the hands of a regime whose crimes will serve as a reminder to never let such atrocities happen again." Ultimately, though, *Germany for the Jewish Traveler* attempts to transform the Jewish sites into simple tourist destinations: "For travelers from all over the world, a visit to Germany is exciting and enormously fulfilling. For Jewish travelers—and particularly for Jewish Americans—it is a country which offers a spectacular, fascinating, poignant, and thought-provoking kaleidoscope of experiences," Bubis concludes.[81]

As an enhancement to its authenticity, Weill inserts his own biography into the text as well—his father was the German Jewish composer Kurt Weill's second cousin, and Weill is able to describe a handful of relevant small towns and villages in addition to well-known centers of Jewish life like Munich, Frankfurt, and Berlin. Weill signals in this way that traveling to Germany can also be an encounter with one's own very personal family history. Kippenheim-Schmieheim, a small town in the state of Baden-Württemberg, is where Weill's grandmother died in 1928, and where Kurt Weill's father was born. Likewise, Weil-der-Stadt, situated southwest of Stuttgart, is where the Weill family's earliest known medieval ancestor, Jacob ben Yehuda Weil, took the name of the city around 1360.[82] For Weill, Worms, too, features "some of the most glorious Jewish sites in Germany, indeed in all of Europe. Worms is 'a must' for Jewish travelers to Germany." The *Judengasse* is described as a "lovely, curving, cobbled street, lined with pastel-colored three-story houses," while the synagogue is presented as a "faithful twentieth-century reconstruction of the synagogue built in 1034," and the tombstones are surrounded by "lush vegetation." As in the previously published guide,

Synagoga, unlike her counterpart, *Ecclesia*, is noted for her endurance and persistence.[83]

These publishing efforts seem indeed to have attracted increasing numbers of tourists.[84] In 2000, Germany and Israel also launched a joint touring program that focuses on major cities of Jewish heritage in each country. Together with Arie Sommer from the Israeli Tourist Office, the manager of the GNTO in New York, Udo Grebe, wrote to 3,600 rabbis in the United States to introduce the program. Aimed at American Jews of German descent, an advertisement for the tours appeared in the *Aufbau* in September 2001. A banner in the middle of the page reads "Germany and Israel," and it is surrounded by four blurbs: "Two unique countries. Two unique destinations. Now closer than ever! More affordable than ever!"[85]

Such initiatives and publications have helped Germany to revamp its international image and increase tourism. Potential Jewish tourists, however, continue to view Worms in particular with profound ambivalence. Leonard J. Lehrman, for example, writing about Jacob Weill's travel guide, notes in the *Aufbau* that the existing historical places may be as important for Germans as they are for Jewish travelers. While the brochure promotes new German Jewish relations, Lehrman concludes that as long as Germans are "not willing to accept foreigners as full fellow citizens, the remnants of that old German so-called 'Jewish problem' will not be solved. Not till then."[86]

Despite this common perspective, Jewish travelers do seek a meeting with the Jewish past in Worms, along the lines of Greenblum's article. The synagogue, but above all the cemetery, offers an encounter with the entire history of German Jewry. While teaching medieval Jewish history at the Hochschule für jüdische Studien (College of Jewish studies) in Heidelberg in the 1990s, Howard Tzvi Adelman explored Germany by drawing upon Tchernichovsky's poetry about medieval martyrdom. Despite some ongoing ambivalence, echoed in the poems, when Adelman visited Worms—the highlight of his "medieval wanderings"—he noted the continuous stream of visitors, who, during the early modern period, marked the Rashi chair and "[lit] candles, [left] slips of paper with prayers, and pile[d] pebbles as a sign of respect." He thought the cemetery was "one of the most beautiful places in the world," where visitors enjoyed "a vista that has not changed much in 900 years" (figs. 42 and 43).[87]

Evyatar Friesel, like other Jewish historians, contemplated the meaning of German Jewish history as he strolled over the Jewish cemetery in

FIGURE 41. *Photo of the plate for twelve community leaders with pebbles.*
Nils Roemer

FIGURE 42. *Photo of tombstone of Meir of Rothenburg with papers and pebbles.*
Nils Roemer

Worms: "Nine hundred years of Jewish existence in Germany lay buried there. A whole dimension of Jewish life and culture, the Ashkenazi branch, had been created in German lands and later carried throughout the world. Some of the greatest creations in modern Jewish history had resulted from the Jewish-German encounter and some of the worst instincts in the German people had been aroused by Jewish presence

FIGURE 43. *Photo of the Jewish cemetery. Nils Roemer*

in their midst. Now it was a finished chapter. But what a chapter!" (fig. 43).[88] For Friesel, Worms stood for the entire German Jewish, or even Ashkenazic, past. As Friesel witnessed its sites, however, the past was "there" and not "here," and the tombstones appear to be timeless monuments of something far away. In line with this perception, postcard and tour guide photos of the cemetery are mostly taken from a distance. This perspective enhances the appearance of the graves as they emerge from the grass and thistle that threaten to overwhelm them. Matthias Hermann's poem "Jewish Cemetery in Worms" describes the tombstones: "In the earth's tides / All entangled like algae / They come dancing / Toward me" (fig. 44).[89]

Despite the overarching rhetoric, both official and commercial, Worms ultimately remains a memorial to destruction. Contrary to early local histories of Jewish communities that neglected the relationship between the community's history and the destruction of the 1930s and 1940s, new research has focused on this reality.[90] Working in Worms itself, Annelore and Karl Schlösser chronicled the fate of the city's Jews and brought this forgotten aspect back from the past.[91] In light of the Schlössers'

FIGURE 44. *Photo of the Jewish cemetery. Nils Roemer*

accomplishments, the German Federal Republic awarded the couple an order of merit. Their research contributed to the knowledge of the fate of Herta Mansbacher as well, who today has a park adjacent to the *Judengasse* named after her.

The Schlössers' work was only one of the many initiatives in the city that made the Jewish past more visible. When in 1989 former student of theology and art history, Heinz Hirndorf, who had been responsible for the windows in the Rashi chapel (as well as numerous other stained-glass windows in churches), began work on the new glass window for the cathedral, he introduced a reminder to the history of the Jews in the city. His "History Window" (*Geschichtsfenster*) depicts various bishops, Luther, and other events from the history of Worms but also features a figure marked by the Jewish star who is being harassed by SA men. Inscribed into the window are the dates 1034 for the building of the first synagogue, 1349 for the Black Death persecution, and 1938 for the destruction of the synagogue.[92] The inclusion of these fairly explicit references to *Kristallnacht* (though not to the actual Holocaust) within a Catholic church (and renowned historical landmark) testifies to the ongoing attempts to remember the past outside of the Jewish sites within the city (fig. 45).

To further the efforts to preserve Jewish history in Worms and educate the public, several citizens of Worms created a society in 1995 called Warmaisa Society for the Promotion and Preservation of Jewish Culture (*Warmaisa, Gesellschaft zur Förderung und Pflege jüdischer Kultur*). The society comprises around one hundred members, with Gerhard Spies as an honorary member; also involved with its various activities are the approximately seventy Russian Jews who live in the city today. Several of these Jews conduct a service in the synagogue every two weeks, aided by the cantor or rabbi from Mainz; they also occasionally celebrate religious festivals like Sukkot with members of the Mainz community. The commingling of Germans and Mainz and Russian Jews blurs the boundaries that otherwise still exist and make it even more difficult to view historical preservation solely as the outcome of Germans' re-creation of a Jewish space.

To further the presence of Jewish culture, the society hosts literary readings and organizes lectures, seminars, concerts, and excursions to sites of Jewish history in Worms. It also commemorates Jewish memorial days, often in conjunction with the city and other associations.[93] Moreover, the society has devoted itself to the ongoing restoration of the Jewish mourning hall at the new cemetery, which was placed under a protection order in 1985.[94] In the new cemetery, several Worms Jews are buried in unnamed graves, prompting Fritz Reuter, the city archivist, to rededicate some of these sites with a stone in 1991, since the "obligation toward these victims continues."[95] Work on the mourning hall, which had been designed by Georg Metzler at the beginning of the twentieth

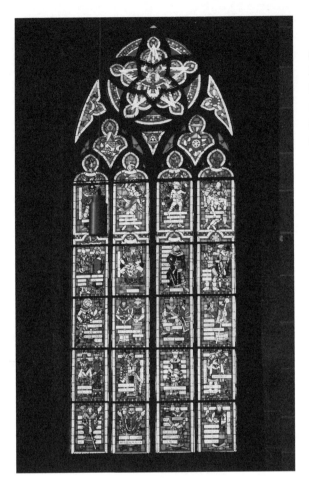

century in the *Jugendstil*, commenced with the help of *Warmaisa*. Today, the hall and the cemetery are again in use for the Russian Jews who reside in the city.[96]

To be sure, the rebuilding of the synagogue and the cultural activities that have been rehabilitated since validate the recent contention that Germans reinvented a Jewish space for themselves in order to regain a sense of normality and promote an image of a pluralistic German society.[97] Yet this view fails to allow for the way Jews adopt and transform this recreated space. For the city, contacts with Jews, whether real or imaginary, played a central role in the process of recovering the Jewish (and larger German) past. Visits by former Jewish members of the community reported in the local press created the illusion of a still extant

Jewish citizenry (though one that exists beyond the city's boundaries). Other Jewish tourists transformed the historical building—however temporarily—into a working house of religious worship. At the same time, for Jews in America, traveling to Worms helps them to confront the Nazi past and reinsert into their own sense of culture the history of German Jewry. While these two groups come to Worms with very different motivations, their temporary presence there ultimately facilitates each other's experience of the city, blurring the lines of presence and absence and mobilizing the realms of memory.

CONCLUSION

This book aims to come to terms with the changing meaning of place, remembrance, and identity over the course of almost a thousand years. Worms was certainly always unique in many ways; the city and its Jewish community thrived on its cultural icons and with little economic power came to possess a formidable cultural capital. Its small and increasingly insignificant regional community featured prominently in debates between Jews and Christians, attempts to fashion and refashion Jewish cultures, and both German and Jewish efforts to confront the legacy of the Holocaust. Indeed, remembrance in Worms not only mattered to its locals but also functioned as a space of negotiation between them and Worms's many visitors.

Today, globalization's international networks of communication and commerce are accused of threatening the very existence of local cultures. Other critics, however, counter that this new media perspective in fact facilitates a reassertion of localism. Far from being symptomatic of an anti-modern backlash, the quest for *Heimat*, for example, appears to be part of the very globalization it might appear to contradict. The virtual reconstruction of the early modern Jewish lane in the Jewish museum in Berlin encourages visitors to follow their inspection of the museum with a visit to Worms. Likewise, the scaled model of Worms's synagogue in the Diaspora Museum in Tel Aviv actually underscores its lasting importance despite its "global" context and aspirations.

Cities, small towns, and villages have always played a formidable role in Jewish history. Local and regional spaces, however, do not always reflect the most stable and hospitable conditions for Jewish life. It was the First Crusade period's experience of destruction, alienation, and (temporary) expulsion that paradoxically bound the reconstituted community of Jews to the physical landscape of Worms, where they remembered their martyrs. The magnitude of the destruction, as well as the elevated self-understanding of the Rhineland community that resulted from it, led the Worms Jews to deviate from standard practice by instituting a new fast day. Building on this model of highly localized forms of remembrance, the community added yet more days of remembrance to their annual cycle in order to recall the destruction of 1349 and 1615.

Alongside these rituals of commemoration emerged narratives about the origin of the community that gave credence to the community's rabbinic

leaders and fended off accusations regarding the medieval Jew's responsibility in the death of Jesus. These narratives expressed both the precarious situation and the self-elevation of a community that increasingly saw itself as a small Jerusalem.

Places have historically shaped the self-understanding of Jewish communities and defined their sense of home, belonging, and tradition. Entrenched in their local cultures of remembrance, then, Worms individuals saw their temporary expulsion from the city during the seventeenth century as a state of exile. In the words of one of the congregation's leading rabbis of this period, the community existed insofar as it observed its customs and fast days, regardless of where it was. Even after the Holocaust, many former Worms Jews linked their upbringing and identity to Worms by readily reciting its particular textual traditions.

Remembrance in Worms was shaped and influenced not just by a local context but also by contacts between geographically distant practitioners; these encounters, however, did not render the local obsolete. The German sociologist Ferdinand Tönnis comprehends the advent of modernity as the weakening of the community (*Gemeinde*), marked by its traditional practices and a personal sense of belonging, and the strengthening of a more individualistic, competitive, and impersonal organization of society (*Gesellschaft*). For Tönnis, however, premodern societies based upon local cultures displayed homogeneity and stability.[1] Yet this was not always the case, of course. Against this romantic depiction of the world, even a small town like Worms, located along a commercial artery like the Rhine, would have appeared already during premodern times to be a tenuous place of both dwellers and travelers and not a place marked by a stable network of social relations. Delineating the boundaries of remembrance therefore highlights the extent to which a small community like Worms was plugged into shifting local, regional, national and transnational contexts.

The production of the past would ultimately emerge in a wider, more diverse geographical space than the individual city itself, a space in which Jews and non-Jews, locals and visitors, historians, poets, tourists, and many others would participate. With the spatial and social dissemination of memory, external influences would also come to bear on the work of remembrance within the community. Already the Hebrew chronicles and the insertion of dirges into the liturgy for *Tisha be-Av* ensured the remembrance of the Worms community outside of the city. The advent of the printing press fundamentally refashioned remembrance, as new means of expressing memory emerged in texts and images. Debates about the veracity of local historical Jewish traditions crossed denominational boundaries and moved from very local contexts into city chronicles, the literature of the Hebraists, and even the early modern travel guides, thus engendering overlapping fields of production and contestation of local memory during this time. Partly inspired by the way the citizenry of Worms had reinvented its past from the fifteenth century onward, these new traditions significantly enlarged the congregation's heritage as well. Isaac Jost, the author of the first comprehensive history of the Jews, wrote an introduction to the first local history of Worms. Notwithstanding his critical attitude toward elements of Worms's Jewish tradition, Leopold Zunz's call upon communities to preserve their tombstones promoted local historical preservation. After the expulsion and destruction of the community during the Nazi era, its former Jews, as well as chaplains, members of the American armed forces, and displaced persons, visited the city as early as 1945. Through these visitors' reports and articles, a wider Jewish public became acquainted with the desolate state of the destroyed synagogue and the remains of the former archive and museum. The presence of these travelers promoted the preservationist work that began at the end of the war and became instrumental in shaping the remembrance of the Jewish past in Worms, which led to the rebuilding of the destroyed synagogue.

Like the city itself, its Jewish community experienced dramatic changes, ruptures, destruction, and rebuilding in the decades after the war, and the continuous push to recall the past should not distract us from the obvious discontinuities. Paradoxically, the trajectory from a culture of remembrance to a space of memory passes through continuities and losses. Worms represents a storehouse from which material can be easily pulled and employed in different contexts, so that the past is always in turn shaped by the present.

Placed at the intersection of local heritage production and the promotion of tourism to the city, Jewish historians during the modern age did not simply study the past but also provided the burgeoning field of tourism with its information, as community officials and scholars assisted in the preservation of historical artifacts. City archivists, who often wrote the most authoritative guides to the city, helped Jewish activities by adding complexity to often overly sanitized stories about what happened.

Interestingly, some channels of remembrance exhibit greater continuity than others, for better or worse, depending upon their relationship to the truth. Tourism, for one, displays an almost uncanny continuity. In his autobiography, the eminent Jewish historian and political scientist Walter Laqueur recalls that when he left Germany in 1938, he brought with him to Palestine Baedeker's guidebook to Germany. When he read an updated version in 1983, he encountered a familiar portrayal of Germany in the opening page. The text had not changed in decades: "The Empire, the Republic, the Hitlers have come and gone . . . but Baedeker still dwells on farmhouse and the old Germanic 'grouped village,' stately castles and the walled towns," Laqueur laconically noted.[2] Similarly, Worms still boasts today of the *Nibelungen*, its relationship to the German emperors, and Martin Luther alongside the synagogue and the cemetery.

Modern critics castigate nostalgia as a failed and wishful sense of desire, one predicated on an imaginary immediacy of the past that negates historical determinacy. As David Lowenthal noted, nostalgia is "a topic of embarrassment and a term of abuse. Diatribe upon diatribe denounces it as reactionary, repressive, ridiculous."[3] These critics trace nostalgia to the advent of modernity, framing it as an anti-modern desire that emerged with the break-up of temporal continuity. Yet the construction of local heritage and invented traditions significantly predates modernity. The local heritage of Worms was as much a product of the Middle Ages and early modern times as it was of the nineteenth and twentieth centuries. Already at the beginning of the seventeenth century, members of the Jewish community rebuilt the synagogue by consciously preserving existing structures and copying older architectural styles. Even the newly built Rashi chapel was erected in a style reminiscent of the Middle Ages. Critical sensibilities toward the reliability of legendary accounts of the community and the invention of new traditions were also not limited to the modern period.

Nevertheless, modernity did fundamentally alter Jewish life and cultures of remembrance. Religious reform, social advancement, and, above all, civic equality changed things. Though the Enlightenment flourished mainly in Jewish urban centers in northern Germany, the arrival of French troops in the Rhineland overwhelmed existing ways of life there. The Jews' emancipation under French occupation represented a discontinuity with previous forms of Jewish self-government and traditional royal alliance. In response to these changed circumstances, Reform Judaism arose and threatened to unravel the cohesiveness of the Jewish community. The revolution of 1848–49 threw the Jews into the turmoil of political conflict as well.

Yet, instead of trying to return to the practices of a distant past, Worms
Jews looked ahead, seeing themselves as culturally integrated members of the city, and of German society. Publicizing their local heritage reconfigured the local memory landscape during the *Kaiserreich* as a realm of German *and* Jewish historical memory, while the Romantics' conception of the Rhineland heightened the visibility of Worms in the increasingly competitive market around Germany's travel destinations. The region's reputation as a quintessential German landscape, shaped by sublime nature and covered by picturesque towns with historical castles and churches, in turn aided Jewish efforts to negotiate these contradictory drives both inward and outward. Nostalgic recollection was less an antidote to the cultural and religious transformation of the Jewish community than an integral element of it.

Worms's venerated community therefore also challenged the West's pervasive enchantment with eastern European Jewry during the first decades of the twentieth century. Whereas twentieth-century German Jewish intellectuals deemed eastern European Jewry to represent a more authentic form of Judaism (in turn buttressing their critical distance regarding the politics of modernization and integration), they found in Worms some comfort in the trappings and narratives of its past, and this place therefore remained intimately connected to the modern projects of cultural and religious change. In the nineteenth century, the recovery of local Jewish tradition helped to overcome existing differences by uniting Jews of various religious orientations. The interest in local lore brought pride to the community as a whole and reaffirmed the Jews' faithfulness to their ancestors even as they departed from their traditions and customs. At the end of the nineteenth century, when David Philippson, for example, published with the Jewish Publication Society in America a book entitled *Old Jewries* (1894), he welcomed the disappearance of the physical remnants of ghettos in Europe. To him this underscored the great improvements that had been made during the nineteenth century. Despite his happiness about the disappearing Jewish lanes, however, his text betrayed a profound ambivalence, comprising his conscious distancing of himself from the past as well as his nostalgic adaptation to it.[4] Arnold Eisen characterizes this eclectic pattern of observance and change as a salient feature of Jews' adjustment to modernity.[5]

With the advent of this modernity, then, newly emerging nation states brought emancipation to the Jews while striving to eliminate legal, cultural, and political differences. The concept of the citizen established a lasting connection between the individual and the state, and the Jews in Germany sought this status. Yet localism and regionalism did not subside. While German Jews vociferously expressed their German patriotism, they ascribed their notions of home and belonging to individual cities. For critics of Jewish modernity, regionalism became *shibboleth* in their debates as they constructed the local as a powerful and pervasive metaphor against the ubiquitous leveling power of larger urban centers.

The deeply ingrained association of the Rhineland with the idea of Germany allowed the inclusion of Jewish tradition into Worms's heritage to authenticate a far more complex construction of German Jewry during the *Kaiserreich*, when regional and national German and Jewish identities coexisted in a contested social, religious, and political space. In this context, local heritage was at once distinctive *and* representative of larger German and German Jewish heritages. As local heritage became even more popular during the Weimar era for Jewish travelers, Worms was celebrated as essentially German and Jewish and came to represent both a birthplace and a symbol of German Jewry.

Today, Worms once again attracts curious travelers and provides an important place for Jews and others to learn about its storied community, but pain and sadness will always echo in the synagogue and in the minds of its visitors. These visitors' interactions with the monuments, however, will continue to prevent a more sanitized version of memory from emerging. Here nostalgia itself is fraught with ambiguities and reminds us that even the vestiges of Jewish life and cultures in Germany are invariably marked by the experience of the Holocaust. The monuments, as much as they invoke the rich legacy of the community, also speak of escape, destruction, and loss. Their history has not ended. In what ways this legacy will continue to matter, we do not know, but that it will seems certain.

NOTES

The following abbreviations are used in the notes.

AZJ	*Allgemeine Zeitung des Judenthums*
BLB	*Bulletin of the Leo Baeck Institute*
CAHJP	Central Archives for the History of the Jewish People
CEH	*Contemporary European History*
HUCA	*Hebrew Union College Annual*
JJGL	*Jahrbuch für jüdische Geschichte und Literatur*
JjLG	*Jahrbuch der jüdisch literarischen Gesellschaft*
JQR	*Jewish Quarterly Review*
JTS	Jewish Theological Seminary
JZfWJ	*Jüdische Zeitschrift für Wissenschaft und Leben*
LBIYB	*Leo Baeck Institute Yearbook*
MGWJ	*Monatsschrift für Geschichte und Wissenschaft des Judentums*
PAAJR	*Proceedings of the American Academy for Jewish Research*
REJ	*Revue des Études Juives*
ZGJD	*Zeitschrift für die Geschichte der Juden in Deutschland*

INTRODUCTION

1. Rolf Vogel, ed., *Der Deutsch-Israeltische Dialog. Dokumentation eines erregenden Kapitels Deutscher Außenpolitik*, 9 vols. (Munich: K. G. Sauer, 1990), 3:1644.

2. See Etienne François and Hagen Schulze, eds., *Deutsche Erinnerungsorte*, 3 vols. (Munich: C. H. Beck, 2001), and Pierre Nora, ed., *Les lieux de mémoire*, 7 vols. (Paris: Gallimard, 1988–92). For succinct criticism, see Peter Carrier, "Places, Politics, and the Archiving of Contemporary Memory in Piere Nora's *Les lieux de mémoire*," in Susannah Radstone, ed., *Memory and Methodology* (Oxford: Berg, 2000), 37, and Steven Englund, "The Ghost of Nation Past," *Journal of Modern History* 64 (1992): 303 and 318.

3. Doreen Massey, "Places and Their Past," *History Workshop Journal* 39 (1995): 183.

4. Lucian Febvre, *Le Rhin: Histoire, myths et réalités*, ed. Peter Schöttler (Paris: Perrin, 1997), 59–64.

5. Clifford Geertz, *The Interpretation of Cultures* (New York: HarperCollins, 1973), 5.

6. James Clifford, *Routes: Travel and Translation in the Late Twentieth Century* (Cambridge, Mass.: Harvard University Press, 1999), 245, and Paul Gilroy, *The Black Atlantic: Modernity and Double Consciousness* (London: Verso, 1993), 111–45.

7. Clifford, *Routes*, 189–219.

8. Maurice Halbwachs, *The Collective Memory*, trans. Francis J. Ditter and Vida Yazdi Ditter (New York: Harper and Row, 1980), 33–34.

9. Aleida Assmann, *Erinnerungsräume. Formen und Wandlungen des kulturellen Gedächtnisses* (Munich: C. H. Beck, 1999), 298–339.

10. Pierre Nora, "Between Memory and History: Les Lieux de Memoire," *Representations* 26 (Spring 1989): 7–25.

11. Yosef Hayim Yerushalmi, "Exile and Expulsion in Jewish History," in Benjamin R. Gampel, ed., *Crisis and Creativity in the Sephardic World, 1391–1648* (New York: Columbia University Press, 1997), 1–22. See also Arnold Eisen, *Galut: Modern Jewish Reflection on Homelessness and Homecoming* (Bloomington: Indiana University Press, 1986), 50; David Myers, "'The Blessing of Assimilation' Reconsidered: An Inquiry into Jewish Cultural Studies," in David Myers and William V. Rowe, eds., *From Ghetto to Emancipation: Historical and Contemporary Reconsiderations of the Jewish Community* (Scranton: University of Scranton Press, 1997), 17–35; and Michael Galchinsky, "Scattered Seeds: A Dialogue of Diaspora," in David Biale, Michael Galchinsky, and Susannah Heschel, eds., *Insider/Outsider: American Jews and Multiculturalism* (Berkeley: University of California Press, 1998), 185–211.

12. On the nobility of memory, see Maurice Halbwachs, *On Collective Memory*, ed. and trans. Lewis A. Coser (Chicago: University of Chicago Press, 1992), 134–35.

13. See Zali Gurevitch and Gideon Aran, "The Land of Israel: Myth and Phenomenon," in Jonathan Frankel, ed., *Reshaping the Past: Jewish History and the Historian* (New York: Oxford University Press, 1994), 195–210. This is an abridged version of the article that originally appeared as "'Al ha-makom," *Alpayim* 4 (1991): 9–44.

14. See Daniel and Jonathan Boyarin, "Diaspora: Generation and the Ground of Jewish Identity," *Critical Inquiry* 19 (1993): 693–725, and Sidra DeKoven Ezrahi, *Booking Passage: Exile and Homecoming in the Modern Jewish Imagination* (Berkeley: University of California Press, 2000).

15. George Steiner, "Our Homeland, the Text," *Salmagundi* 66 (1985): 4–25, and Ezrahi, *Booking Passage*, 17. For a succinct critical review of Ezrahi's book, see Leah Garret, "The Wandering Jew Comes Home," *Prooftexts* 20 (2000): 362–72.

16. See Susan Shapiro, "*Ecriture judaique*: Where Are the Jews in Western Discourse?" in Angelika Bammer, ed., *Displacement: Cultural Identities* (Bloomington: Indiana University Press, 1994), 182–203.

17. Genesis Rabbah 82:10 and Talmud Yerushalmi, Shekalim 47a.

18. Heinrich Graetz, *Die Konstruktion der jüdischen Geschichte*, ed. Nils Roemer (Düsseldorf: Parerga, 2000), 47.

19. Karl Emil Franzos, "Denkmäler deutscher Juden," *AZJ* 66 (1902): 463–65.

20. Nils Roemer, *Between History and Faith: Rewriting the Past—Reshaping Jewish Cultures in Nineteenth-Century Germany* (Madison: Wisconsin University Press, 2005), 129.

I. SACRED REALMS

1. Michael Toch, "*Dunkle Jahrhunderte" Gab es ein jüdisches Frühmittelalter?* (Trier: Arye-Maimon-Institut für Geschichte der Juden, 2001).

2. A. Epstein, "Jüdische Alterthümer in Worms und Speir," *MGWJ* 40 (1895): 513.

3. Julius Aronius, *Regesten zur Geschichte der Juden im fränkischen und deutschen Reiche bis zum Jahre 1273* (Berlin: Leonhard Simion, 1902), 67–68.

4. Fritz Reuter, *Warmaisa. 1000 Jahre Juden in Worms* (Frankfurt am Main: Athenäum, 1987), 22–26.

5. While Mainz Anonymous dates the first attack on May 5 and the second attack on May 18, Salomon gives May 18 and 25, respectively.

6. See Abraham Habermann, ed., *Sefer gezerot ashkenaz ve-tzarfat* (Jerusalem: Tarshish, 1945), 95–96, and Shlomo Eidelberg, ed., *The Jews and the Crusaders:The Hebrew Chronicles of the First and Second Crusade* (Madison: University of Wisconsin Press, 1977), 107.

7. Habermann, *Sefer gezerot ashkenaz ve-tzarfat*, 25; Eidelberg, *Jews and the Crusaders*, 23; and Siegmund Salfeld, *Das Martyrologium des Nürnberger Memorbuches* (Berlin: Leonhard Simion, 1898), 5–8 (Hebrew) and 102–8 (German).

8. Jeremy Cohen, "Between Martyrdom and Apostasy: Doubt and Self-Definition in Twelfth-Century Ashkenaz," *Journal of Medieval and Early Modern Studies* 29 (1999): 431.

9. Regarding authority over the Jews, see Salo Wittmayer Baron, "Plenitude of Apostolic Power and Medieval Jewish Serfdom," in Leon A. Feldman, ed., *Ancient and Medieval Jewish History: Essays by Salo Wittmayer Baron* (New Brunswick: Rutgers University Press, 1963), 284–307. On the charter, see James Parkes, *The Jew in the Medieval Community:A Study of His Political and Economic Situation* (New York: Hermon, 1976), 94, 97 and 392–93.

10. Habermann, *Sefer gezerot ashkenaz ve-tzarfat*, 95, and Eidelberg, *Jews and the Crusaders*, 102.

11. Among the inscriptions on the six existing graves from 1091 (nos. 205, 1010) and 1100 (nos. 938, 969, 987, 1056), only two indicate that the deceased were martyrs (nos. 938 and 969). See *Epithaphien von Grabsteinen des alten israel. Friedhofs in Worms—entziffert und ins Deutsche übersetzt von Prof. David Kaufmann in Budapest in den Jahren 1892–1897 nach dem ihm von dem Vorstandsmitglied Julius Goldschmidt gelieferten Abklatschen* (1901), Stadtarchiv Worms, Judaica 203:3, and Epstein, "Jüdische Alterthümer in Worms und Speir," 559.

12. Judah ben Samuel the Pious, *Sefer Hasidim*, ed. Jehuda Wistinetzki and Jacob Freimann, 2nd ed. (Frankfurt am Main:Wahrmann, 1924), no. 1530.

13. Juda Löw Kirchheim, *Minhagot Vermaiza: Minhagim ve-hanhagot*, ed. Israel Mordechai Peles (Jerusalem: Mif'al torat hakhme Ashkenaz, Mekhon Yerushalayim, 1987), 254. In his book on Jewish custom, Juspa relates that Jews went to the grave of the community leaders on Rosh Hodesh Sivan, the date of the martyrdom of the First Crusade. See Juspa Shammes, *Minhagim di-k.k.Vermaisa le-Rabi Yuzpa Shamash. Mofi'a la-rishonah bi-shelemut mi-kitve ha-yad shel ha-mehaber: Kolel hashlamot ve-hagahot me-Rabenu Yair Hayim Bakharakh'im mekorot, beurim u-fetihah kelalit 'al yede Binyamin Shelomoh Hamburger. Hakhanat tekst u-mavoh histori 'al yede Yitshak Zimer*, 2 vols. (Jerusalem: Mif'al torat hakhme Ashkenaz, Mekhon Yerushalayim, 1988–92), 1: no. 98.

14. Kirchheim, *Minhagot Vermaiza: Minhagim ve-hanhagot*, 254.

15. Whether he based his theory on these traditions or not is unclear, but Moses Mannheimer believed in the nineteenth century that the original burial of these community leaders was close to the grave of Bacharach. See Moses Mannheimer, *Die Juden in Worms, ein Beitrag zur Geschichte der Juden in den Rheingegenden* (Frankfurt am Main: J. S. Adler, 1842), 62.

16. Kirchheim, *Minhagot Vermaiza: Minhagim ve-hanhagot*, 254, and Shammes, *Minhagim di-k.k.Vermaisa*, 1: no. 98.

17. Shammes, *Minhagim di-k.k.Vermais*, 28.

18. Lewysohn, *Nefashot Zadikim*, 94.

19. Ivan G. Marcus, "A Jewish-Christian Symbiosis: The Culture of Early Ashkenaz," in David Biale, ed., *Cultures of the Jews: A New History* (New York: Schocken Books, 2002), 465.

20. Robert Chazan, *European Jewry and the First Crusade* (Berkeley: University of California Press, 1987), 151. For a summary and discussion of the various proposed dates and the interrelationship between the chronicles, see Anna Sapir Abulafia, "The Interrelationship between the Hebrew Chronicles on the First Crusade," *Journal of Semitic Studies* 27 (1982): 221–39.

21. Cohen, *Sanctifying the Name of God*, 60–69.

22. Ivan G. Marcus, "Hierarchies, Religious Boundaries, and Jewish Spirituality in Medieval Germany," *Jewish History* 1 (1986): 7–26; Marcus, "Une communauté pieuse et le doute: Mourir pour la Sanctification du Nom en Achkenaz et l'histoire de rabbi Amnon de Mayence," *Annales: Histoire, sciences socials* 49, no. 5 (1994): 1031–47; Cohen, "Between Martyrdom and Apostasy," 431–71.

23. Habermann, *Sefer gezerot ashkenaz ve-tzarfat*, 96–97; Eidelberg, *Jews and the Crusaders*, 104–5; for the prominence of women as martyrs in the chronicles, see Avraham Grossman, *Pious and Rebellious: Jewish Women in Medieval Europe*, trans. Jonathan Chipman (Hanover, N.H.: University Press of New England, 2004), 199–211.

24. While the *Mishna* is silent on the question of martyrdom, the Talmud discusses the circumstances under which martyrdom becomes a religious obligation. The Talmud Pesahim 53b stipulates several requirements that demand self-sacrifice but also preserves R. Ishmael's view that a Jew should rather submit to idolatry than die.

25. Gershon D. Cohen, "Hannah and Her Seven Sons in Hebrew Literature," in Moshe Davis, ed., *Sefer ha-yovel lekhvod M. M. Kaplan* (New York: JTS, 1953), 109–22.

26. Allan Mintz, *Hurban: Responses to Catastrophe in Hebrew Literature* (New York: Columbia University Press, 1984), 6.

27. Habermann, *Sefer gezerot ashkenaz ve-tzarfat*, 25, and Eidelberg, *Jews and the Crusaders*, 22.

28. Habermann, *Sefer gezerot ashkenaz ve-tzarfat*, 96; Eidelberg, *Jews and the Crusaders*, 103–4; Robert Chazan, *God, Humanity, and History: The Hebrew First Crusade Narratives* (Berkeley: University of California Press, 2000), 33–35.

29. Habermann, *Sefer gezerot ashkenaz ve-tzarfat*, 96; and Eidelberg, *Jews and the Crusaders*, 103; on the exegetical Jewish tradition that Isaac was actually slaugh-

tered, see Shalom Spiegel, *The Last Trial: On the Legends and Lore of the Command to Abraham to Offer Isaac as a Sacrifice; The Akedah*, trans. Judah Goldin (Woodstock, Vt.: Jewish Lights Publishing, 1993).

30. Habermann, *Sefer gezerot ashkenaz ve-tzarfat*, 96, and Eidelberg, *Jews and the Crusaders*, 103.

31. Gerson D. Cohen, "The Hebrew Crusade Chronicles and the Ashkenazic Tradition," in Marc Brettler and Michael Fishbane, eds., *Minhah le-Nahum: Biblical and Other Studies Presented to Nahum Sarna in Honour of His 70th Birthday* (Sheffield: JSOT Press, 1993), 50–51.

32. Habermann, *Sefer gezerot ashkenaz ve-tzarfat*, 42–43, and Eidelberg, *Jews and the Crusaders*, 48.

33. Habermann, *Sefer gezerot ashkenaz ve-tzarfat*, 82, and Eidelberg, *Jews and the Crusaders*, 93.

34. Habermann, *Sefer gezerot ashkenaz ve-tzarfat*, 101; Eidelberg, *Jews and the Crusaders*, 110; Israel Yuval, "Ha-nakam we-ha-kelalah, ha-dam we-ha-alilah: Mealilot kedoshim le-'alilot dam," *Zion* 58 (1993): 33–89.

35. Anna Sapir Abulafia, "Invectives Against Christianity in the Hebrew Chronicles of the First Crusade," in Peter W. Edbury, ed., *Crusade and Settlement: Papers Read at the First Conference of the Society for Study of Crusades and Latin East and Presented to R. C. Smail* (Cardiff: University College Cardiff Press, 1985), 66–72, and Marcus, "Hierarchies, Religious Boundaries and Jewish Spirituality in Medieval Germany," 10–12.

36. Abulafia, "The Interrelationship between the Hebrew Chronicles on the First Crusade," 222–23, and Abraham David, "Zikhronot ve-he-arot 'al gezerot tatnu—bi-defus u-ve kitve yad 'ivriim," in Yom Tov Assis et al., eds., *Yehudim mul ha-zelav: Gezerot 856 ba-historyah uva-historyografiah* (Jerusalem: Y. L. Magnes, 2000), 146–94.

37. S. Bernfeld, *Sefer ha-dema'ot: me'ore'ot ha-gezerot veha-redifot ve-hashmadot*, 3 vols. (Berlin: Eshkol, 1923–26), 1:193–97 and 207–9.

38. Habermann, *Sefer gezerot ashkenaz ve-tzarfat*, 83.

39. Abraham Rosenfeld, ed., *The Authorised Kinot for the Ninth of Av* (New York: Judaica Press, 1979), 132–34, and Daniel Goldschmidt, ed., *Seder ha-kinot le-tisha be-av* (Jerusalem: Mosad Harav Kook, 1972), no. 26.

40. Mishna Ta'anit, 4:6.

41. Marcus, "Une communauté pieuse et le doute," 1031–47.

42. Kirchheim, *Minhagot Vermaiza*, 252.

43. Habermann, *Sefer gezerot ashkenaz ve-tzarfat*, 68, and the translation in Salo Wittmayer Baron, *A Social and Religious History of the Jews* (New York: Columbia University Press, 1957), 4:145.

44. Eleazar bar Yehuda, *Sefer ha-Rokeah ha-gadol al darkhe ha-torah, ha-hasidut yeha-teshuva, hilkhot al kol ha-shana u-minhage ha-rishonim* (Jerusalem, 1960), no. 212.

45. Kirchheim, *Minhagot Vermaiza*, 251–52; Juspa Shammes, *Minhagim di-k.k. Vermaisa le-Rabi Yuzpa Shamash*, 1: no. 98; and Zimer, "Gezerot tatnu be-sifre ha-minhagim be-yeme ha-benayim uv-be-et-ha-hadasha," 157–70.

46. Salfeld, *Das Martyrologium des Nürnberger Memorbuches*, and Moritz Stein-schneider, *Geschichtsliteratur der Juden* (Berlin: J. Kaufmann, 1905), no. 24.

47. Adolf Jellinek, *Worms und Wien. Liturgische Formulare ihrer Todtenfeier aus alter und neuer Zeit, und Namensverzeichnisse der Wormser Maertyrer aus dem Jahre 1096 und 1349* (Wien: Jakob Schlossberg, 1880), 3–5, and Salfeld, *Das Martyrolo-gium des Nürnberger Memorbuches*, 5–8 (Hebrew) and 102–8 (German).

48. Shlomo Spitzer, ed., *Sefer Maharil: Manhigim* (Jerusalem: Mif'al Torath Chachmey Ashkenaz Machon Yerushalayim, 1989), 159.

49. Ivan G. Marcus, *Piety and Society: The Jewish Pietist of Medieval Germany* (Leiden: Brill, 1981).

50. On this most recently, see Hanna Liss, "Copyright im Mittelalter? Die eso-terischen Schriften von R. El'azar von Worms zwischen Traditions- und Autoren-literatur," *Frankfurter Judaistische Beiträge* 21 (1994): 81–108.

51. Judah ben Samuel the Pious, *Sefer Hasidim*, ed. Jehuda Wistinetzki and Jacob Freimann, 2nd ed. (Frankfurt am Main: Wahrmann, 1924), no. 1530, and Talya Fishman, "The Rhineland Pietists' Sacralization of Oral *Torah*," *Jewish Quarterly Review* 96 (2005): 9–16.

52. Stowe, *Alienated Minority*, 164–71.

53. Gershom Scholem, *On the Kabbalah and Its Symbolism* (New York: Schocken, 1969), 136; Hanna Liss, "Offenbarung und Weitergabe des göttlichen Namens und die Rezeption priesterlicher Traditionen im Sefer ha-Shem des R. El'azar ben Ye-huda von Worms," *Frankfurter Judaistische Beiträge* 26 (1999): 25–50; and Elliot R. Wolfson, *Through a Speculum That Shines: Vision and Imagination in Medieval Jew-ish Mysticism* (Princeton: Princeton University Press, 1994), 239–47.

54. Ivan G. Marcus, "History, Story, and Collective Memory: Narrativity in Early Askenazic Culture," in Michael Fishbane, ed., *The Midrashic Imagination: Jewish Exegesis, Thought, and History* (Albany: State University of New York Press, 1993), 265.

55. A. Graboïs, "Le souvenir et la légende de Charlemagne dans les texts hébra-ïques medievaux," *Le moyan âge* 72 (1966): 32–33.

56. A. Neubauer, "Abou Ahron, le Babylonien," *REJ* 23 (1891): 230–37; Hein-rich Gross, "Zwei kabbalistische Traditionsketten des R. Eleasar aus Worms," *MGWJ* 49 (1905): 692–700; Joseph Dan, *Torat ha-sod shel hasidut ashkenaz* (Je-rusalem: Bialik, 1968), 14–20; Marcus, "History, Story, and Collective Mem-ory," 262–63; and Dan, *Iyyunim be-sifrut hasidut ashkenaz* (Ramat-Gan: Massada, 1975), 49.

57. A. Epstein, "Die nach Raschi benannten Gebäude in Worms," *MGWJ* 45 (1901): 48 and 65–66.

58. Habermann, *Sefer gezerot ashkenaz ve-tzarfat*, 164–67, and Judith R. Baskin, "Dolce of Worms: The Lives and Deaths of an Exemplary Medieval Jewish Woman and Her Daughters," in Lawrence Fine, ed., *Judaism in Practice: From the Middle Ages to the Early Modern Period* (Princeton: Princeton University Press, 2001), 429–37.

59. Judith R. Baskin, "Dolce of Worms: Women Saints in Judaism," in Arvin Sharma, ed., *Women Saints in World Religions* (Albany: State University of New

218

York Press, 2000), 39–70. The same fate was met by one of Eleazar's daughters, who lived at Erfurt, where she died as a martyr at the hand of Crusaders on December 6, either 1213 or 1214.

60. Ludwig Lewysohn, *Nefashot Zadikim. Sechzig Epitaphien von Grabsteinen des israelitischen Friedhofes zu Worms regressiv bis zum Jahr 905 übl. Zeitr. nebst biographischen Skizzen* (Frankfurt am Main: Joseph Baer, 1855), 86–87.

61. T. Carmi, ed., *The Penguin Book of Hebrew Verse* (London: Penguin, 1981), 347.

62. Habermann, *Sefer gezerot ashkenaz ve-tzarfat*, 183–85. On the poem, see Susan Einbinder, *Beautiful Death: Jewish Poetry and Martyrdom in Medieval France* (Princeton: Princeton University Press, 2003), 70–99.

63. *Epithaphien von Grabsteinen des alten israel. Friedhofs in Worms*, Stadtarchiv Worms, Judaica 203:3, no. 88.

64. Patrick J. Geary, *Living with the Dead in the Middle Ages* (Ithaca: Cornell University Press, 1994), 163–93.

65. *Epithaphien von Grabsteinen des alten israel. Friedhofs in Worms*, Stadtarchiv Worms, Judaica 203:3, no. 89; David Kaufmann, "Die Grabsteine R. Meir's von Rothenburg und Alexander Wimpfen's in Worms," *MGWJ* 40 (1895): 126–30; Irving A. Agus, *Rabbi Meir of Rothenburg: His Life and His Works as Sources for the Religious, Legal, and Social History of the Jews of Germany in the 13th Century*, 2 vols. (Philadelphia: Dropsie College for Hebrew and Cognate Learning, 1947), 125–50.

66. See Herman Pollack, *Jewish Folkways in Germanic Lands (1648–1806)* (Cambridge: MIT Press, 1971), 46–49, and Sylvie Goldberg, *Crossing the Jabbok: Illness and Death in Ashkenazi Judaism in Sixteenth through Nineteenth-Century Prague*, trans. Carol Cosman (Berkeley: University of California Press, 1996), 139–42.

67. Geary, *Living with the Dead in the Middle Ages*, 77–92.

68. T. B. Sotah 34b.

69. T. B. Ta'anit. 16a. This difference of opinion is explained by the assumption that the first refers to cemeteries in general, whereas the second refers to Jewish cemeteries. See also Rashi on Numbers 13:22.

70. Leon Nemoy, ed., *Karaite Anthology: Excerpt from the Early Literature* (New Haven: Yale University Press, 1952), 115–16. See also Ephraim Shoham-Steiner, "'For a Prayer in That Place Would Be Most Welcome': Jews, Holy Shrines, and Miracles—A New Approach," *Viator* 37 (2006): 369–95.

71. Zohar, 3:71b.

72. Rashi on T.B. Yevamoth 122a.

73. Ismar Elbogen, *Jewish Liturgy: A Comprehensives History*, trans. Raymond P. Scheindlin (Philadelphia: Jewish Publication Society of America, 1993), 80–84 and 162–63.

74. David Berger, ed., *The Jewish-Christian Debate in the High Middle Ages: A Critical Edition of Nizzahon Vetus* (Philadelphia: Jewish Publication Society of America, 1979), 225, no. 240.

75. *Sefer Hasidim*, ed. Re'uven Margaliyot (Jerusalem: Mosa ha-rav Kok, 1956), 450. The fourteenth-century Ashkenaz R. Judah b. Asher of Toledo mentioned in

his will that he had prayed at the graves of the righteous but refrained, however, from directing his prayer to the deceased. See Israel Abrahams, ed., *Hebrew Ethical Wills* (Philadelphia: Jewish Publication Society of America, 1976), 183–84.

76. Judah ben Samuel, *Sefer Hasidim* (Berlin: Bi-defus T. H. Ittskovski, 1891–93), no. 269, and Elliott Horowitz, "Speaking to the Dead: Cemetery Prayer in Medieval and Early Modern Jewry," *Journal of Jewish Thought and Philosophy* 8 (1999): 303–17.

77. *Sefer Hasidim*, ed. Jehuda Wistinetzki and Jacob Freimann, 2nd ed. (Frankfurt am Main: Wahrmann, 1924), no. 1537.

78. See, for example, R. Menahem of Oldendorf's testimony, cited by Israel Ta-Shma, "'Cronika hadasha le-tekufot baali ha-tosofot me-hugo shel R. I. ha-saken': A New Chronography on the Thirteenth-Century Tosaphist," *Shalem* 3 (1981): 324. See also Maharil's responsum, 118.

79. R. Meir of Rothenburg, *She'elot u-teshuvot Maharam bar Barukh* (Lemberg, 1860), no. 164, fol. 13a.

80. Spitzer, *Sefer Maharil: Manhigim*, 270.

81. Ibid., 273.

82. Zvi Avneri, ed., *Germania Judaica. Bd. 2:Von 1238 bis zur Mitte des 14. Jahrhunderts* (Tübingen: J. C. B. Mohr, 1968), 919–27, and Stowe, *Alienated Minority*, 231.

83. See Frantisek Graus, "Historische Traditionen über Juden im Spätmittelalter (Mitteleuropa)," in Alfred Haverkamp and Alfred Heit, eds., *Zur Geschichte der Juden im Deutschland des späten Mittelalters und der frühen Neuzeit* (Stuttgart: Anton Hiersemann, 1981), 1–26.

84. Yosef Hayim Yerushalmi, "Exile and Expulsion in Jewish History," in Benjamin R. Gampel, ed., *Crisis and Creativity in the Sephardic World, 1391–1648* (New York: Columbia University Press, 1997), 3–22, and Shlomo Eidelberg, "Origins of German Jewry: Reality and Legend," in Shlomo Eidelberg, ed. *Medieval Ashkenazic History: Studies on German Jewry in the Middle Ages* (Brooklyn: Sepher-Hermon Press, 1999), 2–3.

85. Heinrich Boos, *Quellen zur Geschichte der Stadt Worms*, 3 vols. (Berlin: Weidmannsche Buchhandlung, 1886–93), 2:74, and Reuter, *Warmaisa*, 57–58.

86. Eduard Sebald, "Das gotische Südportal," in Herbert Dellwing, ed., *Das Südportal des Wormser Doms* (Worms: Wernersche Verlagsgesellschaft, 1999), 36–78.

87. G. Wolf, "Zur Geschichte der Juden in Worms und des deutschen Städtewesens," *MGWJ* 10 (1861): 416, and Heinrich Boos, *Quellen zur Geschichte der Stadt Worms*, 2: no. 370, 258–59.

88. Shlomo Eidelberg, *R. Juspa, Shammash of Warmaisa (Worms): Jewish Life in Seventeenth-Century Worms* (Jerusalem: The Magnes Press, 1991), in the Hebrew section, 85, and in the English section, 77. For a very detailed and very informative discussion of the year 1349 in Worms in Jewish sources, see Lucia Raspe, "The Black Death in Jewish Sources," *JQR* 94 (2004): 471–89.

89. Epstein, "Jüdische Alterthümer in Worms und Speir," 556, and Alfred Haverkamp, "Die Judenverfolgung zur Zeit des Schwarzen Todes im Gesellschaftsgefüge deutscher Städte," in Alfred Haverkamp and Alfred Heit, eds., *Zur*

Geschichte der Juden in Deutschland des späten Mittelalters und der frühen Neuzeit (Stuttgart: Hiersemann, 1981), 27–93.

90. Salfeld, *Das Martyrologium des Nürnberger Memorbuches*, 73–77 (Hebrew) and 259–66 (German).

91. Franz-Josef Ziwes, *Studien zur Geschichte der Juden im mittleren Rheingebiet während des hohen und späten Mittelalters* (Hannover: Verlag Hahnsche Buchhandlung, 1995), 263–65.

92. Boos, *Quellen zur Geschichte der Stadt Worms*, 2: no. 385, 267.

93. Ibid., 2: no. 385, 267, and Reuter, *Warmaisa*, 61.

94. Gerold Bönnen, "Jüdische Gemeinde und christliche Stadtgemeinde," in Christoph Cluse, Alfred Haverkamp, and Israel J. Yuval, eds., *Jüdische Gemeinden und ihr christlicher Kontext in kulturräumlich vergleichender Betrachtung von der Spätantike bis zum 18. Jahrhundert* (Hannover: Hahn, 2003), 313–15.

95. Kirchheim, *Minhagot Vermaiza: Minhagim ve-hanhagot*, 214, and Shammes, *Minhagim di-k.k. Vermaisa*, 1: no. 217.

96. S. Bernfeld, *Sefer ha-dema'ot*, 2:107.

97. The *Memorbuch* lists eleven community leaders, but Salfeld speculated that a rabbi who also functioned as a *parnas* was probably the twelfth. See Salfeld, *Das Martyrologium des Nürnberger Memorbuches*, 73–77 and 259–65, and Adolf Jellinek, *Worms und Wien. Liturgische Formulare ihrer Todtenfeier aus alter und neuer Zeit und Namesverzeichnisse der Wormser Maertyrer aus dem Jahre 1096 und 1349*, 5–7. Yet the *Memorbuch* intersperses *parnasim* rather than listing them consecutively, which makes this account of their shared fate rather dubious.

98. Boos, *Quellen zur Geschichte der Stadt Worms*, 2: no. 723, 463–67.

99. Christopher R. Friedrichs, "Anti-Jewish Politics in Early Modern Germany: The Uprising of Worms, 1613–1617," *Central European History* 21 (1990): 98.

100. Andreas Hanslok, *Die landesherrliche und kommunale Judenschutzpolitik während des späten Mittelalters im Heiligen Römischen Reich Deutscher Nation. Ein Vergleich der Entwicklungen am Beispiel schlesischer, brandenburgischer und rheinischer Städte* (Berlin: Wissenschaftlicher Verlag, 2000), 234–35.

101. Willehad Paul Eckert, "Hoch-und Spätmittelalter. Katholischer Humanismus," in Karl Heinrich Rengstorf and Siegfried Kortzfleisch, eds., *Kirche und Synagoge. Handbuch zur Geschichte von Christen und Juden*, 2 vols. (Stuttgart: Klett, 1968), 251.

102. *Deutsche Reichsakten. Mittlere Reihe. Unter Maximilian I. Fünfter Band. Reichstag von Worms 1495. Band 2. Berichte und Instruktionen*, ed. Heinz Angermeier (Göttingen: Vandenhoeck and Ruprecht, 1981), 5:2, 1680, and A. Epstein, "Die Wormser Minhagbücher," in Marcus Brann, Ferdinand Rosenthal, and David Kaufmann, eds., *Gedenkbuch zur Erinnerung an David Kaufmann* (Breslau: S. Schottlaender, 1900), 311.

103. Friedrich Battenberg, *Quellen zur Geschichte der Juden im Hessischen Staatsarchiv Darmstadt, 1080–1650* (Wiesbaden: Kommission für die Geschichte der Juden in Hessen, 1995), no. 1164.

104. Max Freudenthal, "Dokumente zur Schriftenverfolgung durch Pfefferkorn," *Zeitschrift für die Geschichte der Juden in Deutschland* 3 (1931): 231–32.

105. Heinrich Graetz, *Geschichte der Juden von der Verbannung der Juden aus Spanien und Portugal (1494) bis zur dauernden Ansiedelung der Marranen in Holland (1618)*, 4th ed. (Leipzig: Oskar Leiner, 1907), 185–86.

106. See Lewysohn, *Nefashot Zadikim*, 111–12, and Lewy, "Zur Geschichte der Wormser jüdischen Gemeinde von ihren Anfängen bis zum neunzehnten Jahrhundert," 14–16.

107. Epstein, "Jüdische Alterthümer in Worms und Speir," 511.

108. For a detailed description of the manuscript, see Ernst Róth and Leo Prijs, *Hebräische Handschriften. Teil 1. Die Handschriften der Stadt- und Universitätsbibliothek Frankfurt am Main. Bd. A-C* (Wiesbaden: Steiner, 1982–93), no. 264, 175–82.

109. Jeremy Cohen, "A 1096 Complex: Constructing the First Crusade in Jewish Historical Memory, Medieval and Modern," in Michael A. Signer and John H. van Engen, eds., *Jews and Christians in Twelfth-Century Europe* (Notre Dame: University of Notre Dame Press, 2001), 9–21.

2. BETWEEN RITUALS AND TEXTS

1. Fritz Reuter, *Worms, ehemals, gestern und heute. Ein Stadtbild im Wandel der letzten 100 Jahre* (Stuttgart: J. F. Steinkopf Verlag, 1988), 7.

2. Louis Finkelstein, *Jewish Self-Government in the Middle Ages* (New York: JTSA, 1924), 79–81 and 257–64.

3. This general cultural exchange between Jews and Christian seems to have existed on a considerable scale—by the end of the sixteenth century, there was even an edition of forty-two German folksongs printed in Hebrew letters. See Georg Liebe, *Das Judentum in der deutschen Vergangenheit* (Leipzig: E. Diederichs, 1903), 61, and Avraham Grossman, *Pious and Rebellious: Jewish Women in Medieval Europe*, trans. Jonathan Chipman (Hanover, N.H.: University Press of New England, 2004), 119–20.

4. Christopher R. Friedrichs, "Jewish Household Structure in an Early Modern Town: The Worms Ghetto Census of 1610," *History of the Family* 8 (2003): 481–93; Max Grunwald, "Le Cimetière de Worms," *REJ NS* 4 (1938): 97; and Hermann Pollack, *Jewish Folkways in Germanic Lands* (Cambridge, Mass.: MIT Press, 1971), 9.

5. Schlomo Spitzer, ed., *Sefer Maharil*, 488–89; Juspa Shammes, *Minhagim di-k.k.Vermaisa le-Rabi Yuzpa Shamash*, 2: 69; and Samson Rothschild, "Ein geschichtlich bedeutsamer Fund," *Vom Rhein* 4 (1907): 77.

6. David Kaufmann, *R. Jair Chajjim Bacharach (1638–1702) und seine Ahnen* (Trier: Siegmund Mayer, 1894), 10–13.

7. *Epithaphien von Grabsteinen des alten israel. Friedhofs in Worms—entziffert und ins Deutsche übersetzt von Prof. David Kaufmann in Budapest in den Jahren 1892–1897 nach dem ihm von dem Vorstandsmitglied Julius Goldschmidt gelieferten Abklatschen*, 2 vols. (1901), Stadtarchiv Worms, Judaica 203:3, no. 191.

8. Malachi Beit-Arié, "The Worms Mahzor: Its History and Its Palaeographic and Codicological Characteristics," in Malachi Beit-Arié, ed., *MS. Jewish National and University Library. Heb. 4° 781/1* (London: Cyelar Establishment, Vaduz, 1985), 13–35.

9. Chava Weissler, *Voices of the Matriarchs: Listening to the Prayers of Early Modern Jewish Women* (Boston: Beacon Press, 1998).

10. Sarah Zfatmann, "Ha-siporet be-yiddish me-rishit 'ad shivhei ha-besht (1504–1814)," 2 vols. (Ph.D. diss., Hebrew University, 1983), 1:116–21, and Elchanan Reiner, "The Ashkenazi Élite at the Beginning of the Modern Era: Manuscript Versus Printed Books," *Polin* 10 (1997): 85–98.

11. Isadore Twersky, "The Shulhan Arukh: Enduring Code of Jewish Law," in Jehuda Goldin, ed., *The Jewish Expression* (New York: Bantam Books, 1970), 322–43.

12. Adolf Kober, "Die deutschen Kaiser und die Wormser Juden," *ZGJD* 5 (1935): 139–40; Moritz Stern, "Ein Copialbuch der jüdischen Gemeinde zu Worms," *ZGJD* 1 (1886): 278; and Reuter, *Warmaisa*, 68–84.

13. See Christopher R. Friedrichs, "Anti-Jewish Politics in Early Modern Germany: The Uprising of Worms, 1613–1617," *Central European History* 21 (1990): 101, and Stern, "Ein Copialbuch der jüdischen Gemeinde zu Worms," 278.

14. Sabine Frey, *Rechtsschutz der Juden gegen Ausweisungen im 16. Jahrhundert* (Frankfurt am Main: Peter Lang, 1983), 108–14, and Ronnie Po-Chia Hsia, *The Myth of Ritual Murder: Jews and Magic in Reformation Germany* (New Haven: Yale University Press, 1988), 163–96.

15. Christopher R. Friedrichs, "Urban Conflicts and the Imperial Constitution in Seventeenth-Century Germany," *Journal of Modern History* 58 (1986): 98–123.

16. For detailed descriptions of this conflict, on which I rely here, see Friedrichs, "Anti-Jewish Politics in Early Modern Germany," 91–152, and Ronnie Po-chia Hsia, "Bürgerschaft in Worms 1614. Judenprivilegien und Bürgerrecht in der frühen Neuzeit," in Hans-Jürgen Goertz, Norbert Fischer, and Marion Kobelt-Groch, eds., *Aussenseiter zwischen Mittelalter und Neuzeit. Festschrift für Hans-Jürgen Goertz zum 60. Geburtstag* (Leiden: E. J. Brill, 1997), 101–10.

17. *Kayserlicher Herold / Das ist / Mandatum Poenale Sine Et Respective Cum Clausula, Wormbsische Zünfft / [et]c. Contra Wormbs / Die Abrechnung und Rückraitung auff fünff vom Hundert mit den Juden zu halten. Bey einem Ehrsamen Hochweisen Raht zu Wormbs den 7. Octob. 1614 glücklich ankommen / Allen frommen Christen zur Nachrichtung in Truck publicirt* (Frankfurt: Latomus, 1614), and *Kurtzer bewehrter Außzuch Der letzten Wormser Judenordnung / wie sie Anno 1594. An etlichen orten Corrigiert und gebessert / im Newlich eröffneten Buchstaben geschrieben befunden* (Vallo Francko, 1614).

18. Christopher R. Friedrichs, "Politics or Pogrom? The Fettmilch Uprising in Germany and Jewish History," *CEH* 19 (1986): 186–228.

19. *Wormbsische Acta oder Aussmusterung der Jüden zu Wormbs: Das ist / Historische Relation / wie die Burger zu Wormbs/ ihre Jüden außwiesen / un[n] fortgetrieben / auch wie sie deroselben Tempel Schul / Synagog / unnd Hauße der Reinigung / alsbaldt abzubrechen / . . . Darauß zusehen / aus was Hochwichtigen bewegendten Ursachen solches geschehen / und was die Obrigkeit hierzu gesagt* (1615), 6, and Juda Löw Kirchheim, *Minhagot Vermaiza*, 209.

20. *Wormbsische Acta oder Aussmusterung der Jüden zu Wormbs*, 6.

21. Ibid., 7.

22. Kirchheim, *Minhagot Vermaiza: Minhagim ve-hanhagot*, 209.

23. Reuter, *Warmaisa*, 87. This pamphlet was reprinted in several forms, though typically without the woodcut.

24. Nahman ben Eliezer Puch, *Be-shurat tovot yeshuot we-nahmot me-geulat k. k. Frankfurt a. M. and k.k. Worms* (1616), 28–32, and Chava Turniansky, "The Events in Frankfurt am Main (11612–1616) in *Megillas Vints* in an Unknown Yiddish 'Historical' Song," in Michael Graetz, ed., *Schöpferische Momente des europäischen Judentums in der frühen Neuzeit* (Heidelberg: C. Winter, 2000), 121–37.

25. Kirchheim, *Minhagot Vermaiza: Minhagim ve-hanhagot*, 209.

26. Ibid., 209–10; Shammes, *Minhagim di-k.k. Vermaisa le-Rabi Yuzpa Shamash*, 1: no. 209, and Eidelberg, *R. Juspa, Shammash of Warmaisa (Worms)*, 74–75 (English) and 73–74 (Hebrew).

27. A. Epstein, "Die Wormser Minhagbücher," in Marcus Brann, Ferdinand Rosenthal, and David Kaufmann, eds., *Gedenkbuch zur Erinnerung an David Kaufmann* (Breslau: S. Schottlaender, 1900), 297–98.

28. Kirchheim, *Minhagot Vermaiza: Minhagim ve-hanhagot*, 301, 3–6.

29. Ibid., 3–6.

30. Abraham Berliner, "Sefer Haskarat neshamot," *Kovez 'al yad* 3 (1886): 16; A. Epstein, "Jüdische Alterthümer in Worms und Speir," *MGWJ* 40 (1895): 557, and Eidelberg, *R. Juspa, Shammash of Warmaisa (Worms)*, 75 (English) and 74 (Hebrew).

31. See Michael Schmidt, *Reverentia und Magnificentia. Historität in der Architektur Süddeutschland, Österreichs und Böhmens vom 14. bis 17. Jahrhundert* (Regensburg: Schnell und Steiner, 1999).

32. Gerhard W. Mühlinghaus, "Der Synagogenbau des 17. und 18. Jahrhunderts," in Hans-Peter Schwarz, ed., *Die Architektur der Synagoge* (Frankfurt am Main: Klett-Cotta, 1988), 131–32, and Krautheimer, *Mittelalterliche Synagogen*, 174.

33. Eidelberg, *R. Juspa, Shammash of Warmaisa (Worms)*, 97–98, and L. Löwenstein, "Wormser Gemeindeordnung," *Blaetter für Jüdische Geschichte und Litteratur* 4 (1903): 148.

34. Magnus Weinberg, "Untersuchungen ueber das Wesen des Memorbuches," *JJLG* 16 (1924): 253–320; M. Weinberg, "Memorbücher," *Menorah* 6 (1928): 697–708; Aubrey Pomernace, " 'Bekannt in den Toren.' Namen und Nachruf in Memorbüchern," in Sabine Hoedl and Elenore Lappin, eds., *Erinnerungen als Gegenwart: Jüdische Gedenkkulturen* (Wien: Philo, 2000), 33–53; Cecil Roth, "The Frankfurt Memorbuch," in *Commemoration of the Frankfurt Jewish Community on the Occasion of the Acquisition of the Frankfurt Memorbuch* (Jerusalem: Jewish National and University Library, 1965), 9–16; and Paul Arnsberg, *Die Geschichte der Frankfurter Juden seit der Französischen Revolution*, 3 vols. (Darmstadt: Eduard Roether Verlag, 1983), 1:630–50.

35. The chronicle was written by Samuel of Schebreshin in 1650 and published in the same year in Cracow. It was republished by Chaim Gurland in *Le-korot hageserot 'al yisra'el* (Cracow: Yosef Fisher, 1889), 7–61.

36. Berliner, "Sefer Haskarat neshamot," 15 and 22.

37. Juspa relates, for example, that it was the custom in Worms to place a *mezusah* vertically on the doorpost, as Rashi had taught it there. He also relates that the community did not recite *'akdamut* and the prayer *adon 'olam*. See Shammes, *Minhagim di-k.k.Vermaisa*, 1: no. 7 and 104, and 2: no. 291 and 2:243.

38. B. T. Hullin 18b elaborates on the requirement for a newcomer (or visitors) to observe the customs of a local community.

39. Shammes, *Minhagim di-k.k.Vermaisa*, 1: no. 224 and 1:30–31.

40. Ibid., 1: no. 98. It is not clear which graves Juspa had in mind.

41. Ibid., 2:267–68.

42. Ibid., 1: no. 98. See also Kirchheim, *Minhagot Vermaiza: Minhagim vehanhagot*, 253, and Eric Zimmer, "Gezerot tatnu be-sifre ha-manhigim be-yeme benayim we-be-'et hadasha: Yezirah we-hitpashtut shel teksey ha-'avalut," in *Yom Tov Assis et al., eds., *Yehudim mul ha-zelav: Gezerot 856 ba-historyah uva-historyografiah* (Jerusalem: Y. L. Magnes, 2000), 158.

43. *Sefer Ma'aseh Nissim*, Amsterdam, 1696; Frankfurt, 1702; Amsterdam, 1723; Homberg, 1725; Fürth, 1767; Offenbach, 1777; and Fürth, 1788.

44. His story about the martyrdom of the community is similar to an account of a persecution in an unknown city provided by Shlomo ibn Verga in his *Shevet Yehuda*, ed. A. Shohat with an introduction by Y. Beer (Jerusalem: Mosad Bialik, 1947), 91.

45. Eidelberg, *R. Juspa, Shammash of Warmaisa (Worms)*, 59, 60, 80 (Hebrew) and 53, 54, 82 (English).

46. Ibid., 59 (Hebrew) and 53 (English).

47. Ibid., 76 (Hebrew) and 78 (English).

48. See Eli Yassif, *The Hebrew Folktale: History, Genre, Meaning*, trans. Jacqueline S. Teitelbaum (Bloomington: Indiana University Press, 1999), 298. For discussions of the current scholarship on the *Maysebukh*, see Erika Timm, "Zur Frühgeschichte der jiddischen Erzählprosa. Eine neu aufgefundene Maise-Handschrift," *Beiträge zur Geschichte der deutschen Sprache und Literatur* 117 (1995): 243–80, and Sarah Zfatman, "Ma'ase bukh—kavim lidmuto shel zanr be-sifrut yidish ha-yeshana, im giluyo shel Ma'ase bukh ketav yad Jerushalayim Heb. 8° 5245," *Ha-Sifrut* 28 (1979): 126–52.

49. Joseph Dan, "Le-toldoteha shel 'sifrut ha-shvahim," *Mehkere yerushalaim be-folklor yehudi* 1 (1981): 82–101; Joseph Dan, "Sifrut ha-shvahim mizrah u-ma'arav," *Pe'amim* 26 (1986): 77–86; Ada Rapoport-Albert, "Hagiography with Footnotes: Edifying Tales and the Writing of History in Hasidism," *History and Theory* 27 (Dec. 1988): 119–59; and Lucia Raspe, *Jüdische Hagiographie im mittelalterlichen Aschkenas* (Tübingen: Mohr Siebeck, 2006), 26–58.

50. Eidelberg, *R. Juspa, Shammash of Warmaisa (Worms)*, 70 (Hebrew) and 70 (English).

51. *Maysebukh* (Basel, 1602), 183; Gedaliah Ibn Yahia, *Shalshelet ha-kabbalah* (Yerushalayim: Hotsa'at ha-dorot ha-rishonim ve-korotom, 1962), 112–13; A. Epstein, "Die nach Raschi benannten Gebäude in Worms," *MGWJ* 45 (1901): 52–58; Raspe, *Jüdische Hagiographie im mittelalterlichen Aschkenas*, 199–241.

52. *Maysebuch* (Roedelheim, 1753), folio 55a–b. See also the English transla-

tion, which is based on the Amsterdam edition of 1723: Moses Gaster, ed., *Ma'aseh Book: Book of Jewish Tales and Legends* (Philadelphia: Jewish Publication Society of America, 1981), 396–400. In this form the story also entered the *Alerlei geshihte* (Amsterdam, 1723), no. 184, as Epstein has already noted; see Epstein, "Die nach Raschi benannten Gebäude in Worms," 55–58.

53. Eidelberg, *R. Juspa, Shammash of Warmaisa (Worms)*, 66 (Hebrew) and 64–65 (English). Judah Lewi Kirchheim had quoted the original story verbatim from Rokeah; see 26 (Hebrew) and 91 (English).

54. Ibid., 78–81 (Hebrew) and 80–82 (English).

55. Ibid., 74–76 (Hebrew) and 76–78 (English); Israel Yuval, "'They Tell Lies: You Ate the Man': Jewish Reactions to Ritual Murder Accusations," in *Religious Violence between Christian and Jews: Medieval Roots, Modern Perspectives*, ed. Anna Sapir Abulafia (Basingstoke: Palgrave, 2002), 87.

56. Kirchheim, *Minhagot Vermaiza: Minhagim ve-hanhagot*, 254. See Raspe, "The Black Death in Jewish Sources," 485, who suggests this possibility.

57. Shlomo Eidelberg, "The Jews of Worms during the French Conquest (1688–1697)," in Shlomo Eidelberg, ed., *Medieval Ashkenazic History: Studies on German Jewry in the Middle Ages* (Brooklyn: Sepher-Hermon Press, 1999), 155–77, and Samson Rothschild, "Die jüdische Gemeinde von Worms während der Zerstörung der Stadt Worms durch die Franzosen (1689)," *Blaetter für Jüdische Geschichte und Litteratur* 3 (1902): 65–71.

58. Reuter, *Warmaisa*, 122, and Kaufmann, *R. Jair Chajjim Bacharach (1638–1702) und seine Ahnen*, 72–81.

59. Kaufmann, *R. Jair Chajjim Bacharach (1638–1702) und Seine Ahnen*, 73–75.

60. Fritz Reuter, ed., *Peter und Johann Friedrich Hammann. Handzeichnungen von Worms aus der Zeit vor und nach der Stadtzerstörung 1689 im 'Pfälzischen Erbfolgekrieg'* (Worms: Bressler, 1989), 18. For non-Jewish descriptions, see Johann Jacob Schudt, *Jüdische Merkwürdigkeiten Vorstellende was sich Curieuses und denckwürdiges in den neuern Zeiten bey einigen Jahr-hunderten mit denen in alle IV. Theile der Welt / sonderlich durch Teutschland / zerstreuten Juden zugetragen. Sammt einer vollständigen Frankfurter Juden-Chronik / Darinnen der zu Franckfurt am Mayn wohnenden Juden / von eingen Jahr-hunderten / bis auff unsere Zeiten merckwürdigste Begebenheiten enthaltend*, 4 vols. (Frankfurt: S. T. Hocker, 1714–18), 4:420–22. For a non-Jewish elegy, see Friedrich Soldan, *Die Zerstörung der Stadt Worms im Jahre 1689. Im Auftrage der Stadt Worms dargestellt* (Worms: Julius Stern, 1889), 55–58; Oscar Canstatt, *Drangsale der Stadt Worms und deren Zerstörung durch die Franzosen am 31. Mai 1689. Zum 200 jährigen Gedenktage* (Worms: Eugen Kranzbühler, 1889); and Johann Jacob Zoller, *Kurtze Beschreibung seines Wandels und vornehmster Begebenheiten / So er Nach Einäscherung seiner Geburtsstadt Wormbs Anno 1689 biß daher in seinem Exilio gehabt: Und denn darauf Eine kurtze und einfältige Verantwortung auf das / was ihn Herr D. Samuel Schelwig / Pastor und Rector zu Dantzig / in seinem so genannten Itinerario Antipietistico beschuldigt* (Halle, 1696).

61. Yair Hayyim ben Moses Samson Bacharach, *Havot Ya'ir*, introduction and 134, Bar-Ilan, Responsa Project, Version 8.0.

62. David Oppenheim, *Nishal David*, 3 vols. (Jerusalem: Mekon Hatam Sofer, 1972–81), 2:197.

63. Jacob Shatsky, "Das kloglied oif dem hurban fun Worms," *Filologische Shriften* (Vilna, 1929), 3: 49–55.

64. Kaufmann, R. *Jair Chajjim Bacharach (1638–1702) und seine Ahnen*, 74–75, and Berthold Rosenthal, "Das 'Grüne Buch' in Worms," Leo Baeck Institute, New York, AR C.222, 225a.

65. Yair Hayyim ben Moses Samson Bacharach, Havot Ya'ir, 126, Bar-Ilan, Responsa Project, Version 8.0.

66. "Zur Geschichte der Juden in Worms," *Blaetter für jüdische Geschichte und Litterature* 2 (1900): 71–72. Juspa's other son, Eliezer, still referred to himself in 1710 as an expellee of Worms. See Moritz Steinschneider, *Catalogus librorum Hebraeorum in Bibliotheca Bodleiana* (Berlin: A. Friedlaender, 1852–60), no. 8070.

67. August Weckerling, "Verzeichnis der durch den Stadtbrand 1689 zerstörten Häuser," *Vom Rhein* 12 (1913): 57–61 and 66–76, here 71.

68. Epstein, "Die nach Raschi benannten Gebäude in Worms," 59; "Zur Geschichte der Juden in Worms," *Blaetter für jüdische Geschichte und Litterature* 2 (1900): 63; and Berthold Rosenthal, *Heimatgeschichte der badischen Juden seit ihrem geschichtlichen Auftreten bis zur Gegenwart* (Bühl-Baden: Konkordia A. G., 1927), 151.

69. Shatsky, "Das Kloglied oif dem Hurban fun Worms," 53. About these negotiations, see Reuter, *Warmaisa*, 124–28.

70. Gerhard W. Mühlinghaus, "Der Synagogenbau des 17. und 18. Jahrhunderts," in Hans-Peter Schwarz, ed., *Die Architektur der Synagoge* (Frankfurt am Main: Klett-Cotta, 1988), 131, and Otto Böcher, *Die Alte Synagoge zu Worms* (Worms: Verlag Stadtbibliothek Worms, 1960), 77–78.

71. Berliner, "Sefer Haskarat neshamot," 22 and 21, and M. Horovitz, *Die Inschriften des alten Friedhofs der israelitischen Gemeinde zu Frankfurt a. M.*, 4 vols. (Frankfurt J. Kauffmann, 1901), 2:136.

72. Berliner, "Sefer Haskarat neshamot," 22, and Lewysohn, *Nefashot Zadikim*, no. 38.

73. Bernhard Wachstein, *Die Inschriften des alten Judenfriedhofs in Wien. Im Auftrage der historischen Kommission der israelitischen Kultusgemeinde in Wien*, 2 vols. (Vienna: Wilhelm Braumüller, 1917), 2: no. 860, 280. For his generosity, the Worms *Memorbuch* extolled his accomplishments and named and blessed him and his wife. See Berliner, "Sefer Haskarat neshamot," 40–41.

74. Epstein, "Die nach Raschi benannten Gebäude in Worms," 60, and Siegmund Salfeld, *Das Martyrologium des Nürnberger Memorbüches* (Berlin: Leonhard Simion, 1898), xxxvi and xxxviii.

75. Yair Hayyim ben Moses Samson Bacharach, *Havot Ya'ir*, introduction and 134, Bar-Ilan, Responsa Project, Version 8.0.

76. Otto Böcher, "Die Alte Synagoge zu Worms, mit 79 Abb.," in Roth, *Festschrift zur Wiedereinweihung der Alten Synagoge zu Worms*, 86–87.

77. Adolf Kober, "Die deutschen Kaiser und die Wormser Juden," *ZGJD* 5 (1935): 144.

3. CHRISTIAN INTERLOCUTORS AND JEWISH MEMORY

1. Paul Hazard, *The European Mind, 1680–1715* (Cleveland: World Publishing Company, 1952), 3–28.

2. Jürgen Osterhammel, *Die Entzauberung Asiens. Europa und die asiatischen Reiche im 18. Jahrhundert* (Munich: C. H. Beck, 1998).

3. Adolf Kober, "Die deutschen Kaiser und die Wormser Juden," *ZGJD* 5 (1935): 146, and Stephan Wendehorst, "Imperial Spaces as Jewish Spaces: The Holy Roman Empire, the Emperor, and the Jews in the Early Modern Period; Some Preliminary Observations," *Jahrbuch des Simon-Dubnow-Instituts / Simon Dubnow Institute Yearbook* 2 (2003): 454 and 466.

4. Samson Rothschild, *Aus Vergangenheit und Gegenwart der Israel. Gemeinde Worms*, 5th ed. (Frankfurt am Main: J. Kauffmann, 1913), 23.

5. Max Grunwald, "Le Cimetière de Worms," *REJ NS* 4 (1938): 97.

6. *Epithaphien von Grabsteinen des alten israel. Friedhofs in Worms—entziffert und ins Deutsche übersetzt von Prof. David Kaufmann in Budapest in den Jahren 1892–1897 nach dem ihm von dem Vorstandsmitglied Julius Goldschmidt gelieferten Abklatschen*, nos. 421, 358, and 360.

7. Ernst Roth, "Das Wormser Mahzor," in Ernst Roth, Georg Illert, and Hans Lamm, eds., *Festschrift zur Wiedereinweihung der Alten Synagoge zu Worms* (Frankfurt am Main: Ner Tamid, 1961), 218–21.

8. Böcher, "Die Alte Synagoge zu Worms, mit 79 Abb.," 77, 84–85, and Annette Weber, "Das Museum der israelitischen Gemeinde in der Alten Synagoge zu Worms," *Aschkenas* 12 (2002): 57–59.

9. See the title page of *Ma'aravot yotzrot ve-zulatot u-selihot 'im pesuke we-manhigim de-k.k. Vermisa* (Frankfurt am Main: Johanan Koelner, 1714).

10. *Ma'aravot yotzrot ve-zulatot u-selihot 'im pesuke ve-manhigim de-k.k. Vermisa* and *Seder selihot 'im pesukim ve-ma'aravot ve-yotzrot ve-sulat ve-yom kipur katan a.p. seder ve-minhag k"k Virmeisa* (Sulzbach: Meshalem Salman, 1737); this edition was written by the community leader Aharon ha-Levi.

11. For the routes and attractions in Germany, see Malcolm Letts, "Germany and the Rhine," in R. S. Lambert, ed., *Grand Tour: A Journey in the Tracks of the Age of Aristocracy* (London: Faber and Faber Limited, 1935), 119–36, and Jeremy Black, *The British Abroad: The Grand Tour in the Eighteenth Century* (New York: St. Martin's Press, 1992), 60–61.

12. Gilbert Burnet, *Some Letters Containing an Account of What Seemed Most Remarkable in Traveling through Switzerland, Italy, and Germany: Three Letters Concerning the Present State of Italy, &c. in the years 1685 and 1686* (London: J. Robinson and A. Churchil, 1689), 295.

13. Fynes Moryson, *An Itinerary Containing His Ten Yeeres Travell through the Twelve Dominions of Germany, Bohmerland, Switzerland, Netherland, Denmarke, Poland, Italy, Turkey, France, England, Scotland & Ireland* (1617), 4 vols. (Glasgow: James MacLehose and Sons, 1907), 1:69.

14. Misson's book appeared initially in French in 1691, in English in 1695, and in German in 1701. For his description of Worms and its Jewish history, see the English edition, titled *A New Voyage to Italy: With Curious Observation on Several*

Other Countries; As Germany, Switzerland, Savoy, Geneva, Flanders, and Holland; To-gether, With Useful Instructions for Those Who Shall Travel Thither, 4 vols. (London: Printed for R. Bonwicke et al., 1714), 2:100–106.

15. Josef Giesen, "Thomas Coryats Eindrücke von Worms im Jahre 1608," *Der Wormsgau* 2 (1934/1943): 41–48; Fritz Arens, "Alte Reiseberichte über Worms. Worms im Jahre 1660," *Der Wormsgau* 2 (1934/1943): 145–50; Josef Giesen, "Französischer Besuch in Worms im Jahre 1664," *Der Wormsgau* 2 (1934/1943): 151–52; and Josef Giesen, "Alte Reiseberichte über Worms, Frankenthal und Oppenheim," *Der Wormsgau* 2 (1934/1943): 273–74. For references to Jews in early modern travelogues, see Black, *The British Abroad*, 247–49.

16. Israel Zinberg, *A History of Jewish Literature*, trans. Bernard Martin, 12 vols. (New York: Ktav Publishing, 1975), 7:235–40, and Jean Baumgarten, "Testimonia: Jerusalem in Seventeenth-Century Travellers' Accounts in Yiddish," *Mediterranean Historical Review* 7 (1992): 219–26.

17. Compare Menahem ben Judah de Lonzano, *Sefer or torah* (Hamburg, 1738), 2b and 27a, with Juspa Shammes, *Minhagim di-k.k. Vermaisa le-Rabi Yuzpa Shamash*, 1:59–60, fn. 9.

18. Shlomo Berger, *Travels among Jews and Gentiles: Abraham Levie's Travelogue, Amsterdam, 1764; Edition of the Text with Introduction and Commentary* (Leiden: Brill, 2002), 65.

19. See Benjamin Cymerman, ed., *The Diaries of Rabbi Ha'im Yosef David Azulai ('Ma'gal Tov'—the Good Journey)* (Jerusalem: Bnei Issakhar Institute, 1997), 85–86.

20. See the entry on Shimon bar Yitzhak in Hayyim Joseph Azulai, *Shem ha-gedolim* (Vilna: Y. R. Rom, 1853).

21. Joseph Schatzmiller, "Jews, Pilgrimage, and the Christian Cult of Saints: Benjamin of Tudela and His Contemporaries," in Alexander Callander Murray, ed., *After Rome's Fall: Narrators and Sources of Early Medieval History; Essays Presented to Walter Goffart* (Toronto: University of Toronto Press, 1998), 337–47.

22. Jacob Rader Marcus, in his *Communal Sick-Care in the German Ghetto* (Cincinnati: Hebrew Union College Press, 1947), 228, posits that more than forty editions of these works appeared in Hebrew and Yiddish before 1800. On the medieval and early modern debate about visiting the graves of sages and other dignitaries, see Shoham-Steiner, " 'For a Prayer in That Place Would Be Most Welcome': Jews, Holy Shrines, and Miracles—A New Approach."

23. Joel ben Samuel Sirkes, *Bayit hadash on Tur Yoreh De'ah*, no. 217.

24. Herman Pollack, *Jewish Folkways in Germanic Lands (1648–1806)* (Cambridge, Mass.: MIT Press, 1971), 48.

25. Simeon Frankfurt, *Sefer ha-hayyim* (Amsterdam, 1715), 128–29; see also Chava Weissler, *Voices of the Matriarchs: Listening to the Prayers of Early Modern Jewish Women* (Boston: Beacon Press, 1998), 140–43.

26. R. Joseph ben Moses, *Sefer leket yosher*, 2:25a, Bar-Ilan, Responsa Project, Version 8.0.

27. Solomon ben Jechiel Luria, *She'ulot u-tshuvot*, 29, Bar-Ilan, Responsa Project, Version 8.0.

28. Eidelberg, *R. Juspa, Shammash of Warmaisa*, 80–81 (Hebrew) and 82 (English).

29. David Kaufmann, "Die Grabsteine R. Meir's von Rothenburg und Alexander Wimpfen's in Worms," *MGWJ* 40 (1895): 127.

30. Kaufmann, "Der Grabstein des R. Jakob b. Mose ha-Levi (Maharil) in Worms Breslau," 229, and Otto Böcher, *Die Alte Synagoge zu Worms* (Worms: Verlag Stadtbibliothek Worms, 1960), 112–13.

31. Misson, *A New Voyage to Italy*, 2:103.

32. Weber, "Das Museum der israelitischen Gemeinde in der Alten Synagoge zu Worms," 62–63.

33. A. Epstein, "Jüdische Alterthümer in Worms und Speir," *MGWJ* 40 (1895): 512, and Annette Weber, "Katalog der Kultgegenstände aus dem Museum der israelitischen Gemeinde Worms anhand der Angaben und Fotos von Isidor Kiefer," *Aschkenas* 12 (2002): 83.

34. See Otto Böcher, "Ein barocker Wormser Toradeuter und seine Mannheimer Stifterin," *Wormsgau* 7 (1965–66): 66, and Böcher, "Varia zu Bau und Ausstattung der Wormser Synagogue," *Wormsgau* 10 (1972–73): 59–61.

35. James Beck, "The Anabaptists and the Jews: The Case of Hätzer, Denck, and the 'Worms Prophets,'" *Mennonite Quarterly Review* 75 (2001): 407–27.

36. For general background, see Elisheva Carlebach, *Divided Souls: Converts from Judaism in Germany, 1500–1750* (New Haven: Yale University Press, 2001).

37. Johannes Jacob Huldreich, *Toledoth Yeshu* (Leyden, 1705), 790. Huldrich's manuscript of *Toldot Jeshu* was identical to the text used by the convert Brentz and the Christian Hebraist Johann Jakob Schudt. See Samuel Krauss, *Das Leben Jesu nach jüdischen Quellen* (Berlin: S. Calvary and Co., 1902), 33–34.

38. See Salo Wittmayer Baron, *A Social and Religious History of the Jews*, 18 vols. (New York: Columbia University Press, 1958–83), 8:194–95, and František Graus, "Historische Traditionen über Juden im Spätmittelalter (Mitteleuropa)," in Alfred Haverkamp, ed., *Zur Geschichte der Juden in Deutschland des späten Mittelalters und der frühen Neuzeit* (Stuttgart: Anton Hiersemann, 1981), 1–26.

39. *Die Chroniken der oberrheinischen Staedte: Strassburg*, 2 vols. (Leipzig: Salomon Hirzel, 1871), 2:758, and Ilse Haari-Oberg, *Die Wirkungsgeschichte der Trierer Gründungssage vom 10. bis 15. Jahrhundert* (Bern: Lang, 1994).

40. Gerold Bönnen, "Wormser Stadtmythen im Spiegel spätmittelalterlicher Ueberlieferungen," *Stadt in der Geschichte* 28 (2003): 9–28.

41. See Heinrich Boos, *Monumenta Wormatiensia—Annalen und Chroniken* (Berlin: Weidmann, 1893), 5.

42. See Bernhard Walde, *Christliche Hebraisten Deutschlands am Ausgang des Mittelalters* (Münster: Aschedorffsche Verlagsbuchhandlung, 1916), 560–65.

43. Shammes, *Minhagim di-k.k. Vermaisa*, 1: no. 7 and 2:243.

44. Eidelberg, *R. Juspa, Shammash of Warmaisa (Worms)*, 60–61 (Hebrew section) and 54–56 (English).

45. Gedaliah Ibn Yahia, *Shalshelet ha-kabalah* (Jerusalem: Hotsa'at ha-dorot ha-rishonim ve-korotam, 1962), 112–13 and 123.

46. Samuel Friedrich Brentz, "Jüdischer abgestreiffter Schlangen-Balg," in *The-*

riaca Judaica Ad Examen Revocata, Sive Scripta Amoibaea Samuelis Friderici Brenzii, Conversi Judaei, & Salomonis Zevi, Apellae astutissimi, a Viris Doctis hucusque desiderata = Jüdischer abgestreiffter Schlangen-Balg | nunc primum Versione Latina, Justisque Animadversionibus aucta & in publicum missa studio Johannes Wülferi (Nuremberg: Knorz, 1681), 3–4.

47. R. Salomon Zevi, *Yudisher Theriac* (Hannover, 1615), 10–11.

48. Martin Diefenbach, *Judaeus Conversus, Oder: Umständliche und glaubhafte Erzehlung | was sich vormahls mit einem allhier im Hospital Dieb-Stahls halben | gefänglich gesesse n| und auff sein instendiges Begehren im Christenthumb wohl unterwiesene n| darauf gehörig getaufften und so nochmals am Hoch-Gericht in Glauben an CHR Jesum selig Bekehrten Juden begeben. Sammt fernen Erläuterungen und weitlaufftigen Ausführungen des von Ihm allbereit Anno 1696 herauß gegebenen Judaei Convertendi. Zu Endt findet sich: Die Nachricht wegen des vor 5. Jahren allhier geschehenen Tauffe | Asel zum Hinter-Hecht | hiesigen seshaften Juden Sohns | nochmals Johann Zacharias Heylwart genanndt | und der mit Ihm seithero vorgefallenen bedencklichen Begebenheiten. Mit Zweyen dahin gehörigen Juden-Predigten | und behorigen Register,* 2nd ed. (Frankfurt am Main: Knoch, 1709), 282–83.

49. Diefenbach, *Judaeus Conversus,* 282.

50. Ibid., 288–89.

51. Caesarius of Heisterbach, *The Dialogue on Miracles,* trans. H. von E. Scott and C. C. Swinton Bland, 2 vols. (London: Routledge and Sons, 1929), 2:24. See also Ivan G. Marcus, "Images of the Jews in the *Exempla* of Caesarius of Heisterbach," in Jeremy Cohen, ed., *From Witness to Witchcraft: Jews and Judaism in Medieval Christian Thought* (Wiesbaden: Harrassowitz Verlag, 1996), 247–56, and Joseph Dan, "Rabbi Judah the Pious and Caesarius of Heisterbach: Common Motifs in Their Stories," *Scripta Hierosolymitana* 22 (1971): 18–27.

52. Eidelberg, *R. Juspa, Shammash of Warmaisa (Worms),* 58–60 (English) and 62–63 (Hebrew).

53. Johann Andreas Eisenmenger, *Entdecktes Judenthum,* 2 vols. (Königsberg, 1700), 2:664–66.

54. For the prominence of Jewish female martyrs, see Avraham Grossman, *Pious and Rebellious: Jewish Women in Medieval Europe,* trans. Jonathan Chipman (Hanover, N.H.: University Press of New England, 2004), 199–211. For the medieval Christian sources, see Mary Minty, "Kidush ha-shem be-eney nozrim begermania be-yeme ha-benayim," *Zion* 59 (1994): 209–66.

55. Johann Jacob Schudt, *Jüdische Merkwürdigkeiten Vorstellende was sich Curieuses und denckwürdiges in den neuern Zeiten bey einigen Jahr-hunderten mit denen in alle IV. Theile der Welt | sonderlich durch Teutschland | zerstreuten Juden zugetragen. Sammt einer vollständigen Frankfurter Juden-Chronik | Darinnen der zu Franckfurt am Mayn wohnenden Juden | von eingen Jahr-hunderten | bis auff unsere Zeiten merckwürdigste Begebenheiten enthaltend,* 4 vols. (Frankfurt: S. T. Hocker, 1714–18), 3:411–14.

56. Eidelberg, *R. Juspa, Shammash of Warmaisa (Worms),* 89–90 (English) and 86–87 (Hebrew).

57. Diefenbach, *Judaeus Conversus,* 284.

58. Johann Christoph Wagenseil, *Belehrung der Juedisch-Teutschen Red- und Schreibart* (Königsberg, 1699), 5.

59. Gerold Bönnen, "Jüdische Gemeinde und christlichen Stadtgemeinde," in Christoph Cluse, Alfred Haverkamp, and Israel J. Yuval, eds., *Jüdische Gemeinden und ihr christlicher Kontext in kulturräumlich vergleichender Betrachtung von der Spätantike bis zum 18. Jahrhundert* (Hannover: Hahn, 2003), 326.

60. Moritz Stern, "Ein Copialbuch der jüdischen Gemeinde zu Worms," *ZGJD* 1 (1886): 279.

61. Samson Rothschild, "Eine Eingabe der Wormser Judenschaft an die Vertreter der Allerchristlichsten Majestät des Königs aus dem Jahre 1646," *Blaetter für Jüdische Geschichte und Litteratur* 5 (1904): 30–31.

62. Johann-Georg Kern, *Kurtzer und bewehrter Außzug An alle Geistliche un[d] Weltliche | hohe und niderstandes Personen | von der Welt unerhörte | beydes freudige und erschröckliche Zeitung | alles dessen | so in deß Heyligen Reichs Freystat Wormbs | gemeine Bürgerschafft daselbsten | mit den darin wohnenden Juden sich deroselben rechtmesig zuerledigen | in Anno 1613. fürgangen. in welchem dero Bürger Bitt und Beschwerung für Augen gestelt | auch die geschwinde Practicen der Juden | sampt deroselben zugethanen und verwandten etlicher massen entdeckt | und dann Ihrer Käys. Mayest. unterschidene ernstmesig ergangene Befehl wegen der Juden | wie auch der Bürgerschafft theils habenden Privilegiis. Freyen Judenschanckung. Item. In der Käys. Cammer von der Bürgerschafft wider sie Jüden außbrachten Mandatis: Außschaffung der Jüden. Einnehmung der Stadt Wormbs. Sampt Ihrer Käys. Mayest. uber etzliche zwey Jähriger gefangener Bürger Execution | und verfolgung wegen der Jüden: durch die hochansehnlichsten Herrn Ihrer Churfürstl. Gn. Pfaltzgraff Friderichen den V. und Ihre Fürstl. Gn. Bischoff zu Speyer | verordnete Käys. Com[m]issarien | in grosser anzahl Volcks | mit verschwerung deß gantzen Römischen Reichs | den 26. Martii | Im Jahr 1617. wircklich vollzogen | Zur Warnung | und künfftigen nachrichtung . . . In offnen Druck verfertigt* (1617), Eii, recto.

63. Schudt, *Jüdische Merkwürdigkeiten*, 3:397.

64. Ibid., 3:329.

65. Ibid., 3:329 and 398.

66. Ibid., 3:397.

67. Ibid., 3:400–403.

68. Misson, *A New Voyage to Italy*, 2:101–2 and 10–106.

69. Jacques Basnage, *The History of the Jews, from Jesus Christ to the Present Time: Containing Their Antiquities, Their Religion, Their Rites, the Dispersion of the Ten Tribes in the East, and the Persecutions This Nation Has Suffer'd in the West. Being a Supplement and Continuation of the History of Josephus*, trans. Tho. Taylor (London: Printed for J. Beaver and B. Lintot, R. Knaplock, J. Sprint, A. Bell, R. Smith, and J. Round, 1708), 505.

70. Ludvig Holberg, *Jüdische Geschichte von Erschaffung der Welt bis auf gegenwärtige Zeiten*, trans. Georg August Detharding (Altona: Korte, 1747), 3:329–30, 397, 399–401, and 417–20.

71. Johann Hermann Dielhelm, *Denkwürdiger und nützlicher Rheinischer Antiquarius, welcher die wichtigsten und angenehmsten geograph-, histor- und politischen*

Merkwürdigkeiten des ganzen Rheinstroms von seinem Ursprunge an, samt allen seinen Zuflüssen, bis er sich endlich nach und nach wieder verlieret, darstellet. Zum Nutzen der Reisenden und anderer Liebhaber sehenswürdiger Sachen, so man an jedem an demselben gelonen Ort als etwas rares zu bemerken und was sich bis in das Jahr 1743 damit zugetragen hat, gesammlet, und Nebst einer kurzen Beschreibung der vornehmsten Städte in Holland, mit einigen Anm., wie auch genauen Landkarten, dazu gehörigen Kupfern und Registern versehen (Frankfurt am Main: Stoks und Schilling, 1744), 3, 481–82, and 493–95. The guide initially appeared in 1739 and was republished again in 1776.

72. Johann Friedrich Moritz, *Historisch-Diplomatische Abhandlung vom Ursprung derer Reichs-Stätte von der allezeit unmittelbaren und weder unter Herzöglich- und Gräflich- noch unter Bischöflichen-weltlicher Jurisdiction jemahls gestandenen Freyen Reichs-Statt Worms deren offenbaren Irrthümern und Zudringlichkeiten des Schannats in seiner Bischöflichen-Wormsischen Historie entgegen gestellet* (Frankfurt, 1756), 71; Zorn-Wilksche Chronik, Stadtarchiv Worms 1b, 687; and Otto Böcher, "Ein jüdischer Grabstein aus vor christlicher Zeit in Worms," *Wormsgau* 3 (1951–58): 412–13.

73. Moritz, *Historisch-Diplomatische Abhandlung vom Ursprung derer Reichs-Stätte*, 71–75, and Johanne Friderico Schannat, *Historia Episcopatus Wormatiensis, Pontificum Romanorum Bullis, Regum, Imperatorum Diplomatibus, Episcoporum AC Principum Chaartis, Aliisque Pluribus Documentis Athenticis Asserta ac Illustrata* (Frankfurt am Main: Franciscum Varrentrapp, 1737), 204.

74. Menahem Mann ben Salomon Amelander, *Sefer she'erit yisra'el* (Amsterdam, 1743), 2–3, 48b, 93b and 96. See Leo and Rena Fuks, "Jewish Historiography in the Netherlands," Saul Lieberman, ed., *Salo Wittmayer Baron Jubilee Volume on the Occasion of his Eightieth Birthday*, 3 vols. (New York: Columbia University Press, 1975), 1: 432–466, here 453–456 and R. G. Fuks-Mansfeld, "Yiddish Historiography in the Time of the Dutch Republic," *Studia Rosenthaliana* 15 (1981): 9–19, esp. 13–15.

75. *Sefer Ma'ase nissim* (Fuerth: Itzig ben Loeb, 1767), cover page.

76. Ibid., introduction.

77. Ibid., 65.

78. In his *Seder ha-dorot* (Karlsruhe, 1769), Heilperin describes the community as arrogant in his entry for the year 1620 due to the prosperity they enjoyed.

79. See Abraham M. Tendlau, *Sprichwörter und Redensarten deutsch-jüdischer Vorzeit. Ein Beitrag zur Volks-, Sprach- und Sprichwörter- Kunde. Aufgezeichnet aus dem Munde des Volkes und nach Wort und Sinn erläutert* (Frankfurt am Main: J. Kauffmann, 1860), 347.

80. G. W. Böhmer, "Ludwig der Große, Mordbrenner in Worms, im J. 1689," *Stats-Anzeigen* 1 (1789): 367–77.

81. Oscar Canstatt, *Drangsale der Stadt Worms und deren Zerstörung durch die Franzosen am 31. Mai 1689: Zum 200 jährigen Gedenktage* (Worms: Eugen Kranzbühler, 1889), 186–87, and Samson Rothschild, "Samuel Levi. Ein Wormser Rabbiner aus der zweiten Hälfte des 18. Jahrhunderts. Mitglied des Pariser Sanhedrin," *Vom Rhein* 12 (1913): 21.

82. See Berthold Rosenthal, "Die letzten Wormser Judenbischöfe," *MGWJ* 83 (1939): 313–24.

83. A. Kober, "Die deutschen Kaiser und die Wormser Juden," *ZGJD* 5 (1935): 148; Samson Rothschild, "Samuel Levi. Ein Wormser Rabbiner," 15–16 and 21–22; and "Provinzialrabbiner Dr. Levi," *AZJ* 63 (1899): 172–74.

84. Isaac Abraham Euchel, *Gebete der hochdeutschen und polnischen Juden aus dem hebräischen übersetzt und mit Anmerkungen begleitet* (Königsberg, 1786), 440, note 44.

85. Jews from Worms do not appear in any of the subscription lists to the major maskilic publications, such as their bible translations or journal. See Steven M. Lowenstein, "The Readership of the Bible Translation," *HUCA* 103 (1982): 179–213.

86. William Beckford, *Dreams, Waking Thoughts and Incidents; in a Series of Letters from Various Parts of Europe* (London: J. Johnson and P. Elmsly, 1783), 47 and 54; Ann Radcliffe, *A Journey Made in the Summer of 1794, through Holland and the Western Frontier of Germany, with a Return down the Rhine, to Which Are Added Observations during a Tour to the Lakes of Lancashire, Westmoreland and Cumberland* (London, 1794), 238–41. In general on the perception of the Rhineland in the eighteenth century, see Irene Haberland, "Auf der Suche nach der pittoresken Schönheit. Englische Künstler am Rhein im 19. Jahrhundert," in Klaus Honnef et al., eds., *Vom Zauber des Rheins ergriffen. Zur Entdeckung der Rheinlandschaft* (Munich: Klinkhardt and Biermann, 1992), 41–66, and Gertrude Cepl-Kaufmann and Antje Johanning, *Mythos Rhein. Zur Kulturgeschichte eines Stromes* (Darmstadt: Wissenschaftliche Buchgesellschaft, 2003), 99–152.

87. Eoin Bourke, "The Frankfurt Judengasse in Eyewitness Accounts from the Seventeenth to the Nineteenth Century," in Anne Fuchs and Florian Krobb, eds., *Ghetto Writing: Traditional and Eastern Jewry in German-Jewish Literature from Heine to Hilsenrath* (Rochester: Cambden House, 1999), 11–24.

88. On the Romantics' perception of Jews and Judaism, see Alfred D. Low, *Jews in the Eyes of the Germans: From Germany to Imperial Germany* (Philadelphia: Ishi, 1979), 206–14.

89. Philip V. Bohlman and Otto Holzapfel, eds., *The Folksongs of Ashkenaz* (Wisconsin: A-R Editions, 2001), 15–23.

90. Samson Rothschild, *Emancipations-Bestrebungen der juedischen Grossgemeinden des Grossherzogthums Hessen im vorigen Jahrhundert. Auf Grund von Protokollen und Akten des Archivs der jued. Gemeinde zu Worms* (Worms am Rhein: Julius Mannheimer, 1924).

4. RESTORING THE LOST MEMORY

1. See Richard Cohen, *Jewish Icons: Art and Society in Modern Europe* (Berkeley: University of California Press, 1998), 154–85, and Peter Fritzsche, "How Nostalgia Narrates Modernity," in Alon Confino and Peter Fritzsche, eds., *The Work of Memory: New Directions in the Study of German Society and Culture* (Urbana: University of Illinois Press, 2002), 62–85.

2. Rahel Varnhagen to Ludwig Robert, February 5, 1816, in *Rahel Varnhagen*

234

Notes to Pages 64–71

und ihre Zeit (Briefe 1800–1833), ed. Friedhelm Kemp, 4 vols. (Munich: Kösel, 1968), 4:101.

3. Fritz Reuter, *Worms ehemals, gestern und heute. Ein Stadtbild im Wandel der letzten 100 Jahre*, 2nd ed. (Stuttgart: J. F. Steinkopf Verlag, 1988), 13.

4. Heinrich Laube, *Reisenovellen* (1837), ed. Alfred Estermann, 6 vols. (Frankfurt am Main: Athenäum, 1973), 6:223.

5. John Murray, *A Hand-Book for Travellers on the Continent: Being a Guide through Holland, Belgium, Prussia, and Northern Germany, and Along the Rhine, from Holland to Switzerland: Containing Description of the Principal Cities, Their Museums, Picture Galleries etc., the Great High Roads and the Most Interesting and Picturesque Districts, also Directions for Travelers, and Hints for Tours, with an Index Map* (London: John Murray and Son, 1836), 416.

6. Victor Hugo, *Le Rhin* (Strasbourg: Bueb et Reumaux, 1980), 316–17.

7. *Epithaphien von Grabsteinen des alten israel. Friedhofs in Worms—entziffert und ins Deutsche übersetzt von Prof. David Kaufmann in Budapest in den Jahren 1892–1897 nach dem ihm von den Vorstandmitgliede Julius Goldschmidt gelieferten Abklatschen*, 2 vols. (1901), Stadtarchiv Worms, Judaica, 203: 3, no. 1083.

8. Talmud Bavli, Rosh ha-shana, 18b, and Benjamin Auerbach, *Nahal Eshkol*, 2 vols. (Halberstadt: H. Meyer, 1865–67), 2:16.

9. See Moses Mannheimer, *Die Juden in Worms, ein Beitrag zur Geschichte der Juden in den Rheingegenden* (Frankfurt am Main: J. S. Adler, 1842), 19.

10. Reuter, *Warmaisa*, 148–54.

11. Monika Richarz, *Jewish Life in Germany: Memoirs of Three Centuries*, trans. Stella P. Rosenfeld and Sidney Rosenfeld (Bloomington: Indiana University Press, 1991), 250.

12. Fritz Reuter, "Politisches und gesellschaftliches Engagement von Wormser Juden im 19./20. Jahrhundert. Die Familien Eberstadt, Edinger, Rothschild und Guggenheim," *Menora* 10 (1999): 308.

13. On Samuel Adler, see Gershon Greenberg, "The Dimensions of Samuel Adler's Religious View of the World," *HUCA* 46 (1975): 377–412, and Samuel Adler, "Prelude to America," in Stanley F. Chyet, ed., *Lives and Voices: A Collection of American Jewish Memoirs* (Philadelphia: Jewish Publication Society of America, 1972), 3–34. On the involvement in the rabbinical conference, see Steven M. Lowenstein, "The 1840s and the Creation of the German-Jewish Religious Reform Movement," in Werner E. Mosse, Arnold Paucker, and Reinhard Rürup, eds., *Revolution and Evolution: 1848 in German-Jewish History* (Tübingen: J. C. B. Mohr, 1981), 277–78.

14. Isidor Kiefer, "Synagogue 1841. Ein Wendepunkt in der Baugeschichte unserer alten Synagoge," Isidor Kiefer Collection, Leo Baeck Institute in New York, AR 1894–1903, box 2.

15. Kiefer, "Synagogue 1841. Ein Wendepunkt in der Baugeschichte unserer alten Synagoge," and Otto Böcher, *Die Alte Synagoge zu Worms* (Worms: Verlag Stadtbibliothek Worms, 1960), 120.

16. *Gebete zu dem am ersten Tage des Pesach-Festes in der Synagoge zu Worms stattfindenden deutschen Gottesdienstes* (Worms: Steinkühl and Smith, 1847), v.

17. W. Gunther Plaut, *The Rise of Reform Judaism: A Sourcebook of Its European Origin* (New York: World Union for Progressive Judaism, 1963), 61–62.

18. I. M. Jost, *Geschichte der Israeliten seit der Zeit der Maccabäer bis auf unsre Tage nach den Quellen bearbeitet*, 9 vols. (Berlin: Schlesinger, 1820–28), 7:225.

19. C. W. Sp(ieker), "Historische Miscellen," *Sulamith* 2 (1808): 295–97.

20. Leopold Zunz, "Salomon ben Isaac, genannt Raschi," *Zeitschrift für die Wissenschaft des Judentums* 1 (1822): 378.

21. The news of this finding was first noted in "Personalchronik und Miscellen," *Orient* 3 (1842): 296, and was later dismissed in the same periodical. See J. A. Fränkel, "Die Wormser Grabinschrift und unser Zeitrechnung," *Literaturblatt des Orient* 3 (1842): 681–85 and 698–703. The news about the alleged discovery was also reviewed in the *Vossische Zeitung* (August 22, 1842) and in the *Haude- und Spenersche Zeitung* (August 22, 1842). Fränkel apparently also published his rejection of the discovery in the *Haude- und Spenersche Zeitung*.

22. Joseph Schwarz, *Descriptive Geography and Brief Historical Sketch of Palestine*, trans. Isaac Leeser (Philadelphia: A. Hart, 1850), 364–66.

23. Albert Wolf, "Etwas über jüdische Kunst und ältere jüdische Künstler," *Mittheilungen der Gesellschaft für Jüdische Volkskunde* 5 (1902): 69. I have been unable to locate any information about Neu's life or his relationship to this society.

24. Stadtarchiv Worms, Fotoabteilung, F 3175/6. For Hoffmann, see Ulrich Thieme and Felix Becker, *Allgemeines Lexikon der Bildenden Künstler von der Antike bis zur Gegenwart*, 37 vols. (Leipzig: E. A. Seemann, 1938), 17:260.

25. Leopold Zunz, *Die synagogale Poesie des Mittelalters* (Berlin: Springer, 1855), 9.

26. Heinrich Graetz, *Geschichte der Juden von den ältesten Zeiten bis auf die Gegenwart. Aus den Quellen neu bearbeitet*, 3rd ed. (Leipzig: O. Leiner, 1893), 4:1.

27. Mannheimer, *Die Juden in Worms*, 1–8.

28. Mannheimer, *Die Juden in Worms*, 11.

29. Ibid., 11–12.

30. Ibid., 13–16; Auerbach, *Nahal Eshkol*, 2:56; and Auerbach, *Geschichte der israelitischen Gemeinde Halberstadt* (Halberstadt: H. Meyer, 1866), 184.

31. Auerbach, *Geschichte der israelitischen Gemeinde Halberstadt*, 32. Whether this observance reflected a new or rehabilitated practice is unclear. It may be that the Worms community's particular emphasis on commemorating the memory of the Jewish martyrs explains why Ludwig Lewysohn too indicates that this fast day was still observed in the 1850s. See Lewysohn, "Scenen aus dem Jahr 1096," *MGWJ* 5 (1856): 167–77; Lewysohn, *Nefashot Zadikim. Sechzig Epitaphien von Grabsteinen des israelitischen Friedhofes zu Worms regressiv bis zum Jahr 905 übl. Zeitr. nebst biographischen Skizzen* (Frankfurt am Main: J. Baer, 1855), 15–18; and Lewysohn, "Worms," *AZJ* 19 (1855): 295.

32. Mannheimer, *Die Juden in Worms*, 15 and 17.

33. Ibid., 12.

34. Ibid., 56 and 64.

35. Nils Roemer, "Turning Defeat into Victory: *Wissenschaft des Judentums* and the Martyrs of 1096," *Jewish History* 13 (1999): 68.

36. Isaac Jost, "Vorwort," in Mannheimer, *Die Juden in Worms*, 2.

37. Wolf Pascheles, *Sippurim. Eine Sammlung jüdischer Volkssagen, Erzählungen, Mythen, Chroniken, Denkwürdigkeiten*, 4th ed. (Prague: Wolf Pascheles, 1870), 27.

38. Abraham M. Tendlau, *Das Buch der Sagen und Legenden jüdischer Vorzeit. Nach den Quellen bearbeitet nebst Anmerkungen und Erläuterungen*, 3rd ed. (Frankfurt am Main: J. Kauffmann, 1873), 223–25, 226–29, and 230–41. Tendlau's anthology originally appeared in 1842 and was reprinted in 1846 as well.

39. Ludwig Lewysohn, "Wormser Sagen," *Jüdische Volksblatt* 2 (1854–55): 66–67, 91–92, 94–95, 112, 123–24, and 77–178.

40. Heinrich Heine, "Der Rabbi von Bacherach. Ein Fragment," in Klaus Briegleb, ed., *Heinrich Heine: Sämtliche Schriften*, 7 vols. (München: Deutscher Taschenbuchverlag, 1997), 1: 471. I follow here the English translation in Heinrich Heine, "Rabbi of Bacherach," in Elizabeth Petuchowski, ed., *Jewish Stories and Hebrew Melodies by Heinrich Heine* (New York: M. Wiener, 1987), 36.

41. I follow here the English translation in Heine, "Rabbi of Bacherach," 39, with a slight modification.

42. Heine, "Rabbi of Bacherach," 60–62.

43. Hermann Reckendorf, *Die Geheimnisse der Juden*, 5 vols. (Leipzig: Wolfgang Gerhard, 1856–1857), 4: 26–32.

44. Getrude Cepl-Kaufmann and Antje Johanning, *Mythos Rhein. Kulturgeschichte eines Stromes* (Darmstadt: Wissenschaftliche Buchgesellschaft, 2003), 168–79.

45. Ludwig Bechstein, *Deutsches Sagenbuch* (Leipzig: Georg Wigand, 1853), iii.

46. Bechstein, *Deutsches Sagenbuch*, 39–40, and Karl Geib, *Die Sagen und Geschichten des Rheinlandes in umfassender Auswahl gesammelt und bearbeitet* (Mannheim: Heinrich Hoff, 1836), 136–39.

47. "Rabbi Juda Chasid's Mauer zu Worms," *AZJ* 7 (1843): 743; "Die Märtyrer," *Der Israelit des 19. Jahrhunderts* 5 (1844): 40; and L. H. Lehmann, "Das Licht der zwei Fremden (Eine Legende)," *AZJ* 7 (1843): 29–31.

48. "The Synagogue at Worms and the Two Martyrs," *Occident* 1 (1843): 82.

49. Ibid., 84.

50. See the dedication in Celia and Marion Moss, *The Romance of Jewish History*, 2nd ed., 3 vols. (London: A. K. Newman, 1843). On the Moss sisters, see Michael Galchinsky, *The Origin of the Modern Jewish Woman Writer: Romance and Reform in Victorian England* (Detroit: Wayne State University Press, 1996), 105–33.

51. Celia Moss, "The Martyrs of Worms: A German Tale," *Occident* 5 (1847–48): 344.

52. Ibid., 245–46.

53. See Michael Ragussis, *Figures of Conversion: "The Jewish Question" and English National Identity* (Durham: Duke University Press, 1995).

54. Moss, "The Martyrs of Worms: A German Tale," 344.

55. Leopold Zunz, *Zur Geschichte und Literatur* (Berlin: Veit and Co., 1845), 304–458; see pages 404 and 415 for indications that Zunz had been in Worms.

56. "Aufruf," *AZJ* 17 (1853): 423–24; "Worms," *Jewish Chronicle* 9 (August 26, 1853): 375; "Appel," *L'Univers Israélite* 9 (1853): 70–72; and "Les monuments du Judaisme," *Archives Israélites* 14 (1853): 634–36. Rabbi Kolmar apparently pre-

pared the French translation of the circular; see "Worms," *AZJ* 17 (1853): 379. See also the introduction to Lewysohn's book, which also mentions Leopold Zunz's *Zur Geschichte und Literatur*, Lewysohn, *Nefashot Zadikim*, no pagination.

57. "Aufruf," *AZJ* 17 (1853): 424.

58. Ibid.

59. "Worms," *AZJ* 18 (1854): 16, 77, 255, 349; "Worms," *AZJ* 19 (1855): 295, 437–38, and 512; and "Worms," *AZJ* 20 (1856): 469.

60. "Worms," *AZJ* 18 (1854): 128, 385–86, 432–33, 445–46, 511, and 670–71, and "Worms," *AZJ* 19 (1855): 151–52, 215, 257 and Otto Böcher, *Die Alte Synagoge zu Worms*, 120–21.

61. Lewysohn, *Nefashot Zadikim*, 18 and 93–94, and Lewysohn, "Scenen aus dem Jahr 1096," 168–69 and 174. The review in the prestigious *MGWJ* lauded the work and agreed that the historical monuments deserved to be recognized both inside and outside of Worms. See the review by B. Beer in *MGWJ* 5 (1856): 316–18; "Worms," *AZJ* 19 (1855): 56–57; and "Literaturbericht," *AZJ* 19 (1855): 266–67.

62. Lewysohn, *Nefashot Zadikim*, 69.

63. Lewysohn, "Scenen aus dem Jahre 1096," 177.

64. Böcher, *Die Alte Synagoge zu Worms*, 121–22, and A. Epstein, "Jüdische Alterthümer in Worms und Speier," *MGWJ* 40 (1895): 558.

65. Abraham M. Tendlau, *Sprichwörter und Redensarten deutsch-jüdischer Vorzeit. Als Beitrag zur Volks-, Sprach- und Sprichwörterkunde. Aufgezeichnet aus dem Munde des Volkes und nach Wort und Sinn erläutert* (Frankfurt am Main: J. Kauffmann, 1860), 347.

66. Marcus Lehmann, "Prospectus," *Der Israelit* 1 (1860): 1–2.

67. Marcus Lehmann, "Eine Geschichte der Juden in orthodoxen Sinne und Geiste," *Der Israelit* 1 (1860): 281–83, and S. Lipschütz, "Einiges über das Bedürfnis einer jüdischen Geschichte und deren Darstellung," *Der Israelit* 5 (1864): 371–73 and 383–85.

68. Abraham Tendlau, "Maharam Merothenburg," *Israelit* 6 (1865): 51–52, 66–67, 79–81; Tendlau, "Die Familie Dalberg," *Israelit* 7 (1866): 34–35; and Tendlau, "Die erste jüdische Colonie in Worms," *Israelit* 7 (1866): 420–21.

69. A number of new books and articles appeared on the history of the community during this period. See G. Wolf, *Juden in Worms und des deutschen Städtewesens. Nach archivalischen Urkunden des K. K. Ministeriums des Aeussern in Wien* (Breslau: Schletter, 1861); G. Wolf, "Zur Geschichte der Juden in Worms und des deutschen Städtewesens," *MGWJ* 10 (1861): 321–33, 361–76, 410–30, and 453–63; review of G. Wolf, "Juden in Worms," *JZfWJ* 1 (1862): 273–76; Ludwig Lewysohn, "Zur Geschichte der Juden in Worms," *Jeschurun* 4 (1864): 99–107; Lewysohn, "Culturhistorische Notizen," *Jüdische Volksblatt* 3 (1856): 176; "Die erste jüdische Colonie in Worms," *Israelit* 7 (1866): 420–21; "Die Familie Dalberg," *Israelit* 7 (1866): 34–35; Lewysohn, "Literarische Notizen," *Jüdisches Literaturblatt* 5 (1876): 22, 30; Lewysohn, "Literarische Notizen," *Jüdisches Literaturblatt* 6 (1877): 106–7.

70. "Literarische Nachrichten," *AZJ* 15 (1851): 462.

71. Zunz, *Monatstage des Kalenderjahres*, 65–66.

72. Heinrich Graetz, *History of the Jews*, 6 vols. (Philadelphia: Jewish Publication Society of America, 1967), 3:41, 518, 301–2, and 4:108–9.

73. See the extensive bibliography by C. A. H. Burkhardt and M. Stern, "Aus der Zeitschriftenliteratur zur Geschichte der Juden in Deutschland," *ZGJD* 2 (1888): 1–46 and 109–49.

74. Cepl-Kaufmann and Johanning, *Mythos Rhein. Kulturgeschichte eines Stromes*, 153–93.

75. Rudy Koshar, *German Travel Cultures* (Oxford: Berg, 2000), 24.

76. "Briefe aus Oesterreich," *MGWJ* 6 (1857): 215, and "Briefe aus Süddeutschland," *MGWJ* 6 (1857): 412.

77. "Briefe aus Süddeutschland," 256. See also Isaac Rosenmeyer, "Meine Reise über Galizien nach Deutschland," *AZJ* 22 (1858): 39–41, 151–53, 220–22, 277–78; "Briefe aus Wien," *MGWJ* 6 (1857): 175–81; "Briefe aus Oesterreich-Italien," *MGWJ* 6 (1857): 392–98; and "Jüdische Alterthümer in Berlin," *AZJ* 50 (1886): 732–34.

78. "Briefe aus Süddeutschland," 256.

79. Ibid., 134.

80. Fritz Reuter, *Worms zwischen Reichsstadt und Industriestadt, 1800–1882* (Worms: Stadtarchiv Worms, 1993), 64–65, 78, 88–89.

81. Karl Klein, *Die Hessische Ludwigsbahn oder Worms, Oppenheim und die anderen an der Bahn liegenden Orte. Topographisch und historisch dargestellt nebst einer übersichtlichen Beschreibung von Mainz* (Mainz: Seifert'schen Buchdruckerei, 1856), 98, 120–121. On this see "Worms," *AZJ* 20 (1856): 524.

82. See *A Handbook for Travellers on the Continent: Being a Guide to Holland, Belgium, Prussia, Northern Germany, and the Rhine from Holland to Switzerland*, 17th ed. (London: John Murray, 1871), 542–43, and Karl Baedeker, *Deutschland und Österreich. Handbuch für Reisende*, 11th ed. (Coblenz: Karl Baedeker, 1869), 377.

83. "Altes und Neues. Die alte Synagoge zu Worms," *Illustrierte Zeitung* 679 (July 5, 1856), 12, Stadtarchiv Worms, Abt. 203, Nr. 40; "Worms," *AZJ* 20 (1856): 469–70; Ludwig Lewysohn, "Die israeltischen Denkmäler in Worms," *Israelitische Jugendbibliothek* 1 (1858): 25–32; and "Worms—The Jews There," *Jewish Messenger* 3 (1858): 78.

84. "Projektierte Synagogen Umbau 1862," Isidor Kiefer Collection, Leo Baeck Institute in New York, AR 1894–1903, box 2.

85. Reuter, *Worms zwischen Reichsstadt und Industriestadt, 1800–1882*, 79.

86. "Alterthumsverein," *Rheinischer Herold* 80 (July 5, 1860).

87. "Inauguration of the Luther Monument at Worms—Imposing Ceremonies," *The Times* (July 13, 1868): 1b-c; "The Luther Monument at Worms," *The Times* (July 25, 1868): 5c, and Christiane Theiselmann, *Das Wormser Lutherdenkmal Ernst Rietschels (1856–1868) im Rahmen der Lutherrezeption des 19. Jahrhunderts* (Frankfurt am Main: P. Lang, 1992).

88. Friedrich Fuchs, *Geschichte der Stadt Worms. Nebst einer Analyse der Nibelungensage und einem Anhang. "Führer durch Worms"* (Worms: Julius Stern, 1868).

89. Reuter, *Worms ehemals, gestern und heute*, 13–15.

5. JEWISH TRAVELING CULTURES OF REMEMBRANCE

1. See Maiken Umbach, "Reich, Region und Föderalismus als Denkfiguren
in politischen Diskursen der Frühen und der Späten Neuzeit," in Dieter Lange-
wiesche and Georg Schmidt, eds., *Föderative Nation. Deutschlandkonzepte von der
Reformation bis zum Ersten Weltkrieg* (München: Oldenbourg, 2000), 191–214, and
Abigail Green, *Fatherlands, State-Building, and Nationhood in Nineteenth-Century
Germany* (Cambridge: Cambridge University Press, 2001), 11 and 97–98.

2. See David Sorkin, *The Transformation of German Jewry, 1780–1840* (Oxford:
Oxford University Press, 1987).

3. "Das Deutsche Reich und die Juden," *AZJ* 35 (1871): 41–43.

4. Ismar Schorsch, *Jewish Reactions to German Anti-Semitism, 1870–1914* (New
York: Columbia University Press, 1972), 23–52, and Nils Roemer, *Between His-
tory and Faith: Rewriting the Past—Reshaping Jewish Cultures in Nineteenth-Century
Germany* (Madison: Wisconsin University Press, 2005), 81.

5. "Verzeichnis sämmtlicher Vereine für jüdische Geschichte und Literatur in
Deutschland, deren Mitgliederzahl und Vorstände," *JJGL* 3 (1900): 295; the 1901
edition of the same source no longer lists the local branch in Worms.

6. Ismar Schorsch, "Moritz Güdemann, Rabbi, Historian and Apologist,"
LBIYB 11 (1966): 46.

7. George L. Mosse, "The Image of the Jew in German Popular Culture: Felix
Dahn and Gustav Freytag," *LBIYB* 2 (1957): 218–27.

8. For the importance of the local, see Celia Applegate, *Heimat in the Pfalz: A
Nation of Provincials: The German Idea of Heimat* (Berkeley: University of California Press, 1990); Alon Confino, *The Nation as a Local Metaphor: Württemberg, Imperial Germany, and National Memory, 1871–1918* (Chapel Hill: University of North
Carolina Press, 1997); James Retallack, ed., *Saxony in German History: Culture, Society, and Politics, 1830–1933* (Ann Arbor: University of Michigan Press, 2000); and
Nancy R. Reagin, "Recent Work on German National Identity: Regional? Imperial? Gendered? Imaginary?" *Central European History* 37 (2004): 273–89.

9. Adolf Jellinek, *Worms und Wien. Liturgische Formulare ihrer Todtenfeier aus alter
und neuer Zeit, und Namensverzeichniss der Wormser Maertyrer aus den Jahren 1096
und 1349* (Wien: J. Schlossberg, 1880).

10. Abraham Berliner, "Das Gedaechtnis der Gerechten," *Der Israelit* 13 (1872):
901–2, and *Der Israelit* 14 (1873): 952.

11. Moritz Kayserling, *Die Jüdischen Frauen in der Geschichte, Literatur und
Kunst. Bibliothek des deutschen Judentums* (Hildesheim: Olms, 1991), 68 and 138.

12. Herbert Blume, "Blaugelb und Schwarzweißrot. Wilhelm Brandes als Schriftsteller," in Herbert Blume, ed., *Von Wilhelm Raabe und anderen. Vorträge aus dem
Braunschweiger Raabe-Haus* (Bielefeld: Verlag für Regionalgeschichte, 2001), 95–129.

13. *Wilhelm Brandes, Die Jüdin von Worms. Mit begleitender Musik für Klavier von
Robert Heger. Op. 13.* (Berlin: Bote und G. Bock, 1913).

14. Theodor Gassmann, "Die Juden von Worms. Volks-Drama in fünf Aufzügen," in Gassmann, *Dramatisches* (Hamburg: H. F. Richter, 1872), 213–335.

15. Carl Trog, *Rheinlands Wunderhorn: Sagen, Geschichte und Legenden, auch
Schwänke aus den alten Ritterburgen, Klöstern und Städten der Rheinufer und des*

Notes to Pages 91–94

Rheingebietes von den Quellen bis zur Mündung des Stromes. Dem deutschen Volk gewidmet, 15 vols. (Essen: Silbermann, 1882–84), 6:154–57, and Stadtarchiv Worms, F2522/8 and F2522/6.

16. Harold Hammer-Schenk, "Die Architektur der Synagoge von 1780 bis 1933," in Hans-Peter Schwarz, ed., *Die Architektur der Synagoge* (Frankfurt am Main: Klett-Cotta, 1988), 247–48.

17. "Worms," *New Wormser Zeitung* (August 15, 1875), and Abschrift: Ausfertigung. Schenkung, Stadtarchiv Worms, Fritz Reuter Sammlung, Abt. 214/13.

18. Nathan Stein, Lebenserinnerungen, Nathan Stein Collection, Leo Baeck Institute, New York, ME 618, 9–10, and Samson Rothschild, *Beamte der Wormser jüdischen Gemeinde Mitte des 18. Jahrhunderts bis zur Gegenwart* (Frankfurt am Main: J. Kauffmann, 1920), 37–49.

19. Fritz Reuter, "Leopold Levy und seine Synagoge von 1875," *Der Wormsgau* 11 (1974–75): 61–65.

20. Monika Richarz, *Jewish Life in Germany: Memoirs of Three Centuries,* trans. Stella P. Rosenfeld and Sidney Rosenfeld (Bloomington: Indiana University Press, 1991), 249.

21. Fritz Reuter, "Altertumsverein und Paulusmuseum. Aspekte der Wormser Wissenschafts-, Personen-und Stadtgeschichte im 19. Jahrhundert als Beitrag zur hundertjährigen Jubiläum des Museums der Stadt Worms 1881–1981," *Wormsgau* 13 (1979–81): 20–38.

22. Julius Goldschmidt, "Der alte israelitische Friedhof zu Worms," *Vom Rhein* 1 (1902): 3–5. On the importance of the *Nibelungen* as part of the local heritage production around the turn of the century, see Gerold Bönnen, "Die Nibelungenstadt. Rezeption und Stadtbild in Worms im 19. und 20. Jahrhundert," *Blätter für deutsche Landesgeschichte* 136 (2000): 37–49. On the *Nibelungen* song and Germany's national heritage, see Peter Wapnewski, "Das Nibelungslied," in Etienne François and Hagen Schulze, eds., *Deutsche Erinnerungsorte,* 3 vols. (München: C. H. Beck, 2001), 1:159–69.

23. Theodor Mommsen, "Auch ein Wort über unser Judentum, Berlin 1880," in Walter Boehlich, ed., *Der Berliner Antisemitismusstreit* (Frankfurt am Main: Suhrkamp, 1965), 212.

24. Reuter, *Warmaisa,* 177, and Otto Böcher, *Die alte Synagoge zu Worms* (Worms: Verlag Stadtbibliothek Worms, 1960), 66.

25. Ernst Wörner, *Die Kunstdenkmäler im Großherzogtum Hessen. Inventarisirung und beschreibende Darstellung der Werke der Architektur, Plastik, Malerei und des Kunstgewerbes bis zum Schluss des XVIII. Jahrhunderts. Kreis Worms* (Darmstadt: Bergsträsser, 1887), 258.

26. Maiken Umbach, *Federalism and Enlightenment in Germany, 1740–1806* (London: Hambledon, 1998), 42–69.

27. Fritz Reuter, *Karl Hoffmann und "das neue Worms." Stadtentwicklung und Kommunalbau, 1882–1918* (Darmstadt: Hessische Historischen Kommission Darmstadt und der Historischen Kommission für Hessen, 1993), 113–20.

28. Fritz Reuter, "Wormser Historiker aus dem 19. und 20. Jahrhundert," *Der Wormsgau* 19 (2000): 89–92.

29. Böcher, *Die Alte Synagoge zu Worms*, 122; Samson Rothschild, "Ein geschichtlich bedeutsamer Fund," *Vom Rhein* 4 (1907): 77; "Epithaphien von Grabsteinen des alten israel. Friedhofs in Worms—entziffert und ins Deutsche übersetzt von Prof. David Kaufmann in Budapest in den Jahren 1892–1897 nach dem ihm von dem Vorstandsmitglied Julius Goldschmidt gelieferten Abklatschen," Worms Stadtarchiv, Judaica 203:3; and Samson Rothschild, "Der israelitische Friedhof in Worms," *AZJ* 73 (1909): 354–55.

30. Reuter, *Warmaisa*, 179.

31. Fritz Reuter established the origin of the Rashi Chapel museum based on Rothschild's *Aus Vergangenheit und Gegenwart* (Mainz: Wirth, 1895), which already includes a photo of the museum. See Fritz Reuter, "Vom Erwachen des historischen Interesses am jüdischen Worms bis zum Museum des Isidor Kiefers," *Aschkenas* 12 (2002): 13–44.

32. Friedrich Soldan, *Die Zerstörung der Stadt Worms im Jahre 1689. Im Auftrage der Stadt Worms dargestellt* (Worms: Julius Stern, 1889), 49. Heinrich Boos was much more critical of Jewish behavior during the occupation in the fourth volume of his *Geschichte der rheinischen Städtekultur von den Anfängen bis zur Gegenwart mit besonderer Berücksichtigung Worm* (Berlin: Stargardt, 1901). Samson Rothschild responded critically in a review of Boos's book; see Rothschild, "Die jüdische Gemeinde von Worms während der Zerstörung durch die Franzosen," *Blaetter für jüdische Geschichte und Litteratur* 3 (1902): 65–71.

33. Canstatt's articles appeared originally in 1889 in *Wormser Zeitung* and were afterward published as a book; see Canstatt, *Drangsale der Stadt Worms und deren Zerstörung durch die Franzosen am 31. Mai 1689. Zum 200 jährigen Gedenktage* (Worms: Eugen Kranzbühler, 1889), introduction and 99. The Jewish account of the destruction was reprinted on pages 99–103 and 147–48.

34. Karl Baedeker, *The Rhine from Rotterdam to Constance: Handbook for Travellers*, 13th ed. (Leipzig, 1896), 264, and 14th ed. (Leipzig: Karl Baedeker, 1900), 276–79.

35. Leo Woerl, *Führer durch Worms und Umgebung*, 6th ed. (Leipzig, 1900), 29. The book was first published in 1885. August Weckerling, *Beckmann-Führer. Worms am Rhein und Umgebung. Mit Stadt-Plan und vielen Abbildungen*, 3rd ed. (Heilbronn am Neckar: Otto Weber Verlag, 1908). This guide appeared in 1902, 1904, 1908, 1910, and 1915, and the fourth French edition appeared in 1919 as *Worms sur le Rhin et ses Environs: Avec un plan de la Ville et de Nombreuses Illustrations*, trans. Tony Kellen (Heilbronn: Weber, 1919).

36. *Illustrirter Führer durch Worms. Ein Gedenkbüchlein für Fremde und für Einheimische. Mit über 50 Illustrationen* (Worms: Heinrich Fischer, 1900), 14–15 and 22; Ludwig Heilmann, *Führer durch Worms und Umgebung für Fremde und Einheimische* (Worms: Reiss, 1899), 18, 37–38, and 79–80; and *Neuester Führer durch Worms am Rhein und Umgebung (mit Plan) und 55 Illustrationen* (Worms: Christian Herbst, 1906), 39–40 and 63.

37. Heilmann, *Führer durch Worms*, introduction and 18.

38. Richarz, *Jewish Life in Germany*, 250.

39. On the narrative construction of German Jewish autobiographies, see Mir-

iam Gebhardt, *Das Familiengedächtnis. Erinnerung im Deutsch-Jüdischen Bürgertum 1890 bis 1932* (Stuttgart: F. Steiner, 1999).

40. "Bonn," *AZJ* 49 (March 17, 1885): 196; Barbara Suchy, "The Verein zur Abwehr des Antisemitismus (I)—From Its Beginnings to the First World War," *LBIYB* 28 (1983): 205–40; Schorsch, *Jewish Reactions to German Anti-Semitism*, 79–101; and Protokollbuch des Vereins zur Abwehr des Antisemitismus, 1909–1910, 1913, 1916, 1917, 1921, 1922, Neue Synagoge Berlin—Centrum Judaicum Oranienburger Strasse #9127.

41. See Rudy Koshar, *Germany's Transient Pasts: Preservation and National Memory in the Twentieth Century* (Chapel Hill: University of North Carolina Press, 1998), 64–66.

42. Many of these photos had already been taken during the 1890s, and they served as the basis for illustrations that appeared in *Jüdische Presse* 38–39 (1894): 151–53, 155. The fact that several photographers competed to produce these images indicates great interest in the sites. See also the postcard of Worms in the Postcard Collection at Jewish Theological Seminary; the Sally Bodenheimer Postcard Collection, LBI AR 7169; and the Synagogue Collection: Worms, LBI. See also Fritz Reuter, ed., *Worms in alten Ansichtskarten* (Frankfurt am Main: Flechsig Verlag, 1979), and Stadtarchiv Worms 209:3.

43. *Neuester Führer durch Worms am Rhein und Umgebung (mit Plan) und 55 Illustrationen* (Worms: Christian Herbst, 1906), 3.

44. Ibid., 39–40 and 62–63.

45. Samson Rothschild, *Aus Vergangenheit und Gegenwart der Israel. Gemeinde Worms* (Mainz, [1895]). The work appeared in Mainz in 1901 and then in Frankfurt in 1905, 1909, 1913, 1926, and 1929.

46. Rothschild, *Aus Vergangenheit und Gegenwart der Israel* (1895).

47. Rothschild, *Aus Vergangenheit und Gegenwart der Israel. Gemeinde Worms*, 5th ed. (Frankfurt am Main: J. Kauffmann, 1913).

48. August Weckerling, *Beckmann-Führer. Worms am Rhein und Umgebung. Mit Stadt-Plan und vielen Abbildungen*, 4th ed. (Heilbronn am Neckar: Otto Weber Verlag, 1908), 102.

49. Ludwig Schaper, "Worms," *Illustrirte Zeitung* 116 (June 20, 1901): 977–979 and *Neuester Führer durch Worms am Rhein und Umgebung (mit Plan) und 55 Illustrationen* (Worms: Christian Herbst, 1906), and 62.

50. Marion Kaplan, "Redefining Judaism in Imperial Germany: Practices, Mentalities, and Community," *Jewish Social Studies* 9 (2002): 9–11.

51. Leo Schönmann, "Das war in Worms im Monat Mai" (1960), Leo Baeck Institute, New York, ME573, p. 2.

52. David Philippson, *Old European Jewries* (Philadelphia: Jewish Publication Society of America, 1894), 1.

53. Abraham Epstein, "Jüdische Alterthümer in Worms und Speier," *MGWJ* 40 (1896): 512, and Epstein, "Die nach Raschi benannten Gebäude in Worms," *MGWJ* 45 (1901): 44–75.

54. See Ludwig Lewysohn, "Die Raschi-Kapelle in Worms," *Laubhütte* (1898):

Notes to Pages 102–108

613–14, and Abraham Epstein's response, "Die sogenannte Raschi-Capelle in Worms" *Dr. Bloch's Oesterreichische Wochenschrift*, Feb. 10, 1899, 113–14.

55. Moritz Güdemann, "Raschi," *Ost und West* 5 (1905): 433–40, which reprints the illustration of the chapel from Lewysohn's book, and Abraham Berliner, *Blicke in die Geisteswerkstatt Raschis. Vortrag im Verein für jüdische Geschichte und Literatur zu Berlin gehalten* (Frankfurt am Main: Kauffmann, 1905).

56. The two winning entries were later published. See Max Beermann and Max Doktor, *Raschis Leben und Wirken. zwei Preisschriften* (Worms: H. Kraeuter'schen Buchhandlung, 1906), and Reuter, 180.

57. Julius Goldschmidt, "Der alte israelitische Friedhof zu Worms," *Vom Rhein* 1 (1902): 3–5.

58. Bernard Lazare, *Job's Dungheap: Essays on Jewish Nationalism and Social Revolution* (New York: Schocken Books, 1948), 50.

59. J. D. Eisenstein, *Ozar Yisrael: An Encyclopaedia of All Matters Concerning Jews and Judaism in Hebrew*, 10 vols. (New York: J. D. Eisenstein, 1910), 4:191.

60. "Worms," *Der Israelit* 16 (1885): 669–70.

61. Samson Rothschild, "Die Synagogue zu Worms," *Der Israelit* 22 (1891): 1697–98.

62. Shalom Asch, "Baym taykh reyn," *Gezamlte shriften*, 30 vols. (Warsaw: Kultur-lige, 1930–38), 13:165–172.

63. Israel Zangwill, "Moods of the Year," *The Jewish Year Book* 5657 (1896): 233–34.

64. Asch, "Maynz un Openhaym," *Gezamlte shriften*, 13:155–64.

65. Asch, "Di elteste shul in der velt," *Gezamlte shriften*, 13:173–85.

66. Ibid., 175.

67. Ibid., 177.

68. Karlfried Gründer and Friedrich Niewöhner, eds., *Gershom Scholem, Tagebücher nebst Aufsätzen und Entwürfen bis 1923. 1. Halband, 1913–1917* (Frankfurt am Main: Jüdischer Verlag, 1995), 30.

69. Benas Levy, *Die Juden in Worms. Ein Vortrag* (Berlin: M. Poppelauer, 1914), 3.

70. S. Rothschild, "Eine seltene Frau," *Der Israelit* (March 20, 1902), 542. This guest book unfortunately does not exist any more. See *Sefer ha-minhagim: The Book of Chabad-Lubavitch Customs (1994)*, http://www.sichosinenglish.org/books/sefer-haminhagim/01.htm, fn. 252, accessed July 2002.

71. "Ausstellung der Wormser jüdischen Altertümer und Denkwürdigkeiten," *Wormser Zeitung* 139 (June 4, 1914): 2. The importance of this event is apparent from the fact that a short account was included in a report of the city; see *Verwaltungs-Rechenschaftsbericht des Oberbürgermeisters der Stadt Worms für 1914* (Worms am Rhein: A. K. Boechinger, 1916), 12–13.

72. Samson Rothschild, *Die Synagoge in Worms und ihre berühmten Altertümer in 21 Bildern* (Worms: Christian Herbst, 1914).

73. "Verzeichnis der Mitglieder der isr. Gemeinde Worms (aufgestellt am 23. September 1911)," Worms Collection, Leo Baeck Institute, New York, AR 145, folder 3.

74. *Zur Geschichte der Wormser jüdischen Gemeinde, ihrer Friedhöfe u. ihres Begräb-*

niswesens. Gedenkschrift zur Eröffnung des neuen Friedhofs (Worms: H. Kräuter'schen Buchhandlung, 1911), and *Der alte israelitische Friedhof zu Worms am Rhein. Zwölf Kunstblätter mit Vorwort von Max Levy*, October 1913 (Worms: Christian Herbst, 1913). | 245

75. Stadtarchiv Worms, Neg. NR. CH 427.

76. Fritz Reuter, "Kunsthistoriker und Heimatforscher aus dem 19./20. Jahrhundert und ihre Grabstätten," *Wormsgau* 19 (2000): 88–92 and 20 (2001): 137.

77. "Der letzte Rest der Judengasse in Frankfurt a. M.," *AZJ* 49 (1885): 230, and "Noch einmal die Judengasse in Frankfurt a. M.," *AZJ* 49 (1885): 726–27.

78. "Das Ende der Frankfurter am Main Judengasse," *AZJ* 48 (1884): 386; "Die Judengasse in Frankfurt am Main," *Die jüdische Presse* 15 (1884): 104; and Roemer, *Between History and Faith*, 122.

79. "Der Verein für Geschichte der Juden in Deutschland," *AZJ* 49 (1885): 717–18.

80. See the letter by the Vorstand der israelitischen Religionsgmeinde Worms, October 19, 1885, DIGB: Historische Commission, 1885–1917, CAHJP M1/24, and Roemer, *Between History and Faith*, 95–96.

81. A. Neubauer and Moritz Stern, *Hebräische Berichte über die Judenverfolgung während der Kreuzzüge* (Berlin: Simion, 1892), and Siegmund Salfeld, *Das Martyrologium des Nürnberger Memorbuches* (Berlin: Simion, 1898).

82. "Bericht über die sechste Plenarsitzung der Historischen Comission für die Geschichte der Juden in Deutschland," *ZGJD* 5 (1892): 408–9.

83. C. A. H. Burkhardt and M. Stern, "Aus der Zeitschriftenliteratur zur Geschichte der Juden in Deutschland," *ZGJD* 2 (1888): 1–46 and 109–49.

84. Rudy Koshar, *From Monuments to Traces: Artifacts of German Memory, 1870–1990* (Berkeley: University of California Press, 2000), 23–24.

85. Bernhard Brilling, "Das jüdische Archivwesen in Deutschland," *Der Archivar* 13 (1960): 271–90.

86. Ezechiel Zivier, "Eine archivalische Informationsreise," *MGWJ* 49 (1905): 209–54. On Worms see Samson Rothschild, "Das Archiv der jüdischen Gemeinde von Worms," *Vom Rhein* 1 (1902): 21–22. This article was reprinted in *Blätter für jüdische Geschichte und Literatur* 2 (1902): 8–11.

87. Gustav Karpeles, "Ein allgemeines Archiv der deutschen Juden," *AZJ* (1904): 13.

88. "Bericht über die Tätigkeit des Gesamtarchivs der deutschen Juden," *Mitteilungen des Gesamtarchivs der deutschen Juden* 3 (1911): 55–84.

89. Ibid., 60, 65, 70, 58 and 61.

90. Ibid., 63.

91. Ibid., 59.

92. Samson Rothschild, "Das Archiv der jüdischen Gemeinde von Worms," *Vom Rhein* 1 (1902): 21–22. A list of those Jewish communities that handed over their archives up until 1927 was published in "Geschäftsbericht," *Mitteilungen des Gesamtarchivs der deutschen Juden* 6 (1926): 114–20.

93. Adolf Kohut, *Geschichte der deutschen Juden. Ein Hausbuch für die jüdische Familie* (Berlin: Deutscher Verlag, 1898).

94. Till van Rahden, "'Germans of the Jewish Stamm': Visions of Community Between Nationalism and Particularism, 1850 to 1933," in Neil Gregor, Nils Roemer, and Mark Roseman, eds., *German History from the Margins, 1800 to the Present* (Bloomington: Indiana University Press, 2006), 27–48.

95. "Die Juden am Rhein," *Die Welt* (October 22, 1897): 5.

96. Felix Theilhaber, *Der Untergang der deutschen Juden. Eine volkswirtschaftliche Studie* (Munich: Reinhardt, 1911), 122; Arthur Ruppin, *Die Juden in der Gegenwart. Eine sozialwissenschaftliche Studie* (Berlin: S. Calvary, 1904); and Steven M. Lowenstein, "Was Urbanization Harmful to Jewish Tradition and Identity in Germany?" *Studies in Contemporary Jewry* 15 (1999): 80–106.

97. Gershom Scholem, *From Berlin to Jerusalem: Memories of My Youth* (New York: Schocken Books, 1980), 18.

98. *Gabriel Riesser. Eine Auswahl aus seinen Schriften und Briefen. Mit Geleitwort des Herrn Justizrat Dr. M. Horwitz, ersten Vorsitzenden des Zentralvereines Deutscher Staatsbürger Jüdischen Glaubens* (Frankfurt am Main: Kauffmann, 1913). This was the title of a once well-known play by Karl Schönherr (1910) that glorified the peasant, who is deeply rooted in the soil of his land and believes in the eternal values of religion, in contrast to those decadent townsfolk.

99. Kurt Blumenfeld, *Erlebte Judenfrage. Ein Vierteljahrhundert Deutscher Zionismus* (Stuttgart: Deutsche-Verlags-Anstalt, 1962), 85–99.

100. Eugen Fuchs, "Glaube und Heimat," *Im deutschen Reich* (September 1917): 343; Fuchs, "Glaube und Heimat," *Im deutschen Reich* (November 1917): 443–47; Fuchs, "Glaube und Heimat," *Neue jüdische Monatshefte* 1 (1917): 629–41.

101. Gustav Karpeles, "Ein allgemeines Archiv der deutschen Juden," *AZJ* (1904): 13.

102. [Gustav Karpeles], "Hundert Literaturvereine," *AZJ* 62 (1898): 553.

103. J. Herzberg, "Ueber jüdische Jugendliteratur," *Israelitisches Familienblatt* 10 (February 2, 1907): 9. See also J. Wiener, "Warum und womit erhalten wir unsere Kinder dem Judenthum," *AZJ* 56 (1892): 233.

104. Abraham Shalom Friedberg, *Zikhronot le-beyt David* (Tel Aviv: Masada, 1960), 247–64; Niza Ben-Ari, *Roman 'im ha-'avar: Ha-Roman ha-histori ha-yehudi-ha-germani min ha-meah ha-19 we-yezirato shel sifrut leumit* (Tel Aviv: Devir, 1997), 147–86 and 225–28; Dan Miron, *Ashkenaz: Modern Hebrew Literature and the Pre-Modern German Jewish Experience* (New York: Leo Baeck Institute, 1989), 23–31; and Allan Mintz, *Hurban: Responses to Catastrophe in Hebrew Literature* (New York: Columbia University Press, 1984), 126–29.

6. WORMS: A JEWISH *HEIMAT* ON BORROWED TIME

1. Peter Fritzsche, "Cities Forget, Nations Remember: Berlin and Germany and the Shock of Modernity," in Paul Betts and Greg Eghigian, eds., *Pain and Prosperity: Reconsidering Twentieth-Century German History* (Stanford: Stanford University Press, 2003), 35–60 and 227–32.

2. Georg Hermann, "Großstad oder Kleinstadt," *CV-Zeitung*, no. 22 (June 3, 1927): 309–10; Ludwig Basnitzki, "Der Dorfjude," *CV-Zeitung*, no. 24 (June 17,

1927): 338; and "Großstadt oder Kleinstadt," *CV-Zeitung*, no. 6 (July 1, 1927): 369–70, (July 22, 1927): 413–14, and (October 7, 1927): 566–67.

3. "Großstadt oder Kleinstadt," *CV-Zeitung*, no. 6 (July 1, 1927): 369.

4. Leo Baeck, "Gemeinde in der Großstadt," in *Wege im Judentums. Aufsätze und Reden*, ed. Werner Licharz (Gütersloh: Gütersloher Verlagshaus, 1997), 218–25.

5. Svetlana Boym, *The Future of Nostalgia* (New York: Basic Books, 2001), xiii.

6. Adolf Kober, "Die Geschichte der deutschen Juden in der historischen Forschung der letzten 35 Jahre," *ZGJD* 1 (1929): 19.

7. See, for example, Ismar Elbogen, *Geschichte der Juden in Deutschland* (Berlin: E. Lichtenstein, 1935); Jacob R. Marcus, *The Rise and Destiny of the German Jew* (Cincinnati: Union of American Hebrew Congregations, 1934); Bruno Weil, *Der Weg der deutschen Juden* (Berlin: Centralverein deutscher Staatsbürger Jüdischen Glaubens, 1934); Marvin Lowenthal, *The Jews of Germany: A Story of Sixteen Centuries* (New York: Jewish Publication Society of America, 1936); and Guy Miron, "The Emancipation 'Pantheon of Heroes' in the German Jewish Public Memory in the 1930s," *German History* 21 (2003): 476–504.

8. Bertha Pappenheim, *Allerlei Geschichten, Maasse-Buch. Buch der Sagen und Legenden aus Talmud und Midrasch nebst Volkserzählungen in Jüdisch-Deutscher Sprache* (Frankfurt am Main: J. Kauffmann, 1929); Shalom Asch, "Jossel, der Schammes," *Menorah* 5 (1927): 511–16; and Asch, "Der gefangene Rabbi von Rothenburg," *Menorah* 6 (1928): 153–55.

9. His first collection appeared under the pseudonym Micha Josef bin Gorion as *Die Sagen der Juden* in five volumes beginning in 1913 (Frankfurt: Rütten and Loening, 1913–27).

10. Buber's journal took particular trouble to introduce Berdyczewski to that public with articles like Baruch Krupaick's "Micha Josef Berdyczewski. Seine Wahrheiten und Dichtung," *Der Jude* 3 (1918): 266–77, and Markus Ehrenpreis's "Gespräche mit Berdyczewski," *Der Jude* 6 (1921): 174–80.

11. Arnold Zweig, "Der Born Judas," *Jüdische Rundschau* (September 9, 1924): 15–16. See also Michael Brenner, *The Renaissance of Jewish Culture in Weimar Germany* (New Haven: Yale University Press, 1996), 140–41.

12. Micha Josef bin Gorion, "Eine Wormser Geschichte" and "Rabbi Meir aus Rothenburg," *Der Born Judas. Legenden, Märchen und Erzählungen*, 2nd ed., 6 vols. (Leipzig: Insel Verlag, 1919), 1:305–6 and 6:127–28.

13. Saul Tchernichovsky, "Metim ha-rishonim," in *Kol kitve Sha'ul Tshernihovski: Shirim we-baladot* (Tel Aviv: 'Am 'Oved, 1990), 471–73.

14. Isidor Kiefer, "Das Museum der israelitischen Gemeinde Worms," *ZGJD* 5 (1934): 182–86; Samson Rothschild, "Das jüdische Museum in Worms," *Israelitisches Familienblatt* 25 (June 21, 1925): 172–73; and Rothschild, *Führer durch Worms und Umgebung (mit Plan) mit ausführlichen Beschreibungen des Lutherdenkmals, Domes, Paulusmuseums u.s.f. Mit 70 Abbildungen und Plan von Worms*, 6th ed. (Worms: Christian Herbst, 1925), 82–83. Kiefer himself gives November 12, 1924, as the opening date. See his "Das Museum der Israelitischen Gemeinde Worms am Rhein (1938)," Stadtarchiv Worms, Abt. 203/10b, p. 16. For the celebration of

Notes to Pages 118–20

the synagogue, see *Wormser Volkszeitung* (November 21, 1924), Stadtarchiv Worms, Abt. 228.

248

15. Stadtarchiv Worms, F2776/71 and 73; Stadtarchiv Worms, CH 267–268; and Isidor Kiefer's letter to Friedrich Illert, January 13, 1949, Stadtarchiv Worms, Abt. 20, Nr. 71.

16. Rüdiger Haude, *"Kaiseridee" oder "Schicksalsgemeinschaft." Geschichtspolitik beim Projekt "Aachener Krönungsausstellung 1915" und bei der Jahrtausendausstellung Aachen 1925* (Aachen: Aachener Geschichtsverein, 2000), 121–31.

17. Elisabeth Moses, "Jahrtausend-Ausstellung, Köln," *Soncino-Blätter* 1 (1925): 87. On the exhibition, see Katharina Rauschenberger, *Jüdische Tradition im Kaiserreich und in der Weimarer Republik. Zur Geschichte des jüdischen Museumswesens in Deutschland* (Hannover: Hahnsche Buchhandlung, 2002), 205–14.

18. Adolf Kober, "Von der Jahrtausendausstellung der Rheinlande im Köln," *C.V.-Zeitung* 4 (June 26, 1925): 448, and Kober, "Die jüdische Abteilung auf der Kölner Jahrtausend-ausstellung," *Israelitisches Familienblatt* (July 23, 1925): 194–96.

19. W. Ewald and B. Kuske, eds., *Führer durch die Jahrtausend-Ausstellung der Rheinlande in Köln 1925* (Cologne: M. Dumont Schauberg, 1925), 133–42.

20. Artur Schweriner, "Köln—ein Markstein in der Geschichte des C. V. Glänzender Verlauf der Kundgebung und Verbandstagung," *C.V.-Zeitung* 4 (July 3, 1925): 469, and Kurt Alexander, "Von der Wesensart des rheinischen Juden," *C.V.-Zeitung* 4 (June 26, 1925): 453. *Der Schild* also dedicated its September 3 edition to the exhibition as a special issue.

21. Betty Stern, "Die jüdische Abteilung in der Jahrtausend-Feier zu Köln," *Die jüdische Frau* 1 (1925): 1–2.

22. "Der 8. Lehrerverbandstag in Köln," *C.V.-Zeitung* 4 (June 12, 1925): 416.

23. "Auf nach Köln," *C.V.-Zeitung* 4 (June 12, 1925): 414.

24. Ludwig Holländer, "Der westdeutschen Tagung zum Gruss!" *C.V.-Zeitung* 4 (June 26, 1925): 447.

25. Bernhard Falk, "Der deutsche Jude auf rheinischer Erde," *C.V.-Zeitung* 4 (June 26, 1925): 445.

26. Leo Löwenstein, "Die deutschen Juden und der deutsche Rhein," *Der Schild* 4 (September 3, 1925): 317. See also Ruth Pierson, "Embattled Veterans—The Reichsbund jüdischer Frontsoldaten," *LBIYB* 19 (1974): 151.

27. "Worms auf der Kölner Jahrtausendaustellung," *Wormser Zeitung* (June 30, 1925).

28. Samson Rothschild, "Aus jüdischen Gassen," *Israelitisches Familienblatt* (March 19, 1925): 113–14; Rothschild, "Der jüdische Friedhof," *Israelitisches Familienblatt* (May 28, 1925): 164; and Rothschild, "Das jüdische Museum in Worms," *Israelitisches Familienblatt* (June 11, 1925): 172–73.

29. Samson Rothschild, "Jüdische Altertümer in Worms und Speyer," *C.V.-Zeitung* 4 (June 26, 1925): 460.

30. "Die Rheinlandtagung des Reichsbundes jüdischer Frontsoldaten," *Der Schild* 4 (September 11, 1925): 341.

31. Samson Rothschild, "Ausstellung jüdischer Altertümer in der Wormser

Stadtbibliothek anläßlich der Rheinlandtagung des Reichsbundes jüdischer Front-soldaten," *Israelitisches Familienblatt* (September 24, 1925): 236; see also the program and notes for his tour in "Synagoge in Worms, Führungsvortrag," Isidor Kiefer Collection, Leo Baeck Institute, New York, AR 1894–1903, Box 2: 22 and 23.

32. Siegfried Guggenheim, *Offenbacher Haggadah* (Offenbach am Main: Guggenheim, 1927), 77 and 79, and Brenner, *The Renaissance of Jewish Culture in Weimar Germany*, 171–72.

33. Guggenheim, *Offenbacher Haggadah*, 1.

34. "Die Haggadah eines Wormser," *Wormser Zeitung* (June 19, 1928).

35. *Der Orden Bne Briss. Mitteilungen der Grossloge für Deutschland. U. O. B. B.* (February 1928): 31; *Jüdische Liberale Zeitung* 8 (January, 13, 1928) makes a similar point.

36. Siegfried Guggenheim Collection, Leo Baeck Institute, New York, AR 180, D/C 8.

37. "Die neue Offenbacher Haggadah," *C.V.-Zeitung* 6 (December 16, 1927): 702–3, and Siegfried Guggenheim Collection, Leo Baeck Institute, New York, AR 180, D/C 8. See also Dr. Haupt (Darmstadt), "Die Offenbach Haggadah," *C.V.-Zeitung*, 7 (March 23, 1928): 158–59.

38. "Die neue Offenbacher Haggadah," *C.V.-Zeitung* 6 (December 16, 1927): 703.

39. Adolf Kober, "Die Geschichte der deutschen Juden in der historischen Forschung der letzten 35 Jahre," *ZGJD* 1 (1929): 23.

40. Peter Metz, "Ein Gang durch das Museum Jüdischer Altertümer," *Menorah* 12 (December 1927): 767–84; Rudolf Hallo, "Das Jüdische Museum in Kassel," *Der Schild* 6 (September 12, 1927): 285–86.

41. Erich Toeplitz, "Jüdische Museum," *Der Jude* 8 (1924): 339–46.

42. Jakob Seifensieder, "Wohin mit den deutsch-jüdischen Altertümern," *C.V.-Zeitung* 6 (June 24, 1927): 359. For more on the ongoing debate between local and centralized Jewish museums, see Rauschenberger, *Jüdische Tradition im Kaiserreich und in der Weimarer Republik*, 53–59.

43. "Wohin mit den jüdischen Altertümern?" *C.V.-Zeitung* 6 (September 9, 1927): 515.

44. Jakob Seifensieder, "Sammelt die jüdischen Altertümer!" *C.V.-Zeitung* 6 (September 16, 1927): 526.

45. Walter Benjamin, "The Work of Art in the Age of Mechanical Reproduction" (1935), in Benjamin, *Illuminations*, ed. Hannah Arendt, trans. Harry Zohn (New York: Schocken, 1969), 217–51.

46. Toeplitz, "Jüdische Museum," 339.

47. Hilaire Belloc, *Many Cities* (London: Constable, 1928), 210.

48. Paul Arnsberg, *Die jüdischen Gemeinden in Hessen. Anfang, Untergang, Neubeginn* (Frankfurt am Main: Societäts-Verlag, 1971), 427–28.

49. Isaak Holzer, "Das jüdische Worms und seine Sehenswürdigkeiten," *Der Jugendbund* 18 (December 1932): 2–3. See also Friedrich Illert, "Worms," *C.V.-Zeitung* 6 (August 5, 1927): 439–40; Georg Simmel, "Die Ruine," in Jürgen Habermas, ed., *Georg Simmel. Philosphische Kultur. Über das Abenteuer, die Geschlechter und*

die Krise der Moderne (Berlin: Klaus Wagenbach, 1986), 118–24; and Rudy Koshar, *From Monuments to Traces: Artifacts of German Memory, 1870–1990* (Berkeley: University of California Press, 2000), 80–83.

50. Christine Keitz, *Reisen als Leitbild: Die Entstehung des modernen Massentourismus in Deutschland* (Munich: Deutscher Taschenbuchverlag, 1997), 30–53, and Rudy Koshar, *German Travel Cultures* (Oxford: Berg, 2000), 65–114.

51. Samson Rothschild, "Aus jüdischen Gassen," *Israelitisches Familienblatt* (March 19, 1925): 113–14. See also Isaac Holzer, "Die Juden in Worms. Ein Rückblick auf ihre Geschichte," *Der Orden Bne Briss* (January 1, 1926): 1–2.

52. *Führer durch Worms und Umgebung* (1921), 39, 76–79; Friedrich M. Illert, *Offizieller Führer des Verkehrsvereins. Worms am Rhein und der Wonnegau mit vielen Abbildungen und Stadtplan*, 9th ed. (Worms: Verlag Christian Herbst, 1935), 27 and 57–58; and *Worms a. Rh. Deutschland-Bildheft Nr. 57* (Berlin: Berlin-Tempelhof-Universum-Verlagsanstalt, 1933), 24 and 27.

53. Arnsberg, *Die jüdischen Gemeinden in Hessen*, 427–28; Georg Salzberger, "Zwischen zwei Weltkriegen. Die Gesellschaft für jüdische Volksbildung und das Jüdische Lehrhaus," in Albert H. Friedländer, ed., *Georg Salzberger, Leben und Lehre* (Frankfurt am Main: Waldemar Kramer, 1982), 100–101. At the Talmud Tora Realschule, Joseph Carlebach also combined traditional teaching with, for example, a Rhineland excursion for his students. See Haim H. Cohn, "Joseph Carlebach," *LBIYB* 5 (1960): 66.

54. Karl Guggenheim, "Deutschtum und Judentum. Vortrag gehalten in der Freimauererloge Worms am 25. Januar 1930," Karl Guggenheim Collection, Leo Baeck Institute, New York, AR 179.

55. "Grundsteinlegung zum 118er Denkmal in Worms," *Wormser Zeitung* (May 9, 1932), and "Die Denkmalsweihe der 118er in Worms," *Wormser Zeitung. Morgenblatt* (August 22, 1932).

56. "Das innere des neuen jüdischen Museums in Worms," *Wormser Zeitung* (October 22, 1932); "Wiedereröffnung des jüdischen Museums in Worms," *Wormser Zeitung* (October 26, 1932); and Isidor Kiefer, "Das Museum der israelitischen Gemeinde Worms," *ZGJD* 5 (1935): 182–86.

57. Frank Bajohr, *"Unser Hotel ist judenfrei": Bäder-Antisemitismus im 19. und 20. Jahrhundert* (Frankfurt am Main: Fischer Verlag, 2003), 53–115, and Saul Lilienthal, *Jüdische Wanderungen in Frankfurt am Main, Hessen, Hessen-Nassau* (Frankfurt am Main: J. Kauffmann, 1938), introduction.

58. Manfred Lehmann, "Worms—One of Our 'Mother Cities,'" http://www.manfredlehmann.com/sieg278.html (accessed June 2004).

59. Martin Buber, *Die Stunde und die Erkenntnis. Reden und Aufsätze* (Berlin: Schocken, 1936), 164.

60. Ibid., 164–65.

61. See the postcard "Worms—Der aelteste israelitische Friedhof Deutschlands.—Blick auf den Dom (1016)" (Worms: Christian Herbst, 1914).

62. Jack Kugelmass, ed., *Going Home* (New York: YIVO Institute, 1993); Daniel Soyer, "The Travel Agent as Ethnic Broker Between Old World and New: The Case of Gustave Eisner," *YIVO Annual* 21 (1993): 345–68; Daniel Soyer, *Jewish*

Immigrant Associations and American Identity in New York, 1880–1939 (Cambridge, Mass.: Harvard University Press, 1997), 190–205.

63. See the advertisement leaflet in Marvin Lowenthal Collection, American Jewish Archives, New York, 140, box 13, folder 5. See also Lowenthal, "The First Jews in Germany," *Menorah* 22 (1934): 147–58. ⸽ 251

64. Marvin Lowenthal, *A World Passed By: Scenes and Memories of Jewish Civilization in Europe and North Africa* (New York: Harper and Brothers Publishers, 1933), xv–xvi.

65. Ibid., xvii, 276, and 285.

66. Koshar, *German Travel Cultures*, 129. See also the chapter "Berlin Jews Speak" in the Gordon Bolitho's travel guide titled *The Other Germany* (New York: D. Appleton-Century Company, 1934), 249–64, as well as I. Burrows, *The Intelligent Traveler's Guide to Germany* (New York: Knight Publication, 1936), 6.

67. Vladimir Kagan, *The Complete Vladmir Kagan: A Lifetime of Avant-Garde Design* (New York: Pointed Leaf Press, 2004), 23; see also Tanya Josefowitz, *I Remember* (London: Published by the author, 1999), 37.

68. Henry Huttenbach, "The Reconstruction and Evaluation of a Social Calendar as a Primary Source for the History of the Jewish Community of Worms (1933–1938)," *Proceedings of the Sixth World Congress of Jewish Studies* (Jerusalem 1975): 2:367–97.

69. Jacob Boas, "Germany or Diaspora: German Jewry's Shifting Perception in the Nazi Era (1933–1938)," *LBIYB* 27 (1986): 109–26.

70. "Die 900-Jahr-Feier in Worms. Ein Bericht und eine Betrachtung von unserem nach Worms entsandten Spezialberichterstatter Dr. M. Spitzer," *Jüdische Rundschau* 39 (June 8, 1934): 3, and "Bericht des Pressedienste der israelitschen Religionsgemeinde Worms über die Weihe-Stunde aus Anlass des 900jährigen Bestehens der Synagoge in Worms," Stadtarchiv Worms: Abt. 203, Nr. 8.

71. See Isaak Holzer's speech in Stadtarchiv Worms: Abt. 203, Nr. 8.

72. Leo Baeck, "Rede des Rabbiners Dr Baeck," Stadtarchiv Worms: Abt. 203, Nr. 8, and "Der Geist von Worms. Die 900-Jahrfeier der Synagoge—Eine erhebenden Weihestunde—Dr. Baecks Ansprache," *Jüdisch-liberale Zeitung* (June 8, 1934), Stadtarchiv Worms: Abt. 203, Nr. 8.

73. "Die 900-Jahr-Feier in Worms," *Israelitisches Gemeindeblatt. Offizielles Organ der Isr. Gemeinden Mannheim u. Ludwigshafen* (June 14, 1934); see also Stadtarchiv Worms: Abt. 203, Nr. 8; and "Schabbath in Worms," *Jüdische Rundschau* (September 28, 1934): 1–5.

74. Excerpts of Max Grünewald's table talk appear in his letter dated July 8, 1934, to the board of the Jewish community of Worms, Stadtarchiv Worms: Abt. 203, Nr. 8.

75. A letter from the Centralverein to Karl Guggenheim, May 15, 1934, Stadtarchiv Worms: Abt. 203, Nr. 8 lists the various action points. Guggenheim employed a newspaper clipping service to collect all of the articles, which were subsequently reproduced in a specially bound volume. See the letter by Max Goldschmidt to Karl Guggenheim, June 16, 1934, Stadtarchiv Worms: Abt. 203, Nr. 8. All subsequent articles about the celebrations are from this volume unless otherwise stated.

76. "Baeck über den Geist von Worms," *Gemeindeblatt für die jüdischen Gemeinden in Rheinland und Westfalen* (June 8, 1934); "900 Jahre Synagoge Worms," *Frankfurter Israelitsches Gemeindeblatt* (June 1934); "Die 900-Jahr-Feier in Worms," *Bayerische Israelitische Gemeindezeitung* (June 15, 1934); Stadtarchiv Worms: Abt. 203, Nr. 8.

77. "900 Jahre Synagoge Worms, 1034–1934," *C.V.-Zeitung* 13 (May 31, 1934), and "900 Jahre Wormser Synagoge," *Israelitisches Familienblatt* (May 31, 1934).

78. "Zum Geleit," *Zum 900jährigen Bestehen der Synagoge zu Worms. Eine Erinnerungsausgabe des Vorstandes der Israelitischen Religionsgemeinde Worms. Sonderheft der Zeitschrift für die Geschichte der Juden in Deutschland* 5 (1934): 85.

79. "Das Judengespenst. Vor 900 Jahren—und heute," *Jüdische Rundschau* 39 (June 1, 1934): 1, and "Die 900-Jahr-Feier in Worms. Ein Bericht und eine Betrachtung von unserem nach Worms entstandten Spezialberichterstatter Dr. M. Spitzer," *Jüdische Rundschau* 39 (June 8, 1934): 3.

80. "Die 900-Jahrfeier in Worms," *Der Israelit* (June 7, 1934): 11.

81. See the folder "Glückwünsche," Stadtarchiv Worms, Abt. 203, Nr. 8.

82. See the letter by the *Reichsvertretung der deutschen Juden,* May 28, 1934, to the board of the Jewish community of Worms, Stadtarchiv Worms: Abt. 203, Nr. 8.

83. See the letter by the chair of the C.V. from June 2, 1934, to the council of the *Religionsgemeinschaft Württenbergs* and the letter by the chair of the Jewish community of Braunschweig from June 1, 1934, to the board of the Jewish community of Worms, Stadtarchiv Worms: Abt. 203, Nr. 8.

84. Letter by the Spanish and Portuguese Synagogue, Bevis Marks, London from June 27, 1934, to the board of the Jewish community of Worms, Stadtarchiv Worms: Abt. 203, Nr. 8.

85. Letter by the Congregation She'arith Israel in the City of New York, September 9, 1934, to the board of the Jewish community of Worms, Stadtarchiv Worms: Abt. 203, Nr. 8. See also the letter by the Jewish community of Jastrow from June 1, 1934, and the note by the Verband Van Liberaal Religieuse Joden in Nederland from June 4, 1934, both to the board of the Jewish community of Worms, Stadtarchiv Worms: Abt. 203, Nr. 8.

86. Michael Brodhaecker, *Menschen zwischen Hoffnung und Verzweiflung. Der Alltag jüdischer Mitmenschen in Rheinhessen, Mainz und Worms während des "Dritten Reiches"* (Mainz: Gesellschaft für Volkskunde in Rheinland-Pfalz, 1999), 221 and 233–74, and Fritz Reuter, ed., *Worms 1933. Zeitzeugnisse und Zeitzeugen. Mit dem Lebens-Erinnerungen von Oberbürgermeister Wilhelm Rahn* (Worms: Stadtarchiv Worms, 1995), 14–16.

87. See the letters by Karl Guggenheim to the Jewish community of Worms, February 22, 1934, to Leo Baeck, *Reichsvertretung der deutschen Juden,* from March 2, 1933, and to the *Centralverein deutschen Staatsburgers jüdisches Glaubens,* May 3, 1934, Stadtarchiv Worms: Abt. 203, Nr. 8.

88. Fritz Reuter, "Politisches und gesellschaftliches Engagement von Wormser Juden im 19./20. Jahrhundert. Die Familien Eberstadt, Edinger, Rothschild und Guggenheim," *Menora* 10 (1999): 337, and Henry R. Huttenbach, *The Destruction of the Jewish Community of Worms, 1933–1945: A Study of the Holocaust Experience*

in Germany (New York: Memorial Committee of Jewish Victims of Nazism from Worms, 1981), v.

89. "Der Geist von Worms," *Pariser Tageblatt* 1, no. 5 (December 14, 1933): 2.

90. See the letter from Isidor Kiefer from March 20, 1933, to the *Altertumsverein* in Stadtarchiv Worms, Abt. 75/1, and Stadtarchiv Worms, Abt. 75, Anhang 1, which includes a list of the members and their resignations, and the letter from Isidor Kiefer to the *Vorstand der israel. Religionsgemeinde Worms*, September 22, 1934, Isidor Kiefer Collection at the Leo Baeck Institute, New York, AR 1894–1903, box 1.

91. Brodhaecker, *Menschen zwischen Hoffnung und Verzweiflung*, 367.

92. See Henry R. Huttenbach, *The Emigration Book of Worms: The Character and Dimension of the Jewish Exodus from a Small German Jewish Community, 1933–1941* (Koblenz: Landesarchivverwaltung Rheinland-Pfalz, 1974), 5–6.

93. Friedrich M. Illert, *Offizieller Führer des Verkehrsvereins. Worms am Rhein und der Wonnegau*, 9th ed. (Worms: Christian Herbst, 1935), 9, 27, and 59.

94. Gerold Bönnen, "Die Nibelungenstadt: Rezeption und Stadtbild in Worms im 19. und 20. Jahrhundert," *Blätter für deutsche Landesgeschichte* 136 (2000): 37–49.

95. Bajohr, *"Unser Hotel ist judenfrei,"* 132–41; Keitz, *Reisen als Leitbild*, 248–49; *Reichsstatthalter in Hessen*, September 11, 1937, *Jüdische Kurgäste in Baedern und Kurorten*, Worms Stadtarchiv, Abt. 5, Nr. 3778.

96. See Eva Reichmann-Jungmann, "Jüdische Gemeinden an Ruhr und Rhein," *Die jüdische Gemeinde* (July 8, 1937): 5–8; the letter by the *Jüdischen Lehrhaus* on May 14, 1935, to the board of the community of Worms; and the letter by the board to the *Lehrhaus* on the same day; Stadtarchiv Worms: Abt. 203, Nr. 8.

97. Karl Guggenheim, *Reichsbund Juedischer Frontsoldaten; Ortsgruppe Worms. Ansprache des Vorsitzenden [bei der] Toten-Gedenkfeier in der alten Synagoge zu Worms, February 21, 1937* (Worms, 1937), and "Der Heldengedenktag im Judentum Deutschlands," *Der Schild* 16 (1937): 1.

98. "Wormser jüdische Altertümer," *Der Schild* (September 16, 1936): 4.

99. Lilienthal, *Jüdische Wanderungen in Frankfurt am Main, Hessen, Hessen-Nassau*, introduction.

100. Brodhaecker, *Menschen zwischen Hoffnung und Verzweiflung*, 325–66, and Gerold Bönnen, " 'Es ist mein Lebenszweck': Isidor Kiefer und sein Anteil am Wiederaufbau der Wormser Synagoge, 1957–1961," *Aschkenas* 12 (2002): 93.

101. Kagan, *The Complete Vladmir Kagan*, 24; Josefowitz, *I Remember*, 5–13; and Brodhaecker, *Menschen zwischen Hoffnung und Verzweiflung*, 367.

102. Huttenbach, *The Emigration Book of Worms*, 6–9.

103. Max Guggenheim, "Abschied von Worms," *Jüdische Wochenschau* (November 8, 1940): 7.

104. Helmut Frank, "As a German Rabbi to America," in *Paul Lazarus Gedenkbuch—Beiträge zur Würdigung der letzten Rabbinergeneration in Deutschland* (Jerusalem: Jerusalem Post Press, 1961), 135–42, and "Worms," *C.V.-Zeitung* 17 (March 24, 1938): 4.

105. Huttenbach, *The Destruction of the Jewish Community of Worms*, 26.

106. Jacob Jacobson, "Schützet Euer Archivgut," *C.V.-Zeitung* 17 (June 2, 1938): 3–4.

107. Isidor Kiefer to Friedrich Illert, September 21, 1946, Stadtarchiv Worms, Abt. 20, Nr. 71.

108. "Herr Samson Rothschild: Historian of the Jews of Worms," *The Times* (June 17, 1939): 14, col. 4; "A Rothschild Master," *Palestine Post* (June 25, 1939): 4–5, and Fritz Reuter, "Wormser Historiker aus dem 19. und 20. Jahrhundert," *Der Wormsgau* 19 (2000): 91.

109. Museum d. israel. Gemeinde Worms, Isidor Kiefer, New York, 1938, Stadtarchiv Worms, Judaica-Sammlung, 203:10b.

110. Richarz, *Jewish Life in Germany*, 424–29; for the historical background to the deportation, see Peter Longerich, *Krieg der Vernichtung. Eine Gesamtdarstellung der nationalsozialistischen Judenverfolgung* (Munich: Piper, 1998), 282–83.

111. Henry R. Huttenbach, *The Life of Herta Mansbacher: A Portrait of a Jewish Teacher, Heroine, and Martyr* (New York: Memorial Committee of Jewish Victims of Nazism from Worms, 1980); Huttenbach, *The Destruction of the Jewish Community of Worms*, 35, and Brodhaecker, *Menschen zwischen Hoffnung und Verzweiflung*, 372–408.

112. See the copy of Kiefer's inventory of the museum's collection from September 9, 1965, Stadtarchiv Worms, Abt. 214, Nr. 15.

113. "Bericht ueber die Rettung dreier silberner Gegenstände der Jüdischen Gemeinde in Worms," in the Michael Oppenheim Collection, Stadtarchiv Mainz, 50 II:14.

114. "Kannst Du's ertragen?" Leo Baeck Institute, New York, Worms Collection.

115. Saul Tchernichovsky, "Metim ha-rishonim," in Tchernichovsky, *Kol kitve Sha'ul Tshernihovski: Shirim we-baladot* (Tel Aviv: 'Am 'Oved, 1990), 471–73.

116. S. Y. Agnon, "On the Road," in Nahum N. Glatzer, ed., *Twenty-One Stories: S. Y. Agnon* (New York: Schocken Books, 1970), and Dan Miron, *Ashkenaz: Modern Hebrew Literature and the Pre-Modern German Jewish Experience* (New York: Leo Baeck Institute, 1989), 8–13.

117. Abraham Habermann, ed., *Sefer gezerot ashkenaz ve-tzarfat* (Jerusalem: Tarshish, 1945), ix–xii.

7. PLACE AND DISPLACEMENT OF MEMORY

1. Frank Stern, "The Historic Triangle: Occupiers, Germans and Jews in Postwar Germany," *Tel Aviver Jahrbuch für deutsche Geschichte* 19 (1990): 47–76.

2. *Resolution Adopted by the Second Plenary Assembly of the World Jewish Congress, Montreux, June 27th–July 6th, 1948* (London, 1948), 7.

3. Robert Weltsch, "Judenbetreuung in Bayern," *Mitteilungsblatt des Irgun Olei Merkas Europa* 10 (May 10, 1946): 5.

4. C. Yahil, "All Jews Must Leave Germany," *Jewish Frontier* (May 1951): 18–21.

5. Henry R. Huttenbach, *The Destruction of the Jewish Community of Worms, 1933–1945: A Study of the Holocaust Experience in Germany* (New York: Memorial Committee of Jewish Victims of Nazism from Worms, 1981), 242–43.

6. Huttenbach, *The Destruction of the Jewish Community of Worms*, 239–41.

7. Elisabeth Young-Bruehl, *Hannah Arendt: For Love of the World* (New Haven: Yale University Press, 1982), 186.

8. Maurice Halbwachs, "The Legendary Topography of the Gospels," in Halbwachs, *On Collective Memory*, ed. and trans. Lewis A. Coser (Chicago: University of Chicago Press, 1992), 219.

9. *Bücher, die zu Buche schlagen. Der Beitrag jüdischer Mitbürger zu Literatur und Wissenschaft. Ausstellung der Stadtbibliothek Worms* (Worms: Stadtbibliothek, [1984]), 134.

10. Huttenbach, *The Destruction of the Jewish Community of Worms*, 242–43.

11. Max Guggenheim, "Worms," *Jüdische Rundschau* (March 28, 1945), Collection of American Federation of Jews from Central Europe, Leo Baeck Institute, New York, AR 4420, folder xvii.

12. Ibid.

13. Mordechai Narkiss, the director of the museum, told Guggenheim that he contemplated the physical transfer of the synagogue to Israel, since the Talmud says that in messianic times all synagogues would come to Eretz Israel. Max Guggenheim, "Episoden aus der Geschichte meiner Vaterstadt. Worms am Rhein und ihrer jüdischen Gemeinde" (1950), pp. 5 and 9, Leo Baeck Institute, New York, ME 222; "Precious at Random," *Palestine Post* (February 2, 1947): 4; and "At Random," *Palestine Post* (April 1, 1947): 4.

14. Stephen S. Kayser's letter to Michael Oppenheim, July 24, 1951, Michael Oppenheim Collection, Stadtarchiv Mainz, 50 II:14

15. Christhard Hoffmann, ed., *Preserving the Legacy of German Jewry: A History of the Leo Baeck Institute, 1955–2005* (Tübingen: Mohr Siebeck, 2005), 27–28.

16. Selma Stern, "Problems of American-Jewish and German Jewish Historiography," in Erich E. Hirshler, ed., *Jews from Germany in the United States* (New York: Farrar, Straus and Cuddahy, 1955), 4–5.

17. Robert Liberles, *Salo Wittmayer Baron: Architect of Jewish History* (New York: New York University Press, 1995), 240.

18. Cecil Roth, "The Restoration of Jewish Libraries, Archives and Museums," *Contemporary Jewish Record* 7 (1944): 253–57.

19. "Jewish Trusteeship over Property of Exterminated Jews Demanded by the Board of Deputies," *JTA News* 8 (November 8, 1944): 3; Board of Deputies of British Jews, *Statement of Postwar Policy* (London, 1944), 10–11; Michael J. Kurtz, "Resolving a Dilemma: The Inheritance of Jewish Property," *Cardozo Law Review* 20 (1998): 625–55.

20. See the letter by Saperstein to Walter Zander, October 18, 1945, and Walter Zander's letter to Cecil Roth, September 26, 1945, Cecil Roth Letters, Brotherton Library, University of Leeds.

21. American Federation of Jews from Central Europe, December 30, 1944, to Isidor Kiefer, Isidor Kiefer Collection, Leo Baeck Institute, New York, AR 1894–1903, box 2, folder 4; "Registry of Property of Former Jewish Communities in Germany: Worms," American Federation of Jews from Central Europe: Worms, Leo Baeck Institute, New York, AR 4420, xvii.

22. Salo Baron to Isidor Kiefer, August 8, 1945, Isidor Kiefer Collection, Leo Baeck Institute, New York, AR 1894–1903, box 2, folder 4, and the report by

M. Bernstein, Stuttgart, May 25, 1949, Salo Baron Archive M580, Stanford University, box 231, folder 17.

23. "Commission on European Jewish Cultural Reconstruction, Tentative List of Jewish Cultural Treasures in Axis-Occupied Countries," *Jewish Social Studies* 8 (1946): 13. Subsequently, the commission also published "Tentative List of Jewish Periodicals in Axis-Occupied Countries" in *Jewish Social Studies* (1947) and "Addenda and Corrigenda to Tentative List of Jewish Cultural Treasures in Axis-Occupied Countries" in *Jewish Social Studies* (1948).

24. See E. G. Loewenthal's letter to Friedrich Illert, April 23, 1958, Stadtarchiv Worms, Alter Judenfriedhof am Andreasring, Abt. 20, Nr. 14.

25. Hannah Arendt, "Field Report No. 15, February 10, 1950," Jewish Theological Seminary, New York, IF-86–15–1950, p. 6.

26. Kurtz, "Resolving a Dilemma," 648; Liberles, *Salo Wittmayer Baron*, 237–42.

27. Hannah Arendt to Friedrich Illert, September 27, 1950, April 8, 1951, and July 19, 1961, Stadtarchiv Worms, Abt. 20 (Kulturinstitute), p. 72; report by Eliahu Ben-Horin to Hannah Arendt, September 5, 1950, Salo Baron Archives M580, Stanford University, box 232, folder 5; and Hannah Arendt to Friedrich Illert, May 15, 1950, Stadtarchiv Worms, Abt. 20 (Kulturinstitute), p. 72.

28. Gerold Bönnen, "'Es ist mein Lebenszweck': Isidor Kiefer und sein Anteil am Wiederaufbau der Wormser Synagoge, 1957–1961," *Aschkenas* 12 (2002): 93 and 108.

29. "Yesterday: The Jews in Germany and Today," *Newsweek* (July 9, 1956): 100–103, and K. R. Grossmann, "Der Retter der Wormser Synagoge. Dr. Illerts Kampf um den Sieg," *Aufbau*, July 27, 1956, p. 21.

30. "In der stat fun Rashi," *Das Vort* (September 28, 1949): 4.

31. "Protocoll of the Torah-Uebergabe of May 28, 1948," Stadtarchiv Worms, Abt. 203, Nr. 12, and Friedrich Illert to Isidor Kiefer, March 20, 1949, Stadtarchiv Worms, Abt. 20, Nr. 71.

32. Jens Hoppe, "Das jüdische Museum in Worms. Seine Geschichte bis 1938 und die anschliessenden Bemühungen um die Wiedererrichtung der Wormser Synagoge," *Wormsgau* 21 (2002): 92–97.

33. Prominent among the potential returnees in such a case would have been Erwin Mayer and his wife, former citizens of Worms who went back in 1946. See Annelore and Karl Schlösser, *Die Wormser Juden 1933–1945. Dokumentation*, CD (Worms: Stadtarchiv, 2002).

34. Letter from Frau Lilli Blumenthal to Friedrich Illert, November 4, 1954; Friedrich Illert to Karl Guggenheim, July 25, 1953, Stadtarchiv Worms, Abt. 20 (Kulturinstitute), p. 72; Jüdische Betreuungstelle der Stadt Frankfurt a. M. to Friedrich Illert, December 24, 1945, Stadtarchiv Worms, Alter Judenfriedhof am Andreasring, Abt. 20, Nr. 15.

35. Karl D. Darmstaedter to Friedrich Illert, February 20, 1954, Stadtarchiv Worms, Abt. 20, Nr. 72.

36. Letter by Isidor Kiefer to Max and Siegfried Guggenheim, December 9, 1953, Isidor Kiefer Collection, Leo Baeck Institute, New York, AR 1894–1903, Nr. 24; Dr. K., "Lieber Besuch aus Neuyork. Mit 88 Jahren hält Isidor Kiefer seiner

Vaterstadt Worms die Treue," *Wormser Zeitung* (August, 17, 1958), Siegfried Guggenheim Collection, Leo Baeck Institute, New York, AR 180, B2, 23.

37. "Ein guter Freund seiner Wormser Heimat. Heute wird Alfred Langenbach in London 80 Jahre alt," *Wormser Zeitung* (September 10, 1959), Alfred Langenbach Collection, Leo Baeck Institute, New York, AR 2186, and Friedrich Illert, "Dr. Siegfried Guggenheim zum 80. Geburtstag. Über den Ozean grüßt Worms seinen hervorrangenden Bürgersohn," *Wormser Zeitung* (October 12, 1953).

38. Otto Böcher, "Das jüdische Worms," *Humanitas. Mitteilungsblatt der ehemaligen Lehrer und Schüler des Gymnasiums zu Worms* 7 (June 1957): 10–13; Otto Böcher, "Ein jüdischer Grabstein aus vorchristlicher Zeit in Worms?" *Der Wormsgau* 3 (1957): 412–13; Otto Böcher, "Sechs neugefundene Grabsteine vom Wormser 'Judensand,'" *Der Wormsgau* 3 (1957): 413–15; Otto Böcher, "Dauerhafteste Tradition der mittelalterlichen Reichstadt. Geschichte und Leben der Wormser Juden. Gemeinschaft, der ein grausames Ende gesetzt wurde," *Wonnegauer Heimatsblätter* 8 (August 1958): 1–2; Carl J. H. Villinger, "Die schwimmende Kiste," *Wonnegauer Heimatsblätter* 3 (March 1958): 54; and Richard Wisser, "Altwormser Sehenswürdigkeiten in neuer Sicht. Kaum bekannt—im Herzen der Stadt: Der Alte Judenfriedhof," *Wonnegauer Heimatsblätter* 6 (June 1958): 1–2.

39. Isaac Ratner, "Mir szeinen doh," *Undser Veg* 2 (October 19, 1945): 3.

40. Koppel S. Pinson, "Jewish Life in Liberated Germany: A Study of the Jewish DPs," *Jewish Social Studies* 9 (1947): 110.

41. Shmuel Krawkowski, "Memorial Projects and Memorial Institutions Initiated by She'erith Hapletah," in Yisrael Gutman and Avital Saf, eds., *She'erith Hapletah, 1944–1948: A Rehabilitation and Political Struggle; Proceedings of the 6th Yad Vashem International Conference, Jerusalem, October 1985* (Jerusalem: Yad Vashem, 1990), 391.

42. Georg Illert, "Die jüdischen Altertümer in Worms in den Jahren 1938–1961," Stadtarchiv Worms, Abt. 20, Nr. 9, p. 2, and Georg Illert, "Die jüdischen Altertümer in Worms in den Jahren 1938–1961," in Ernst Roth, ed., *Festschrift zur Wiedereinweihung der Alten Synagoge zu Worms* (Frankfurt am Main: Ner Tamid Verlag, 1961), 230. See the list of DP camps in Germany in Angelika Königseder and Juliane Wetzel, *Waiting for Hope: Jewish Displaced Persons in Postwar II Germany*, trans. John A. Broadwin (Evanston: Northwestern University Press, 2001), 215–55.

43. Königseder and Wetzel, *Waiting for Hope: Jewish Displaced Persons in Postwar II Germany*, 74–77 and 128–30.

44. Fotographien jüdischen Besucher in Worms, Stadtarchiv Worms, Abt. 203, 12/10.

45. A. Browar, "Worms," *Frayhayt* 2 (1946).

46. Ibid.

47. "Worms heute: 'Die Klagemauer des 20. Jahrhunderts,'" *Jüdische Gemeindeblatt* 1 (August 1, 1949). See also "In der stat fun Rashi," *Dos Vort* (September 28, 1949): 4.

48. Fotographien jüdischer Besucher in Worms, Stadtarchiv Worms, Abt. 203, 12/10.

49. Steven S. Schwarzschild, "Besuch in Schum" (1948–1950), Isidor Kiefer Collection, Leo Baeck Institute, New York, AR 1898, box 2, folder ix.

50. "Worms, jüdische Heiligtümer gerettet," *Aufbau* 11 (June 22, 1945): 7. See also Max Gumbel's short description of his visit to Worms, where he grew up, in *The Fountain*, 194–96, Leo Baeck Institute, New York, ME 994.

51. Dr. Illert, "Aus allen Erdteilen kommen Juden nach Worms. Vor den Grabstätten des Maharam und Maharil—Große Tage des Lebens," *Allgemeine Wochenzeitung des Judentums* (January 23, 1951): 5.

52. Friedrich Illert to Dr. Neuhaus, Leiter der jüdischen Betreuungsstelle der Stadt Frankfurt a. M., September 29, 1946, Stadtarchiv Worms, Alter Judenfriedhof am Andreasring, Abt. 20, Nr. 14.

53. Bruno Weil, Die drei Synagogen (Aus dem Tagebuch einer Deutschlandreise), Bruno Weil Collection, Leo Baeck Institute, New York, MF 516, 1–3.

54. Marvin Lowenthal, *A World Passed By* (New York: National Jewish Welfare Board and A. Behrmann House Publication, 1945). While apparently already inundated with requests from schools, Lowenthal suggested promoting the book to Jewish army chaplains in a letter to his publisher Behrmann; see the letter by Behrmann House, Inc., Publishers, October 26, 1945, to Marvin Lowenthal, American-Jewish Archives, New York, Marvin Lowenthal Papers 140, box 6.

55. *A Pocket Guide to Germany* (Washington, D.C.: U. S. Government Printing Office, 1944) and *A Pocket Guide to Germany* (Washington, D.C.: U. S. Government Printing Office, 1951).

56. See Frank L. Weil, introduction to Lowenthal, *A World Passed By*.

57. See Lowenthal's introduction to *A World Passed By*.

58. Lowenthal, *A World Passed By*, 120–22.

59. Friedrich M. Illert, *Noteworthy and Memorable Facts about Worms*, trans. K. Th. Hirsch (Worms: Published by the Municipal Archives, 1945), 10–14, Isidor Kiefer Collection, Leo Baeck Institute, New York, AR 1894–1903, box 2.

60. Andre Soutou, *Worms am Rhein. Führer durch die Stadt und ihre Sehenswürdigkeiten* (Worms: Erich Norberg, 1949), 54.

61. Ibid., 22–52, and Illert, *Worms am Rhein*, 84–85.

62. *The Jewish Chronicle Travel Guide* 1 (1954). The most recent edition is Michael Zaidner, ed., *Jewish Travel Guide 2000* (London: Valentine and Mitchell, 2000).

63. *The Jewish Travel Guide: The Jewish Life in Germany* (Frankfurt am Main: Paneuropean Edition, 1954), 4–8, 10–19, 19–20, 79.

64. *Neugegründete Fremdenverkehrsverbände in Deutschland. Stand vom 10.2.1947*, Institute for Tourism, Berlin. The *Deutsche Zeitschrift für Fremdenverkehr* was first published in July 1949.

65. Hannah Arendt, "Field Report No. 15, February 10, 1950," Jewish Theological Seminary, New York, IF-86-15-1950, p. 6; M. Bernstein, "Worms—Sage und Wirklichkeit," *Allgemeine Jüdische Illustrierte* 1 (May 1951), 3; "Worms heute: 'Die Klagemauer des 20. Jahrhunderts,'" *Jüdische Gemeindeblatt* 1 (August 1, 1949); "In der stat fun Rashi," *Dos Vort* (September 28, 1949), 4; and "Worms," *Frayheyt* 2 (1946).

66. Ernest Namenyi, "Pierres de Rhenanie," *La Vie Juive* (January 1953): 19.

67. "Die Rashi-Synagoge in Worms," *Aufbau* 15 (October 14, 1949): 8; Helmut Rödler, "Worms aus der Asche," *Aufbau* (December 4, 1953): 9; Ricarda Schloss-han, "Verwitterte Gräber im Haus des Lebens," *Frankfurter Allgemeine Zeitung* (July 10, 1955): 7; Erwin Kleine, "Verjüngung der Erde zu Schauen. Ein Gang über den ältesten Judenfriedhof Europas—Worms war einst Mittelpunkt Jüdisches Lebens," *Kölnische Rundschau* (November 25, 1956), Press Cuttings on the History of German Jewry: Worms, Wiener Library, London, Press Archives Pc 8, 146; and Peter Ratazzi, "Ancient Records in the City of Worms: Burial Ground of Jews Dates Back 900 Years," *Herald Tribune*, November 24, 1959, Worms Stadtarchiv, Abt. 20 (Kulturinstitute): 72.

68. John McCloy, "Remarks," *Conference on "the Future of Jews in Germany"* (Heidelberg, 1949), 20.

69. Eva G. Reichmann, "Germany's New Nazis: Impressions from a Recent Journey through Germany's Danger Zones," Wiener Library, August 1951, and Hannah Arendt, "The Aftermath of Nazi-Rule: Reports from Germany," *Commentary* 10 (1950): 342–53.

70. See, for example, "German Nazis Are Active Again: Desecrations of Cemeteries," *Wiener Library Bulletin* 2 (November 1947), 3; "The Old Iniquity Writ Large: Desecrations of Cemeteries in Germany," *Wiener Library Bulletin* 3 (March 1949): 26.

71. "Cemetery Desecrated in Worms: From Our Correspondent," *Jewish Chronicle* (May 15, 1953): 1. See also "Jüdische Friedhof in Worms geschändet," *Frankfurter Rundschau* (May 13, 1952): 138; "Jüdische Gräber geschändet," *Frankfurter Rundschau* (May 22, 1952), in Press Cuttings Archive 8, Reel 185, Ka, Wiener Library, London; Max Guggenheim to Isidor Kiefer, November 12, 1953, Isidor Kiefer Collection, Leo Baeck Institute, New York, AR 1894–1903, p. 23; Friedrich Illert to the Städtische Presseamt Worms, May 19, 1952, Stadtarchiv Worms, Alter Judenfriedhof am Andreasring, Abt. 20, Nr. 15; and Friedrich Illert to August Gallinger, July 7, 1953, Stadtarchiv Worms, Alter Judenfriedhof am Andreasring, Abt. 20, Nr. 15.

72. Rudy Koshar, *Germany's Transient Pasts: Preservation and National Memory in the Twentieth Century* (Chapel Hill: University of North Carolina Press, 1998), 208.

73. Susanne Kittel, "Spuren der Übergangszeit: Der Wiederaufbau von Worms nach 1945," *Bausubstanz* 14 (1988): 40–45, and Beverly Heckart, "The Cities of Avignon and Worms as Expressions of the European Community," *Comparative Studies in Society and History* 31 (1989): 462–90.

74. See, for example, Illert, *Worms am Rhein*.

75. Walter Koehler, *Worms am Rhein. Das Wesen der Stadt—Ihr Zustand. Erste Gedanken über den späteren Wiederaufbau* (January 1946); *Worms am Rhein. Ein Beispiel* (October, 1948); *Worms am Rhein. Der Wiederaufbau* (December 31, 1951); and *Tradition und Fortschritt im Aufbau. Aufbau-Verein Worms e.V. Gemeinnützige Vereinigung Wormser Bürger zum Wiederaufbau ihrer Stadt Worms am Rhein* (Worms: Erich Norberg, 1957).

76. Mahnmahl des Faschismus, Stadtarchiv Worms, Stadtverwaltung 6:109.

77. Fritz Reuter, "Leopold Levy und seine Synagoge von 1875. Ein Beitrag zu Geschichte und Selbstverständis der Wormser Juden im 19. Jahrhundert," *Wormsgau* 11 (1974–75): 66–67.

78. See letter by the *Jüdische Betreuungstelle der Stadt Frankfurt a. M.* to Friedrich Illert, December 24, 1945, Stadtarchiv Worms, Alter Judenfriedhof am Andreasring, Abt. 20, Nr. 14, and Friedrich Illert's letters to Dr. E. G. Löwenthal, August 13, 1958, and October 1, 1958, Stadtarchiv Worms, Alter Judenfriedhof am Andreasring, Abt. 20, Nr. 14.

79. Friedrich Illert to Heinrich Völker, June 14, 1945, Stadtarchiv Worms, Alter Judenfriedhof am Andreasring, Abt. 20, Nr. 15; Friedrich Illert to Heinrich Völker, March 4, 1946; Friedrich Illert to Dr. Neuhaus, September 29, 1946, and Illert's letter to Finanzamt Worms, July 21, 1946, Stadtarchiv Worms, Alter Judenfriedhof am Andreasring, Abt. 20, Nr. 14.

80. Finanzamt Worms to Friedrich Illert, August 12, 1946, Stadtarchiv Worms, Alter Judenfriedhof am Andreasring, Abt. 20, Nr. 14.

81. Auszug aus der Niederschrift über die öffentliche Sitzung des Stadrats vom 18. Dezember 1946, Stadtarchiv Worms, Friedhof am Andreasring, Abt. 20, Nr. 14.

82. Isidor Kiefer to Heinrich Völker, October 11, 1947, Stadtarchiv Worms, Alter Judenfriedhof am Andreasring, Abt. 20, Nr. 14. See also Friedrich Illert letters to E. G. Löwenthal, August 13, 1958, and October 1, 1958, Stadtarchiv Worms, Alter Judenfriedhof am Andreasring, Abt. 20, Nr. 14, and "Gewährung von Landeszuschüssen zur Instantsetzung jüdischer Friedhöfe," *Ministerialblatt der Landesregierung von Rheinland-Pfalz* 7 (June 8, 1955): 697–700.

83. Otto Böcher, *Der alte Judenfriedhof in Worms. Ein Führer durch seine Geschichte und Grabmäler* (Worms: Stadtarchiv Worms, 1958). This guide reappeared in 1960, 1962, 1968, 1976, 1979, 1984, 1987, and 1992.

84. Isidor Kiefer to Friedrich Illert, November 21, 1946, Stadtarchiv Worms, Abt. 20, Nr. 71.

85. Friedrich Illert to Isidor Kiefer, February 24, 1946, Stadtarchiv Worms, Abt. 203, Nr. 12.

86. Friedrich Illert to Isidor Kiefer, December 20, 1947, Stadtarchiv Worms Abt. 20, Nr. 71.

87. Illert, *Worms am Rhein. Führer durch die Geschichte und Sehenswürdigkeiten*, 85.

88. Eleonore Sterling to Guido Kisch, July 5, 1954, Guido Kisch Collection, Leo Baeck Institute, New York, AR 787, Folder 7/13.

8. WORMS OUT OF THE ASHES

1. See Norbert Frei, *Adenauer's Germany and the Nazi Past: The Politics of Amnesty and Integration*, trans. Joel Golb (New York: Columbia University Press, 2002).

2. Celia Applegate, *Heimat in the Pfalz: A Nation of Provincials; The German Idea of Heimat* (Berkeley: University of California Press, 1990), 229.

3. Robert Möller, *War Stories: The Search for a Usable Past in the Federal Republic of Germany* (Berkeley: University of California Press, 2001).

4. Peter Reichel, *Vergangenheitsbewältigung in Deutschland. Die Auseinandersetzung mit der NS-Diktatur von 1945 bis heute* (Munich: Beck, 2001); Mary Fulbrook, *German National Identity after the Holocaust* (Cambridge: Polity Press, 1999); Alf Lüdtke, "'Coming to Terms with the Past': Illusions of Remembering, Ways of Forgetting Nazism in West Germany," *Journal of Modern History* 65 (1993): 542–72.

5. See, for example, Harold Marcuse, *Legacies of Dachau: The Uses and Abuses of a Concentration Camp, 1933–2001* (Cambridge: Cambridge University Press, 2001); Peter Reichel, ed., *Das Gedächtnis der Stadt. Hamburg im Umgang mit seiner nationalsozialistischen Vergangenheit* (Hamburg: Dölling und Galitz Verlag, 1997); and Rudy Koshar, *From Monuments to Traces: Artefacts of German Memory, 1870–1900* (Berkeley: University of California Press, 2000), 226–85.

6. Hannah Arendt, "The Aftermath of Nazi Rule: Report from Germany," *Commentary* (October 1950): 342.

7. Alexander and Margarete Mitscherlich, *Inability to Mourn*, trans. Beverly R. Placzek (New York: Grove Press, 1975), 10–11. On the rebuilding of historical monuments, see Koshar, *Germany's Transient Pasts*, 199–243.

8. Between 1945 and 1987, for example, 63 out of 245 synagogues that had survived the war were torn down in the state of Hessen alone. See Thea Altaras, *Synagogen in Hessen: Was geschah seit 1945?* (Königstein/Taunus: K. Langewiesche, 1988), 35.

9. Gavriel Rosenfeld, *Munich and Memory: Architecture, Monuments, and the Legacy of the Third Reich* (Berkeley: University of California Press, 2000).

10. Ibid., xvii.

11. James E. Young, *Holocaust Memorials and Meaning* (New Haven: Yale University Press, 1993), xii.

12. Friedrich Illert to Isidor Kiefer, March 29, 1948, Stadtarchiv Worms, Abt. 20, Nr. 71.

13. Friedrich Illert to the French military government, March, 24, 1948, Stadtarchiv Worms, Abt. 20, Nr. 71.

14. See Isidor Kiefer's letter on behalf of the Jewish Museum in New York (undated), Leo Baeck Institute, New York, Isidor Kiefer Collection, AR 1894–1903, box 2; Isidor Kiefer to Friedrich Illert, April 12, 1949, and March 11, 1950, Stadtarchiv Worms, Abt. 20, Nr. 71.

15. Schriftwechsel mit der Israel-Mission, 1958–1963, Stadtarchiv Worms, Abt. 6, Nr. 140, and Jens Hoppe, "Das jüdische Museum in Worms. Seine Geschichte bis 1938 und die anschliessenden Bemühungen um die Wiederrichtung der Wormser Synagoge," *Wormsgau* 21 (2002): 97–99.

16. Georg Illert, "Die jüdischen Altertümer in Worms in den Jahren 1938–1961," in Ernst Roth, ed., *Festschrift zur Wiedereinweihung der Alten Synagoge zu Worms* (Frankfurt am Main: Ner Tamid Verlag, 1961), 231–232, and Stadtarchiv Worms, Abt. 20:7, Jüdische Altertümer: Rechtsstreit der Branche Française gegen die Stadt Worms, Nr. 67–69.

17. Gutachten des Herren Isidor Kiefer aus New York, Nachlaß Dr. Friedrich Maria Illert (1892–1966), Stadtarchiv Worms, 170/16, Nr. 8.

18. "An die ehemaligen Wormser jüdischen Familien," Leo Baeck Institute, New York, Isidor Kiefer Collection, AR 1894–1903, box 1.

19. Stadtarchiv Worms, Abt. 20, Nr. 70, and Stadtarchiv Worms, Abt. 6, Nr. 77. Gerald Bönnen quite rightly questions Illert's self-fashioned image as Worms's cultural custodian and further implies that Illert pressured the former Jews of Worms regarding his personal agenda. See Gerald Bönnen, " 'Es ist mein Lebenszweck': Isidor Kiefer und sein Anteil am Wiederaufbau der Wormser Synagoge, 1957–1961," *Aschkenas* 12 (2002): 101.

20. Hoppe, "Das jüdische Museum in Worms," 98.

21. "Anmerkungen zur Denkschrift des Herrn Oberbürgermeister der Stadt Worms über die jüdischen Altertümer dortselbst," Salo Baron Archives, M580, Stanford University, JRC, 1954–1955, box 44, folder 1, 1–3.

22. Friedrich Illert to Isidor Kiefer, March 27, 1956, in which Illert notes that the question of the ownership of the archives had become a matter of foreign policy. Leo Baeck Institute, New York, Isidor Kiefer Collection, AR 1894–1903, box 2.

23. "Vorentwurft betr. Vereinbarung zwischen Branche Française und Stadt Worms und Abkommen zwischen Bundesrepublik Deutschland und Israel, September 1958," Leo Baeck Institute, New York, Isidor Kiefer Collection, AR 1894–1903, box 2, and Friedrich Illert to Isidor Kiefer, August 29, 1956, Leo Baeck Institute, New York, Isidor Kiefer Collection, AR 1894–1903, box 2.

24. "Jüdische Kulturschätze von Worms nach Jerusalem. Stadtrat stimmte der Vereinbarung mit Israel zu. Isolierbaracke im Krankenhaus abgezogen," *Wormser Zeitung* (December 21, 1956): 3.

25. Quoted in Daniel Cohen, "Jewish Records from Germany in the Jewish Historical Archives in Jerusalem," *LBIYB* 1 (1956): 331–45, here 332.

26. "Wormser Dokumente in Jerusalem. Geschichtliche Zeugen der jüdischen Gemeinde. Ein Beweis des Willens der Wiedergutmachung," *Wormser Zeitung* (April 19–20, 1958): 4, and the newspaper articles from the *Badische Neuste Nachrichten* (March 29, 1958) and *Frankfurt Allgemeine Zeitung* (October 31, 1957), Press Cuttings on the History of German Jewry: Worms, Wiener Library, London Press Archives, PC 8, 146.

27. "Wormser Kulturgegenstände bleiben," *Allgemeine Wochenzeitung der Juden in Deutschland* 11 (March 22, 1957): 14.

28. "Prime Minister's Office. The Archivist. Ceremony at the State Archives on the Occasion of the Transfer of the Worms Antiquities, October 29, 1957," Press Cuttings on the History of German Jewry: Worms, Wiener Library, London Press Archives, PC 8, 146.

29. Dr. Ernst Tryfus, "Das Archiv der Gemeinde Worms in Israel," *Mitteilungsblatt* 25 (November 22, 1957): 8, and Daniel Cohen, "Das Archiv der Gemeinde Worms," *BLBI* 1 (1958): 118–22.

30. Friedrich Illert to Isidor Kiefer, August 29, 1956, Leo Baeck Institute, New York, Isidor Kiefer Collection, AR 1894–1903, box 2.

31. See, for example, Friedrich Illert, "Die Synagoge in Worms," *N.Y. Staatszeitung und Herold* (March 27, 1955): 21c–22c, and Isidor Kiefer, "Raschikapelle im

jüdischen Friedhof Worms erneuert," *N.Y. Staats-Zeitung und Herold* (February 7, 1958): 15.

32. Friedrich Illert, "Das kleine Jerusalem: Aelteste jüdische Gedenkstätten in Worms," *Boletin Informativo der Sociedad Cultural Israelita B'ne Jisroel* (July 1952), Stadtarchiv Worms, Stadtarchiv Abt. 20 (Kulturinstitute): 72.

33. Kiefer, "Raschikapelle im jüdischen Friedhof Worms erneuert," 15.

34. Georg Illert, "Die jüdischen Altertümer in Worms in den Jahren 1938–1961," 237.

35. Eugen Mayer to Heinrich Völker, October 15, 1959, Einweihung der wieder aufgebauten alten Wormser Synagoge am 3.12.1961 [1961–1965], Stadtarchiv Worms, Abt. 6, Nr. 72.

36. Isaak Holzer to Friedrich Illert, July 22, 1947, Stadtarchiv Worms, Abt. 20, 71.

37. See the letter by Richard Krautheimer to Friedrich Illert, April 30, 1947. Karl Darmstaedter rejected the idea of rebuilding the synagogue altogether. See Karl Darmstaedter to Friedrich Illert, February 20, 1954, Stadtarchiv Worms, Abt. 20, Nr. 72.

38. Elke Spies, "Die zerstörte Raschi-Synagoge," *Aufbau* (undated), Isidor Kiefer Collection, AR 1894–1903, box 2, Leo Baeck Institute, New York.

39. See her letter to Baron Ludwig von Heyl, November 14, 1955, Stadtarchiv Worms, Briefwechsel mit Anlagen mit Carola Kaufmann, geb. Levy, 1947–1955, 170/16, Nr. 7.

40. Ibid.

41. See the undated letter by Ferdinand Kaufmann to Isidor Kiefer, Stadtarchiv Worms, Briefwechsel mit Anlagen mit Carola Kaufmann, geb. Levy, 1947–1955, 170/16, Nr. 7.

42. Rudolf Morsey and Hans-Peter Schwarz, eds., *Adenauer-Heuss. Unter vier Augen. Gespräche aus den Gründerjahren* (Berlin: Siedler, 1997), 78 and 371 n. 34. See the copy of Isidor Kiefer's letter to Konrad Adenauer, March 21, 1954, Leo Baeck Institute, New York, Isidor Kiefer Collection, AR 1894–1903, box 2, and the copy of Kiefer's letter to Konrad Adenauer, September 28, 1957, Stadtarchiv Worms, Stadtverwaltung Worms: Hauptverwaltung, Hauptamt: Abt. 6, 70.

43. "Worms Synagogue to Be Rebuilt: Fundraising Campaign," *Jewish Chronicle* (July 29, 1955): 10.

44. Heinrich Völker, "An die im Ausland lebenden ehemaligen Bürger der Stadt Worms," (August 1959), Worms Stadtarchiv, Abt. 6, Nr. 73.

45. E. M. Orland (Eleonore Sterling), "West Germany," *American Jewish Year Book* 63 (1963): 355. Much to the dismay of the local Worms newspaper, the exhibition contained only a few items that pertained to Worms, due to the "saddening events of November 9th," apparently referring to the destruction during Kristallnacht. See "Wormser Kulturgut auf den Synagoga. Weinkrüge, Silberpokal und Gemälde in Rechlinghausen zu sehen," *Wormser Zeitung* (December 5, 1960): 5. On the exhibition, see *Synagoga. Kultgeräte und Kunstwerke von der Zeit der Patriarchen bis zur Gegenwart. Städtische Kunsthallte Recklinghausen, 3. November 1960–15. Januar 1961* (Recklinghausen: Städtische Kunsthalle, 1960), and Sabine Offe,

Ausstellungen, Einstellungen, Entstellungen: Jüdische Museen in Deutschland und Österreich (Berlin: Philo, 2000), 72.

46. Ulrich Brochhagen, *Nach Nürnberg. Vergangenheitsbewältigung und Westintegration in der Ära Adenauer* (Berlin: Ullstein, 1999), 319–67, and Detlef Siegfried, "Zwischen Aufarbeitung und Schlußstrich. Der Umgang mit der NS-Vergangenheit in den beiden deutschen Staaten 1958 bis 1969," in Axel Schmidt et al., eds., *Dynamische Zeiten. Die 60er Jahre in den beiden deutschen Gesellschaften* (Hamburg: Christians, 2000), 77–113.

47. Theodor W. Adorno, "What Does Coming to Terms with the Past Mean?" in *Bitburg in Moral and Political Perspective*, ed. Geoffrey H. Hartman (Bloomington: Indiana University Press, 1986), 115.

48. "Prominente Gäste besuchen Worms: Gesellschaft für christlich-jüdische Zusammenarbeit schickt Vertreter," *Wormser Zeitung* (September 24, 1959): 4; "Grundsteinlegung für Wormser Synagogue," *Generalanzeiger Ludwigshafen* (September 23, 1959); "Dokumente tausendjähriger Geschichte," *Darmstädter Echo* (September 24, 1959), Press Cuttings on the History of German Jewry: Worms, Wiener Library, London Press Archives, PC 8, 146.

49. Ernst Roth, "Grundsteinlegung zum Wiederaufbau der Wormser Synagoge am 27. September 1959," in Ernst Roth, ed., *Festschrift zur Wiedereinweihung der Alten Synagoge zu Worms* (Frankfurt am Main: Ner Tamid Verlag, 1961), 245–46. The Worms celebration is also captured in a sound recording by Südwestfunk, Stadtarchiv Worms, Abt. 211a, Nr. 146.

50. Heinrich Völker, "In der Synagogenruine. Ansprache des Oberbürgermeisters H. Völker," in Roth, *Festschrift zur Wiedereinweihung der Alten Synagoge zu Worms*, 246–47.

51. Karl Guggenheim to Heinrich Völker, September 9, 1959, and Renate Heidelberger geb. Hirsch, September 20, 1959, Einweihung der wieder aufgebauten alten Wormser Synagoge am 3.12.1961 (1961–1965), Stadtarchiv Worms, Abt. 6, Nr. 72, and Völker, "In der Synagogenruine," 248–49.

52. Ludwig Erhard, "Feierliche Ansprache"; Ernst Roth, "Zur Wiedereinweihung der Alten Wormser Synagoge vor 20 Jahren," *Udim* 11–12 (1981/1982): 200–203; and "Synagoge in Worms eingeweiht," *Süddeutsche Zeitung* (December 12, 1961), Press Cuttings on the History of German Jewry: Worms, Wiener Library, London Press Archives, PC 8, 146.

53. Fritz Reuter, "Dr. Friedrich M. Illert (1892–1966). Zu seinem 100. Geburtstag," *Der Wormsgau* 16 (1991/1995): 23.

54. Recording of the Südwestfunk, Stadtarchiv Worms, Abt. 211a, Nr. 146, and Isidor Kiefer in Roth, *Festschrift zur Wiedereinweihung der Alten Synagoge zu Worms*, 258–59.

55. Roth, *Festschrift zur Wiedereinweihung der Alten Synagoge zu Worms*, 252.

56. Ibid., 251.

57. Daniela Schäfer, "Grundsteinlegung in Worms. Das älteste jüdische Gotteshaus in Deutschland entsteht wieder," *Allgemeine Wochenzeitung der Juden in Deutschland* (October 8, 1959): 4.

58. Roth, *Festschrift zur Wiedereinweihung der Alten Synagoge zu Worms*, 254;

"Eine Stätte frommer Pilgerschaft," *Allgemeine Wochenzeitung der Juden in Deutschland* (September 28, 1959); and "Innenminister Schröder brandmarkt Rassenhaß," *Frankfurter Allgemeine Zeitung* (September 28, 1959), Press Cuttings on the History of German Jewry: Worms, Wiener Library, London Press Archives, PC 8, 146. Heinrich Lübke's address noted that the rebuilding of the synagogue would be a sign for the "good neighborliness of Germans and Jews in their shared fatherland." See the undated letter by Heinrich Lübke, Wiederaufbau der Synagoge, 1959–1961, Stadtarchiv Worms, Abt. 6, Nr. 73.

59. Roth, *Festschrift zur Wiedereinweihung der Alten Synagoge zu Worms*, 255.

60. F. Ziegellaub and I. Wenger in Roth, *Festschrift zur Wiedereinweihung der Alten Synagoge zu Worms*, 262–65. See also "Freude und Besinnung: Ansprache von Dr. F. E. Schinnar, Botschafter Israels," *Allgemeine Wochenzeitung der Juden in Deutschland* (October 8, 1959): 4.

61. Richard Lewisohn to Heinrich Völker, October 7, 1959, Einweihung der wieder aufgebauten alten Wormser Synagoge am 3.12.1961 (1961–1965), Stadtarchiv Worms, Abt. 6, Nr. 72, and similar letters addressed to the mayor of the city.

62. See Heinrich Völker's letter to Kurt Koehler, September 30, 1959, Einweihung der wieder aufgebauten alten Wormser Synagoge am 3.12.1961 (1961–1965), Stadtarchiv Worms, Abt. 6, Nr. 72. A similar critical voice appeared also in the left newspaper *Vorwärts* (October 2, 1959). See Kurt Koehler's letter to Heinrich Völker, September 28, 1959, Einweihung der wieder aufgebauten alten Wormser Synagoge am 3.12.1961 (1961–1965), Stadtarchiv Worms, Abt. 6, Nr. 72.

63. See the correspondence with Heinrich Völker in Einweihung der wieder aufgebauten alten Wormser Synagoge am 3.12.1961 (1961–1965), Stadtarchiv Worms, Abt. 6, Nr. 72.

64. Annelore and Karl Schlösser, *Die Wormser Juden 1933–1945. Dokumentation,* CD (Worms: Stadtarchiv, 2002).

65. Daniela Schäfer, "Grundsteinlegung in Worms. Das älteste jüdische Gotteshaus in Deutschland entsteht wieder," *Allgemeine Wochenzeitung der Juden in Deutschland* (October 8, 1959): 4. In addition to E. G. Lowenthal, theologian and art historian Otto Böcher, who had been born in Worms, reviewed the history of the community in the *Allgemeine*. See E. G. Lowenthal, "Die jüdische Gemeinde in Worms," *Allgemeine Wochenzeitung der Juden in Deutschland* (September 25, 1959), and Otto Böcher, "Aus der Geschichte der Alten Synagogue zu Worms," *Allgemeine Wochenzeitung der Juden in Deutschland* (September 25, 1959), Press Cuttings on the History of German Jewry: Worms, Wiener Library, London Press Archives, PC 8, 146.

66. Norman Bentwich, "Jewish Relics at Worms," *Jewish Chronicle* (December 19, 1958): 19.

67. Isidor Kiefer, "Zum Wiederaufbau der zerstoerten Synagoge in Worms" (July 1954), Stadtarchiv Worms, Abt. 20 (Kulturinstitute): 72 Abt. 203, Nr. 11.

68. Ernst Borgward and Wolfgang Teuchert, "Tagung der deutschen Denkmalpfleger," *Deutsche Kunst und Denkmalpflege* 21 (1963): 65–67, and Koshar, *Germany's Transient Pasts*, 264.

69. Otto Böcher, "Zum Wiederaufbau der Wormser Synagoge," *Der Wormsgau* 19 (2000): 205–27.

70. Letter by Isidor Kiefer to Otto Böcher, May 30, 1961, in Böcher, "Zum Wie-deraufbau der Wormser Synagoge," 219.

71. Otto Böcher reprints his article, as well as the correspondence with Isidor Wenger, in "Zum Wiederaufbau der Wormser Synagoge," 223–27.

72. Karl Guggenheim, "Erinnerungen," *Aufbau* (December 1, 1961): 17–18; Guggenheim, "Erinnerungen an Worms. Die Wormser Synagoge eingeweiht," *Aufbau* (December 8, 1961): 9–10; Guggenheim, "Erinnerungen," *Allgemeine Wochenzeitung der Juden in Deutschland* (December 1, 1961): 17–18; and Leo Schonmann, "Das war in Worms im Monat Mai" (1960), Stadtarchiv Worms, Abt. 203, 81.

73. Isidor Kiefer, "Ein alter Mann erzählt von Worms seiner Jugend," *Won-negauer Heimatblätter* 4 (September 1959): 2–3.

74. Koshar, *Germany's Transient Pasts*, 247.

75. The debates in the German public about the trial, as well as the *Festschrift* on the occasion of the synagogue's reconsecration, appeared with the same publisher in Frankfurt in 1961; see Hans Lamm, ed., *Der Eichmann-Prozess in der deutschen öffentlichen Meinung. Eine Dokumentensammlung* (Frankfurt am Main: Ner Tamid, 1961).

76. "Chanukkah—ein demokratisches Fest. Oberbürgermeister Völker beschenkt als Versöhnungsgeste junge Juden," *Wormser Zeitung* (December 5, 1964): 4.

77. *Wiedereinweihung der Alten Synagogue zu Worms* (1961), Stadtarchiv Worms, Abt. 203, Nr. 82.

78. Heinrich Völker, "Begrüßungsansprache"; Ernst Roth, "Zur Wiederein-weihung der Alten Wormser Synagoge vor 20 Jahren," *Udim* 11–12 (1981/1982): 184–89; Sybil Henning, "Der heilige Sand von Worms," *Heidelberger Tageblatt* (September 23, 1960): 19.

79. "Prominente Gäste besuchen Worms. Gesellschaft für christlich-jüdische Zusammenarbeit schickt Vertreter," *Wormser Zeitung* (September 24, 1959): 4.

80. "Ein denkwürdiges Ereignis in der Geschichte der Stadt Worms: Die Syna-goge—Symbol der Liebe und Verständigung. Feierliche Einweihung des wiede-raufgebauten Gotteshauses in Gegenwart hoher Repräsentanten und Juden aus aller Welt," *Wormser Zeitung* (December 4, 1961): 4, and "Prominenz aus aller Welt in der Nibelungenstadt. Im Zeltbau standen sieben Fernsehempfänger / Glatteis verzögerte die Anfahrt des Ministerpräsidenten," *Wormser Zeitung* (December 4, 1961): 4.

81. Gaston Coblentz, "Synagogue Sacked by Nazis Rebuilt in City of Only 22 Jews," *Herald Tribune* (December 1961): 2; Siegfried Guggenheim Archive 180, Nr. 39, and "Presseberichte. Alte Synagoge zu Worms. Grundsteinlegung. Wiederein-weihung, 1959–1962," Stadtarchiv Worms, Abt. 6, Nr. 79.

82. Erhard Becker, "Die alte Synagoge zu Worms," *Stuttgarter Zeitung* (Decem-ber 2, 1961): 50; Sybil Henning, "Der heilige Sand von Worms," *Heidelberger Tage-blatt* (September 23, 1960), 19; "Ein denkwürdiges Ereignis in der Geschichte der Stadt Worms: Die Synagoge—Symbol der Liebe und Verständigung. Feierliche Einweihung des wiederaufgebauten Gotteshauses in Gegenwart hoher Repräsent-anten und Juden aus aller Welt," *Wormser Zeitung* (December 4, 1961): 4.

266

Notes to Pages 175–76

83. Otto Böcher, "Heilige Gemeinde Worms," Press Cuttings on the History of German Jewry: Worms, Wiener Library, London Press Archives, PC 8, 146.

84. Ernst Roth, "Zur Wiedereinweihung der Alten Wormser Synagoge vor 20 Jahren," *Udim* 11–12 (1981/1982): 194–95.

85. "Einweihung der wiedererrichteten Raschi-Synagoge," *Münchener Jüdische Nachrichten* (December 8, 1961), in Presseberichte. Alte Synagoge zu Worms. Grundsteinlegung. Wiedereinweihung, 1959–1962, Stadtarchiv Worms, Abt. 6, Nr. 79, and Otto Simon, "Einweihung der wieder aufgebauten Wormser Synagoge," *Jewish Way* (December 1961): 5.

86. Frederick R. Lachmann, "Ein jüdischer Tempel in der Stadt ohne Juden," *Aufbau* (December 1, 1961): 27–28.

87. "Europe's Oldest Synagogue Is Reconsecrated: Reminder of Nazi Crimes," *Jewish Chronicle* (December 8, 1961): 14.

88. E. G. Lowenthal, "Festtage in Worms," *Aufbau* (December 29, 1961): 17–18.

89. E. G. Lowenthal, "Tat der Gesinnung—Tag der Besinnlichkkeit," *Allgemeine Wochenzeitung der Juden in Deutschland* (December 8, 1961): 5.

90. Friedrich Illert, *Worms am Rhein. Führer durch die Geschichte und Sehenswürdigkeiten* (Worms: Erich Norberg, 1964), 95–96.

91. Elisabeth Domansky, "Die gespaltene Erinnerung," in Manuel Köppen, ed., *Kunst und Literatur nach Auschwitz* (Berlin: Erich Schmidt, 1993), 178–97.

92. "Bewohnerin der Judengasse. Sanieren heißt nicht abreißen, sondern erhalten so gut es eben geht," *Wormser Zeitung* (March 31, 1973): 11.

93. *Stadtsanierung Worms. Die Judengasse. 5. Bürgerinformationen der Stadtverwaltung Worms zur Altstadtsanierung* (Worms: 1978), 8–17.

94. Fritz Reuter's list of publications on Worms and its Jewish history is too long to be cited here completely. Among his more important publications are *Warmaisa. 1000 Jahre Juden in Worms* (Worm: Stadtarchiv Worms, 1984), which was republished in 1987, as well as various guides to the city including *Worms am Rhein. Historische Stadtspaziergänge für Einheimische und Gäste* (Hamm: Kehl, 2000). Reuter also published separate guides to the Jewish sites: see *Jüdisches Worms. Rashi-Haus und Judengasse* (Worms: H. Fischer, 1992, 1993, and 1998), which also appeared recently in an English edition, as well as *Jewish Worms: Rashi House and Judengasse* (Worms, 1992), published again in 1999.

95. Fritz Reuter, "Thesen des Altertumsvereins Worms e. V. zur Sanierung der Judengasse," *Der Wormsgau* 10 (1972–73): 86; Reuter, *Jüdisches Worms. Raschi-Haus und Judengasse*, 10–13; and Otto Böcher, "Thesen des Altertumsvereins Worms e.V. zur Sanierung der Judengasse," *Der Wormsgau* 10 (1972–73): 86.

96. Reuter, *Jüdisches Worms. Raschi-Haus und Judengasse*, 15–20 and 22–25.

97. Henry R. Huttenbach, *The Emigration Book of Worms: The Character and Dimension of the Jewish Exodus from a Small German Jewish Community, 1933–1941* (Coblenz: Landesarchivverwaltung Rheinland-Pfalz, 1974), v.

98. Miriam Gerber, "Talk on Memorial Weekend in Worms (November 9–11, 1980) for Scott Tower B'nai B'rith—March, 11, 1981," Worms Stadtarchiv, Abt. 214/13, Nr. 10.

99. Henry R. Huttenbach, *The Destruction of the Jewish Community of Worms,*

1933–1945: A Study of the Holocaust Experience in Germany (New York: Memorial Committee of Jewish Victims of Nazism from Worms, 1981), 77–216.

100. Ibid., xvi.

101. Ibid., n.p.

102. Ibid., 242.

103. Gerber, "Talk on Memorial Weekend in Worms."

104. Ibid.; see also the circular letter from the Memorial Committee for Jewish Victims of Nazism from Worms, February 1, 1981, Worms Stadtarchiv Abt. 6/47, Nr. 92.

105. See the letter by Fritz Reuter to Otto Böcher, April 9, 1980, Stadtarchiv Worms, Ehemalige Wormser Juden, Abt. 6–47 A, Nr. 92.

106. "Deutsch-jüdische Begegnung—in drei Veranstaltungen," *Wormser Zeitung* (September 19–20, 1959), Stadtarchiv Worms, Abt. 20 (Kulturinstitute): 72.

107. "Die Kontake aus der Israel-Reise gut nutzen. Das Programm der Wormser Sozialdemokraten-Gruppen war in den zwei Wochen sehr vielseitig," *Wormser Zeitung* (December 2, 1985): 15; "Wormser Laute sehr weit vom Rhein entfernt: Ehemalige Mitbürger jüdischen Glaubens waren in Israel zahlreich bei der Reisegruppe," *Wormser Zeitung* (November 26, 1985): 11.

9. THE PRESENCE OF ABSENCE

1. Klaus F. Schmidt-Mâcon, *Steinzeichen. Gedichte mit Fotographien von Günther Sydow* (Heppenheim: Otto KG, 1982), 57.

2. Ibid., 58–59.

3. Ibid., 9. See also the poem "allen menschen," 49.

4. Ibid., 24.

5. Ibid., 20–21. Thus, one poem is also dedicated to Martin Buber, 46.

6. Ibid., 42–43.

7. "Nine Historic Synagogues," *New York Times* (August 20, 1961): 74.

8. Geoffrey Wigoder, *The Story of the Synagogue: A Diaspora Museum Book* (London: Weidenfeld and Nicolson, 1986), 44–45, and Wigoder, "Beth Hatefutsoth: The First Decade," *Ariel* 77–78 (1989): 99–110.

9. Jutta Strauss, "Das Jüdische Museum Berlin. 'Leben Nicht Tod,'" *Wormsgau* 21 (2002): 158–63.

10. Otto Böcher, *Die alte Synagoge in Worms am Rhein* (Worms: Stadtbibliothek Worms, 1960). Subsequently, the book was republished in 1963, 1969, 1974, 1978, 1982, 1985, 1988, 1992, and 2001. See also Böcher, *The Old Synagogue in Worms on the Rhine* (Munich: Deutscher Kunstverlag, 2001).

11. Albrecht Goes, "Morgenstunden in Worms," *BLBI* 1 (1958): 117.

12. Rudy Koshar, *Germany's Transient Pasts: Preservation and National Memory in the Twentieth Century* (Chapel Hill: University of North Carolina Press, 1998), 316, and Dieter Wilhelm, *Worms. Mittelstadt am Rande des Rhein-Neckar-Ballungsraumes. Eine stadtgeographische Betrachtung seiner Entwicklung im 19. und 20. Jahrhundert* (Worms: Stadtbibliothek, 1971), 90–91.

13. *Warmaisa—Heilige Gemeinde am Rhein* (2002).

14. See "Walking Tours," http://www.worms.de/touristinfo/site/touren/touieng .htm (accessed August 2002).

15. "Hoher Wasserstand im Tauchbad. Zustand früherer Jahrhunderte erreicht. Jüdische Stätte für kultische Reinigung," *Wormser Zeitung* (January 28, 1994): 13.

16. Gerrard Breitbart, "Die Alte Synagoge zu Worms nach ihre Wiedereinweihung," *Udim* 11–12 (1981): 215–18, and "Festakt für eine junge Jüdin," *Wormser Zeitung* (July 1, 1989): 14.

17. Klaus Brill, "Reisen an einen denkwürdigen Ort. Der Gast aus Israel begegnet einer Vergangenheit, die geprägt ist von großen kulturellen Leistungen und schrecklicher Verfolgung," *Süddeutsche Zeitung* (April 9, 1986): 3; "Der wird mal US-Präsident. Bill Clinton stattet der Nibelungenstadt vor fünf Jahren als Gouverneur von Arkansas eine Besuch ab," *Rhein-Main Presse* 13, World Jewish Community Collection, Leo Baeck Institute, New York, AR 145, box 1, folder 9; "Juden—Deutsche: Befangenheit bei Älteren, Hoffnung gilt der Jugend," *Wormser Zeitung* (September 6, 1988): 11; "Worms war ein beeindruckendes Erlebnis," *Wormser Zeitung* (September 28, 1996): 17; "Raschi-Haus: Gäste aus aller Welt," *Wormser Zeitung* (March 1, 1984): 1; and "Der Große im 'kleinen Jerusalem.' Teddy Kollek von Worms bewegt," *Wormser Zeitung* (October 15, 1985): 1.

18. Rolf Vogel, ed., *Der Deutsch-Israeltische Dialog. Dokumentation eines erregenden Kapitels Deutscher Außenpolitik,* 9 vols. (Munich: K. G. Sauer, 1990), 3:1615–84.

19. Interview with Gerhard Spies, September 3, 2003.

20. *Offenbacher Haggadah* (Verlag des Herausgebers Dr Guggenheim, Flushing, N.Y. in Kommission bei Otto Harrassowitz Wiesbaden, 1960), 85–86 and 130–31.

21. Correspondence with Paul Gusdorf (January 25, 2004); interview with Miriam Gerber, January 17, 2004. See also "Tracing your Family," *LBI News* 17 (Summer 1977): 4–5.

22. Fritz Reuter, "Wormser Historiker aus dem 19. und 20. Jahrhundert," *Der Wormsgau* 19 (2000): 91. See also Otto Böcher, "Varia zu Bau und Ausstattung der Wormser Synagogue," *Wormsgau* 10 (1972–73): 61.

23. Stadtarchiv Worms, Fotoabteilung F 5779/2 (P6283422).

24. Private correspondence and interview with Liselotte Wahrburg, March 16, 2004.

25. Interview with Paul Gusdorf, January 20, 2004. See also the interview with Paul Gusdorf, 41207, Shoah Foundation, Los Angeles, CA.

26. Memorial Services, November 9, 1988, Synagogue in Worms, Germany, Paul A. Gusdorf, Private Collection.

27. Y. Michael Bodemann, "Reconstructions of History: From Jewish Memory to Nationalized Commemoration of Kristallnacht in Germany," in Y. Michael Bodemann, ed., *Jews, Germans, Memory: Reconstruction of Jewish Life in Germany* (Ann Arbor: University of Michigan Press, 1996), 179–223, and Elisabeth Domansky, "'Kristallnacht,' the Holocaust, and German Unity: The Meaning of November 9 as an Anniversary in Germany," *History and Memory* 4 (1992): 60–94.

28. Interview with Frank Gusdorf, January 19, 2003; "Frank A. Gusdorf, My Story. A Visit to Germany in 2002," made available by the author; and interview with Frank Gusdorf, 36406, Shoah Foundation, Los Angeles, CA.

29. *Friday Evening Service Remembered*, audiocassette, Worms Synagogue, Worms Jewish Community Collection, Leo Baeck Institute, New York, AR 145.

30. See, for example, "Der jüdischen Geschichte in Worms nachgehen. Koordinierungsrat von 52 Gesellschaften tagt und bereitet die 'Woche der Brüderlichkeit' vor," *Wormser Zeitung* (November 11, 1983): 9; *Jüdisches Erbe in Deutschland. Botschaft und Herausforderung. Woche der Brüderlichkeit* (Frankfurt am Main: Deutscher Koordinierungsrat der Gesellschaften für Christlich-Jüdiscche Zusammenarbeit, 1984); "Juden—Deutsche: Befangenheit bei Älteren, Hoffnung gilt der Jugend," *Wormser Zeitung* (September 6, 1988): 11.

31. Jack Zipes, "The Contemporary German Fascination for Things Jewish: Toward a Minor Jewish Culture," in Sander L. Gilman and Karen Remmler, eds., *Re-emerging Jewish Culture in Germany: Life and Literature since 1989* (New York, 1994), 15–45.

32. Thomas F. Klein, "Ein Stück gerettetes Vergessen," *Frankfurter Allgemeine Zeitung* (November 5, 1995): 11.

33. Entry made in June 1996, Guestbook of the Rashi-Haus, Stadtarchiv Worms, Abt. 203, Nr. 80/5.

34. Entry made on May 30, 1996, Guestbook of the Rashi-Haus, Stadtarchiv Worms, Abt. 203, Nr. 80/5.

35. Elisabeth Oggel, *Martin Buber 1878–1978. Leben, Werk und Wirkung. Eine Ausstellung. Herausgegeben vom Deutschen Koordinierungsrat der Gesellschaft für Christlich-Jüdische Zusammenarbeit* (Worms: Selbstverlag, 1978).

36. "Buber-Blick wieder frei: Pflegearbeiten auf dem Judenfriedhof bis zum Frühjahr fertig," *Wormser Zeitung* (December 18, 1997), 9.

37. Björn Krondorfer, *Remembrance and Reconciliation: Encounters between Young Jews and Germans* (New Haven: Yale University Press, 1995), 157.

38. Ibid., 158.

39. This entry was made on May 10, 1996. Guest book of the Rashi-Haus, Stadtarchiv Worms, Abt. 203, Nr. 80/5, and Ulrike Schäfer, "Plötzlich kommen dann doch die vielen Fragen. Wenn jüdische Schüler und ihre christlichen Klassenkammeraden gemeinsam Worms besuchen," *Wormser Zeitung* (July 20, 1996): 13.

40. See for example, Norman Bentwich, "Wiedersehen mit der Synagogue in Worms," Stadtarchiv Worms, Abt. 6, Nr. 70, 3, which appeared in São Paulo's Jewish periodical *Crônica Israelita* (April 26, 1963).

41. For an account of one of these "reunions" see, for example, Michael Ryan, "Child of the Holocaust: Celia Appel of America Returns for Reunion to the Germany She Fled 50 Years Ago," *People Weekly* 30 (November 7, 1988): 1–4; Gideon Greif, Colin McPherson, and Laurence Weinbaum, eds., *Die Jeckes. Deutsche Juden aus Israel erzählen* (Köln: Böhlau, 2000), 48–58, 73, 88, 130–31, 140, 163–64, 199, 208 and 286–87; "Jüdische Mitbürger kamen im ganzen Jubiläumsjahr," *Wormser Zeitung* (January 10, 1985): 13; and Miriam Rosenkranz, "Wo einst die berühmte Talmudhochschule stand," *Allgemeine jüdische Wochenzeitung* (July 21, 1989): 11.

42. For example, the Jewish community of Karlsruhe, a Hillel group, and the Jewish History Tours from America both visited Worms. See the entries on June

8 and July 8, 1997, in the guestbook of the Rashi-Haus, Stadtarchiv Worms, Abt. 203, Nr. 80/5.

43. Cecil Roth, "Places of Jewish Interest in Europe for This Year's Tourist," *National Jewish Monthly* (January 1961): 24, and Roth, "Travel Is Broadening: Jewish Tourists Overseas Should Visit Synagogues; Some Helpful Advice; What to See, How to Act in England, France, Italy, Holland, Israel," *National Jewish Monthly* (June 1960): 22–25.

271

44. Roth, "Places of Jewish Interest in Europe," 27.

45. Mark H. Elovitz, "Germany's Little Jerusalem," *Jewish Spectator* (January 1967): 24–26.

46. Julie Neuberger, "The Bitter Memories That Still Affect German Jews," *The Times* (May 18, 1977): 13.

47. Judith Marcus, Joseph B. Maier, and Zoltán Tarr, "Introduction: Werner J. Cahnman on the Historical Sociology of the Jews," in Judith Marcus, Joseph B. Maier, and Zoltán Tarr, eds., *German Jewry, Its History and Sociology: Selected Essays of Werner J. Cahnman* (New Brunswick: Transaction Publishers, 1989), ix–xxiv.

48. Werner J. Cahnman, "Germany in 1970," *Reconstructionist* 36 (December 25, 1970): 17.

49. Werner J. Cahnman, "The Reconstruction of Eleventh-Century Jewish Presence on the Rhine," *National Jewish Monthly* (June 1978): 11.

50. "Geschichte und Verantwortung stellen: Amerikanische Wochenzeitung 'Aufbau' würdigt Wiederaufbau des Rashi-Hauses," *Wormser Zeitung* (January 21, 1983): 11, and "Beitrag zur Völkerverständigung. American Jewish Committee: Was Worms tut, sehen wir positiv," *Wormser Zeitung* (June 25, 1984): 11.

51. Gabe Levenson, "Travel: Remembering Herta," *Jewish Week and American Examiner* (May 27, 1983).

52. Erica Stachelberg, "Travel Diary of a Visit to Germany in 1982," Leo Baeck Institute, New York, Erica B. Stachelberg Collection, AR 11268, 2.

53. Ibid., 57.

54. Krondorfer, *Remembrance and Reconciliation*, 156.

55. Bernard Postal and Samuel H. Abrahams, *The Landmark of a People: A Guide to Jewish Sites* (New York: Hill and Wang, 1962), vi.

56. See Ruth Ellen Gruber, *Jewish Heritage Travel: A Guide to East-Central Europe*, 2nd ed. (New York: John Wiley and Sons, 1994), and Gruber, *Virtually Jewish: Reinventing Jewish Culture in Europe* (Berkeley: California University Press, 2002), 131–54.

57. Eric Davidson Collection, Leo Baeck Institute New York, AR 7245, box 5: 4,

58. Alan E. Steinweis, "Dead Jews: Depictions of European History and Culture in Contemporary American Travel Guides," *Shofar* 15 (1997): 57–63; Jack Kugelmass, "Why We Go to Poland: Holocaust Tourism as Secular Ritual," in James E. Young, ed., *The Art of Memory: Holocaust Memorials in History* (New York: Prestel, 1994), 175–85; James E. Young, "Broken Tablets and Jewish Memory in Poland," in *The Texture of Memory: Holocaust Memorials and Meaning* (New Haven: Yale University Press, 1993), 185–208.

59. There is by now an endless array of guides to Jewish historical sites. See,

Notes to Pages 192–94

for example, Bernard Postal and Samuel H. Abramson, *Traveler's Guide to Jewish Landmarks in Europe* (New York: Fleet Press Corp., 1971); Matthew Reisz, *Europe's Jewish Quarters* (London: Simon and Schuster, 1991); Ben G. Frank, *A Travel Guide to Jewish Europe*, 2nd ed. (Gretna: Pelican, 1996); Oscar Israelowitz, *Guide to Jewish Europe: Western Europe*, 9th ed. (Brooklyn: Israelowitz, 1997); and Don and Linda Freedman, "European Jewish Heritage Tours," http://www.thetravelzine.com/ejht5.htm (accessed August 2003).

60. Gruber, *Virtually Jewish: Reinventing Jewish Culture in Europe*, 131–54.

61. The first edition appeared in 1992. Ben G. Frank, *A Travel Guide to Jewish Europe*, 2nd ed. (Gretna: Pelican Publishing Company, 1999), 319–21. Following this introduction, the guide provides in-depth descriptions only of cities that have a Jewish community, like Berlin, Düsseldorf, Frankfurt, and Munich, with Dachau included as well (328–55). Worms is only introduced through a summary of its sites.

62. Joseph Greenblum, "A Pilgrimage to Germany," *Judaism* 44 (1955): 1.

63. See, for example, Peter Hirsch and Billie Ann Lopez, *Reiseführer durch das jüdische Deutschland* (Munich: Verlag Roman Kovar, 1993), which appeared in 1998 in English translation as *Traveler's Guide to Jewish Germany* (Gretna: Pelican Pub Co., 1998).

64. Greer Fay Cashman, "Traffic through Lod: Drops for September," *Jerusalem Post* (October 5, 1990); Elizabeth Wissner-Gross, "On the Go," *Newsday* (May 13, 1990), 3; "Travel Advisory," *New York Times* (July 22, 1990): section 5, p. 3, col. 1; and Jerry Morris, "The '90s: A Decade of Extravaganzas for Travelers Here and Abroad: Globe-Trotting," *Boston Globe* (September 2, 1990), A16.

65. *Germany for the Jewish Traveler* (New York: GNTO, [1990]), 3.

66. Ibid., 13.

67. "'Noch 10 Sekunden . . .' bis Worms live. S3-Regional sendet direkt aus der Raschi-Synagoge. Talk am Thoraschrein über das Erbe der Judengemeinde," *Wormser Zeitung* (January 26, 1990): 14.

68. Entry, June 1996, Guestbook of the Rashi-Haus, Stadtarchiv Worms, Abt. 203, Nr. 80/5.

69. Entry, November 10, 1993, Guestbook of the Rashi-Haus, Stadtarchiv Worms, Abt. 203, Nr. 80/5.

70. Entry, November 10, 1993, Guestbook of the Rashi-Haus, Stadtarchiv Worms, Abt. 203, Nr. 80/5.

71. Entry made on November 10, 1993, Guestbook of the Rashi-Haus, Stadtarchiv Worms, Abt. 203, Nr. 80/5.

72. Greenblum, "A Pilgrimage to Germany," 1 and 4.

73. "Retracing History on Heritage Mission to Berlin, Prague, and Lithuania," *YIVO News* (Summer 2001): 10.

74. See the advertisement in *YIVO News* (Winter 2000–2001): 13.

75. Greenblum, "A Pilgrimage to Germany," 1 and 4.

76. Ruth Rovner, *Exploring Jewish Germany: A Reporter's Notebook* (New York: GNTO, 1996), iii.

77. "Was die jüdischen Stätten auslösen. Amerikanische Journalisten recher-

chiert in Worms. Schreiben gegen pauschale Urteile," *Wormser Zeitung* (September 2, 1997), 11.

78. Maria Lisella, "Looking Back to Go Forward," *Travel Agent* (March 10, 1997): E6; Carol Sottili, "WorldWise," *Washington Post* (February 16, 1997): EO3; and Marilyn H. Karfeld, "Transforming Memory to Remembrance," *Cleveland Jewish News* (November 6, 1998): 23.

79. Daniel Goldhagen, *Hitler's Willing Executioners: Ordinary Germans and the Holocaust* (London: Abacus, 1997), 466; see also Gabe Levenson, "A Changed Spirit: Germany," *Jewish Week* (May 29, 1998): 35. For a discussion of the public debate surrounding Goldhagen's book, see Johannes Heil and Rainer Erb, eds., *Geschichtswissenschaft und Öffentlichkeit. Der Streit um Daniel J. Goldhagen* (Frankfurt am Main: Fischer Taschenbuch Verlag, 1998), and Geoff Eley, ed., *The Goldhagen Effect: History, Memory, Nazism—Facing the German Past* (Ann Arbor: University of Michigan Press, 2000).

80. *Germany for the Jewish Traveler* (New York: GNTO, 1998), 2–3.

81. Ibid., 1 and 4.

82. Ibid., 28 and 33.

83. Ibid., 14–15.

84. See William I. Weisberg, "To the Editor," *New York Times* (August 16, 1998): 11.

85. Melissa Radler, "New Tours Package Israel with Germany," *Jerusalem Post* (July 11, 2001): 4; Abby Ellin, "A Germany-Israel Heritage Travel Program: So Why Not?" *New York Times* (December 5, 2001): C7, col. 1; "Jewish Traveler Resource: Germany—Tracing Jewish Roots," http://emcoinc.com/travel/html/JewishTravel/Germany.htm (accessed July 2002).

86. Leonard J. Lehrman, "Germany for the Jewish Traveler," *Aufbau* (July 17, 1998): 14.

87. Howard Tzvi Adelman, "Germany as Museum of Jewish History and a Laboratory for Jewish-Christian Relations," in Leonard H. Ehrlich et al., eds., *Textures and Meanings: Thirty Years of Judaic Studies at University of Amherst*, available at http://www.umass.edu/judaic/anniversaryvolume/2004, pp. 35–36.

88. Evyatar Friesel, *The Days and the Seasons: Memoirs* (Detroit: Wayne State University Press, 1996), 217.

89. Matthias Hermann, "Jewish Cemetery in Worms," in Elena Lappin, ed., *Jewish Voices, German Words: Growing Up Jewish in Postwar Germany and Austria*, trans. Krishna Winston (North Haven: Catbird Press, 1994), 230.

90. See Monika Richarz, "Luftaufnahme—oder die Schwierigkeit der Heimatforscher mit der jüdischen Geschichte," *Babylon* 8 (1991): 30.

91. Annelore and Karl Schlösser, *Die Judenverfolgung 1933–1945 in Worms* (Worms: Stadtarchiv Worms, 1987).

92. Fritz Reuter, "Das 'Geschichtsfenster' von Heinz Hindorf in Wormser Dom—Beschreibung und Betrachtung," *Wormsgau* 18 (1999): 230, and "Gegen Vergessen: Vor Synagoge: Gedenken an die Pogromnacht," *Wormser Zeitung* (November 11, 1997): 9.

93. See http://www.warmaisa.de, and interview with Ulrike Schäfer, May 3, 2004.

94. "Neuer Glanz für jüdische Trauerhalle. Innenräume renoviert. Weitere Sanierungsbedarf. Arbeiten auf dem Friedhof," *Wormser Zeitung* (September 7, 1999): 14; "Jugendstil inzwischen alt genug. Jüdische Trauerhalle ein Schmuckstück," *Wormser Zeitung* (February 17, 1999): 15; "Mit Sensibilität restauriert. Eingangsportal der jüdischen Trauerhalle behält seine Geschichte," *Wormser Zeitung* (August 25, 1998): 13; "Ein Projekt der kleinen Schritte. Sanierung der jüdischen Trauerhalle: Anfang ist gemacht," *Wormser Zeitung* (August 12, 1998): 9; and "Bald wieder Juwel. Jüdische Trauerhalle wird restauriert. Spenden," *Wormser Zeitung* (June 16, 1998): 13.

95. Fritz Reuter, "Zum Gedenken an die Opfer," *Allgemeine Wochenzeitung der Juden in Deutschland* (September 19, 1991), Press Cuttings on the History of German Jewry: Worms, Wiener Library, London Press Archives, PC 8, 146.

96. "Mit Sensibilität restauriert. Eingangsportal der jüdischen Trauerhalle behält seine Geschichte," *Wormser Zeitung* (August 25, 1998): 13; "Neuer Glanz für jüdische Trauerhalle. Innenräume renoviert. Weitere Sanierungsbedarf. Arbeiten auf dem Friedhof," *Wormser Zeitung* (September 7, 1999): 14.

97. See Gruber, *Virtually Jewish*, and Diana Pinto, "The Third Pillar? Toward a European Jewish Identity," in A. Kovacs, ed., *Jewish Studies at the Central European University: Public Lectures, 1996–1999* (Budapest: Central European University, 2000), 198–200.

CONCLUSION

1. Ferdinand Tönnis, *Gemeinschaft und Gesellschaft*, 3rd ed. (Darmstadt: Wissenschaftliche Buchgesellschaft, 1991).

2. Walter Laqueur, *Germany Today: A Personal Report* (London: Weidenfeld and Nicolson, 1985), 20–21.

3. David Lowenthal, *The Imagined Past: History and Nostalgia*, ed. Christopher Shaw and Malcolm Chase (Manchester: Manchester University Press, 1989), 20.

4. David Philippson, *Old European Jewries* (Philadelphia: Jewish Publication Society of America, 1894).

5. Arnold Eisen, *Rethinking Modern Judaism: Ritual, Commandment, Community*, Chicago Studies in the History of Judaism (Chicago: Chicago University Press, 1998), 2.

BIBLIOGRAPHY

PERIODICALS

Allgemeine Jüdische Illustrierte, 1951
Allgemeine Jüdische Wochenzeitung, 1989
Allgemeine Wochenzeitung der Juden in
    Deutschland, 1951–61, 1991
Allgemeine Zeitung des Judentums,
    1837–1910
American Jewish Year Book, 1963
Archives Israélites, 1853
Aufbau, 1945–56, 1961, 1998
Blätter für jüdische Geschichte und
    Litteratur, 1902–4
Boston Globe, 1990
Cleveland Jewish News, 1998
Contemporary Jewish Record, 1944
C.V.-Zeitung, 1922–38
Deutsche Kunst und Denkmalpflege,
    1963
Frankfurter Allgemeine Zeitung, 1955
Frankfurter Rundschau, 1952
Frayhayt, 1946
Heidelberger Tageblatt, 1960
Herald Tribune, 1959 and 1961
Illustrierte Zeitung, 1856 and 1901
Der Israelit, 1860–1910, and 1934
Israelit des 19. Jahrhunderts, 1839–48
Israelitische Annalen, 1839–41
Israelitische Jugendbibliohthek, 1858
Der israelitische Volkslehrer, 1851–60
Israelitische Wochenschrift, 1870–94
Israelitisches Familienblatt, 1898–1910
    and 1924–34
Jahrbuch für die Geschichte der Juden,
    1860–69
Jahrbuch für jüdische Geschichte und
    Literatur, 1898–1910
Jahrbuch zur Belehrung und
    Unterhaltung, 1892
Jahrbücher für deutsche Theologie,
    1865–67

Jedidja, 1817–31
Jerusalem Post, 1990 and 2001
Jeschurun, 1854–1870
Jewish Chronicle, 1853, 1953, 1955,
    and 1958
Jewish Frontier, 1951
Jewish Messenger, 1858
Jewish Social Studies, 1946–48
The Jewish Spectator, 1967
Jewish Way, 1961
Jewish Week, 1990 and 1998
Jewish Week and American Examiner,
    1983
Jewish Year Book 5657 (1896)
JTA News, 1944
Der Jude, 1918–24
Die jüdische Frau, 1925
Die jüdische Gemeinde, 1937
Jüdische Gemeindeblatt, 1949
Jüdische Liberale Zeitung, 1928
Jüdische Presse, 1894
Jüdische Rundschau, 1902–34
Jüdische Wochenschau, 1940
Jüdische Zeitschrift für Wissenschaft
    und Leben, 1862–75
Jüdischer Almanach, 1902–4
Jüdisches Volksblatt, 1854–66
Der Jugendbund, 1932
Kölnische Rundschau, 1956
Die Laubhütte, 1884–1910
LBI News, 1977
L'Univers Israélite, 1853
Magazin für Geschichte, Literatur und
    Wissenschaft des Judentums, 1874–93
Menorah, 1923–32
Ministerialblatt der Landesregierung von
    Rheinland-Pfalz, 1955
Mitteilungen der Gesellschaft für jüdische
    Volkskunde, 1898–1910

Mitteilungen des Gesamtarchivs der deutschen Juden, 1909–26

Mitteilungsblatt des Irgun Olei Merkas Europa, 1946–57

Monatsblätter zur Belehrung des Judentums, 1881–98

Monatsschrift für Geschichte und Wissenschaft des Judentums, 1851–1939

National Jewish Monthly, 1960, 1961, and 1978

Neue Wormser Zeitung, 1875

Newsday, 1990

Newsweek, 1956

New York Times, 1961, 1990, 1998, and 2001

N.Y. Staats-Zeitung und Herold, 1955 and 1958

Der Orden Bne Briss. Mitteilungen der Grossloge für Deutschland. U.O.B.B., 1926–28

Der Orient, 1840–51

Ost und West, 1901–10

Palestine Post, 1939 and 1947

Pariser Tageblatt, 1933

People Weekly, 1988

Populär-wissenschaftliche Monatsblätter, 1881–1908

Reconstructionist, 1970

Revue des Études Juives, 1880

Rheinischer Herold, 1860

Der Schild, 1925–37

Soncino-Blätter, 1925

Stuttgarter Zeitung, 1961

Süddeutsche Zeitung, 1986

Sulamith, 1806–46

The Times, 1868, 1937, 1939, and 1977

Travel Agent, 1997

Undser Veg, 1945

La Vie Juive, 1953

Vom Rhein, 1907–13

Dos Vort, 1949

Vorwärts, 1959

Washington Post, 1997

Die Welt, 1897–1910

Wiener Library Bulletin, 1947–49

Wissenschaftich Zeitschrift für jüdische Theologie, 1835–47

Wonnegauer Heimatsblätter, 1958–59

Wormser Volkszeitung, 1912–24

Wormser Zeitung, 1912–2000

Der Wormsgau, 1957

Zeitschrift für die Geschichte der Juden in Deutschland, 1882–92 and 1929–35

Zeitschrift für die Wissenschaft des Judentums, 1822–23

YIVO News, 2000–2001

INTERVIEWS AND CORRESPONDENCE

Interview with Gerold Bönnen, October 1, 2003

Interview with Miriam Gerber, January 17, 2004

Interview with Frank Gusdorf, January 19, 2004

Interview with Paul Gusdorf, January 20, 2004

Correspondence with Paul Gusdorf, January 25, 2004

Interview with Helmut Izhak Kraemer, February 2004

Interview with Hilde Licht, May 20, 2004

Interview with Fritz Reuter, August 23, 2001

Interview with Ulrike Schäfer, May 3, 2004

Interview with Annelore Schloesser, December 30, 2003

Interview with Gerhard Spies, September 3, 2003

Interview with Liselotte Wahrburg, March 16, 2004

INTERVIEWS, SHOAH FOUNDATION, LOS ANGELES, CA
Interview of Inge Davidson, 26653
Interview of Edith Dietz, 10495
Interview of Fritz Edgar Froehlich, 29849
Interview of Frank Gusdorf, 36406
Interview of Paul Gusdorf, 41207
Interview of Yizhak Kremer, 44794
Interview of Inga Johanna Lieb, 10488
Interview of Edith Lucas Pagelson, 9806
Interview of Suse Margot Rosenstock, 11067
Interview of Ellen Ruth Schalkowsky, 33877
Interview of Elsbeth Schmidt, 19528

ARCHIVAL MATERIAL
American Jewish Archives, New York, Marvin Lowenthal, Papers *–140.
Central Archives for the History of the Jewish People, Jerusalem. Deutsch-
    Israelitischer. Gemeindebund: Historische Commission. Correspondence mit
    Gemeinden, M1/24.
————. Deutsch-Israelitischer Gemeindebund: Historische Commission, 1885–
    1917, M1/23.
Jewish Theological Seminary, New York, Hannah Arendt, Field Reports.
Leo Baeck Institute, New York. American Federation of Jews from Central
    Europe Archives; 1944–1947, AR 4420 and AR 126.
————. Hermann Baerwald Collection, AR 744.
————. Sally Bodenheimer Postcard Collection, LBI AR 7169.
————. Karl Darmstaedter Archives, AR 15.
————. Eric Davidson Collection, AR 7245.
————. Karl Guggenheim Archives, AR 179.
————. Max Guggeheim, Episoden aus der Geschichte meiner Vaterstadt Worms
    am Rhein und ihrer juedischen Gemeinde, ME 222.
————. Siegried Guggenheim Collection, AR 180.
————. Max Gumbel, The Fountain, ME 994.
————. Isaak Holzer Collection, AR 3464.
————. Isidor Kiefer Collection, AR 1894–1903 and AR 3912.
————. Guido Kisch Collection, AR 787.
————. Alfred Langenbach Collection, AR 2186.
————. Herta Mansbacher Collection, AR 6198.
————. Berthold Rosenthal, Das "Grüne Buch" in Worms, AR C.222, 225a.
————. Leo Schonmann, "Das war in Worms im Monat Mai" (1960), ME573.
————. Else Spies Collection, AR 1081.
————. Erica B. Stachelberg Collection, AR 11268.
————. Nathan Stein, Lebenserinnerungen, ME 618.
————. Synagogue Collection: Worms, AR 145.
————. Bruno Weil Collection, MF 516.
————. Inge Worth Collection, AR 11134.

Brotherton Library, University of Leeds, Cecil Roth Letters.

Neue Synagoge Berlin—Centrum Judaicum Oranienburger.

Protokollbuch des Vereins zur Abwehr des Antisemitismus, 1909–10, 1913, 1916, 1917, 1921, 1922, Nr. 9127.

Stadtarchiv Mainz, Nachlaß Oppenheim, Die silbernen Gegenstände der jüdischen Gemeinde in Worms.

Stanford Archives, Salo Baron Wittmayer Collection, M580.

Wiener Library, London. Eva G. Reichmann, "Germany's New Nazis: Impressions from a Recent Journey through Germany's Danger Zones." Wiener Library, August 1951.

———. Press Cuttings on the History of German Jewry: Worms, Press Archives PC 8, 146.

Worms Stadtarchiv. Alter Judenfriedhof am Andreasring, Abtl. 20, Nr. 15.

———. Altertumsverein, Abt. 75/1.

———. Archiv der jüdischen Gemeinde, Abt. 140.

———. Briefwechsel m. Anlagen mit Carola Kaufmann, geb. Levy, 1947–1955, 170/16 Nr. 7.

———. Ehemalige Wormser Juden, Abt. 6–47 A., Nr 92.

———. Fotoabteilung.

———. Fotographien jüdischen Besucher in Worms, Abt. 203, 12/10.

———. Gästebuch, Synagoge, Feb. 1962–May 1971, 203, Nr. 79/1.

———. Gästebuch, Raschihaus, 1993–2002, 203, Nr. 80/5.

———. Miriam Gerber, "Talk on Memorial Weekend in Worms (November 9–11, 1980) for Scott Tower B'nai B'rith—March, 11, 1981," Abt. 214/13, Nr. 10.

———. Dr. Friedrich Maria Illert, Abt. 170/16.

———. Judenfriedhof am Andreasring, Abt. 20, Nr. 14.

———. Jüdische Altertümer: Rechtsstreit der Branche Française gegen die Stadt Worms, Abt. 20: 7: Nr. 67–69.

———. Reichsstatthalter in Hessen, September 11, 1937, Jüdische Kurgäste in Baedern und Kurorten, Abt. 5, Nr. 3778.

———. Judaica-Sammlung, Abt. 203.

———. Walter Koehler. *Worms am Rhein. Das Wesen der Stadt—Ihr Zustand. Erste Gedanken über den späteren Wiederaufbau* (January 1946); *Worms am Rhein. Ein Beispiel* (October 1948); *Worms am Rhein. Der Wiederaufbau* (December 31, 1951); and *Tradition und Fortschritt im Aufbau. Aufbau-Verein Worms e.V. Gemeinnützige Vereinigung Wormser Bürger zum Wiederaufbau ihrer Stadt Worms am Rhein.* Worms: Erich Norberg, 1957, Abt. 6.

———. Mahnmal des Faschismus, Stadtverwaltung 6: 109.

———. Papiere betr. Dr Ludwig Lewysohn, Judaica 203: 32.

———. Polizeidirektion, Abt. 13.

———. Recording of the Südwestfunk, Abt. 211a, Nr. 146.

———. Fritz Reuter, Abtl. 214/13.

———. Leo Schonmann, Das war in Worms im Monat Mai (1960), Abt. 203, 81.

———. Schriftwechsel mit der Israel-Mission, 1958–1963, Abt. 6, Nr. 140.

———. Stadtarchiv: Einweihung des Kriegerdenkmals 1932, Abteilung 204, Nr. 3/16.

———. Stadtarchiv Worms, Abt. 20, Nr. 71; Abt. 203, Nr. 8; and Abt. 204, Nr. 3/16.

———. Stadtarchiv: Laufende Registratur, Synagoge: Besucherstatisktik, Amt 47 A.

———. Städtische Kulturinstitute, Abt. 20, 72.

———. Stadtverwaltung, 1815–1945, Abteilung 4 and 5.

———. Stadtverwaltung Worms: Hauptverwaltung. Allgemeine Verwaltung. Betr. Amerikanischen Militärregierung, 1945–1963, Abt. 6, Nr. 118.

———. Stadtverwaltung Worms: Hauptverwaltung, Hauptamt, Abt. 6, 70.

———. Stadtverwaltung Worms: Hauptverwaltung, Hauptamt: Wiederaufbau der Synagoge, 1959–1961, Abt. 6.

———. Wiederaufbau der Synagoge, 1959–1961, Abt. 6, Nr. 73.

———. Carl Johann Heinrich Villinger Nachlass, Abt. 212.

———. Worms: Korrespondenz, H-M, Abt. 47 A.

———. Zeitungsartikel ueber die Feierlichkeiten von 1939, Abt. 204, Nr. 1/0.

PRIVATE COLLECTIONS
Frank A. Gusdorf, *My Story: A Visit to Germany in 2002*. Frank A. Gusdorf, Private Collection.
Memorial Services, November 9, 1988, Synagogue in Worms, Germany. Paul A. Gusdorf, Private Collection.

MANUSCRIPTS
Nahman ben Eliezer Puch, Be-shurat tovot yeshuot we-nahmot me-geulat k.k. Frankfurt a. M. and k. k. Worms (1616), Universitätsbibliothek Erlangen-Nuernberg, 8⁰ Rab. I 225⁴.
Pinkas shel kahal Warmaisa, Bodleian Library, MS Opp. 716.

SOURCES ON THE INTERNET
"Jewish Traveler Resource: Germany—Tracing Jewish Roots." http://emcoinc .com/travel/html/JewishTravel/Germany.htm. Accessed July 2002.
Sefer ha-minhagim: The Book of Chabad-Lubavitch Customs (1994), http://www .sichosinenglish.org/books/sefer-haminhagim/01.htm. Accessed July 2002.
WARMAISA—Gesellschaft zur Förderung und Pflege jüdischer Kultur in Worms. http://www.warmaisa.de. Accessed July 2002.
"Walking Tours." http://www.worms.de/touristinfo/site/touren/touieng.htm. Accessed August 2002.
"European Jewish Heritage Tours." Don and Linda Freedman. http://www .thetravelzine.com/ejht5.htm. Accessed August 2003.

CDS AND DVDS
Bar-Ilan, Responsa Project, Version 8.0.
Sauer, Wilfried, and Werner Schlieter. *Warmaisa: Worms; Holy Community on the Rhine River*. Worms: Mediumzentrum, 2003.

Schlösser, Karl and Annelore. *Die Wormser Juden, 1933–1945.* Worms: Stadtarchiv Worms, 2002.

PRINTED SOURCES

Abrahams, Israel, ed. *Hebrew Ethical Wills.* Philadelphia: Jewish Publication Society of America, 1976.

Adelman, Howard Tzvi. "Germany as Museum of Jewish History and a Laboratory for Jewish-Christian Relations." In *Textures and Meanings: Thirty Years of Judaic Studies at University of Amherst.* Edited by Leonard H. Ehrlich, Shmuel Bolozky, Robert A. Rothstein, Murray Schwartz, Jay R. Berkovitz, and James E. Young. Available at http://www.umass.edu/judaic/ anniversaryvolume/2004. 27–44.

Adler, Samuel. "Prelude to America." In *Lives and Voices: A Collection of American Jewish Memoirs.* Edited by Stanley F. Chyet. Philadelphia: Jewish Publication Society of America, 1972. 3–34.

Agnon, S. Y. "On the Road." In *Twenty-One Stories: S.Y. Agnon.* Edited by Nahum N. Glatzer. New York: Schocken Books, 1970. 182–193.

Der alte israelitische Friedhof zu Worms am Rhein. Zwölf Kunstblätter mit Vorwort von Max Levy, October 1913. Worms: Christian Herbst, 1913.

Arendt, Hannah. "The Aftermath of Nazi-Rule: Reports from Germany." *Commentary* 10 (1950): 342–53.

Aronius, Julius. *Regesten zur Geschichte der Juden im fränkischen und deutschen Reich bis zum Jahre 1273.* Berlin: Simion, 1902.

Asch, Sholem. *Gezamlte shriftn.* 30 vols. Warsaw: Kultur-lige, 1930–38.

Auerbach, Benjamin. *Geschichte der israelitischen Gemeinde Halberstadt.* Halberstadt: H. Meyer, 1866.

———. *Nahal Eshkol.* 2 vols. Halberstadt: H. Meyer, 1865–67.

Azulai, Hayyim Joseph. *Shem ha-gedolim.* Vilna: Y. R. Rom, 1853.

Baedeker, Karl. *Berlin und Umgebung: Handbuch für Reisende.* Leipzig: Karl Baedeker, 1894.

———. *Deutschland und Österreich: Handbuch für Reisende.* 11th ed. Coblenz: Karl Baedeker, 1869.

———. *The Rhine from Rotterdam to Constance: Handbook for Travellers.* 13th ed. Leipzig: Karl Baedeker, 1896.

———. *The Rhine from Rotterdam to Constance. Handbook for Travellers.* 14th ed. Leizig: Karl Baedeker 1900.

Baerwald, B. *Der alte Friedhof der israelitischen Gemeinde zu Frankfurt am Main.* Frankfurt am Main: St. Goar, 1883.

Battenberg, Friedrich. *Quellen zur Geschichte der Juden im Hessischen Staatsarchiv Darmstadt, 1080–1650.* Wiesbaden: Kommission für die Geschichte der Juden in Hessen, 1995.

Bechstein, Ludwig. *Deutsches Sagenbuch.* Leipzig: Georg Wigand, 1853.

Beermann, Max, and Max Doktor. *Raschis Leben und Wirken. Zwei Preisschriften.* Worms: H. Kraeuter'schen Buchhandlung, 1906.

Belloc, Hilaire. *Many Cities.* London: Constable, 1928.

Berdyczewski, Micha Josef (Micha Josef bin Gorion). *Der Born Judas. Legenden, Märchen und Erzählungen.* 2nd ed. 6 vols. Leipzig: Insel Verlag, 1919.

——. *Die Sagen der Juden.* 5 vols. Frankfurt: Rütten and Loening, 1913–27.

Berger, David, ed. *The Jewish-Christian Debate in the High Middle Ages: A Critical Edition of Nizzahon Vetus.* Philadelphia: Jewish Publication Society of America, 1979.

Berliner, Abraham. *Aus dem inneren Leben der deutschen Juden im Mittelalter. Nach den gedruckten und ungedruckten Quellen. Zugleich ein Beitrag zur deutschen Kulturgeschichte.* Berlin: Benzian, 1871.

——. *Blicke in die Geisteswerkstatt Raschis. Vortrag im Verein für jüdische Geschichte und Literatur zu Berlin gehalten.* Frankfurt am Main: Kauffmann, 1905.

——. *Raschi. Vortrag im Verein für jüdische Geschichte und Literatur zu Berlin gehalten.* Berlin: M. Poppelauer, 1906.

——. "Sefer Haskarat neshamot." *Kovez 'al yad* 3 (1886): 3–62.

Bernfeld, S. *Sefer ha-dema'ot: me'ore'ot ha-gezerot veha-redifot ve-hashmadot.* 3 vols. Berlin: Eshkol, 1923–26.

Blumenfeld, Kurt. *Erlebte Judenfrage. Ein Vierteljahrhundert Deutscher Zionismus.* Stuttgart: Deutsche-Verlags-Anstalt, 1962.

Board of Deputies of British Jews. *Statement of Post-War Policy.* London, 1944.

Bodenschatz, Johann Christoph G. *Kirchliche Verfassung der heutigen Juden sonderlich derer in Deutschland in IV. Haupt-Theile abgefasset aus ihren eigenen und anderen Schriften umständlich dargethan und mit 30 sauberen Kupfern erläutert.* Frankfurt am Main: Becker, 1748–49.

Böcher, Otto. "Das jüdische Worms." *Humanitas. Mitteilungsblatt der ehemaligen Lehrer und Schüler des Gymnasiums zu Worms* 7 (June 1957): 10–13.

——. *Der alte Judenfriedhof in Worms. Ein Führer durch seine Geschichte und Grabmäler.* Worms: Stadtarchiv Worms, 1958.

——. *Die alte Synagoge in Worms am Rhein.* Worms: Stadtbibliothek Worms, 1960.

——. *The Old Synagogue in Worms on the Rhine.* Munich: Deutscher Kunstverlag, 2001.

Bolitho, Gordon. *The Other Germany.* New York: D. Appleton-Century Company, 1934.

Boos, Heinrich. *Geschichte der rheinischen Städtekultur von den Anfängen bis zur Gegenwart mit besonderer Berücksichtigung Worms.* 4 vols. Berlin: Stargardt, 1897–1901.

——. *Quellen zur Geschichte der Stadt Worms.* 3 vols. Berlin: Weidmannsche Buchhandlung, 1893.

Brandes, Wilhelm. *Die Jüdin von Worms. Mit begleitender Musik für Klavier von Robert Heger. Op. 13.* Berlin: Bote und G. Bock, 1913.

Buber, Martin. *Die Stunde und die Erkenntnis. Reden und Aufsätze.* Berlin: Schocken, 1936.

Burkhardt, C. A. H., and M. Stern. "Aus der Zeitschriftenliteratur zur Geschichte der Juden in Deutschland." *ZGJD* 2 (1888): 1–46 and 109–49.

Bücher, die zu Buche schlagen. Der Beitrag jüdischer Mitbürger zu Literatur und Wissenschaft. Ausstellung der Stadtbibliothek Worms. Worms: Stadtbibliothek, 1984.

Burnet, Gilbert. *Some Letters Containing an Account of What Seemed Most Remarkable in Traveling through Switzerland, Italy, and Germany. Three Letters Concerning the Present State of Italy, & c. in the years 1685 and 1686.* London: J. Robinson and A. Churchil, 1689.

Burrows, I. *The Intelligent Traveler's Guide to Germany.* New York: Knight Publication, 1936.

Canstatt, Oscar. *Drangsale der Stadt Worms und deren Zerstörung durch die Franzosen am 31. Mai 1689. Zum 200jährigen Gedenktage.* Worms: Eugen Kranzbühler, 1889.

Carmi, T., ed. *The Penguin Book of Hebrew Verse.* London: Penguin, 1981.

Cohen, Daniel. "Das Archiv der Gemeinde Worms." *BLBI* 1 (1958): 118–22.

Cohen, Daniel. "Jewish Records from Germany in the Jewish Historical Archives in Jerusalem." *LBIYB* 1 (1956): 331–45.

Conference on "the Future of Jews in Germany." Heidelberg, 1949.

Deutsche Reichsakten. Mittlere Reihe. Unter Maximilian I. Fünfter Band. Reichstag von Worms 1495. Edited by Heinz Angermeier. Göttingen: Vandenhoeck and Ruprecht, 1981.

Dielhelm, Johann Hermann. *Denkwürdiger und nützlicher Rheinischer Antiquarius, welcher die wichtigsten und angenehmsten geograph-, histor- und politischen Merkwürdigkeiten des ganzen Rheinstroms von seinem Ursprunge an, samt allen seinen Zuflüssen, bis er sich endlich nach und nach wieder verlieret, darstellet; Zum Nutzen der Reisenden und anderer Liebhaber sehenswürdiger Sachen, so man an jedem an demselben geloenen Ort als etwas rares zu bemerken und was sich bis in das Jahr 1743 damit zugetragen hat, gesammlet, und Nebst einer kurzen Beschreibung der vornehmsten Städte in Holland, mit einigen Anm., wie auch genauen Landkarten, dazu gehörigen Kupfern und Registern versehen.* Frankfurt am Main: Stoks und Schilling, 1744.

Eidelberg, Shlomo, ed. *The Jews and the Crusaders: The Hebrew Chronicles of the First and Second Crusade.* Madison: University of Wisconsin Press, 1977.

———. *R. Juspa, Shammash of Warmaisa (Worms): Jewish Life in Seventeenth-Century Worms.* Jerusalem: The Magnes Press, 1991.

Eisenmenger, Johann Andreas. *Entdecktes Judenthum, Oder Gründlicher und wahrhaffter Bericht, welchergestalt die verstockten Juden die hochheiligen Dreyeinigkeit, Gott Vater, Sohn und Heiligen Geist, erschrecklicher Weise lästern und verunehren, die Heil. Mutter Christi verschmähen, das Neue Testament, die Evangelisten und Aposteln, die Christliche Religion spöttlich durchziehen, un die gantze Christenheit auff das äusserte verachten und verfluchten; dabey noch viele andere, bishero unter den Christen entweder gar nicht, oder nur zum Theil bekant-gewesene Dinge und grosse Irrthüme der Jüdischen Religion und Theologie, wie auch viel lächerliche und kurtzweilige Fabeln, und andere ungereimte Sachen an den Tag kommen; Alles aus ihren eigenen, und zwar sehr vielen, mit großer Mühe und unverdrossenen Fleiß durchgelesenen Büchern, mit Anzeichnunng der Hebräischen*

Worte, und deren treuen Uebersetzung in die teutsche Sprach, kräfftiglich erwiesen, und in zweyen Theilen verfasset, deren jeder seine behörige allemal von einer gewissenen Materie außführlich handelnde Capitel enthält. Allen Christen zur treuhertzigen Nachricht verfertiget, und mit vollkommenen Registern versehen. 2 vols. Königsberg, 1700.

Eisenstein, J. D., ed. *Ozar Yisrael: An Encyclopaedia of All Matters Concerning Jews and Judaism in Hebrew.* 10 vols. New York: J. D. Eisenstein, 1910.

Eleazar bar Yehuda. *Sefer ha-rokeah ha-gadol al darkhe ha-torah, ha-hasidut ve-hateshuva, hilkhot al kol ha-shana u-minhage ha-rishonim.* Jerusalem, 1960.

Elbogen, Ismar. *Geschichte der Juden in Deutschland.* Berlin: E. Lichtenstein, 1935.

Euchel, Isaac Abraham. *Gebete der hochdeutschen und polnischen Juden aus dem hebräischen übersetzt und mit Anmerkungen begleitet.* Königsberg, 1786.

Ewald, W., and B. Kuske, eds. *Führer durch die Jahrtausend-Ausstellung der Rheinlande in Köln 1925.* Köln: M. Dumont Schauberg, 1925.

Frank, Ben G. *A Travel Guide to Jewish Europe.* 2nd ed. Gretna: Pelican Publishing Company, 1999.

Frank, Helmut. "As a German Rabbi to America." In *Paul Lazarus Gedenkbuch— Beiträge zur Würdigung der letzten Rabbinergeneration in Deutschland.* Jerusalem: Jerusalem Post Press, 1961. 135–42.

Freudenthal, Max. "Dokumente zur Schriftenverfolgung durch Pfefferkorn." *Zeitschrift für die Geschichte der Juden in Deutschland* 3 (1931): 227–32.

Friedberg, Abraham Shalom. *Zikhronot le-beyt David.* Tel Aviv: Masada, 1960.

Friesel, Evyatar. *The Days and the Seasons: Memoirs.* Detroit: Wayne State University Press, 1996.

Fuchs, Friedrich. *Geschichte der Stadt Worms. Nebst einer Analyse der Nibelungensage und einem Anhang. "Führer durch Worms."* Worms: Julius Stern, 1868.

Führer durch Worms und Umgebung mit ausführlichen Beschreibungen des Lutherdenkmals, Domes, Paulusmuseum u.s.f. Mit 70 Abbildungen und Plan von Worms. 6th ed. Worms: Christian Herbst, 1921.

Führer durch Worms und Umgebung (mit Plan) mit ausführlichen Beschreibungen des Lutherdenkmals, Domes, Paulusmuseums u.s.f. Mit 70 Abbildungen und Plan von Worms. 6th ed. Worms: Christian Herbst, 1925.

Gassmann, Theodor. "Die Juden von Worms. Volks-Drama in fünf Aufzügen." In *Dramatisches.* Hamburg: H. F. Richter, 1872. 213–335.

Gaster, Moses, ed. *Ma'aseh Book: Book of Jewish Tales and Legends.* Philadelphia: Jewish Publication Society of America, 1981.

Gebete zu dem am ersten Tage des Pesach-Festes in der Synagoge zu Worms stattfindenden deutschen Gottesdienstes. Worms: Steinkühl and Smith, 1847.

Geib, Karl. *Die Sagen und Geschichten des Rheinlandes in umfassender Auswahl gesammelt und bearbeitet.* Mannheim: Heinrich Hoff, 1836.

Germany for the Jewish Traveler. New York: GNTO, 1990.

Germany for the Jewish Traveler. New York: GNTO, 1998.

Goes, Albrecht. "Morgenstunden in Worms." *BLBI* 1 (1958): 117.

Goldschmidt, Daniel, ed. *Seder ha-kinot le-tisha be-av.* Jerusalem: Mosad Harav Kook, 1972.

Graetz, Heinrich. *Geschichte der Juden von den ältesten Zeiten bis auf die Gegenwart. Aus den Quellen neu bearbeitet.* 11 vols. Leipzig: O. Leiner, 1853–74.

———. *Geschichte der Juden von den ältesten Zeiten bis auf die Gegenwart. Aus den Quellen neu bearbeitet.* 3rd ed. Leipzig: O. Leiner, 1893.

———. *History of the Jews.* 6 vols. Philadelphia: Jewish Publication Society of America, 1967.

———. *Volkstümliche Geschichte der Juden.* 3 vols. Leipzig: O. Leiner, 1888.

Greenblum, Joseph. "A Pilgrimage to Germany." *Judaism* 44 (1995): 1–4.

Greif, Gideon, Colin McPherson, and Laurence Weinbaum, eds. *Die Jeckes. Deutsche Juden aus Israel erzählen.* Köln: Böhlau, 2000.

Gross, Heinrich. "Zwei kabbalistische Traditionsketten des R. Eleasar aus Worms." *MGWJ* 49 (1905): 692–700.

Gruber, Ruth Ellen. *Jewish Heritage Travel: A Guide to East-Central Europe.* 2nd ed. New York: John Wiley and Sons, 1994.

Guggenheim, Karl. *Reichsbund Juedischer Frontsoldaten. Ortsgruppe Worms. Ansprache des Vorsitzenden [bei der] Toten-Gedenkfeier in der alten Synagoge zu Worms, February 21, 1937.* Worms, 1937.

Guggenheim, Siegfried. *Offenbacher Haggadah.* Offenbach am Main: Guggenheim, 1927.

———. *Offenbacher Haggadah.* Wiesbaden: Otto Harrassowitz, 1960.

Gurland, Chaim. *Le-korot ha-gezerot 'al yisra'el.* Cracow: Yosef Fisher, 1889.

Habermann, Abraham, ed. *Sefer gezerot ashkenaz ve-tzarfat.* Jerusalem: Tarshish, 1945.

Heilmann, Ludwig. *Führer durch Worms und Umgebung für Fremde und Einheimische.* Worms: Reiss, 1889.

Heilperin, Yehiel ben Solomon. *Seder ha-dorot.* Karlsruhe, 1769.

Heine, Heinrich. "Der Rabbi von Bacherach. Ein Fragment." In Klaus Briegleb, ed., *Heinrich Heine: Sämtliche Schriften.* 7 vols. München: Deutscher Taschenbuchverlag, 1997. 1:461–501.

———. *Jewish Stories and Hebrew Melodies by Heinrich Heine.* Edited by Elizabeth Petuchowski. New York: M. Wiener, 1987.

Hirsch, Peter, and Billie Ann Lopez. *Reiseführer durch das jüdische Deutschland.* Munich: Verlag Roman Kovar, 1993.

———. *Traveler's Guide to Jewish Germany.* Gretna: Pelican Pub. Co., 1998.

Holberg, Ludvig. *Jüdische Geschichte von Erschaffung der Welt bis auf gegenwärtige Zeiten.* Translated by Georg August Detharding. Altona: Korte, 1747.

Horovitz, M. *Die Inschriften des alten Friedhofs der israelitischen Gemeinde zu Frankfurt a. M.* 4 vols. Frankfurt am Main: J. Kauffmann, 1901.

Hugo, Victor. *Le Rhin.* Preface by Michel Le Bris. Strasbourg: Bueb et Reumaux, 1980.

Illert, Friedrich M. *Noteworthy and Memorable Facts about Worms.* Translated by K. Th. Hirsch. Worms: Published by the Municipal Archives, 1945.

———. *Offizieller Führer des Verkehrsvereins. Worms am Rhein und der Wonnegau mit vielen Abbildungen und Stadtplan.* 9th ed. Worms: Verlag Christian Herbst, 1935.

————. *Worms am Rhein. Führer durch die Geschichte und Sehenswürdigkeiten.* Worms: Erich Norberg, 1954.

————. *Worms am Rhein. Führer durch die Geschichte und Sehenswürdigkeiten.* Worms: Erich Norberg, 1964.

Illustrierter Führer durch Worms. Ein Gedenkbüchlein für Fremde und für Einheimische. Mit über 50 Illustrationen. Worms: Heinrich Fischer, 1900.

Israelowitz, Oscar. *Guide to Jewish Europe: Western Europe.* 9th ed. Brooklyn: Israelowitz, 1997.

Jellinek, Adolf, ed. *Kreuzzüge. Nach handschriftlichen hebräischen Quellen.* Leipzig: J. M. Goldberg, 1854.

————. *Worms und Wien. Liturgische Formulare ihrer Todtenfeier aus alter und neuer Zeit, und Namensverzeichniss der Wormser Maertyrer aus den Jahren 1096 und 1349.* Wien: J. Schlossberg, 1880.

The Jewish Travel Guide: The Jewish Life in Germany. Frankfurt am Main: Paneuropean, 1954.

Josefowitz, Tanya. *I Remember.* London: Private publication, 1999.

Jost, I. M. *Geschichte der Israeliten seit der Zeit der Maccabäer bis auf unsre Tage nach den Quellen bearbeitet.* 9 vols. Berlin: Schlesinger, 1820–28.

Jüdisches Erbe in Deutschland. Botschaft und Herausforderung. Woche der Brüderlichkeit. Frankfurt am Main: Deutscher Koordinierungsrat der Gesellschaften für Christlich-Jüdissche Zusammenarbeit, 1984.

Kagan, Vladimir. *The Complete Vladimir Kagan: A Lifetime of Avant-Garde Design.* New York: Pointed Leaf Press, 2004.

Kayserlicher Herold / Das ist / Mandatum Poenale Sine Et Respective Cum Clausula, Wormbsische Zünfft / [et]c. Contra Wormbs / Die Abrechnung und Rückraitung auff fünff vom Hundert mit den Juden zu halten. Bey einem Ehrsamen Hochweisen Raht zu Wormbs den 7. Octob. 1614 glücklich ankommen / Allen frommen Christen zur Nachrichtung in Truck publicirt. Franckfurt: Latomus, 1614.

Kayserling, Moritz. *Die Jüdischen Frauen in der Geschichte, Literatur und Kunst. Bibliothek des deutschen Judentums.* Hildesheim: Olms, 1991.

Kirchheim, Juda Löw. *Minhagot Vermaiza: Minhagim ve-hanhagot.* Edited by Israel Mordechai Peles. Jerusalem: Mif'al torat hakhme Ashkenaz, Mekhon Yerushalayim, 1987.

Klein, Karl. *Die Hessische Ludwigsbahn oder Worms, Oppenheim und die anderen an der Bahn liegenden Orte. Topographisch und historisch dargestellt nebst einer übersichtlichen Beschreibung von Mainz.* Mainz: Seifert'schen Buchdruckerei, 1856.

Kohut, Adolph. *Geschichte der deutschen Juden. Ein Hausbuch für die jüdische Familie. Illustriert von Th. Kutschmann.* Berlin: Deutscher Verlag, 1898.

Krondorfer, Björn. *Remembrance and Reconciliation: Encounters between Young Jews and Germans.* New Haven: Yale University Press, 1995.

Kurtzer bewehrter Außzuch Der letzten Wormbser Judenordnung / wie sie Anno 1594. an etlichen orten Corrigiret und gebessert / im Newlich eröffneten Buchstaben geschrieben befunden. Vallo Francko, 1614.

Kurtzer unvergreifflicher Bericht wie Der Durchleuchtigst Hochgeborne Fürst und

Herr | Herr Friderich Der Fünfft | Pfaltzgraff bey Rhein | [et]c. Churfürst | Montags den 24. Aprilis | alten Calenders, diß 1615. Jahrs | nachts zwischen 12. und 1. Uhren | mit etlichem volck vor die Stadt Wormbs kommen | und wie dasselbe uff Dinstag den 25. eiusdem, umb 10. Uhren | vor Mittag daselbst | eingelassen worden | auch wie solches alles zugangen | und was sich gedenckwürdiges dabey begeben und zugetragen hat. 1615.

Lappin, Elena, ed. *Jewish Voices, German Words: Growing Up Jewish in Postwar Germany and Austria.* Translated by Krishna Winston. North Haven: Catbird Press, 1994.

Lazare, Bernard. *Job's Dungheap: Essays on Jewish Nationalism and Social Revolution.* New York: Schocken Books, 1948.

Lehmann, Manfred R. "Worms—One of Our 'Mother Cities.'" Available at http://www.manfredlehmann.com/sieg278.html. Accessed June 2004.

Levy, Benas. *Die Juden in Worms. Vortrag, gehalten beim Verein für jüdische Geschichte und Literatur.* Berlin: M. Poppelauer, 1914.

Lewysohn, Ludwig. *Nefashot Zadikim. Sechzig Epitaphien von Grabsteinen des israelitischen Friedhofes zu Worms regressiv bis zum Jahr 905 übl. Zeitr. nebst biographischen Skizzen.* Frankfurt am Main: Baer, 1855.

———. "Scenen aus dem Jahr 1096." *MGWJ* 5 (1856): 167–77.

———. "Zur Geschichte der Juden in Worms." *MGWJ* 7 (1858): 37–53.

Liebe, Georg. *Das Judentum in der deutschen Vergangenheit.* Leipzig: Diedrichs, 1903.

Lilienthal, Saul. *Jüdische Wanderungen in Frankfurt am Main, Hessen, Hessen-Nassau.* Frankfurt am Main: J. Kauffmann, 1938.

Lowenthal, Marvin. *A World Passed By: Scenes and Memories of Jewish Civilization in Europe and North Africa.* New York: Harper and Brothers Publishers, 1933.

———. *A World Passed By.* New York: National Jewish Welfare Board and A. Behrmann House Publication, 1945.

———. *The Jews of Germany: A Story of Sixteen Centuries.* New York: Jewish Publication Society of America, 1936.

Marcus, Jacob R. *The Rise and Destiny of the German Jew.* Cincinnati: Union of American Hebrew Congregations, 1934.

Marcus, Judith, Joseph B. Maier, and Zoltán Tarr, eds. *German Jewry: Its History and Sociology; Selected Essays of Werner J. Cahnman.* New Brunswick: Transaction Publishers, 1989.

Mannheimer, Moses. *Die Juden in Worms, ein Beitrag zur Geschichte der Juden in den Rheingegenden.* Frankfurt am Main: J. S. Adler, 1842.

Maysebukh. Basel, 1602.

Maysebukh. Roedelheim, 1753.

Misson, Maximilian. *A New Voyage to Italy: With Curious Observation on Several Other Countries: As Germany, Switzerland, Savoy, Geneva, Flanders, and Holland. Together, with Useful Instructions for Those Who Shall Travel Thither.* 4 vols. London: Printed for R. Bonwicke et al., 1714.

Mitscherlich, Alexander and Margarete. *Inability to Mourn.* Translated by Beverly R. Placzek. New York: Grove Press, 1975.

Morsey, Rudolf, and Hans-Peter Schwarz, eds. *Adenauer-Heuss. Unter vier Augen. Gespräche aus den Gründerjahren*. Berlin: Siedler, 1997.

Moryson, Fynes. *An Itinerary Containing His Ten Yeeres Travell through the Twelve Dominions of Germany, Bohmerland, Switzerland, Netherland, Denmarke, Poland, Italy, Turkey, France, England, Scotland and Ireland*. 4 vols. Glasgow: James MacLehose and Sons, 1907.

Moses, Siegfried. "Leo Baeck Institute of Jews from Germany." *LBIYB* 1 (1956): xi–xviii.

Moss, Celia. "The Martyrs of Worms: A German Tale." *Occident* 5 (1847–48): 200–204, 244–52, 295–300, and 339–44.

———. "The Synagogue at Worms and the Two Martyrs." *Occident* 1 (1843): 82–84.

Moss, Celia, and Marion Moss. *The Romance of Jewish History*. 2nd ed. 3 vols. London: A. K. Newman, 1843.

Muhlen, Norbert. *The Survivors: A Report on the Jews in Germany Today*. New York: Crowell, 1962.

Murray, John. *A Hand-Book for Travellers on the Continent: Being a Guide through Holland, Belgium, Prussia, and Northern Germany, and along the Rhine, from Holland to Switzerland. Containing Descriptions of the Principal Cities, Their Museums, Picture Galleries etc., the Great High Roads and the Most Interesting and Picturesque Districts, also Directions for Travelers, and Hints for Tours, with an Index Map*. London: John Murray and Son, 1836.

———. *A Handbook for Travellers on the Continent: Being a Guide to Holland, Belgium, Prussia, Northern Germany, and the Rhine from Holland to Switzerland*. 17th ed. London: John Murray, 1871.

Nemoy, Leon, ed. *Karaite Anthology: Excerpt from the Early Literature*. New Haven: Yale University Press, 1952.

Neubauer, Adolf, and Moritz Stern, eds. *Hebräische Berichte über die Judenverfolgung während der Kreuzzüge*. Berlin: Simion, 1892.

———. "Abou Ahron, le Babylonien." *REJ* 23 (1891): 230–37.

Neuester Führer durch Worms am Rhein und Umgebung (mit Plan) und 55 Illustrationen. Worms: Christian Herbst, 1906.

Oggel, Elisabeth. *Martin Buber, 1878–1978. Leben, Werk und Wirkung. Eine Ausstellung. Herausgegeben vom Deutschen Koordinierungsrat der Gesellschaft für Christlich-Jüdische Zusammenarbeit*. Worms: Selbstverlag, 1978.

Oppenheim, David. *Nishal David*. 3 vols. Jerusalem: Mekon Hatam Sofer, 1972–81.

Pappenheim, Bertha. *Allerlei Geschichten, Maasse-Buch. Buch der Sagen und Legenden aus Talmud und Midrasch nebst Volkserzählungen in Jüdisch-Deutscher Sprache*. Frankfurt am Main: J. Kauffmann, 1929.

Pascheles, Wolf. *Sippurim. Eine Sammlung jüdischer Volkssagen, Erzählungen, Mythen, Chroniken, Denkwürdigkeiten*. 4th ed. Prague: Wolf Pascheles, 1870.

Philippson, David. *Old European Jewries*. Philadelphia: Jewish Publication Society of America, 1894.

Pinson, Koppel, S. "Jewish Life in Liberated Germany: A Study of the Jewish DPs." *Jewish Social Studies* 9 (1947): 101–26.

Plaut, W. Gunther. *The Rise of Reform Judaism: A Sourcebook of Its European Origin*. New York: World Union for Progressive Judaism, 1963.

A Pocket Guide to Germany. Washington, D.C.: U. S. Government Printing Office, 1944.

A Pocket Guide to Germany. Washington, D.C.: U. S. Government Printing Office, 1951.

Postal, Bernard, and Samuel H. Abrahams. *The Landmark of a People: A Guide to Jewish Sites*. New York: Hill and Wang, 1962.

———. *Traveler's Guide to Jewish Landmarks in Europe*. New York: Fleet Press Corp., 1971.

Protokolle und Aktenstücke der zweiten Rabbiner-Versammlung, abgehalten zu Frankfurt am Main. Frankfurt am Main, 1845.

Puch, Nahman ben Eliezer. *Be-shurat tovot yeshuot we-nahmot me-geulat k. k. Frankfurt a. M. and k.k.* Worms, 1616.

Reckendorf, Hermann. *Die Geheimnisse der Juden*. 5 vols. Leipzig: Wolfgang Gerhard, 1856–57.

Reisz, Matthew. *Europe's Jewish Quarters*. London: Simon and Schuster, 1991.

Resolution Adopted by the Second Plenary Assembly of the World Jewish Congress, Montreux June 27th–July 6th, 1948. London, 1948.

Reuter, Fritz. *Jewish Worms: Rashi House and Judengasse*. Worms: Jüdisches Museum Raschi-Haus, 1992.

———. *Jüdisches Worms. Rashi-Haus und Judengasse*. Worms: H. Fischer, 1992.

———. *Worms am Rhein. Historische Stadtspaziergänge für Einheimische und Gäste*. Hamm: Kehl, 2000.

Richarz, Monika. *Jewish Life in Germany: Memoirs of Three Centuries*. Translated by Stella P. Rosenfeld and Sidney Rosenfeld. Bloomington: Indiana University Press, 1991.

Rosenfeld, Abraham, ed. *The Authorised Kinot for the Ninth of Av*. New York: Judaica Press, 1979.

Roth, Ernst. "Zur Wiedereinweihung der Alten Wormser Synagoge vor 20 Jahren." *Udim* 11–12 (1981/1982): 179–208.

Roth, Ernst, ed. *Festschrift zur Wiedereinweihung der Alten Synagoge zu Worms*. Frankfurt am Main: Ner Tamid Verlag, 1961.

Rothenburg, R. Meir. *She'elot u-teshuvot Maharam bar Barukh*. Lemberg, 1860.

Rothschild, Samson. *Aus Vergangenheit und Gegenwart der israel. Gemeinde Worms*. Mainz: G. Wirth, [1895].

———. *Aus Vergangenheit und Gegenwart der israel. Gemeinde Worms*. 5th ed. Frankfurt am Main: J. Kauffmann, 1913.

———. *Beamte der Wormser jüdischen Gemeinde Mitte des 18. Jahrhunderts bis zur Gegenwart*. Frankfurt am Main: J. Kauffmann, 1920.

———. *Die Synagoge in Worms und ihre berühmten Altertümer in 21 Bildern*. Worms: Christian Herbst, 1914.

Rovner, Ruth. *Exploring Jewish Germany: A Reporter's Notebook*. New York: GNTO, 1996.

Ruppert, Willi. *"Und Worms lebt dennoch." Ein Bericht 1945–1955.* Worms: Wormser Verlagsdruckerei, 1955.

Ruppin, Arthur. *Die Juden in der Gegenwart. Eine sozialwissenschaftliche Studie.* Berlin: S. Calvary, 1904.

Salfeld, Siegmund. *Das Martyrologium des Nürnberger Memorbuches.* Berlin: Simion, 1898.

Salzberger, Georg. "Zwischen zwei Weltkriegen. Die Gesellschaft für jüdische Volksbildung und das Jüdische Lehrhaus." In *Georg Salzberger, Leben und Lehre.* Edited by Albert H. Friedländer. Frankfurt am Main: Waldemar Kramer, 1982, 97–108.

Schaab, Karl Anton. *Diplomatische Geschichte der Juden zu Mainz und dessen Umgebung. Mit Berücksichtung ihres Rechtszustandes in den verschiedenen Epochen.* Mainz, 1855.

Schmidt-Mâcon, Klaus F. *Steinzeichen. Gedichte mit Fotographien von Günther Sydow.* Heppenheim: Otto KG, 1982.

Schudt, Johann Jacob. *Jüdische Merkwürdigkeiten Vorstellende was sich Curieuses und denckwürdiges in den neuern Zeiten bey einigen Jahr-hunderten mit denen in alle IV. Theile der Welt / sonderlich durch Teutschland / zerstreuten Juden zugetragen. Sammt einer vollständigen Frankfurter Juden-Chronik / Darinnen der zu Franckfurt am Mayn wohnenden Juden / von eingen Jahr-hunderten / bis auff unsere Zeiten merckwürdigste Begebenheiten enthaltend.* 4 vols. Frankfurt: S. T. Hocker, 1714–18.

Schwarz, Joseph. *Descriptive Geography and Brief Historical Sketch of Palestine.* Translated by Isaac Leeser. Philadelphia: A. Hart, 1850.

Sefer Hasidim. Edited by Re'uven Margaliyot. Jerusalem: Mosa ha-rav Kok, 1956.

Sefer Hasidim. Edited by Jehuda Wistinetzki and Jacob Freimann. 2nd ed. Frankfurt am Main: Wahrmann, 1924.

Shammes, Juspa. *Minhagim di-k.k. Vermaisa le-Rabi Yuzpa Shamash. Mofi'a la-rishonah bi-shelemut mi-kitve ha-yad shel ha-mehaber. Kolel hashlamot ve-hagahot me-Rabenu Yair Hayim Bakharakh'im mekorot, beurim u-fetihah kelalit 'al yede Binyamin Shelomoh Hamburger. Hakhanat tekst u-mavoh histori 'al yede Yitshak Zimer.* 2 vols. Jerusalem: Mif'al torat hakhme Ashkenaz, Mekhon Yerushalayim, 1988–92.

Soldan, Friedrich. *Die Zerstörung der Stadt Worms im Jahre 1689. Im Auftrage der Stadt Worms dargestellt.* Worms: Julius Stern, 1889.

Soutou, Andre. *Worms am Rhein. Führer durch die Stadt und ihre Sehenswürdigkeiten.* Worms: Erich Norberg, 1949.

Spitzer, Shlomo. *Sefer Maharil: Manhigim.* Jerusalem: Makhon Yerushalayim, 1989.

Stadtsanierung Worms. Die Judengasse. 5. Bürgerinformationen der Stadtverwaltung Worms zur Altstadtsanierung. Worms, 1978.

Stauben, Daniel. *Scènes de la vie juive en Alsace.* Paris: Levy, 1860.

Steinschneider, Moritz. *Catalogus librorum Hebraeorum in Bibliotheca Bodleiana.* Berlin: A. Friedlaender, 1852–60.

Stern, Moritz. "Ein Copialbuch der jüdischen Gemeinde zu Worms." *ZGJD* 1 (1886): 277–80.

Synagoga. Kultgeräte und Kunstwerke von der Zeit der Patriarchen bis zur Gegenwart bis zur Gegenwart. Städtische Kunsthallte Recklinghausen, 3. November 1960–15. Januar 1961. Recklinghausen: Städtische Kunsthalle, 1960.

Tendlau, Abraham M. *Das Buch der Sagen und Legenden jüdischer Vorzeit: Nach den Quellen bearbeitet nebst Anmerkungen und Erläuterungen.* 3rd ed. Frankfurt am Main: J. Kauffmann, 1873.

———. *Sprichwörter und Redensarten deutsch-jüdischer Vorzeit. Ein | Als Beitrag zur Volks-, Sprach- und Sprichwörterkunde. Aufgezeichnet aus dem Munde des Volkes und nach Wort und Sinn erläutert.* Frankfurt am Main: J. Kauffmann, 1860.

Theilhaber, Felix. *Der Untergang der deutschen Juden. Eine volkswirtschaftliche Studie.* Munich: Reinhardt, 1911.

Trog, Carl. *Rheinlands Wunderhorn. Sagen, Geschichte und Legenden, auch Schwänke aus den alten Ritterburgen, Klöstern und Städten der Rheinufer und des Rheingebietes von den Quellen bis zur Mündung des Stromes. Dem deutschen Volk gewidmet.* 15 vols. Essen: Silbermann, 1882–84.

Tchernichovsky, Saul. *Kol kitve Sha'ul Tshernihovski: Shirim we-baladot.* Tel Aviv: 'Am 'Oved, 1990.

Varnhagen, Rahel. *Rahel Varnhagen und ihre Zeit (Briefe 1800–1833).* Edited by Friedhelm Kemp. 4 vols. Munich: Kösel, 1968.

Verga, Shlomo ibn. *Shevet Yehuda.* Edited by A. Shohat with an introduction by Y. Beer. Jerusalem: Mosad Bialik, 1947.

Verwaltungs-Rechenschaftsbericht des Oberbürgermeisters der Stadt Worms für 1914. Worms am Rhein: A. K. Boechinger, 1916.

Vogel, Rolf, ed. *Der Deutsch-Israelitische Dialog. Dokumentation eines erregenden Kapitels Deutscher Außenpolitik.* 9 vols. Munich: K. G. Sauer, 1990.

Wachstein, Bernhard. *Die Inschriften des alten Judenfriedhofs in Wien. Im Auftrage der historischen Kommission der israelitischen Kultusgemeinde in Wien.* 2 vols. Wien: Wilhelm Braumüller, 1917.

Weckerling, August. *Beckmann-Führer. Worms am Rhein und Umgebung. Mit Stadt-Plan und vielen Abbildungen.* 4th ed. Heilbronn am Neckar: Otto Weber Verlag, 1908.

———. *Worms sur le Rhin et ses environs: Avec un plan de la ville et de nombreuses illustrations.* Trans. Tony Kellen. Heilbronn: Weber, 1919.

Weil, Bruno. *Der Weg der deutschen Juden.* Berlin: Centralverein deutscher Staatsbürger Jüdischen Glaubens, 1934.

Woerl, Leo. *Führer durch Worms und Umgebung.* 6th ed. Leipzig, 1900.

Wolf, G. *Juden in Worms und des deutschen Städtewesens. Nach archivalischen Urkunden des K. K. Ministeriums des Aeussern in Wien.* Breslau: Schletter, 1861.

———. "Zur Geschichte der Juden in Worms und des deutschen Städtewesens." *MGWJ* 10 (1861): 321–33, 361–76, 410–30, and 453–63.

Wormbsische Acta oder Aussmusterung der Jüden zu Wormbs: Das ist | Historische Relation | wie die Burger zu Wormbs | ihre Jüden außwiesen | un[n] fortgetrieben | auch wie sie deroselben Tempel Schul | Synagog | unnd Hauße der Reinigung |

alsbaldt abzubrechen / . . . Darauß zusehen / aus was Hochwichtigen bewegendten Ursachen solches geschehen / und was die Obrigkeit hierzu gesagt, 1615.

Worms a. Rh. Deutschland-Bildheft Nr. 57. Berlin: Berlin-Tempelhof-Universum-Verlagsanstalt, 1933.

Worms am Rhein: Führer durch die Geschichte und Sehenswürdigkeiten. Worms: Erich Norberg, 1954.

Wörner, Ernst. *Die Kunstdenkmäler im Großherzogtum Hessen: Inventarisirung und beschreibende Darstellung der Werke der Architektur, Plastik, Malerei und des Kunstgewerbes bis zum Schluss des XVIII. Jahrhunderts. Kreis Worms.* Darmstadt: Bergsträsser, 1887.

Yahia, Gedaliah Ibn. *Shalshelet ha-kabalah.* Jerusalem: Hotsa'at ha-dorot ha-rishonim ve-korotom, 1962.

Zaidner, Michael, ed. *Jewish Travel Guide 2000.* London: Valentine and Mitchell, 2000.

Zoller, Johann Jacob. *Kurtze Beschreibung seines Wandels und vornehmster Begebenheiten / So er Nach Einäscherung seiner Geburtsstadt Wormbs Anno 1689 biß daher in seinem Exilio gehabt: Und denn darauf Eine kurtze und einfältige Verantwortung auf das / was ihn Herr D. Samuel Schelwig / Pastor und Rector zu Dantzig / in seinem so genannten Itinerario Antipietistico beschuldigt.* Halle, 1696.

Zunz, Leopold. *Monatstage des Kalenderjahres: Ein Andenken an Hingeschiedene.* Berlin: Poppelauer, 1872.

———. *Die synagogale Poesie des Mittelalters.* Berlin: Springer, 1855.

———. *Zur Geschichte und Literatur.* Berlin: Veit und Comp., 1845.

Zur Geschichte der Wormser jüdischen Gemeinde, ihrer Friedhöfe u. ihres Begräbniswesens. Gedenkschrift zur Eröffnung des neuen Friedhofs. Worms: H. Kräuter'schen Buchhandlung, 1911.

SECONDARY LITERATURE

Abulafia, Anna Sapir. "The Interrelationship between the Hebrew Chronicles on the First Crusade." *Journal of Semitic Studies* 27 (1982): 221–39.

———. "Invectives against Christianity in the Hebrew Chronicles of the First Crusade." In *Crusade and Settlement: Papers Read at the First Conference of the Society for Study of Crusades and Latin East and Presented to R. C. Smail.* Edited by Peter W. Edbury. Cardiff: University College Cardiff Press, 1985. 66–72.

Adorno, Theodor W. "What Does Coming to Terms with the Past Mean?" In *Bitburg in Moral and Political Perspective.* Edited by Geoffrey H. Hartman. Bloomington: Indiana University Press, 1986. 114–29.

Agus, Irving A. *Rabbi Meir of Rothenburg: His Life and His Works as Sources for the Religious, Legal, and Social History of the Jews of Germany in the 13th Century.* 2 vols. Philadelphia: Dropsie College for Hebrew and Cognate Learning, 1947.

Altaras, Thea. *Synagogen in Hessen: Was geschah seit 1945?* Königstein/Taunus: K. Langewiesche, 1988.

Anderson, Benedict. *Imagined Communities: Reflections on the Origin and Spread of Nationalism.* London: Verso, 1995.

Applegate, Celia. *Heimat in the Pfalz: A Nation of Provincials: The German Idea of Heimat.* Berkeley: University of California Press, 1990.

Arnsberg, Paul. *Die Geschichte der Frankfurter Juden seit der Französischen Revolution.* 3 vols. Darmstadt: Eduard Roether Verlag, 1983.

———. *Die jüdischen Gemeinden in Hessen. Anfang, Untergang, Neubeginn.* Frankfurt am Main: Societäts-Verlag, 1971.

Avneri, Zvi ed. *Germania Judaica. Bd. 2. Von 1238 bis zur Mitte des 14. Jahrhunderts.* Tübingen: J. C. B. Mohr, 1968.

Bajohr, Frank. *"Unser Hotel ist Judenrein." Bäder-Antisemitismus im 19. und 20. Jahrhundert.* Frankfurt am Main: Fischer Verlag, 2003.

Baron, Salo Wittmayer. "Plenitude of Apostolic Power and Medieval Jewish Serfdom." In *Ancient and Medieval Jewish History: Essays by Salo Wittmayer Baron.* Edited by Leon A. Feldman. New Brunswick: Rutgers University Press, 1963. 284–307.

———. *A Social and Religious History of the Jews.* 18 vols. New York: Columbia University Press, 1952–83.

Baskin, Judith R. "Dolce of Worms: The Lives and Deaths of an Exemplary Medieval Jewish Woman and Her Daughters." In *Judaism in Practice: From the Middle Ages to the Early Modern Period.* Edited by Lawrence Fine. Princeton: Princeton University Press, 2001. 429–37.

———. "Dolce of Worms: Women Saints in Judaism." In *Women Saints in World Religions.* Edited by Arvin Sharma. Albany: State University of New York Press, 2000. 39–70.

Beit-Arié, Malachi. "The Worms Mahzor: Its History and Its Palaeographic and Codicological Characteristics." In *MS. Jewish National and University Library. Heb. 4° 781/1.* Edited by Malachi Beit-Arié. London: Cyelar Establishment, Vaduz, 1985. 13–35.

Ben-Ari, Niza. *Roman 'im ha-'avar: Ha-Roman ha-histori ha-yehudi-ha-germani min ha-meah ha-19 we-yezirato shel sifrut leumit.* Tel Aviv: Devir, 1997.

Benjamin, Walter. *Illuminations.* Edited by Hannah Arendt and translated by Harry Zohn. New York: Schocken, 1969.

Berliner, Abraham. *Aus dem Leben der deutschen Juden im Mittelalter zugleich als Beitrag für deutsche Culturgeschichte. Nach gedruckten und ungedruckten Quellen.* Berlin: M. Poppelauer's Buchhandlung, 1900.

Blume, Herbert. "Blaugelb und Schwarzweißrot. Wilhelm Brandes als Schriftsteller." In *Von Wilhelm Raabe und anderen. Vorträge aus dem Braunschweiger Raabe-Haus.* Edited by Herbert Blume. Bielefeld: Verlag für Regionalgeschichte, 2001. 95–129.

Boa, Elizabeth, and Rachel Palfreyman. *Heimat: A German Dream; Regional Loyalties and National Identity in German Culture, 1890–1990.* Oxford: Oxford University Press, 2000.

Boas, Jacob. "Germany or Diaspora: German Jewry's Shifting Perception in the Nazi Era (1933–1938)." *LBIYB* 27 (1986): 109–26.

Böcher, Otto. *Die alte Synagoge zu Worms.* Worms: Verlag Stadtbibliothek, 1960.

————. "Thesen des Altertumsvereins Worms e.V. zur Sanierung der Judengasse." *Der Wormsgau* 10 (1972/73): 86.

————. "Varia zu Bau und Ausstattung der Wormser Synagogue." *Wormsgau* 10 (1972–73): 59–61.

————. "Zum Wiederaufbau der Wormser Synagoge." *Der Wormsgau* 19 (2000): 205–27.

Bodemann, Y. Michael, ed. *Jews, Germans, Memory: Reconstruction of Jewish Life in Germany.* Ann Arbor: University of Michigan Press, 1996.

Boehlich, Walter, ed. *Der Berliner Antisemitismusstreit.* Frankfurt am Main: Suhrkamp, 1965.

Bönnen, Gerold. "Die Nibelungenstadt. Rezeption und Stadtbild in Worms im 19. und 20. Jahrhundert." *Blätter für deutsche Landesgeschichte* 136 (2000): 37–49.

————. "'Es ist mein Lebenszweck': Isidor Kiefer und sein Anteil am Wiederaufbau der Wormser Synagoge, 1957–1961." *Aschkenas* 12 (2002): 91–113.

————. "Jüdische Gemeinde und christliche Stadtgemeinde." In *Jüdische Gemeinden und ihr christlicher Kontext in kulturräumlich vergleichender Betrachtung von der Spätantike bis zum 18. Jahrhundert.* Edited by Christoph Cluse, Alfred Haverkamp, and Israel J. Yuval. Hannover: Hahn, 2003. 309–40.

Boym, Svetlana. *The Future of Nostalgia.* New York: Basic Books, 2001.

Breitbart, Gerrard."Die Alte Synagoge zu Worms nach ihre Wiedereinweihung." *Udim* 11–12 (1981): 215–18.

Brenner, Michael. *After the Holocaust: Rebuilding Jewish Lives in Postwar Germany.* Translated by Barbara Harshav. Princeton: Princeton University Press, 1997.

————. *The Renaissance of Jewish Culture in Weimar Germany.* New Haven: Yale University Press, 1996.

Brilling, Bernhard. "Das jüdische Archivwesen in Deutschland." *Der Archivar* 13 (1960): 271–90.

Brochhagen, Ulrich. *Nach Nürnberg. Vergangenheitsbewältigung und Westintegration in der Ära Adenauer.* Berlin: Ullstein, 1999.

Brodhaecker, Michael. *Menschen zwischen Hoffnung und Verzweiflung. Der Alltag jüdischer Mitmenschen in Rheinhessen, Mainz und Worms während des "Dritten Reiches."* Mainz: Gesellschaft für Volkskunde in Rheinland-Pfalz, 1999.

Burnett, Stephen. "Distorted Mirrors: Antonious Margaritha, Johann Buxtorf and Christian Ethnographies of Judaism." *Sixteenth Century Journal* 25 (1994): 275–87.

Cahn, Walter. "The 'Bimah' of Worms Synagogue Reconsidered." *Jewish Art* 12–13 (1987): 266–68.

Chazan, Robert. *European Jewry and the First Crusade.* Berkeley: University of California Press, 1987.

————. *God, Humanity, and History: The Hebrew First Crusade Narratives.* Berkeley: University of California Press, 2000.

————. "Representation of Events in the Middle Ages." *History and Theory* 27 (1988): 40–55.

Cohen, Gershon D. "Hannah and Her Seven Sons in Hebrew Literature." In *Sefer ha-Yovel le-khevod M. M. Kaplan.* Edited by Moshe Davis. New York: JTS, 1953. 109–22.

———. "The Hebrew Crusade Chronicles and the Ashkenazic Tradition." In *Minhah le-Nahum: Biblical and Other Studies Presented to Nahum Sarna in Honour of his 70th Birthday.* Edited by Marc Brettler and Michael Fishbane. Sheffield: JSOT Press, 1993. 36–53.

Cohen, Jeremy. "A 1096 Complex: Constructing the First Crusade in Jewish Historical Memory, Medieval and Modern." In *Jews and Christians in Twelfth-Century Europe.* Edited by Michael A. Signer and John H. van Engen. Notre Dame: University of Notre Dame Press, 2001. 9–21.

———. "Between Martyrdom and Apostasy: Doubt and Self-Definition in Twelfth-Century Ashkenaz." *Journal of Medieval and Early Modern Studies* 29 (1999): 431–71.

———. *Sanctifying the Name of God: Jewish Martyrs and Jewish Memories of the First Crusade, Jewish Culture and Contexts.* Philadelphia: University of Pennsylvania Press, 2004.

Cohen, Richard I. *Jewish Icons: Art and Society in Modern Europe.* Berkeley: University of California Press, 1998.

Cohn, Haim H. "Joseph Carlebach." *LBIYB* 5 (1960): 58–72.

Confino, Alon. "Collective Memory and Cultural History: Problems and Methods." *AHR* 102 (1997): 1386–1403.

———. "Dissonance, Normality, and the Historical Method: Why Did Some Germans Think of Tourism after May 8, 1945?" In *Life After Death: Approaches to a Cultural and Social History of Europe During the 1940s and 1950s.* Edited by Richard Bessel and Dirk Schumann. Cambridge: Cambridge University Press, 2003. 323–47.

———. *The Nation as a Local Metaphor: Württemberg, Imperial Germany and National Memory, 1871–1918.* Chapel Hill: University of North Carolina Press, 1997.

———. "Traveling as a Culture of Remembrance: Traces of National Socialism in West Germany, 1945–1960." *History and Memory* 12 (2001): 92–121.

Confino, Alon, and Ajay Skaria. "The Local Life of Nationhood." *National Identities* 4 (2002): 7–24.

Dan, Joseph. *Iyyunim be-sifrut hasidut ashkenaz.* Ramat-Gan: Massada, 1975.

———. "Le-toldoteha shel 'sifrut ha-shvahim." *Mehkere yerushalaim be-folklor yehudi* 1 (1981): 82–101.

———. "Sifrut ha-shvahim mizrah u-ma'arav." *Pe'amim* 26 (1986): 77–86.

———. *Torat ha-sod shel hasidut' ashkenaz.* Jerusalem: Bialik, 1968.

David, Abraham "Zikhronot ve-he-arot 'al gezerot tatnu—bi-defus u-ve kitve yad 'ivriim." In *Yehudim mul ha-zelav: Gezerot 856 ba-historyah uva-historyografiah.* Edited by Yom Tov Assis, Michael Toch, Jeremy Cohen, Ora Limor, and Aaron Kedar. Jerusalem: Y. L. Magnes, 2000. 146–94.

DeKoven Ezrahi, Sidra. *Booking Passage: Exile and Homecoming in the Modern Jewish Imagination.* Berkeley: University of California Press, 2000.

Domansky, Elisabeth. "'Kristallnacht,' the Holocaust, and German Unity: The Meaning of November 9 as an Anniversary in Germany." *History and Memory* 4 (1992): 60–94.

Eckert, Willehad Paul. "Hoch-und Spätmittelalter. Katholischer Humanismus." In *Kirche und Synagoge. Handbuch zur Geschichte von Christen und Juden.* Edited by Karl Heinrich Rengstorf and Siegfried Kortzfleisch. 2 vols. Stuttgart: Klett, 1968. 210–306.

Eidelberg, Shlomo. "Origins of German Jewry: Reality and Legend." In *Medieval Ashkenazic History: Studies on German Jewry in the Middle Ages.* Edited by Shlomo Eidelberg. Brooklyn: Sepher-Hermon Press, 1999. 1–10.

Einbinder, Susan. *Beautiful Death: Jewish Poetry and Martyrdom in Medieval France.* Princeton: Princeton University Press, 2003.

Eisen, Arnold. *Rethinking Modern Judaism: Ritual, Commandment, Community.* Chicago Studies in the History of Judaism. Chicago: Chicago University Press, 1998.

Elbogen, Ismar. *Jewish Liturgy: A Comprehensive History.* Edited and translated by Raymond P. Scheindlin. Philadelphia: Jewish Publication Society of America, 1993.

Elbogen, Ismar, Aron Freimann, and Haim Tykocinski, eds. *Germania Judaica.* Tübingen: J.C.B. Mohr, 1963–2003.

Eley, Geoff, ed. *The Goldhagen Effect: History, Memory, Nazism—Facing the German Past.* Ann Arbor: University of Michigan Press, 2000.

Enzensberger, Hans Magnus. "Eine Theorie des Tourismus." In *Einzelheiten I: Bewußtseins-Industrie.* Frankfurt am Main: Suhrkamp, 1964. 179–205.

Epstein, Abraham. "Jüdische Alterthümer in Worms und Speier." *MGWJ* 40 (1895): 509–15 and 554–59.

———. "Die nach Raschi benannten Gebäude in Worms." *MGWJ* 45 (1901): 44–75.

———. "Die Wormser Minhagbücher." In *Gedenkbuch zur Erinnerung an David Kaufmann.* Edited by Marcus Brann, Ferdinand Rosenthal, and David Kaufmann. Breslau: S. Schottlaender, 1900. 288–317.

Finkelstein, Louis. *Jewish Self-Government in the Middle Ages.* New York: Jewish Theological Seminary of America, 1924.

Fishman, Talya. "The Rhineland Pietists' Sacralization of Oral *Torah.*" *Jewish Quarterly Review* 96 (2005): 9–16.

Frei, Norbert. *Adenauer's Germany and the Nazi Past: The Politics of Amnesty and Integration.* Translated by Joel Golb. New York: Columbia University Press, 2002.

Frey, Sabine. *Rechtsschutz der Juden gegen Ausweisungen im 16. Jahrhundert.* Frankfurt am Main: Peter Lang, 1983.

Friedrichs, Christopher R. "Anti-Jewish Politics in Early Modern Germany: The Uprising of Worms, 1613–1617." *Central European History* 21 (1990): 91–152.

———. "German Town Revolts and the 17th Century Crisis." *Renaissance and Modern Studies* 26 (1982): 27–51.

———. "Jewish Household Structure in an Early Modern Town: The Worms Ghetto Census of 1610." *History of the Family* 8 (2003): 481–93.

————. "Jews in Imperial Cities." In *In and Out of the Ghetto: Jewish-Gentile Relations in Late Medieval and Early Modern Germany*. Edited by Ronnie Po-Chia Hsia and Hartmut Lehmann. Cambridge: Cambridge University Press, 1995. 275–88.

————. "Politics or Pogrom? The Fettmilch Uprising in Germany and Jewish History." *CEH* 19 (1986): 186–228.

————. "Urban Conflicts and the Imperial Constitution in Seventeenth-Century Germany." *Journal of Modern History* 58 (1986): 98–123.

Fritzsche, Peter. "Cities Forget, Nations Remember: Berlin and Germany and the Shock of Modernity." In *Pain and Prosperity: Reconsidering Twentieth-Century German History*. Edited by Paul Betts and Greg Eghigian. Stanford: Stanford University Press, 2003. 35–60 and 227–32.

Fulbrook, Mary. *German National Identity after the Holocaust*. Cambridge: Polity Press, 1999.

Galchinsky, Michael. *The Origin of the Modern Jewish Woman Writer: Romance and Reform in Victorian England*. Detroit: Wayne State University Press, 1996.

Geary, Patrick J. *Living with the Dead in the Middle Ages*. Ithaca: Cornell University Press, 1994.

Gebhardt, Miriam. *Das Familiengedächtnis. Erinnerung im Deutsch-Jüdischen Bürgertum 1890 bis 1932*. Stuttgart: F. Steiner, 1999.

Geis, Jael. *Uebrig sein—Leben "danach": Juden deutscher Herkunft in der britischen und amerikanischen Zone Deutschlands, 1945–1949*. Vienna: Philo, 1999.

Gernsheim, Helmut. "The Gernsheim of Worms." *LBIYB* 24 (1979): 247–57.

Gilman, Sander L., and Karen Remmler, eds. *Re-emerging Jewish Culture in Germany: Life and Literature since 1989*. New York: New York University Press, 1994.

Goldberg, Sylvie. *Crossing the Jabbok: Illness and Death in Ashkenazi Judaism in Sixteenth- through Nineteenth-Century Prague*. Translated by Carol Cosman. Berkeley: University of California Press, 1996.

Goldhagen, Daniel. *Hitler's Willing Executioners: Ordinary Germans and the Holocaust*. London: Abacus, 1997.

Graboïs, A. "Le souvenir et la légende de Charlemagne dans les texts hébraïques medievaux." *Le moyen âge* 72 (1966): 5–41.

Graus, Frantisek. "Historische Traditionen über Juden im Spätmittelalter (Mitteleuropa)." In *Zur Geschichte der Juden im Deutschland des späten Mittelalters und der frühen Neuzeit*. Edited by Alfred Haverkamp and Alfred Heit. Stuttgart: Anton Hiersemann, 1981. 1–26.

Green, Abigail. *Fatherlands State-Building and Nationhood in Nineteenth-Century Germany*. Cambridge: Cambridge University Press, 2001.

Greenberg, Gershon. "The Dimensions of Samuel Adler's Religious View of the World." *HUCA* 46 (1975): 377–412.

Gregor, Neil, Nils Roemer, and Mark Roseman, eds. *German History from the Margins, 1800 to the Present*. Bloomington: Indiana University Press, 2006.

Grossman, Avraham. *Pious and Rebellious: Jewish Women in Medieval Europe.* Translated from the Hebrew by Jonathan Chipman. Hanover, N.H.: University Press of New England, 2004.

Gruber, Ruth Ellen. *Virtually Jewish: Reinventing Jewish Culture in Europe.* Berkeley: University of California Press, 2002.

Grunwald, Max. "Le Cimetière de Worms." *REJ* NS 4 (1938): 71–103.

Gurevitch, Zali and Gideon Aran. "The Land of Israel: Myth and Phenomenon." In *Reshaping the Past: Jewish History and the Historian.* Edited by Jonathan Frankel. New York: Oxford University Press, 1994. 195–210.

———. "'Al ha-makom." *Alpayim* 4 (1991): 9–44.

Halbwachs, Maurice. *On Collective Memory.* Edited and translated by Lewis A. Coser. Chicago: University of Chicago Press, 1992.

Hammer-Schenk, Harold. "Die Architektur der Synagoge von 1780 bis 1933." In *Die Architektur der Synagoge.* Edited by Hans-Peter Schwarz. Frankfurt am Main: Klett-Cotta, 1988. 157–285.

———. "Edwin Opplers Theorie des Synagogenbaus: Emanzipationsversuche durch Architektur." *Hannoversche Geschichtsblätter* 32 (1978): 1014–1117.

Hanslok, Andreas. *Die landesherrliche und kommunale Judenschutzpolitik während des späten Mittelalters im Heiligen Römischen Reich Deutscher Nation. Ein Vergleich der Entwicklungen am Beispiel schlesischer, brandenburgischer und rheinischer Städte.* Berlin: Wissenschaftlicher Verlag, 2000.

Haude, Rüdiger. *"Kaiseridee" oder "Schicksalsgemeinschaft": Geschichtspolitik beim Projekt "Aachener Krönungsausstellung 1915" und bei der Jahrtausendausstellung Aachen 1925.* Aachen: Aachener Geschichtsverein, 2000.

Heckart, Beverly. "The Cities of Avignon and Worms as Expressions of the European Community." *Comparative Studies in Society and History* 31 (1989): 462–90.

Heil, Johannes, and Rainer Erb, eds. *Geschichtswissenschaft und Öffentlichkeit. Der Streit um Daniel J. Goldhagen.* Frankfurt am Main: Fischer Taschenbuch Verlag, 1998.

Hoffmann, Christhard, ed. *Preserving the Legacy of German Jewry: A History of the Leo Baeck Institute, 1955–2005.* Tübingen: Mohr Siebeck, 2005.

Honnef, Klaus, Klaus Weschenfelder, and Irene Haberland, eds. *Vom Zauber des Rheins ergriffen. Zur Entdeckung der Rheinlandschaft.* Munich: Klinkhardt and Biermann, 1992.

Hoppe, Jens. "Das jüdische Museum in Worms. Seine Geschichte bis 1938 und die anschliessenden Bemühungen um die Wiedererrichtung der Wormser Synagoge." *Wormsgau* 21 (2002): 81–101.

———. *Jüdische Geschichte und Kultur in Museen. Zur nichtjüdischen Museologie des Jüdischen in Deutschland.* Münster: Waxmann, 2002.

Horowitz, Elliott. "Speaking to the Dead: Cemetery Prayer in Medieval and Early Modern Jewry." *Journal of Jewish Thought and Philosophy* 8 (1999): 303–17.

Hsia, R. Po-Chia. "Bürgerschaft in Worms 1614: Judenprivilegien und Bürgerrecht in der frühen Neuzeit." In *Aussenseiter zwischen Mittelalter und*

Neuzeit. Festschrift für Hans-Jürgen Goertz zum 60. Geburtstag. Edited by
Hans-Jürgen Goertz, Norbert Fischer, and Marion Kobelt-Groch. Leiden: E. J.
Brill, 1997. 101–10.

———. *The Myth of Ritual Murder: Jews and Magic in Reformation Germany.* New
Haven: Yale University Press, 1988.

Huttenbach, Henry R. *The Destruction of the Jewish Community of Worms, 1933–*
1945: A Study of the Holocaust Experience in Germany. New York: Memorial
Committee of Jewish Victims of Nazism from Worms, 1981.

———. *The Emigration Book of Worms: The Character and Dimension of the*
Jewish Exodus from a Small German Jewish Community, 1933–1941. Koblenz:
Landesarchivverwaltung Rheinland-Pfalz, 1974.

———. *The Life of Herta Mansbacher: A Portrait of a Jewish Teacher, Heroine, and*
Martyr. New York: Memorial Committee of Jewish Victims of Nazism from
Worms, 1980.

———. "The Reconstruction and Evaluation of a Social Calendar as a Primary
Source for the History of the Jewish Community of Worms (1933–1938)."
Proceedings of the Sixth World Congress of Jewish Studies 2 (Jerusalem 1975):
367–97.

Kaplan, Marion. *The Making of the Jewish Middle Class: Women, Family, and*
Identity in Imperial Germany. New York: Oxford University Press, 1991.

———. "Redefining Judaism in Imperial Germany: Practices, Mentalities, and
Community." *Jewish Social Studies* 9 (2002): 1–33.

Kaufmann, David. "Die Grabsteine R. Meir's von Rothenburg und Alexander
Wimpfen's in Worms." *MGWJ* 40 (1895): 126–30.

———. *R. Jair Chajjim Bacharach (1638–1702) und seine Ahnen.* Trier: Siegmund
Mayer, 1894.

Keitz, Christine. *Reisen als Leitbild. Die Entstehung des modernen Massentourismus*
in Deutschland. Munich: Deutscher Taschenbuchverlag, 1997.

Kirshenblatt-Gimblett, Barbara. *Destination Culture: Tourism, Museums, and*
Heritage. Berkeley: University of California Press, 1998.

Kittel, Susanne. "Spuren der Übergangszeit. Der Wiederaufbau von Worms nach
1945." *Bausubstanz* 14 (1988): 40–45.

Kober, Adolf. "Die deutschen Kaiser und die Wormser Juden." *ZGDJ* 5 (1935):
134–51.

———. "Jewish Monuments of the Middle Ages in Germany." *PAAJR* 14 (1944):
149–220 and 15 (1945): 1–91.

Königseder, Angelika, and Juliane Wetzel. *Waiting for Hope: Jewish Displaced*
Persons in Post-War II Germany. Translated by John A. Broadwin. Evanston:
Northwestern University Press, 2001.

Koshar, Rudy. *From Monuments to Traces: Artifacts of German Memory, 1870–1990.*
Berkeley: University of California Press, 2000.

———. *German Travel Cultures.* Oxford: Berg, 2000.

———. *Germany's Transient Pasts: Preservation and National Memory in the*
Twentieth Century. Chapel Hill: University of North Carolina Press, 1998.

———. " 'What Ought to Be Seen': Tourists' Guidebooks and National Identities in Modern Germany and Europe." *Journal of Contemporary History* 33 (1998): 323–40.

Krautheimer, Richard. *Mittelalterliche Synagogen*. Berlin: Frankfurter Verlags-Anstalt, 1927.

Krawkowski, Shmuel. "Memorial Projects and Memorial Institutions Initiated by She'erith Hapletah." *She'erith Hapletah, 1944–1948: A Rehabilitation and Political Struggle; Proceedings of the 6th Yad Vashem International Conference, Jerusalem, October 1985*. Edited by Yisrael Gutman and Avital Saf. Jerusalem: Yad Vashem, 1990. 388–98.

Kugelmass, Jack, ed. *Going Home*. New York: YIVO Institute, 1993.

———. "Why We Go to Poland: Holocaust Tourism as Secular Ritual." In *The Art of Memory: Holocaust Memorials in History*. Edited by James E. Young. New York: Prestel, 1994. 175–85.

Kurtz, Michael J. *Nazi Contraband: American Policy on the Return of the European Cultural Treasures, 1945–1955*. New York: Garland Publishing, 1985.

———. "Resolving a Dilemma: The Inheritance of Jewish Property." *Cardozo Law Review* 20 (1998): 625–54.

Lamm, Hans, ed. *Der Eichmann-Prozess in der deutschen öffentlichen Meinung. Eine Dokumentensammlung*. Frankfurt am Main: Ner Tamid, 1961.

Liberles, Robert. "Emancipation and the Structure of the Jewish Community in the Nineteenth Century." *LBIYB* 31 (1986): 51–67.

———. *Salo Wittmayer Baron: Architect of Jewish History*. New York: New York University Press, 1995.

Liss, Hanna. "Copyright im Mittelalter? Die esoterischen Schriften von R. El'azar von Worms zwischen Traditions- und Autorenliteratur." *Frankfurter Judaistische Beiträge* 21 (1994): 81–108.

———. "Offenbarung und Weitergabe des göttlichen Namens und die Rezeption priesterlicher Traditionen im Sefer ha-Shem des R. El'azar ben Yehuda von Worms." *Frankfurter Judaistische Beiträge* 26 (1999): 25–50.

Longerich, Peter. *Krieg der Vernichtung. Eine Gesamtdarstellung der nationalsozialistischen Judenverfolgung*. Munich: Piper, 1998.

Lowenstein, Steven M. "The 1840s and the Creation of the German-Jewish Religious Reform Movement." In *Revolution and Evolution: 1848 in German-Jewish History*. Edited by Werner E. Mosse, Arnold Paucker, and Reinhard Rürup. Tübingen: J. C. B. Mohr, 1981. 255–97.

———. "The Readership of the Bible Translation." *HUCA* 103 (1982): 179–213.

———. "The Rural Community and the Urbanization of German Jewry." *Central European History* 8 (1980): 218–36.

———. "The Yiddish Written Word in Nineteenth-Century Germany." *LBIYB* 34 (1979): 172–92.

Lowenthal, David. *The Past Is a Foreign Country*. Cambridge: Cambridge University Press, 1985.

Lüdtke, Alf. " 'Coming to Terms with the Past': Illusions of Remembering, Ways of Forgetting Nazism in West Germany." *Journal of Modern History* 65 (1993): 542–72.

Marcus, Ivan. "Hierarchies, Religious Boundaries and Jewish Spirituality in
Medieval Germany." *Jewish History* 1 (1986): 7–26.

———. "History, Story and Collective Memory: Narrativity in Early Askenazic
Culture." In *The Midrashic Imagination: Jewish Exegesis, Thought, and History.*
Edited by Michael Fishbane. Albany: State University of New York Press, 1993.
255–79.

———. "A Jewish-Christian Symbiosis: The Culture of Early Ashkenaz." In
Cultures of the Jews: A New History. Edited by David Biale. New York: Schocken
Books, 2002. 449–516.

———. *Piety and Society: The Jewish Pietist of Medieval Germany.* Leiden: Brill,
1981.

———. "Une communauté pieuse et le doute: Mourir pour la sanctification du
Nom en Achkenaz et l'histoire de Rabbi Amnon de Mayence." *Annales* 49
(1994): 1031–47.

Marcuse, Harold. *Legacies of Dachau: The Uses and Abuses of a Concentration Camp,
1933–2001.* Cambridge: Cambridge University Press, 2001.

Meyer, Michael. *The Origins of the Modern Jew: Jewish Identity and European
Culture in Germany, 1749–1824.* Detroit: Wayne State University Press, 1967.

———. *Response to Modernity: A History of the Reform Movement in Judaism.* New
York: Oxford University Press, 1988.

Meyer, Michael, and Michael Brenner, eds. *German-Jewish History in Modern
Times.* 4 vols. New York: Columbia University Press, 1996–2000.

Minty, J. M. "*Judengasse* to Christian Quarter: The Phenomena of the Converter
Synagogue in the Late Medieval and Early Modern Holy Empire." In *Popular
Religion in Germany and Central Europe, 1400–1800.* Edited by Bob Scribner
and Trevor Johnson. New York: Martin's Press, 1996. 58–86 and 220–39.

Mintz, Allan. *Hurban: Responses to Catastrophe in Hebrew Literature.* New York:
Columbia University Press, 1984.

Miron, Dan. *Ashkenaz: Modern Hebrew Literature and the Pre-Modern German-
Jewish Experience.* New York: Leo Baeck Institute, 1989.

Miron, Guy. "The Emancipation 'Pantheon of Heroes' in the German-Jewish
Public Memory in the 1930s." *German History* 21 (2003): 476–504.

Möller, Robert. *War Stories: The Search for a Usable Past in the Federal Republic of
Germany.* Berkeley: University of California Press, 2001.

Moltke, Johannes v. "Identities on Display: Jewishness and the Representational
Politics of the Museum." In *Jews and Other Differences.* Edited by Jonathan
Boyarin and David Boyarin. Minneapolis: University of Minnesota Press,
1997. 79–107.

Mosse, George L. "The Image of the Jew in German Popular Culture: Felix
Dahn and Gustav Freytag." *LBIYB* 2 (1957): 218–27.

Mühlinghaus, Gerhard W. "Der Synagogenbau des 17. und 18. Jahrhunderts."
In *Die Architektur der Synagoge.* Edited by Hans-Peter Schwarz. Frankfurt am
Main: Klett-Cotta, 1988. 115–56.

Myers, David N. "'Mehabevin et ha-tsarot': Crusade Memories and Modern
Jewish Martyrologies." *Jewish History* 13 (1999): 49–64.

Neiss, Marion. "Diffamierung mit Tradition—Friedhofschändungen." In
Antisemitismus in Deutschland. Zur Aktualität eines Vorurteils. Edited by Wolgang
Benz. Munich: Dtv Verlag, 1995. 140–56.

Offe, Sabine. *Ausstellungen, Einstellungen, Entstellungen. Jüdische Museen in
Deutschland und Österreich.* Berlin: Philo, 2000.

Parkes, James. *The Jew in the Medieval Community: A Study of His Political and
Economic Situation.* New York: Hermon, 1976.

Peck, Abraham J. "'Our Eyes Have Seen Eternity': Memory and Self-Identity
among the She'erith Hapletah." *Modern Judaism* 17 (1997): 57–74.

Pierson, Ruth. "Embattled Veterans—The Reichsbund jüdischer Frontsoldaten."
LBIYB 19 (1974): 139–54.

Pollack, Herman. *Jewish Folkways in Germanic Lands (1648–1806).* Cambridge:
MIT Press, 1971.

Pomernace, Aubrey. "'Bekannt in den Toren': Namen und Nachruf in
Memorbüchern." In *Erinnerungen als Gegenwart: Jüdische Gedenkkulturen.*
Edited by Sabine Hoedl and Elenore Lappin. Wien: Philo, 2000. 33–53.

Ragussis, Michael. *Figures of Conversion: "The Jewish Question" and English
National Identity.* Durham: Duke University Press, 1995.

Rahden, Till van. "'Germans of the Jewish Stamm': Visions of Community
between Nationalism and Particularism, 1850 to 1933." In *German History
from the Margins, 1800 to the Present.* Edited by Neil Gregor, Nils Roemer, and
Mark Roseman. Bloomington: Indiana University Press, 2006. 27–48.

Rapoport-Albert, Ada. "Hagiography with Footnotes: Edifying Tales and the
Writing of History in Hasidism." *History and Theory* 27 (Dec. 1988): 119–59.

Raspe, Lucia. "The Black Death in Jewish Sources." *JQR* 94 (2004): 471–89.

———. "Emmeran von Regensburg, Amram von Main. Ein christlicher Heiliger
in der jüdischen Überlieferung." In *Neuer Anbruch. Zur deutsch-jüdischen
Geschichte und Kultur.* Edited by Michael Brocke, Aubrey Pomerance, and
Andrea Schatz. Berlin: Metropol, 2001. 221–41.

———. *Jüdische Hagiographie im mittelalterlichen Aschkenas.* Tübingen: Mohr
Siebeck, 2006.

Rauschenberger, Katharina. *Jüdische Tradition im Kaiserreich und in der Weimarer
Republik. Zur Geschichte des jüdischen Museumswesens in Deutschland.* Hannover:
Verlag Hahnsche Buchhandlung, 2002.

Reichel, Peter, ed. *Das Gedächtnis der Stadt. Hamburg im Umgang mit seiner
nationalsozialistischen Vergangenheit.* Hamburg: Dölling und Galitz Verlag,
1997.

———. *Vergangenheitsbewältigung in Deutschland. Die Auseinandersetzung mit der
NS-Diktatur von 1945 bis heute.* Munich: Beck, 2001.

Reiner, Elchanan. "The Ashkenazi Élite at the Beginning of the Modern Era:
Manuscript Versus Printed Books." *Polin* 10 (1997): 85–98.

Reuter, Fritz. "Altertumsverein und Paulusmuseum. Aspekte der Wormser
Wissenschafts-, Personen- und Stadtgeschichte im 19. Jahrhundert als Beitrag
zur hundertjährigen Jubiläum des Museums der Stadt Worms 1881–1991."
Wormsgau 13 (1979–81): 20–38.

———. "Dr. Friedrich M. Illert (1892–1966). Zu seinem 100. Geburtstag."
Der Wormsgau 16 (1991/1995): 20–27.

———. "Das 'Geschichtsfenster' von Heinz Hindorf in Wormser Dom—
Beschreibung und Betrachtung." *Wormsgau* 18 (1999): 223–51.

———. *Jüdisches Worms. Raschi-Haus und Judengasse.* Worms: H. Fischer, 1993.

———. *Karl Hoffmann und "das neue Worms." Stadtentwicklung und Kommunalbau,
1882–1918.* Darmstadt: Hessische Historischen Kommission Darmstadt und
der Historischen Kommission für Hessen, 1993.

———. "Kunsthistoriker und Heimatforscher aus dem 19./20. Jahrhundert und
ihre Grabstätten." *Wormsgau* 19 (2000): 88–92 and 20 (2001): 127–42.

———. "Leopold Levy und seine Synagoge von 1875." *Der Wormsgau* 11 (1974–
75): 58–68.

———. "Politisches und gesellschaftliches Engagement von Wormser Juden
im 19./20. Jahrhundert. Die Familien Eberstadt, Edinger, Rotschild und
Guggenheim." *Menora* 10 (1999): 305–45.

———. "Thesen des Altertumsvereins Worms e. V. zur Sanierung der
Judengasse." *Der Wormsgau* 10 (1972–73): 86.

———. "Vom Erwachen des historischen Interesses am jüdischen Worms bis zum
Museum des Isidor Kiefers." *Aschkenaz* 12 (2002): 13–44.

———. *Warmaisa. 1000 Jahre Juden in Worms.* Frankfurt am main: Jüdischer
Verlag bei Athenäum, 1987.

———. *Worms ehemals, gestern und heute. Ein Stadtbild im Wandel der letzten 100
Jahre.* 2nd ed. Stuttgart: J. F. Steinkopf Verlag, 1988.

———. *Worms in alten Ansichtskarten.* Frankfurt am Main: Flechsig Verlag, 1979.

———. *Worms zwischen Reichsstadt und Industriestadt, 1800–1882.* Worms:
Stadtarchiv Worms, 1993.

———. "Wormser Historiker aus dem 19. und 20. Jahrhundert." *Der Wormsgau* 19
(2000): 63–102.

Reuter, Fritz, ed. *Peter und Johann Friedrich Hammann. Handzeichnungen von
Worms aus der Zeit vor und nach der Stadtzerstörung 1689 im "Pfälzischen
Erbfolgekrieg."* Worms: Bressler, 1989.

———. *Worms 1933. Zeitzeugnisse und Zeitzeugen. Mit dem Lebens-Erinnerungen
von Oberbürgermeister Wilhelm Rahn.* Worms: Stadtarchiv Worms, 1995.

Richarz, Monika. "Jews in Today's Germanies." *LBIYB* 30 (1985): 265–74.

———. "Luftaufnahme—oder die Schwierigkeit der Heimatforscher mit der
jüdischen Geschichte." *Babylon* 8 (1991): 27–33.

Röckelein, Hedwig. "'Die grabstein, so vil tausent guldin wert sein': Vom Umgang
der Christen mit Synagogen und jüdischen Friedhöfen im Mittelalter und am
Beginn der Neuzeit." *Aschkenas* 5 (1995): 11–45.

Roemer, Nils. *Between History and Faith: Rewriting the Past—Reshaping Jewish
Cultures in Nineteenth-Century Germany.* Madison: University of Wisconsin
Press, 2005.

———. "Turning Defeat into Victory: *Wissenschaft des Judentums* and the
Martyrs of 1096." *Jewish History* 13 (1999): 65–80.

Rosenfeld, Gavriel D. *Munich and Memory: Architecture, Monuments, and the Legacy of the Third Reich.* Berkeley: University of California Press, 2000.

Rosenthal, Berthold. *Heimatgeschichte der badischen Juden seit ihrem geschichtlichen Auftreten bis zur Gegenwart.* Bühl-Baden: Konkordia A. G., 1927.

Roth, Cecil. "The Frankfurt Memorbuch." In *Commemoration of the Frankfurt Jewish Community on the Occasion of the Acquisition of the Frankfurt Memorbuch.* Jerusalem: Jewish National and University Library, 1965. 9–16.

Róth, Ernst, and Leo Prijs. *Hebräische Handschriften. Teil 1. Die Handschriften der Stadt- und Universitätsbibliothek Frankfurt am Main. Bd. A-C.* Wiesbaden: Steiner, 1982–93.

Rothschild, Samson. "Das Archiv der jüdischen Gemeinde von Worms." *Vom Rhein* 1 (1902): 21–22.

———. *Emancipations-Bestrebungen der jüdischen Großgemeinden des Großherzogthums Hessen im vorigen Jahrhundert. Auf Grund von Protokollen und Akten des Archivs der jüd. Gemeinde zu Worms.* Worms am Rhein: Julius Mannheimer, 1924.

Schäfter, Peter. "The Ideal of Piety of the Ashkenazi Hasidim and Its Roots in Jewish Tradition." *Jewish History* 4 (1990): 9–23.

Schlösser, Annelore and Karl. *Die Judenverfolgung 1933–1945 in Worms.* Worms: Stadtarchiv Worms, 1987.

———. *Die Wormser Juden 1933–1945. Dokumentation, CD.* Worms: Stadtarchiv, 2002.

Schmidt, Michael. *Reverentia und Magnificentia. Historität in der Architektur Süddeutschland, Osterreichs und Böhmens vom 14. bis 17. Jahrhundert.* Regensburg: Schnell und Steiner, 1999.

Scholem, Gershom. *On the Kabbalah and Its Symbolism.* New York: Schocken, 1969.

Schorsch, Ismar. *Jewish Reactions to German Anti-Semitism, 1870–1914.* New York: Columbia University Press, 1972.

———. "Moritz Güdemann, Rabbi, Historian and Apologist." *LBIYB* 11 (1966): 42–66.

Sebald, Eduard. "Das gotische Südportal." In *Das Südportal des Wormser Doms.* Edited by Herbert Dellwing. Worms: Wernersche Verlagsgesellschaft, 1999.

Shatsky, Jacob. "Das Kloglied oif dem Hurban fun Worms." *Filologische Shriften* 3 (1929): 44–55.

Shoham-Steiner, Ephraim. "'For a Prayer in That Place Would Be Most Welcome': Jews, Holy Shrines, and Miracles—A New Approach." *Viator* 37 (2006): 369–95.

Siegfried, Detlef. "Zwischen Aufarbeitung und Schlußstrich. Der Umgang mit der NS-Vergangenheit in den beiden deutschen Staaten 1958 bis 1969." In *Dynamische Zeiten. Die 60er Jahre in den beiden deutschen Gesellschaften.* Edited by Axel Schmidt, Detlef Siegfried, and Karl Christian Lammers. Hamburg: Christians, 2000. 77–113.

Simmel, Georg. "Die Ruine." In *Georg Simmel. Philosphische Kultur. Über*

das Abenteuer, die Geschlechter und die Krise der Moderne. Edited by Jürgen
Habermas. Berlin: Klaus Wagenbach, 1986. 118–24.

Smith, Helmut Walser. "The Boundaries of the Local in Modern German History."
In *Saxony in German History: Culture, Society, and Politics, 1830–1933.* Edited by
James Retallack. Ann Arbor: University of Michigan Press, 2000. 63–95.

Smith, Helmut Walser, ed. *Protestants, Catholics and Jews in Germany, 1800–1914.*
Oxford: Berg, 2001.

Sorkin, David. *The Transformation of German Jewry, 1780–1840.* Oxford: Oxford
University Press, 1987.

Soyer, Daniel. *Jewish Immigrant Associations and American Identity in New York,
1880–1939.* Cambridge: Harvard University Press, 1997.

———. "The Travel Agent as Ethnic Broker between Old World and New:
The Case of Gustave Eisner." *YIVO Annual* 21 (1993): 345–68.

Spiegel, Shalom. *The Last Trial: On the Legends and Lore of the Command to
Abraham to Offer Isaac as a Sacrifice; The Akedah.* Translated by Judah Goldin.
Woodstock: Jewish Lights Publishing, 1993.

Steinschneider, Moritz. *Die Geschichtsliteratur der Juden.* Frankfurt am Main:
J. Kaufmann, 1905.

Steinweis, Alan E. "Dead Jews: Depictions of European History and Culture in
Contemporary American Travel Guides." *Shofar* 15 (1997): 57–63.

Stern, Frank. "The Historic Triangle: Occupiers, Germans and Jews in Postwar
Germany." *Tel Aviver Jahrbuch für deutsche Geschichte* 19 (1990): 47–76.

———. *The Whitewashing of the Yellow Badge: Antisemitism and Philosemitism in
Postwar Germany.* Translated by William Templer. Oxford: Pergamon Press,
1992.

Stowe, Kenneth R. *Alienated Minority: The Jews of Medieval Latin Europe.*
Cambridge, Mass.: Harvard University Press, 1992.

Strauss, Jutta. "Das Jüdische Museum Berlin: 'Leben Nicht Tod.'" *Wormsgau* 21
(2002): 155–75.

Suchy, Barbara. "The Verein zur Abwehr des Antisemitismus (I)—From Its
Beginnings to the First World War." *LBIYB* 28 (1983): 205–40.

Ta-Shma, Israel. "A New Chronography on the Thirteenth Century Tosaphist."
Shalem 3 (1981): 319–24.

Theiselmann, Christiane. *Das Wormser Lutherdenkmal Ernst Rietschels (1856–
1868) im Rahmen der Lutherrezeption des 19. Jahrhunderts.* Frankfurt am Main:
P. Lang, 1992.

Thieme, Ulrich, and Felix Becker. *Allgemeines Lexikon der Bildenden Künstler von
der Antike bis zur Gegenwart.* 37 vols. Leipzig: E. A. Seemann, 1938.

Timm, Erika. "Zur Frühgeschichte der jiddischen Erzählprosa: Eine neu
aufgefundene Maise-Handschrift." *Beiträge zur Geschichte der deutschen Sprache
und Literatur* 117 (1995): 243–80.

Toch, Michael. *"Dunkle Jahrhunderte" Gab es ein jüdisches Frühmittelalter?* Trier:
Arye-Maimon-Institut für Geschichte der Juden, 2001.

Tönnis, Ferdinand. *Gemeinschaft und Gesellschaft.* 3rd ed. Darmstadt:
Wissenschaftliche Buchgesellschaft, 1991.

Turniansky, Chava. "The Events in Frankfurt am Main (11612–1616) in *Megillas Vints* in an Unknown Yiddish 'Historical' Song." In *Schöpferische Momente des europäischen Judentums in der frühen Neuzeit*. Edited by Michael Graetz. Heidelberg: C. Winter, 2000. 121–37.

Twersky, Isadore. "The Shulhan Arukh: Enduring Code of Jewish Law." In *The Jewish Expression*. Edited by Jehuda Goldin. New York: Bantam Books, 1970. 322–43.

Umbach, Maiken. *Federalism and Enlightenment in Germany, 1740–1806*. London: Hambledon, 1998.

———. "Reich, Region und Föderalismus als Denkfiguren in politischen Diskursen der Frühen und der Späten Neuzeit." In *Föderative Nation. Deutschlandkonzepte von der Reformation bis zum Ersten Weltkrieg*. Edited by Dieter Langewiesche and Georg Schmidt. Munich: Oldenbourg, 2000. 191–214.

Wapnewski, Peter. "Das Nibelungslied." In *Deutsche Erinnerungsorte*. Edited by Etienne François and Hagen Schulze. 3 vols. München: C. H. Beck, 2001. 1:159–69.

Weinberg, Magnus. "Memorbücher." *Menorah* 6 (1928): 697–708.

———."Untersuchungen ueber das Wesen des Memorbuches." *JJLG* 16 (1924): 253–320.

Weissler, Chava. *Voices of the Matriarchs: Listening to the Prayers of Early Modern Jewish Women*. Boston: Beacon Press, 1998.

Wendehorst, Stephan. "Imperial Spaces as Jewish Spaces: The Holy Roman Empire, the Emperor and the Jews in the Early Modern Period; Some Preliminary Observations." *Jahrbuch des Simon-Dubnow-Instituts/Simon-Dubnow-Institute Yearbook* 2 (2003): 437–74.

Wigoder, Geoffrey. "Beth Hatefutsoth: The First Decade." *Ariel* 77–78 (1989): 99–110.

———. *The Story of the Synagogue: A Diaspora Museum Book*. London: Weidenfeld and Nicolson, 1986.

Wilhelm, Dieter. *Worms. Mittelstadt am Rande des Rhein-Neckar-Ballungsraumes. Eine stadtgeographische Betrachtung seiner Entwicklung im 19. und 20. Jahrhundert*. Worms: Verlag Stadtbibliothek Worms, 1971.

Wirsching, Andreas. "Jüdische Friedhöfe in Deutschland, 1933–1957." *Vierteljahrshefte für Zeitgeschichte* 50 (2002): 1–40.

Wolfson, Elliot R. *Through a Speculum That Shines: Vision and Imagination in Medieval Jewish Mysticism*. Princeton: Princeton University Press, 1994.

Yassif, Eli. *The Hebrew Folktale: History, Genre, Meaning*. Translated by Jacqueline S. Teitelbaum. Bloomington: Indiana University Press, 1999.

———. "Rashi Legends and Medieval Popular Culture." In *Rashi 1040–1990: Hommage à Ephraïm E. Urbach*. Edited by Gabrielle Sed-Rajna. Paris: Cerf, 1993. 483–92.

Yates, Frances. *The Art of Memory*. London: Routledge and Kegan Paul, 1966.

Yerushalmi, Yosef H. "Exile and Expulsion in Jewish History." In *Crisis and*

Creativity in the Sephardic World, 1391–1648. Edited by Benjamin R. Gampel. New York: Columbia University Press, 1997. 3–22.

——. *Zakhor: Jewish History and Jewish Memory*. New York: Schocken, 1989.

Young, James E. "Broken Tablets and Jewish Memory in Poland." In *The Texture of Memory: Holocaust Memorials and Meaning*. Edited by James E. Young. New Haven: Yale University Press, 1993. 185–208.

Young, James E., ed. *Holocaust Memorials and Meaning*. New Haven: Yale University Press, 1993.

Young-Bruehl, Elisabeth. *Hannah Arendt: For Love of the World*. New Haven: Yale University Press, 1982.

Yuval, Israel. "Ha-nakam we-ha-kelalah, ha-dam we-ha-alilah: Me-alilot kedoshim le-alilot dam." *Zion* 58 (1993): 33–89.

——. "Heilige Städte, heilige Gemeinden—Mainz als das Jerusalem Deutschlands." In *Jüdische Gemeinden und Organisationsformen von der Antike bis zur Gegenwart*. Edited by Robert Jütte and Abraham P. Kustermann. Wien: Böhlau, 1996. 91–101.

——. "'They Tell Lies: You Ate the Man': Jewish Reactions to Ritual Murder Accusations." In *Religious Violence between Christian and Jews: Medieval Roots, Modern Perspectives*. Edited by Anna Sapir Abulafia. Basingstoke: Palgrave, 2002. 86–106.

Zfatmann, Sarah. "Ha-siporet be-yiddish me-rishit 'ad 'Shivhei ha-besht (1504–1814)." 2 vols. Ph.D. diss., Hebrew University, 1983.

——. "Ma'ase bukh—kavim lidmuto shel zanr be-sifrut yidish ha-yeshana, im giluyo shel Ma'ase bukh ketav yad Jerushalayim Heb. 8° 5245." *Ha-Sifrut* 28 (1979): 126–52.

Zimer, Yizhak. "Gezerot tatnu be-sifre ha-minhagim be-yeme ha-benayim we-be-et-ha-hadasha: Yezira u-hitpashtut shel teksi ha-avalut." In *Yehudim mul ha-zelav: Gezerot 856 ba-historyah uva-historyografyah*. Edited by Yom Tov Assis, Michael Toch, Jeremy Cohen, Ora Limor, and Aaron Kedar. Jerusalem: Magnes Press, 2000. 157–70.

Ziwes, Franz-Josef. *Studien zur Geschichte der Juden im mittleren Rheingebiet während des hohen und späten Mittelalters*. Hannover: Verlag Hahnsche Buchhandlung, 1995.

INDEX

311